Mesopotamian Civilizations and Empires

An Enthralling Journey Through Sumer, Akkad, Babylon, and Assyria

© Copyright 2024 - All rights reserved.

The content contained within this book may not be reproduced, duplicated, or transmitted without direct written permission from the author or the publisher.

Under no circumstances will any blame or legal responsibility be held against the publisher, or author, for any damages, reparation, or monetary loss due to the information contained within this book, either directly or indirectly.

Legal Notice:

This book is copyright protected. It is only for personal use. You cannot amend, distribute, sell, use, quote, or paraphrase any part, or the content within this book, without the consent of the author or publisher.

Disclaimer Notice:

Please note the information contained within this document is for educational and entertainment purposes only. All effort has been executed to present accurate, up-to-date, reliable, and complete information. No warranties of any kind are declared or implied. Readers acknowledge that the author is not engaging in the rendering of legal, financial, medical, or professional advice. The content within this book has been derived from various sources. Please consult a licensed professional before attempting any techniques outlined in this book.

By reading this document, the reader agrees that under no circumstances is the author responsible for any losses, direct or indirect, that are incurred as a result of the use of the information contained within this document, including, but not limited to, errors, omissions, or inaccuracies.

Free limited time bonus

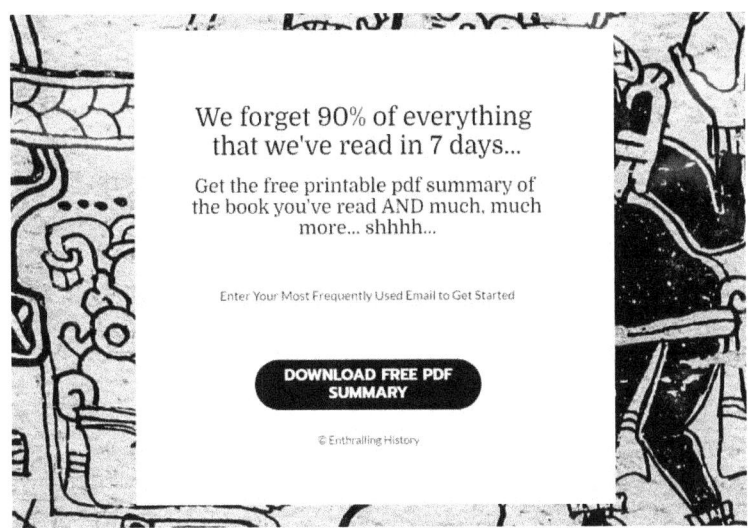

Stop for a moment. We have a free bonus set up for you. The problem is this: we forget 90% of everything that we read after 7 days. Crazy fact, right? Here's the solution: we've created a printable, 1-page pdf summary for this book that you're reading now. All you have to do to get your free pdf summary is to go to the following website: https://livetolearn.lpages.co/enthrallinghistory/

Or, Scan the QR code!

Once you do, it will be intuitive. Enjoy, and thank you!

Table of Contents

PART 1: THE SUMERIAN CIVILIZATION 1
    INTRODUCTION 2
    CHAPTER 1: THE UBAID PERIOD 5
    CHAPTER 2: THE URUK PERIOD 12
    CHAPTER 3: THE EARLY DYNASTIC PERIOD 19
    CHAPTER 4: THE AKKADIAN PERIOD 30
    CHAPTER 5: THE GUTIAN PERIOD 40
    CHAPTER 6: THE SUMERIAN RENAISSANCE 45
    CHAPTER 7: THE DECLINE OF SUMER 50
    CHAPTER 8: SUMERIAN SOCIETY AND FAMOUS RULERS 56
    CHAPTER 9: CULTURE AND INNOVATION 66
    CHAPTER 10: MYTHS AND RELIGION 82
    CONCLUSION 95
PART 2: THE AKKADIAN EMPIRE 98
    INTRODUCTION 99
    CHAPTER 1: THE UBAID PERIOD 102
    CHAPTER 2: THE PRE-AKKADIAN PERIOD 113
    CHAPTER 3: THE RISE OF THE AKKADIAN EMPIRE 124
    CHAPTER 4: THE GOLDEN AGE OF THE AKKADIAN EMPIRE 133
    CHAPTER 5: THE DECLINE AND FALL OF THE AKKADIAN EMPIRE 144
    CHAPTER 6: AKKADIAN SOCIETY AND DAILY LIFE 154
    CHAPTER 7: WARFARE AND THE MILITARY 165

- CHAPTER 8: CULTURE AND ART 175
- CHAPTER 9: FAMOUS RULERS 186
- CHAPTER 10: MYTHS AND RELIGION 195
- CONCLUSION 206

PART 3: THE BABYLONIAN EMPIRE 210
- INTRODUCTION 211
- CHAPTER 1: THE PRE-BABYLONIAN PERIOD 214
- CHAPTER 2: THE FIRST BABYLONIANS 225
- CHAPTER 3: THE RISE OF BABYLON 234
- CHAPTER 4: THE KASSITE DYNASTY 245
- CHAPTER 5: THE ASSYRIAN RULE 255
- CHAPTER 6: A NEW EMPIRE – THE NEO-BABYLONIANS 268
- CHAPTER 7: THE DECLINE AND FALL OF BABYLON 279
- CHAPTER 8: BABYLONIAN SOCIETY AND FAMOUS RULERS 290
- CHAPTER 9: CULTURE AND INNOVATION 301
- CHAPTER 10: MYTHS AND RELIGION 312
- CONCLUSION 323

PART 4: THE ASSYRIAN EMPIRE 325
- INTRODUCTION 326
- CHAPTER 1: NORTH MESOPOTAMIA BEFORE THE ASSYRIANS 335
- CHAPTER 2: THE EARLY PERIOD AND THE AKKADIAN EMPIRE 345
- CHAPTER 3: THE OLD ASSYRIAN EMPIRE AND BABYLON 352
- CHAPTER 4: RESTORATION AND FALL TO THE MITANNI 361
- CHAPTER 5: THE MIDDLE ASSYRIAN EMPIRE 364
- CHAPTER 6: ASSYRIA DURING THE BRONZE AGE COLLAPSE 369
- CHAPTER 7: THE NEO-ASSYRIAN EMPIRE 372
- CHAPTER 8: LANGUAGE DIVERSITY 399
- CHAPTER 9: RELIGION AND BELIEFS 405
- CHAPTER 10: ARTS AND ARCHITECTURE 412
- CONCLUSION 420

HERE'S ANOTHER BOOK BY ENTHRALLING HISTORY THAT YOU MIGHT LIKE 423
FREE LIMITED TIME BONUS 424
BIBLIOGRAPHY 425
IMAGE SOURCES 458

Part 1: The Sumerian Civilization

An Enthralling Overview of Sumer and the Ancient Sumerians

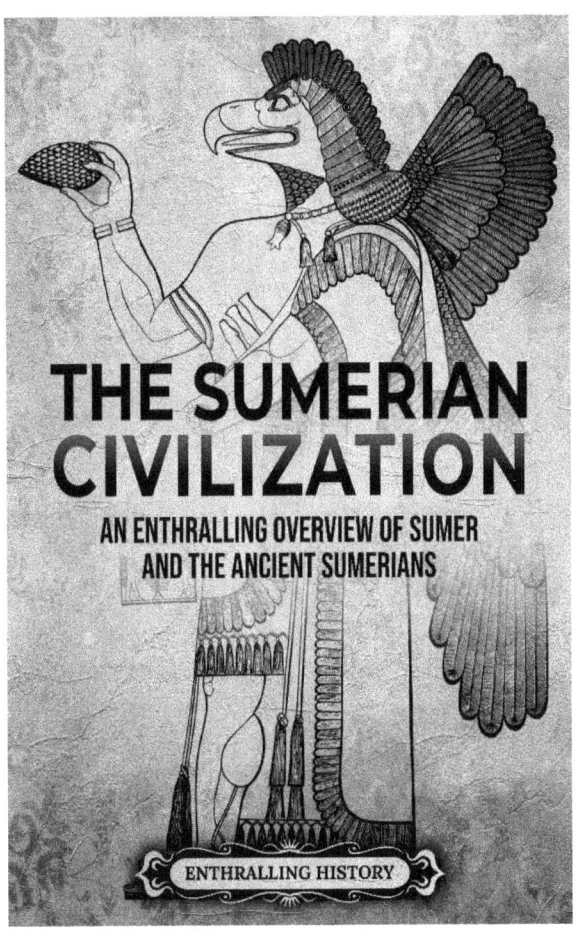

Introduction

In most of us lies a tinge of an adventurous spirit. We crave to investigate the mysterious, the aloof, the unknown. Few of us will ever have the chance to physically follow through on those thoughts. Luckily for us, the busy, technology-driven, and commercialized lives that we are caught up in also provide us with the means to satisfy that conscious or subconscious craving.

Through books and film, we can satisfy our curiosity and enrich our minds. History, as a whole, and ancient history, in particular, is often more mysterious and awe-inspiring than fiction. The higher goal of learning about history, though, is that it should ultimately teach us not to repeat humanity's past mistakes.

Modern ways of cooperation between many different fields of science have clarified much ancient historical data, most of which is relevant today. For example, climate change is a pressing issue today. Palaeobotanists, archaeologists, and other researchers have discovered that our ancient forbearers, without industrialization and large-scale pollution, dealt with climate change on several occasions and thrived again afterward.

With this book, we would like to draw you into the surprisingly sophisticated world of the ancient Sumerians. Reckoned for centuries to be the first people to develop civilization, they flourished at the dawn of history between the Euphrates and Tigris Rivers. They lived, made merry, were sad, and were afraid. They learned, worked, worshiped, fought, and made peace. They invented practical solutions and tools, developed ideas and explanations, and manufactured products from raw materials without external aid or prior knowledge.

The Sumerians invented a list of around thirty-nine "firsts" literally from nothing over a relatively brief period. They solved the challenges of their society through innovation when the need arose. We should not only be in awe of their abilities but also of the fact that we still use some of their innovations, albeit modernized, to this day.

Ancient civilizations sprouted in fertile river valleys on every continent. The most well-known of these is probably the ancient Egyptian civilization of the Nile Valley. Some of these civilizations declined, disappeared, and were forgotten as time passed until their ruins and artifacts were rediscovered by chance—like the Sumerians. In other instances, the deciphering of ancient texts set scholars on the trail of discovery—again, like the Sumerians!

The exact timelines for Sumerian settlements and the development of innovative solutions to ease their lives are not known for sure. The styles and sophistication in the manufacture of pottery are often used to determine timelines and changes in culture during prehistory throughout the ancient Near East. The Sumerian civilization's timeline is based on information gathered from multiple sites.

Carbon-14 dating and other modern scientific dating methods have confirmed some periods. There is little consensus amongst scholars about the exact timeline of events, inventions, and lengths of reigns. Thus, exact chronologies have not been set up and remain a cause of disagreement. We have endeavored to stick to a consistent timeline, but it is important to note that this timeline might not exactly agree with other sources you have read before this. The lack of an exact timeline is part of the Sumerians' intrigue and provides food for speculation, theories, serious history fans, and even ufologists.

In the 19th century, attentive Assyriologists were on the trail of a well-known ancient civilization, the Assyrians. As they investigated the Assyrian culture, they noticed a different culture and legacy. And thus, the magnificent world of the ancient Sumerian civilization was revealed. Biblical scholars and archaeologists jumped at the chance to excavate the land of the biblical and Koranic patriarch Abraham's birth. By this time, they already knew that the Chaldeans of the Bible were later inhabitants of that land.

We still do not know enough about the Sumerians, especially if we consider that their civilization waxed and waned for roughly four thousand years. The bulk of our knowledge stems from archaeological excavations and deciphered clay tablets from the ancient library of King Ashurbanipal of Assyria in Nineveh. More than thirty thousand cuneiform clay tablets were discovered here and elsewhere, and many are still undeciphered. The Assyrian cuneiform tablets were in several languages and styles, and amongst them were lexicons, which set scholars on the path to identify the languages and start deciphering them.

When the Sumerian people, who called themselves the "black-headed people," arrived in the land that would later become Sumer in southern Mesopotamia, there were other groups of nomadic and semi-nomadic people living between the Tigris and Euphrates Rivers and throughout the ancient Near East. Where they came from still baffles scholars. Their genealogy has still not been unraveled despite more than 140 years of excavations and linguistic analysis by many scholars and Sumerologists.

Because the Sumerians invented writing and later recorded the history, myths, and beliefs of earlier generations from oral transmissions, we have their own interpretations and explanations. What did they believe? How did they explain human existence and the purpose of life? How did they explain natural phenomena?

Hypotheses about the origins of the Sumerians vary greatly, and theories and conclusions cover many geographical possibilities. They might have come from the Levant, Anatolia, the Zagros Mountains, ancient East Asia, the Indus Valley, or somewhere in the Indian Ocean. Genetic analysis of ancient Mesopotamian skeletons that compare DNA with modern Marsh Arabs from southern Iraq confirmed that they are closely related. Skeletons from the excavations at Ur by the late Leonard Wooley were recently discovered in still-unpacked crates after nearly a century. One can only hope that DNA from this may finally identify the Sumerians' origins to a reasonably certain degree.

Chapter 1: The Ubaid Period

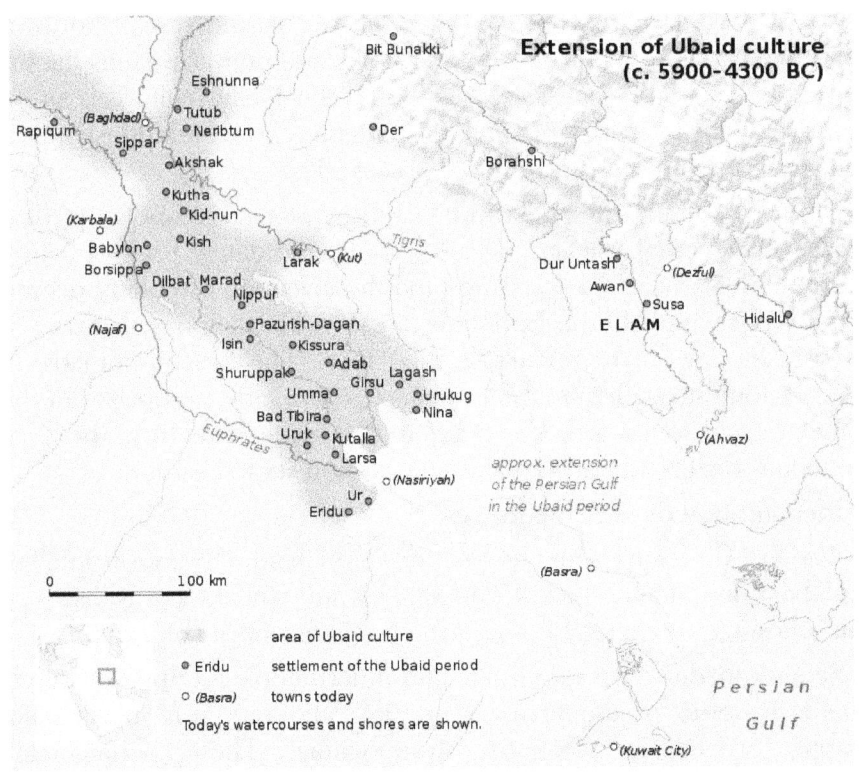

Map showing sites of the Ubaid culture.[1]

How It Began

There is no universally accepted timeline for settlements in ancient Mesopotamia, but it is agreed by scholars that semi-nomadic hunter-gatherers had been settling in Mesopotamia from around 10,000 to 8000 BCE. There are signs of cultivated date palms even before 10,000 BCE in the south, where Sumer would later be founded. The exact origins of these prehistoric people groups and the subsequent development of the Ubaid culture are so interwoven with the rest of the ancient Near East that scholars agreed at a workshop in 2006 that it developed from a mixed heritage diffused peaceably through inter-relationships. The first settlements were made up of nomadic and semi-nomadic groups who started agricultural activities at seasonal settlements.

Mainstream archaeologists and historians believe that the Mesopotamian settlements, which later developed into villages, cities, and civilizations, first happened in the north and then moved south. Other equally qualified scholars and researchers have posited that the Ubaid culture, as the forerunner of the Sumerian culture of southern Mesopotamia, started in the Arabian Gulf region and spread northward from there. This spread from south to north and outward seems the most logical conclusion. What is certain is that the Ubaid culture is present across the entire Fertile Crescent, and timelines are continuously pushed back and sometimes forward by new discoveries.

At the Neolithic site of Jarmo in northeastern Mesopotamia (Iraq), there is evidence of wheat and barley cultivation dating back to between 8000 and 7000 BCE. New cultures and the invention of pottery occurred in the Upper and Middle Euphrates areas at Halaf (today in Syria) and Samarra (today in Iraq) during this time. These semi-nomads also brought domesticated animals like sheep, goats, cattle, and pigs with them as they moved southward. It is believed that some came from the Zagros Mountains region, where animal domestication started earlier.

Identification of Settlement Areas

The first distinctive sedentary period in the land of Sumer is known as the Ubaid period after Tell al-'Ubaid. This substantial tell was discovered four miles (six kilometers) north of the large ancient city of Uruk.

Semi-nomadic tribes of Semitic and other people groups were already settled in some of the areas when the Sumerians or "black-headed people" arrived in southern Mesopotamia. These people called themselves "black-headed people" in later texts after they invented a writing system—the first that we know of in the world.

At some point, the settlers started making clay vessels for domestic use, such as plates, bowls, and containers for food storage. These clay vessels were either lightly or thoroughly fired and in a buff or greenish color. They were decorated with black, brown, or purple geometric lines. This is known as Hassuna-style pottery after the site where it was first discovered in northern Mesopotamia.

Between 6500 and 5000 BCE, settlements continued to spread. By around 6000 BCE, there were signs of sedentary farming communities that relied on irrigation rather than rainfall for crop cultivation in the more arid south of Mesopotamia toward the Persian Gulf. The people farmed the land, kept domesticated animals, and fished from the rivers and the sea. Some archaeologists posit that these lifestyles represent three different ethnic groups: those that cultivated crops, those that practiced animal husbandry, and those that fished the marshes.

The material culture of the Ubaid period across most of the Fertile Crescent varies in duration. In southern Mesopotamia, the Ubaid culture is dated from approximately 6500 BCE to 3800 BCE (or 4000 BCE by some) and as late as c. 5300 BCE to 3900 BCE by others. Due to the lengthy Ubaid period, archaeologists have divided it into six stages, from Ubaid 0 to Ubaid 5.

The dating and spread of Ubaid influences across the Levant are primarily identified through pottery styles, similar cultural evidence, and related periods in time. As already mentioned, scholars are not in agreement on whether the Ubaid culture spread from northern Mesopotamia to the south or from south to north.

The oldest Ubaid settlement in southern Mesopotamia so far discovered is a small tell close to Larsa called Tell el-'Oueili, which dates from 6500 BCE to 5400 BCE. It was discovered by André Parrot and excavated between 1976 and 1989 by the French archaeologist Jean-Louis Huot.

This discovery pushed back the timeline of the Ubaid period and necessitated the adding of Ubaid 0 to the already set Ubaid 1 to Ubaid 5 chronology. Most of the oldest Mesopotamian Ubaid sites are located in the south, where other groups had already settled. To date, there is no consensus among scholars regarding the origins of the people, the settlement dates, and how or why the earliest sedentary cultures flourished in the alluvial plains of the more arid south.

The area is poor in natural resources like minerals and timber, and the flooding of the rivers is unpredictable and untimely for crops, necessitating irrigation. And yet, it may be these difficult circumstances that drove the development of excellent and awe-inspiring innovations. The inhabitants used what was available, cleverly innovated technology when needed, and even made sickles from hard-baked clay for harvesting. The fauna and flora indicate that farmers at this earliest Ubaid site of Tell el-'Oueili used draft animals (oxen) and relied on crops like barley, which could tolerate the alluvial silt's salinity.

The following Ubaid periods are typical of a developing society, with every new style leading to the next. Naturally, the egalitarian society adapted since the people needed a group of people with organizational skills and oversight for communal projects, such as canal-building and maintenance. This, in turn, led to societal differentiation and eventually class structures and labor divisions.

Houses were built from mudbricks and straw or reeds. Tripartite dwellings were generally built around a larger centrally situated multi-roomed house, which then formed a central village around which smaller villages developed. It is possible that the main village would then become the leading force, with the sub-villages being subordinate to it in decision-making and labor distribution.

One can imagine how much labor would have been needed for the maintenance of canals, which would have been plagued by regular silting-up from the flooding rivers. Innovations during this phase did not only ease labor-intensive agricultural activities. Canoes and nets for the fishers of the marshes were also improved.

Organized settlements led to the building of communal centers, with an emphasis on religious buildings. Religious centers became the village centers, with each village having its own patron deity. Like the houses, these buildings were constructed of mudbricks and reeds or straw covered with clay.

The Origins of Eridu

For a long time, researchers, historians, and archaeologists believed that the first city in Sumer was Eridu. This assumption appeared to be confirmed by ancient Sumerian texts describing Sumerian beliefs about the beginning of the world. The Sumerians believed that the deities chose the oldest city when they decided to bring kingship down to Earth. The chief deity, Enki, was said to have built his temple in Eridu. It was only later, with more modern dating methods, that it was discovered that the city of Uruk predates Eridu. Nevertheless, the archaeological site of Eridu provides us with the best-illustrated cultural development record of the period.

Eridu was one of five cities that predated the Great Flood of Sumerian myths. Interestingly, this Great Flood myth is remarkably similar to the biblical Great Flood as described in Genesis. A renowned Sumerologist, Thorkild Jacobsen, named the Sumerian creation myth the *Eridu Genesis*. Excavations in Sumer at the ancient city of Ur confirmed that there was a very thick layer of mud with signs of habitation underneath from the time before the flood.

The city of Eridu was located on the Arabian Gulf and was the southernmost city of Sumer. The earliest settlement phase of the Eridu site is dated to around 5400 BCE. The main tell has eight layers. Eridu's ziggurat was rebuilt seventeen times, each time larger and more elaborate until it represented the common style of later temples. This common style is a tripartite building on a platform consisting of a long rectangular room with rooms leading off the long sides. The central room had an altar, and there was a niche in the wall for a statue of the local patron deity; in Eridu's case, it would have been Enki.

The original Eridu village developed into a town and then into a city with surrounding villages during and following the Ubaid period, despite the salinity-prone soil, which limited its agricultural prowess. In later periods when the city became uninhabitable, it was still used as a cult center until almost the end of the 1st millennium BCE. The city was abandoned and taken over by sandy dunes and silt, but the ziggurat was still functional. Building remnants on a small site nearby suggest that the priests who looked after the temple may have lived there.

During the Eridu phase of the Ubaid period, another ethnic group with its own distinctive culture from a different southern settlement became part of Eridu's population. The second period of Eridu culture is called the Hadji Muhammed phase after this group, and it dates from c. 4800 to 4500 BCE. The Ubaid 2 phase saw extensive growth in settlements and agriculture.

Major canals and irrigation channels with levees and sluice gates drove increased food production, which could support larger communities and enabled the storage of surplus crops. The population growth meant that attention could be channeled into other occupations. Through trading, the Sumerians could supplement their lack of natural resources and raw materials, which included certain minerals, obsidian, and timber. This, in turn, led to further innovations. For example, plows were later fitted with metal cutting edges obtained through trade.

A centralized organization and administration were a natural outcome of these developments. Social levels were undoubtedly impacted, and class stratification took over. It is surmised by some scholars that the heads of extended families may have become local chieftains. These positions were sometimes hereditary. In the beginning, the chieftains would have mainly functioned as advisors, managed inter-community squabbles, and functioned as judges in their communities.

It needs to be mentioned that earlier farmers made use of extended family structures to cope with labor-intensive agricultural activities. During the Ubaid period, labor from outside the family became necessary due to increased production and specialization in other occupations, such as the manufacturing of tools and pottery.

Distinctive Styles of Pottery Discovered by Archaeologists

The distinctive Ubaid pottery, after which this period is named and which, in turn, received its name from the site where it was first identified, was meticulously crafted from light-colored clay. It was sometimes only lightly fired. Sometimes, pottery was thoroughly baked in kilns. Traces of such kilns were found at Tell al-'Ubaid.

The clay dried to a neutral buff or gentle greenish hue and was decorated with black, brown, or purple paint. The painted decorations are in the form of lines, geometric shapes, floral patterns, and animal shapes.

Painted shallow dish decorated with geometric designs in dark paint. From Tell al-'Ubaid, Late Ubaid period, c. 5200–4200 BCE.[2]

Grave goods recovered from Tell al-'Ubaid contained plates, bowls, small kraters (also spelled craters; these were open vase-shaped vessels with handles), clay tokens, and more. Handles and spouts were added later to the larger kraters. The decorations are less elaborate than the earlier Halaf-style pottery of northern Mesopotamia but similar in style and execution. The paint of the decorations was often applied by the blade-cut method.

Apart from the practical clay wares, there were also ornaments and figurines made of clay. These were in the shapes of animals and humans—men and women—with strangely shaped lizard-like faces.

Overall, the Ubaid period brought forth population growth and progress in every sphere of life. The ever-larger villages spread out, with smaller village settlements on the outskirts and in surrounding areas. Domestic dwellings were built from reeds and clay and then progressed to clay-covered reeds to mudbrick dwellings in the distinct tripartite style. This style was repeated for communal and religious buildings, such as the distinctive ziggurats.

Chapter 2: The Uruk Period

Sumerian civilization officially started in the Uruk period. This period was characterized by rapid development and numerous cultural and political changes. Settlements had been replaced by villages, which developed, in some cases, into towns. In the Uruk period, it is believed the first cities in the world appeared.

The Uruk period can be divided into two distinct phases. The Early Uruk period dates from c. 4000 to 3500 BCE, and the Late Uruk period dates from c. 3500 to 3000 BCE.

The Sumerians probably arrived during the Ubaid period and took over the already developed villages. The Sumerians developed them into multi-faceted settlements that consisted of hamlets, towns, urban centers, and even cities.

The eastern arm of the Fertile Crescent ends in southern Mesopotamia (modern-day Iraq). As mentioned before, the origins of the Sumerians are not known. All we know for certain is that their language has no connection to any known language group, and their DNA is similar to the modern-day people living in the marshlands in southern Iraq. They called their new country Sumer (*Kengir* in Sumerian), meaning "country of the noble lords."

The Sumerians are thought to be among the most intelligent and innovative peoples of the ancient world because of their numerous inventions and problem-solving skills. According to dictionaries, the historical concept of a civilization is a society characterized by well-developed urban centers, agricultural success, a written language, a central or state government, developed and applied technologies, a common ideology, and shared culture. The Sumerians tick all the boxes; therefore, they are recognized as the first civilization in history.

After settling in southern Mesopotamia, the innovative Sumerians soon invented or modified the plow, which was followed by the invention of the seeder plow. This later plow could distribute the seeds evenly over the plowed soil. A draft animal could also pull it. Later in Sumerian history, after the invention of writing, they produced the first crop cultivation manual, with instructions in the format of a letter from a father to his son. It covered the entire crop cycle—the how and when of every step to be taken from planning to harvesting. It included tips on what to beware of, tasks that should be done, what should not be done, and how to oversee and instruct a laborer.

During the Early Uruk period, the Sumerians followed in the footsteps of their predecessors when it came to architecture. They used the existing tripartite dwellings in which they resided with their extended families. These houses were grouped in proximity to each other and would form a hamlet over time. Small towns were formed as the hamlets started to expand and meet each other, and a new social structure emerged.

Archaeological excavations indicate that Uruk developed from two separate settlements named Eanna and Kullaba, which grew in size and merged to form the first city (Uruk). Further excavations at this site showed that the city was surrounded by walls that were 5.9 miles (9.5 kilometers) long and enclosed an area of 450 hectares (1,111 acres). It is estimated that the population at this time was around fifty thousand people.

Uruk was considered the most prominent of the Mesopotamian cities for a thousand years. Archaeological evidence and texts confirm that Uruk exercised a certain amount of control over the smaller surrounding villages and towns when it came to trade and political power. However, it is unclear how Uruk's power was enforced, as the administration of the region was decentralized and managed by each of the smaller cities.

What Distinguished Uruk from the Other Cities?

Scholars and historians often ask why Uruk was such a dominant city-state when the city-state of Ur was geographically better located for economic power through trade. Ur was located on a channel of the Euphrates River and lay farther south than Uruk. It was closer to the Persian Gulf—a gateway to the possibly lucrative Arabian and

Mediterranean markets. There is no consensus regarding this issue as of yet.

The Late Uruk Period

As the headwaters of the Persian Gulf receded south during the dry spell of the Late Uruk period, the marshlands shrank. Irrigation of the agricultural fields had to be increased. The rivers that used to provide a natural source for irrigation began to shrink due to severe droughts in the north, making it increasingly difficult to feed the growing population. To solve this problem, the Sumerians looked to colonize surrounding and even far-away areas, which was yet another first in history.

Colonization of the neighboring city-states, especially in the Susiana Plain, occurred between 3700 and 3400 BCE. Archaeological evidence of the cultural, artifactual, architectural, and symbolic remains confirm this timeline and location.

Throughout the colonization period, smaller settlements like Tell Brak and Hamoukar in the north of Mesopotamia were colonized by Uruk. Hamoukar was established to the north of Uruk during the Early Uruk period. These city-states were originally part of the extensive trade routes for bitumen and copper.

It is interesting to note that the expansion and colonized areas were not managed from Uruk but were instead run locally through regional administrative centers. These administrative centers were able to control the manufacture and trade of objects. Cylinder seals, pottery, and other materials excavated in these regions confirm that trading colonies in Syria, Anatolia, and Iran shared the same administrative systems and pottery styles at this time. The products from each center were manufactured locally.

The White Temple of Uruk

Visible from a distance, this magnificent ziggurat, known as the Anu Ziggurat, had a magnificent white temple dedicated to the sky god Anu at its top, which would have dominated the skyline. Located in modern-day Warka, Iraq, archaeologists estimate that it would have taken 1,500 laborers around 5 years to complete its construction. These laborers would have had to work ten-hour days. It is surmised that some laborers would have been coerced or forced to do the work and that only some of their labor was paid for.

Remains of the ziggurat at Uruk that had the White Temple.[3]

The White Temple of Uruk is a typical example of a "high temple." It emerged in this region to honor the patron deity of a city. This rectangular temple was built in the tripartite style, with the corners oriented to the four cardinal directions: north, south, east, and west. This exceptional whitewashed temple, measuring 57.4 feet by 76.4 feet (17.5 by 23.3 meters), would have been a spectacular sight under the midday sun.

As was typical in tripartite buildings, a long central hall was flanked by smaller rooms. An altar was located at the end of the hall, and a niche in a prominent wall for a statue of the patron god would have had a place of pride.

Hamoukar

The settlement of this city dates back to the 5th millennium BCE and was inhabited during the Ubaid and Early Uruk periods. The excavated city is in northeastern Syria, near the Iraq and Turkey borders.

Obsidian processing was the main commercial activity at this settlement. This shows us the people's innovation and drive to ensure sustainable living. The raw obsidian was not locally available and had to be imported from southern Anatolia, which was around 70 miles (112.65 kilometers) away. The manufactured obsidian tools and weapons were then exported to southern Mesopotamia, resulting in the generation of income for the inhabitants. The obsidian workshops covered an area of around 692 acres (280 hectares), and chemical analysis of the obsidian found here confirmed that it came from the foothills of Mount Nemrut in modern-day Turkey.

In Hamoukar, evidence shows the emergence of class structures, with the elites accumulating wealth. They bought their food and other supplies from surrounding villages.

After Hamoukar became an established and wealthy city, the inhabitants realized that the city needed more security. They built a wall around it, thus establishing the first walled city of which we are aware. The urbanization process here can be attributed to economic growth rather than people being coerced or forced to live there as laborers.

At its peak, Hamoukar had around 20,000 inhabitants and covered an area of 259 acres (105 hectares). Hamoukar did not only export tools and weapons to the south. New evidence confirms that they also traded with the north. This northern trade was independently undertaken, proving that Hamoukar had its own rulers or at least some form of independence.

Before the battle of Hamoukar, the inhabitants had progressed to manufacturing copper tools and weapons, making it a target for conquerors due to the city's wealth and accomplishments.

Battle of Hamoukar

The battle of Hamoukar is referred to as the first incident of urban warfare. Excavations have indicated that the attack on the city must have been well-planned. It appears as though it took place rather suddenly, though, catching the inhabitants off-guard. Their unpreparedness might be partly due to the surrounding ten-foot (three-meter) thick walls, which likely left them feeling secure. The invaders somehow set fire to the city. Walls and roofs of buildings that were not consumed by the fire collapsed. Archaeologists have uncovered enough artifacts from the rubble to form a good idea of how the city was destroyed.

Fairly recent excavations have uncovered over 2,300 egg-shaped clay sling bullets from two of the collapsed administrative buildings. Further evidence of the battle, such as twelve graves of male victims, was also found underneath the rubble. Archaeologists are confident the fire that destroyed the city was set by an enemy and was not caused by an earthquake or an accident.

Tell Brak

Tell Brak is located in northeastern Syria. It sits on one of the major ancient trade routes connecting Mesopotamia, Anatolia, Euphrates cities, and Mediterranean seaports. This is one of the largest tells in the area that has been excavated to date.

Tell Brak covered an extensive area of 98 acres (40 hectares) and rose to 131 feet (40 meters) before the excavations. During this city-state's peak, it was spread over an area of between 271 and 395 acres (110 and 160 hectares) and had a population of between 17,000 and 24,000.

Suburbs at Tell Brak

The tell was surrounded by smaller hamlets or suburbs where many of its inhabitants lived. These suburbs cover an area of over 741 acres (300 hectares). Archaeological evidence indicates that this area had been inhabited since the Ubaid period and lasted until the middle of the 1st millennium CE.

Excavations at Tell Brak, Hamoukar, and Tepe Gawra provide archaeologists with pottery and architectural evidence that confirms these city-states shared the same religious, administrative, and social behaviors.

An enormous building for non-residential purposes has been excavated at Tell Brak, exposing walls made from red mudbrick. This majestic building has an entrance with a basalt gateway that has towers on each side. The walls are 6 feet thick (1.85 meters) and 5 feet high (1.5 meters) and are still visible today.

Tel Brak Industry

A craft workshop was excavated in which flint manufacturing, basalt grinding, and mollusk shell inlays took place. Another building for the manufacture of ceramic bowls has been identified, and its purpose was confirmed by the substantial number of mass-produced bowls it contained. A unique chalice made from obsidian and white marble held together with bitumen was also found in this building. This same building even housed an ample collection of stamp seals and sling bullets.

Social Gatherings

The Tell Brak feast hall contained a large number of mass-produced plates and tasseled pots. This building has been identified as a feast hall due to the large ovens with animal remains found in the northern courtyard. The interior of the feast hall contains several large hearths, which would have provided heat during communal gatherings and feasts.

Beer made from barley and groats was apparently consumed at these feasts, and copious amounts of meat were devoured. It would appear that the ancient civilization had a work life, a social life, and a religious life.

Religion

Religious practices were centered on the worship of an all-seeing deity, and a temple in Tell Brak was dedicated to this god, which was the city's patron deity. This temple may indicate that Tell Brak was one of the first cities in northern Mesopotamia that practiced an organized religion—at least as far as we know.

The inhabitants of Tell Brak made votive figurines and symbols that they used to worship their all-seeing god. However, it is possible they worshiped a goddess instead. Scholars surmise that the Sumerian goddess Inanna, who is associated with political power, war, justice, beer, love, and beauty, was the goddess the people of Tell Brak worshiped.

Eye figurines and symbols found at the temple in Tell Brak.[4]

Chapter 3: The Early Dynastic Period

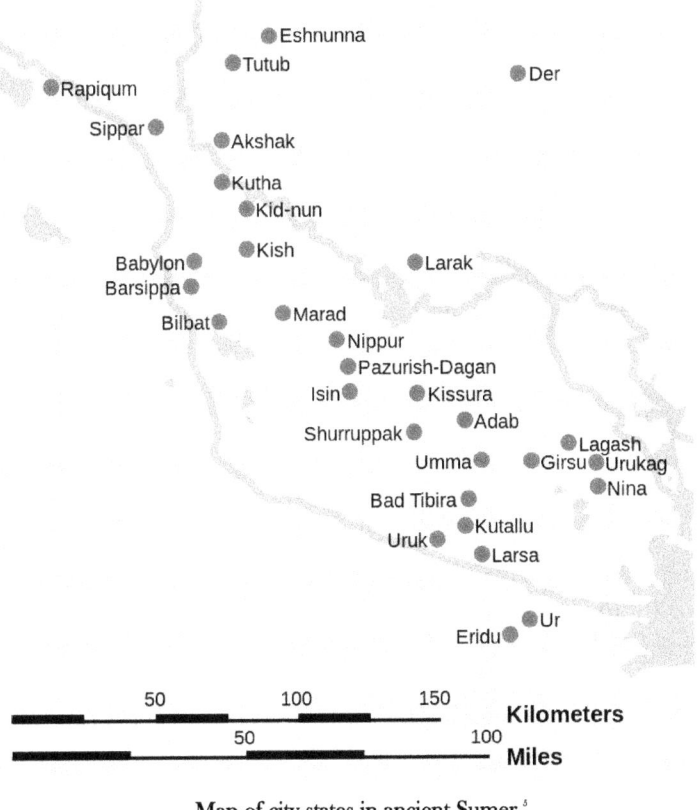

Map of city-states in ancient Sumer.[5]

The Rise of the Early Dynastic Period

Although there are no clearly demarcated eras in the development of Sumer during the Early Dynastic period, scholars have divided it into three phases: Early Dynastic I (c. 2900-2800 BCE), Early Dynastic II (c. 2800-2600 BCE), and Early Dynastic III (c. 2600-2334 BCE). The entire ED (Early Dynastic) period was one of growth and innovations. Many of the "firsts" credited to the Sumerians date to this period and the short bridging phase immediately before it.

Knowledge of this period is largely due to archaeological excavations, later historical records, and deciphering Sumerian writings that date to the later part of the Early Dynastic period. Historians often have to compare several of these sources to come to reasonably reliable conclusions since some of the information, especially from ancient records, is only partly factual.

A good example is the Sumerian King List, which provides valuable information for a discerning researcher, although they are interwoven with impossibly lengthy reigns and lifespans of kings coupled with obviously mythical deeds and beings. Although the Sumerian king list contains several Semitic names of kings and places, it has been reasonably established that the Sumerians were non-Semitic in origin.

Jemdet Nasr Period

During the final phase of the Uruk period and the beginning of the Early Dynastic period, around 3000 BCE to 2900 BCE, a relatively brief overlapping period has been identified. It was named the Jemdet Nasr period after the site that was confirmed to be Sumerian. This period lasted from 3100 to 2900 BCE, and radiocarbon dating confirms these dates. Scholars are divided in their acceptance of the Jemdet Nasr period as a separate phase due to wide cultural similarities with the preceding and following periods.

The scientific world was first alerted to the Jemdet Nasr culture when clay tablets with a proto-cuneiform (Archaic) type of writing were discovered. These tablets had appeared in antiquities markets since around 1903. The writing had already been identified as the Sumerian language due to the discovery of later tablets. An Assyriologist, Stephen Langdon, started excavations at Jemdet Nasr in 1926. The same cultural aspects that were identified at this site were later discovered at many other archaeological sites across southern and central Mesopotamia.

Administrative clay tablet from the Jemdet Nasr Period, Uruk III.[6]

The period seems to be an extension of the Uruk period, as it saw the further development of several inventions and characteristics already evident in the Uruk period. Ceramics are present in polychrome and in the distinct monochrome, which were similar to the Ubaid period. The original pictographic writing invented during the Uruk period had developed into a more abstract style by this time. The distinctive wedge shape of cuneiform writing also dates to this Early Dynastic bridging period.

Early Dynastic Period

The Early Dynastic period started at different times across Sumer, at least according to the archaeological record of the sites so far excavated. The one thing that the beginning of Sumerian history to almost the late Early Dynastic period has in common is the insecurity of the chronology and the dates on which they are hung. More radiocarbon dating and modern scientific methods of dating are sorely needed to enable scholars to refine and correlate these dates.

According to early excavations done in the previous century, there appeared to be a break in cultural deposits and established networks around 2900 BCE. At the time, this was explained by the story of the Great Flood. Legends of a universal flood are recorded in the tales of several ANE (ancient Near East) scripts, as well as the biblical flood. Great and widespread floods from circa 2900 to 2800 BCE seemed to be confirmed by very thick mud deposits (11 feet or 3.35 meters). These deposits were found by Leonard Woolley in his excavations at Ur and at other sites by different archaeologists.

The controversy surrounding the reality of such a flood added to the many arguments involving the Sumerian civilization. The problem with the flood story is that the dates, depths of mud layers, and sites where mud layers are present do not correlate. Furthermore, this mud layer does not appear at all the sites that have been excavated.

The delta area of southern Mesopotamia was prone to seasonal floods, especially by the Euphrates River, which caused the rivers to often change course. Even though the Euphrates was relatively shallow, it was known to have wiped away everything in its path on occasion. The various mud layers are better explained as being the results of different floods at different times. These floods would have varied in intensity. The stories of these floods were then passed down orally and combined with myths and legends before eventually being written down.

Cultural Advancements

The First Dynasty of Egypt has been radiocarbon dated to 3100 BCE and is considered by historians to be the oldest dynasty in the world. The Sumerian Early Dynastic period is the first era in Mesopotamia in which a dynastic ruling line can be traced. At the same time, the earliest settlements and villages started to have leadership. It is widely accepted that this role eventually progressed via a line of kinship, with a family head becoming a chieftain and passing leadership on to members of the same family.

Writing progressed from simple pictographic commercial records and transactions. This was due to the development of syllabic representations, which could be more flexibly used. During the Early Dynastic II and III, the first contemporary extant text that can be described as historical is in praise of Enmebaragesi, King of Kish. However, this wasn't erected by just any person; Enmebaragesi commissioned it himself! It is dated to c. 2600 BCE and is housed in the Iraq Museum in Baghdad.

Religion in Ancient Sumer

Similar to previous Sumerian periods, religion played a large role, and the belief that humans were on Earth to serve the gods was firmly entrenched in every aspect of life. Placating and honoring the deities was paramount in the life of every Sumerian. Interestingly, the first gift dedicated by a king to a god that we have definitive proof of was not dedicated to the patron god of the city or that king! The inscription, which was discovered at Tell al-'Ubaid, was from a king of Ur and dedicated to one of the major Sumerian goddesses who influenced daily life. It stated, "Aanepada King of Ur, son of Mesanepada King of Ur, has built this for his lady Ninhursag."

The priests of local deities played an important role. They advised the people at all levels of society. Since they acted as mouthpieces of the deities, they made the will of the gods clear to the people in all matters, whether it was personal or work-related. The priests had to clarify the reasons for a bad experience or situation, such as a calamity or the infertility of people and/or their livestock. The priests were also the interpreters of what the deities needed to right the matter.

They used several methods of divination; reading the entrails of a sheep or goat is a popular example. They also interpreted the dreams and visions of people in their communities. They received direction from the deities via oracles, dreams, and cosmic signs. The priest-kings and later the kings received, acted upon, and communicated the will of the gods to the people.

Priests were also doctors. Due to their association with the deities, they were believed to have the knowledge to define the cause and prescribe a cure, which would all be communicated to them by the gods.

The ziggurats, which were often in the centers of cities, were not built as places of worship. They did not have space for gatherings, despite their monumental size. They were built as a dwelling for the local patron deity, and in larger cities, there might be more than one ziggurat since the people had to honor the supreme deities as well. Large quantities of votive offerings and statuettes and later cuneiform messages on pieces of clay, stone, or other suitable materials were discovered under floors and inside the walls of these buildings and the temples on their tops. These were presumably placed there by priests on behalf of individuals who wanted to plead, implore, or thank a deity.

A wall plaque depicting libations to a seated god; Ur, 2500 BCE.[7]

Structure of Society

The early Sumerians were not class conscious, and it appears that all citizens were equal. This is confirmed by grave goods from cemeteries that were excavated at several archaeological sites, as well as later texts about the early periods. This changed over time, and class structures developed naturally. Changes in individual responsibilities and communal duties, the implementation of leadership and authority, and an accumulation of wealth created stratification among the people.

Increased agricultural production led to the division of labor and specialization of crafts. This was firmly entrenched by the Early Dynastic period. Four main levels of society can be distinguished. These were the priests, the upper class, the lower class, and the slaves. Archaeologists were able to confirm these distinctions from grave goods interred with the dead.

It appears from the artworks of the ED period that the priests and sometimes kings shaved their heads. Women wore their long hair in braids or elaborate coifs piled on their heads. Men had long hair, which was often tied up in a knot. People dressed in skirts or dresses with scalloped hems that overlapped in layers, slightly reminiscent of the feathers of a bird. Jewelry was worn by both men and women, rich and poor, with clear class distinctions obvious in the materials from which it was made. The upper class and rulers wore exquisite adornments made from gold and other precious materials. This has been confirmed by excavations of grave goods with which they were buried.

Men and women had equal rights during this period, and women participated in all parts of society. Kingship was mostly bestowed on males, but we know of one woman, Ku Bau, an innkeeper or brewer of beer, who received the kingship of Kish.

Rise of the Kings, Cities, and City-States

In the early Mesopotamian towns, the first rulers were priests, but they became kings once villages had progressed and enlarged into urban centers. Kingship became an integral part of the social organization, and by the Early Dynastic I period, the priests, the military, and the entire community were lower in status than the local kings. Kings were more secular in function, but their primary objective of pleasing the city's patron god and the major gods of the Sumerian pantheon remained the same. It should be noted that for the Sumerians, the kingship was divine— a gift bestowed by the gods on an elected subject that could be removed if the gods so wished.

The king claimed his appointment to the throne by the city's deity and was seen as representing that deity. The kings portrayed themselves as subservient to the deity's wishes and acted as part of the community in their service to the gods. In artworks, the kings can be seen participating in communal activities like the building of a temple. But at the same time, the portrayals of kings in personalized and named capacities indicate the growth in the status of those leaders. The grave goods from the royal cemetery at Ur and the building of palaces verify this trend.

Votive Relief of Ur-Nanshe, King of Lagash, as the bird god Anzu.[8]

The first historically verifiable dynastic king, Mesannepada (Mesanepada), is thought to have started the First Dynasty of Ur around 2670 BCE.

Names of kings often come from inscriptions. Ur-Nanshe, the first king of the First Dynasty of Lagash, added to an inscription about how he honored the goddess Nanshe by building a canal. "For Nanshe he dug the Ninadua-canal, her beloved canal, and extended its far end to the sea."

A votive statuette of a musician named Ur-Nanshe was found in the ruins of a temple at the distant site of Mari in Syria around this same period (c. 2520 BCE). An inscription of his name ran across the shoulders. The superbly carved statuette could have been a trade good, as the Sumerians had trade colonies as far away as Tell Brak in Syria since the Uruk period. The statuette is currently claimed to have been made in Mari, but there remains the possibility that there is some connection to Sumer.

Ur-Nanshe, King of Lagash, ruled c. 2520 BCE. Excavations at Lagash (modern-day Telloh) provided archaeologists with a massive number of cuneiform tablets. These tablets, together with inscriptions on monuments and stelae, provided important information about the Sumerian civilization during this period.

Kish was another important city-state in the Early Dynastic period. Kish was founded sometime around the Jemdet Nasr period. Although Kish was impacted by the flood of c. 2900 BCE, it flourished soon after. According to legend, the deities brought kingship down to Earth for a second time after the Great Flood and established it in Kish. Modern scholars first confirmed the title for a king, *lugal* (big man), as opposed to the previous *en* (priest) or *en-lugal* (priest-king), in the records from Kish.

Part of Kish's importance lay in its strategic position. It was situated where the Tigris and Euphrates come close together, so it had control over both rivers. Thus, the people could influence the irrigation waters and river traffic farther south; it was a powerful position that could affect the veritable lifeblood of the southern city-states.

Urbanization developed in the Uruk period, but it increased during the Early Dynastic periods. The Early Dynastic I period saw more innovative developments. New cities were built, and by the Early Dynastic II period, they had become city-states. The central buildings of these city-states were still religious buildings, which by this time were almost entirely ziggurats.

The city of Ur was founded during the Ubaid period. By the Early Dynastic period, it was a highly developed and prosperous city. Several other cities were on par with Ur, and these cities developed into fully-fledged independent city-states.

The city-states were similar in regards to cultural and political ideas and administration, yet they were undoubtedly heterogeneous and independent from each other. In previous eras, towns were recognized by other cities as major political entities, and there were periods when one held sway over others.

Each city-state consisted of a central city with surrounding smaller villages. They had their own armies, central food storage facilities, ziggurats, administrative centers, and specialized industries. They traded with each other, the neighboring world, and far afield.

Apart from the natural river shifts, human changes to the natural watercourses increased. The people diverted the rivers through canals, which had been done in previous eras as well. There are inscriptions from the late Early Dynastic III period, when writing was more developed, attesting to the large and important water diversions and canals. As mentioned above, a king of Lagash added how he honored the goddess Nanshe by building a canal to an inscription.

Conflicts, Battles, and Wars

Skirmishes are as old as the human race itself, and the Sumerians were no exception. As the city-states flourished and the populations grew, so did the need for more—more land, more resources, more control. The city-states also needed more protection against foreign enemies, such as the Gutians and the Elamites, who raided their trade routes and invaded their lands. Armies were created, weapons were developed, and cities were surrounded by defensive walls.

Battles were often fought between neighboring Sumerian city-states and included trade disputes, boundary disputes, resource control, and ownership matters. The conflicts driven by rivalry increased during the Early Dynastic period, which is reflected in the depictions of battles in artworks.

According to the Sumerian King List, rivalries led to battles, which then led to one city taking control of the other after defeating them. This meant the end of a line of kings, as the kingship of the conquered city was removed. Usually, the conquered city would eventually rebel and become autonomous again, thus kicking off a new dynasty.

The first pictographic depiction of a battle dates to around 3500 BCE, and it came from Kish. The first historically recorded war took place after c. 2700 BCE. This conflict was between the Sumerians and the Elamites. The king of Kish at the time, Enembaragesi, defeated the Elamites and carried off their weapons. The famous Stele of the Vultures records one of the many battles fought between the neighboring Sumerian city-states of Lagash and Umma, with this particular battle taking place sometime around 2500 BCE. Apart from the rather gruesome depiction of vultures carrying off the heads of the vanquished, this stele gives historians insight into the weapons and military formation of the victor: Lagash.

Cuneiform Script

During the Early Dynastic II period, clay seals were wider and elaborately decorated with human or animal scenes. The difference in clay seals is one of the few ways scholars distinguish between the Early Dynastic I and Early Dynastic II periods.

The most important invention during the Early Dynastic period is arguably the invention of writing. Cuneiform tablets with the same Archaic script have been found at several sites. These sites are far apart from each other, which indicates that the script did not develop in isolation. City-states were in continuous contact, and they would have shared ideas and inventions, despite their autonomy.

Example of pictographic script.[9]

By c. 2700 BCE, the original pictographic script, also called proto-Sumerian or Archaic, had evolved to include representations of sounds. This enabled the Sumerians to write any word or even abstract concepts. By c. 2500 BCE, the script had developed into a limited number of wedge-shaped lines that could be arranged in various ways and combinations to transmit anything that needed to be communicated.

The script, which originated due to the need to record trade and administrative matters, bloomed into a full-blown written language. Toward the end of the Early Dynastic era, the Sumerians created literature.

Chapter 4: The Akkadian Period

In the northern city of Kish during the 24th century BCE, a foundling raised by the king's gardener became the king's cupbearer. This king was Ur-Zababa. The position of cupbearer had to be filled by someone who was seen as trusted and powerful. Some scholars believe the cupbearer influenced the king's decisions. This cupbearer of Ur-Zababa would later become Sargon the Great.

At this time, the powerful king from Uruk in southern Sumer was Lugal-zage-si. He was in the process of expanding his territory, and his armies were working their way upriver to Kish. According to some sources, Lugal-zage-si had already conquered most of the Sumerian city-states and some areas adjacent to Sumer. Some scholars claim Lugal-zage-si oversaw the world's first empire, but this is refuted by evidence and analysis. It is accepted that Lugal-zage-si gained control over several city-states and then bragged that he had conquered all of Sumer. One must also remember that the fiercely independent city-states of ancient Sumer did not see their geographical locations as part of a whole—in other words, a country—despite having the same language and culture.

Ur-Zababa sent his cupbearer with a message to Lugal-zage-si, supposedly to offer a deal. It turns out that the message actually asked Lugal-zage-si to kill the messenger! Ur-Zababa must have lost his trust in his cupbearer at some point and wanted to get rid of him. Whether the message contained any suggestion of a peace deal is unclear. What is known is that Lugal-zage-si and Sargon joined forces and easily conquered Kish. Sargon became the king of Kish and then had a falling out with his benefactor. He captured Lugal-zage-si and cruelly forced him to wear a yoke around his neck. Sargon then dragged him to Nippur, the city-state of the deity Enlil, in whose name Lugal-zage-si claimed his kingship.

The former cupbearer to the king of Kish took the name Sargon (also spelled as Sarru-kin, which is believed to mean "the king is established/legitimate") as his throne name. According to legend and from Sargon's so-called autobiography, he was born to a priestess of an important temple and did not know his father. He was beloved and selected for kingship as a youth by the Sumerian goddess Inanna or, according to some sources, Ishtar. It must be noted that the records of this version of events date to the Old Babylonian period, which came much later. Thus, its authenticity as coming from Sargon himself must remain in doubt.

The Conquests of King Sargon

Sargon set out on a military expansion campaign across Sumer and later boasted in an inscription that he triumphed in thirty-four battles on his journey to the Persian Gulf. During his travels, he conquered the whole of Sumer. Thus, the first true empire in history was born. Sargon's reign lasted from c. 2334 BCE to 2279 BCE, and his successors ruled after him until the empire was overthrown in c. 2150 BCE.

According to some sources, the socio-political situation in Sumer was not as bright as it had been. The elite and priesthood were abusing their power to the extent that the lower classes were suffering unbelievable hardships. Some are said to have been forced to sell their children to cover their debts. In some states, the rulers became nothing more than warlords ruling with an iron fist. The struggles of the commoners against their elite rulers may have contributed to Sargon's successes.

To the east, the conquest of an Elamite city, Arawa, was recorded in inscriptions, and other Elamite cities followed, although we do not know the exact years or names. On a victory stele found in Susa, Sargon calls himself the conqueror of Elam and Parabium. This might indicate that he had fully conquered Elam to the east of Sumer and Akkad. To the north of Akkad in the Upper Euphrates region, there is evidence of Sargon's conquests in archaeological and textual records. At Mari, for example, the great palace was destroyed shortly after the beginning of Sargon's reign and then later rebuilt during the middle of the Akkadian period. Sargon also made an inscription stating that Mari and Elam obeyed him as the lord of the land.

Some of the wars fought during Sargon's reign appear to be raids rather than a war of conquest. In addition, many of the foreign regions were city-states rather than countries. Sargon's trade ambitions may have been satisfied by having merchants installed in some foreign countries rather than governors.

Many Sargonic inscriptions are known today only through copies made by later Babylonian scribes. From this information, modern-day scholars have ascertained that Sargon indeed conquered and made incursions into most of the ancient Near East. He called himself "king of the world" and the king and/or priest of various areas. One inscription reads that Dagan (the chief deity of several ancient Near East nations) gave Sargon Mari, Yarmuti, Ebla (Irbil), and as far as the cedar forests and the silver mountains. The latter probably indicates Lebanon and the Taurus Mountains.

Sargon created a new capital called Agade to the north of Sumer, and his empire was called the Akkadian Empire. The people of the lands forming Akkad north of the Sumerian city-states were mostly Semitic-speaking tribes. Under the new centralized administration, the official language was Akkadian, although they used the Sumerian cuneiform script. The various languages and dialects of conquered states were still in use, but preference was given to Akkadian, which eventually became the lingua franca of the ancient Near East.

Although the general opinion of later ancient records states that Sargon built his new capital of Agade or Akkad, there are tantalizing clues that the city already existed before Sargon came to power. The earliest written mention of the city can be found during the Second Dynasty of Uruk, dating to the so-called "year date" of Ensakusanna.

The location of Agade remains elusive to this day. The Akkadians undoubtedly inherited their penchant for recording commercial transactions, personal and administrative matters, building projects, trade and trading partners, skirmishes and wars, and religious matters from the Sumerians. The discovery of Agade and its archives will shed light on and clarify much of this period.

The Wealthy Capital of the Akkadian Empire: Agade

The capital of the Akkadian Empire is described in contemporary and copied materials from other Mesopotamian sources as a wealthy, thriving, and bustling metropolis. It had an especially busy harbor. Ships at the docks were described as loading and offloading agricultural produce, various trade goods, scarce resources, and exotic goods from distant lands. The conquest of Sumer opened the route to the Persian Gulf, so all the sea and river trade crafts now docked at Agade. Sea traffic came from Bahrain, the Indus Valley, Egypt, Arabia, and Ethiopia.

Legends of the city's riches and treasures circulated long after it was gone. In later periods, it was a destination for treasure hunters. Extant texts, for instance, describe a three-year-long archaeological excavation undertaken by a scribe during the time of Babylonian King Nabonidus, who ruled c. 555 BCE to 539 BCE.

Sargon wanted to extend trade and diplomatic relationships from his capital city across the entire ancient Near East. Sargon's armies were said to have marched as far as the Mediterranean, Syria, Anatolia, the sources of the Tigris and Euphrates, and areas around the Arabian Gulf, conquering all in their path. Sargon controlled most of the trade routes across the ancient Near East.

Much of Sargon's rule has become so intertwined with legends that it is difficult to discern fact from fiction. Sargon was a legend in his own time, and rulers of other kingdoms and later eras would claim descendancy to Sargon's lineage to legitimize their rule or gain higher standing and respect.

The Semitic Akkadians had mingled with and learned from the Sumerians over a long period of time, and Sargon's new empire flourished with the new additional territories, his new capital city, and a new centralized government. The brilliant Sargon realized that the fiercely independent Sumerian city-states would soon be clamoring for their independence once more. As a countermeasure, he installed family members and trusted leaders in various prominent positions in the cities. Nevertheless, part of his army was kept busy putting down recurring revolts, especially toward the end of his reign.

After unifying the south of Mesopotamia, Sargon conquered the rest of the loosely associated cities in ancient Mesopotamia and other regions of the ancient Near East. The chronology and the exact extent of these conquests remain elusive. It appears that battles in distant places were not followed up with the continued rule of that state; it is possible these battles were brief military follow-up incursions to subdue the areas that tried to regain independence. Records from cities like Mari, Ebla, and others confirm Sargon's conquests and influence across the Fertile Crescent and beyond. Tablets from Ebla indicate that it was a province of

Akkad at one time.

Akkad – A Centralized Imperial Government

Local governors across the Akkadian Empire were appointed by Sargon, and they implemented the policies dictated by the central government in Agade. Standard units of measure and tax systems were implemented across the empire.

The implemented policies and changes included overhauling and centralizing the administration of agricultural production. Agricultural lands were enlarged by relocating people to nearby urban centers, thus centralizing the labor force. These newly extended urban centers were enclosed by city walls. Agricultural production from the dry fields in the north of Mesopotamia was supplemented with irrigation.

Part of Sargon's strategy to limit revolts included relocating Akkadian people to Sumerian and other city-states. He used propaganda to keep people in awe of him by describing wars, detailing the number of enemies slain and the number of people enslaved during campaigns. These records were inscribed on statues and stelae. Revolts were brutally crushed, and entire cities were punished by tearing down their city walls. In southern Mesopotamia, that meant flooding the cities with river water. The people who remained loyal to the Akkadian Empire during revolts were rewarded with land taken from the rebels and the slain.

Art from the Akkadian period shows a marked swing to more naturalistic scenes, monumental art, and sculpture. Seals were created with backgrounds and realistic drawings of people and animals. Sculptures and reliefs portrayed real people, which is evident from the remains of similar, if not identical, representations of kings placed in the temple precincts of many cities across the empire. It can be assumed that these statues served as a constant reminder to the people of who the king was. Like the statues of the patron deities, the statues of the king were always present in cities.

A magnificent bronze head, which is thought to have been part of a statue, was recovered during excavations at Nineveh in 1931. It is believed to portray Sargon of Akkad. Bronze statues were cast by the lost wax technique, in which the melted metal was cast in a wax mold. The Akkadian kings used visual arts, including statues of themselves with inscriptions of their deeds and religious devotion, as a propaganda device.

The Akkadian Empire gave us the first "named" poet in history! Enheduanna was a princess and a high priestess, and she wrote poems and hymns during the reign of Sargon the Great. She was actually Sargon's daughter. Luckily, her literary contributions formed part of the later Old Babylonian and Assyrian scribal curriculums, so copies of her work were saved for posterity.

As part of Sargon's strategic appointments after he conquered Sumer, Sargon appointed his daughter, Enheduanna, as the high priestess of the patron deity of Ur in southern Mesopotamia. It is speculated that the appointment was partly to link the Semitic religion of Akkad to the Sumerian religion. Sargon did not replace the Sumerian gods; he adopted them into the Akkadian culture, sometimes under Akkadian names. During Leonard Woolley's excavations at Ur, he discovered an alabaster disc that named Enheduanna as the high priestess of the Sumerian moon god, Inanna. It also stated that Sargon was her father.

Rimush – The Usurper

When Sargon died after ruling for around fifty-five years, his younger son, Rimush, became the ruler. Why Rimush became the ruler and not Sargon's eldest son is a mystery. Conquered states saw Sargon's death as a chance to get their autonomy back, so rebellions broke out across the empire.

Rimush gathered his father's forces and brutally crushed the rebels. He dealt harshly with the Sumerian city-states. Mass deportations and seizure of lands were the order of the day. Temple lands, which were the primary source of income for priests, were confiscated and given to Akkadians. According to records recovered from Umma, survivors from rebellions and other deportees were put in labor camps and worked to death. Could concentration camps be counted as another Sumerian first?

Victory stelae of Rimush have been found in several places, including Elam. He called himself "king of the world" and "king of the universe." And like his father, he inscribed the exact numbers of soldiers and civilians killed, deported, and enslaved. One inscription, for instance, at the city of Kazallu, where a rebellion had broken out, recorded that twelve thousand people were killed in battle and that five thousand were taken as slaves. Inscriptions also recorded the types and quantities of booty confiscated by the king's forces.

Rimush only ruled for nine turbulent years before he was assassinated in his palace. According to legend, he was strangled with cylinder seals, which were probably tied in a string. The culprits were never identified, but speculation includes his older brother, Manishtushu.

Manishtushu – Rightful Heir of Sargon?

Manishtushu declared that Enlil, one of the Sumerian chief deities, had called him to kingship. After the continuous wars of his brother's short reign, he arranged a feast in Agade for representatives of various cities and regions. Legend has it that a total of 964 rulers gathered at Agade for a lavish feast, with beer flowing abundantly. Manishtushu's guards and soldiers looked on to prevent skirmishes from breaking out. Manishtushu managed to convince them to accept a land deal. The details of it are not clear, but it was highly favorable to Manishtushu. The beer probably helped!

Nevertheless, Manishtushu tried to promote peace, unlike his brother before him. He appears to have had peaceful trade relations with cities and states in the Iranian desert, Anatolia, the Mediterranean region, the Indus Valley, Arabia, Egypt, and perhaps Ethiopia.

Records recovered at Tell Brak in Syria detail large-scale land reforms, which were done under the military's supervision. The most important stele from this period is the Manishtushu Obelisk. This magnificent object was made from black diorite stone imported from ancient Magan (Oman). It details the king's gift to four officials. An inscription states that Manishtushu sent a fleet of ships to Magan and successfully fought against thirty-two cities that had gathered to fight his forces. He destroyed their cities "as far as the silver mines."

Manishtushu, like his brother Rimush, was assassinated in Agade by members of his court.

Naram-Sin – Classical Period

The third ruler of Akkad was Manishtushu's son, Naram-Sin. The Akkadian Empire reached its peak during his reign. He was a rather controversial figure according to later sources, and he was blamed in *The Curse of Agade* for being responsible for the empire's fall. Like his grandfather, Sargon, Naram-Sin was ruthless at times but also the epitome of a true warrior king.

Naram-Sin recorded an inscription about a revolt of Sumerian cities led by Uruk and Kish. The inscription recounts that Naram-Sin fought nine battles at the beginning of his reign. The goddess Ishtar helped him to be victorious, and his people asked him to become the god of the city of Agade, where he built a temple for himself. Protective walls were demolished, cities were flooded, and many of the captives were brutally killed and enslaved.

Naram-Sin's reign is known as the Classical period of the Akkadian Empire due to its magnificent art and the size and achievements reached during this time. He expanded the empire to include the Zagros Mountains and their rich mineral resources and also possibly Cyprus. A destruction layer at Ebla in Syria dates to Naram-Sin's reign.

A cylinder seal depicts hunting scenes with Naram-Sin, which may indicate that he did not accompany his troops everywhere or that wars and conflicts tapered down sometimes.

Naram-Sin was credited with many building projects. He demolished the temple of Enlil in Nippur and replaced it with a larger and elaborately decorated temple. The majestic project was overseen by his son. There is a detailed account of the building materials, the progression of the work, and the numbers of different craftsmen, like carpenters, sculptors, metal workers, and more. The best craftsmen were commandeered from every corner of the empire to complete this temple.

At some point in his reign, Naram-Sin started to look at himself as a demi-god and is portrayed with the horned helmet that was once reserved for depicting deities. This can be seen, for example, on the famous pink limestone Victory Stele of Naram-Sin, which was originally from Sippar but discovered in Susa. Today, it is on display in the Louvre in Paris.

It is generally believed that an ancient treaty between the Egyptians and the Hittites after the Battle of Kadesh was the first treaty in the world. However, it is possible that the peace treaty was yet another first for Mesopotamia. It was concluded between Akkad and Elam during Naram-Sin's reign. It appears that he made a peace treaty with an Elamite king named Khita. The king of Elam stated that the enemy of Naram-Sin would be his enemy and that the friend of Naram-Sin would also be his friend. The treaty was sealed by the marriage of Naram-Sin to Khita's daughter.

Naram-Sin ruled for thirty-six years and died of natural causes around 2218 BCE.

Shar-Kali-Sharri

After Naram-Sin's death, his son, Shar-Kali-Sharri, became king. Yet again, the transition of power presented an opportunity for the Sumerian city-states to regain their independence. Shar-Kali-Sharri put down these revolts, and scholars are often forced to piece together bits and pieces of his twenty-five-year reign from records of year names. These include references such as the year in which Shar-Kali-Sharri captured Sarlagab, the king of Gutium, or the year Shar-Kali-Shari laid the foundation of the temple.

It is clear that the nomadic Gutians, who came from the foothills of the Zagros Mountains, intensified their incursions into the Akkadian territories. They were a menace during Naram-Sin's reign. Shar-Kali-Sharri collected high taxes from the empire to keep his armies equipped and ready to fight these incursions. This led to increased uprisings in the states under his rule. It was a vicious cycle, and he could not subdue every revolt, leading to the once-mighty Akkadian Empire losing control over much of its territory.

The End of an Empire

It behooves us to quote the author of the Sumerian King List at this point: "Then, who was king? Who was not king? Igigi, Nanum, Imi, and Elulu, the four of them were kings but ruled for a total of only 3 years."

Sargon and his dynasty connected the entire ancient Near East, allowing these regions to trade and exchange ideas. It seems that the Akkadians and Sumerians traveled in person to many parts of the inhabited world without playing the middleman as in pre-Sargonic times. Imports from outside the ancient Near East were recovered from the Akkadian era, and horses were imported for the first time, which could mean they had contact with people from the Eurasian Steppe.

The Akkadian language remained the lingua franca, especially for international correspondence, for millennia to come.

More recent studies show that there are indications of severe droughts and other climatic changes, like lower levels of the vital rivers, which contributed to the demise of the Akkadian Empire. It stands to reason that a slump in food production would have increased internal riots and general unrest across much of the ancient Near East beginning around 2200 BCE.

The Gutians seized their opportunity.

This mask is thought to be of Sargon the Great.[10]

Chapter 5: The Gutian Period

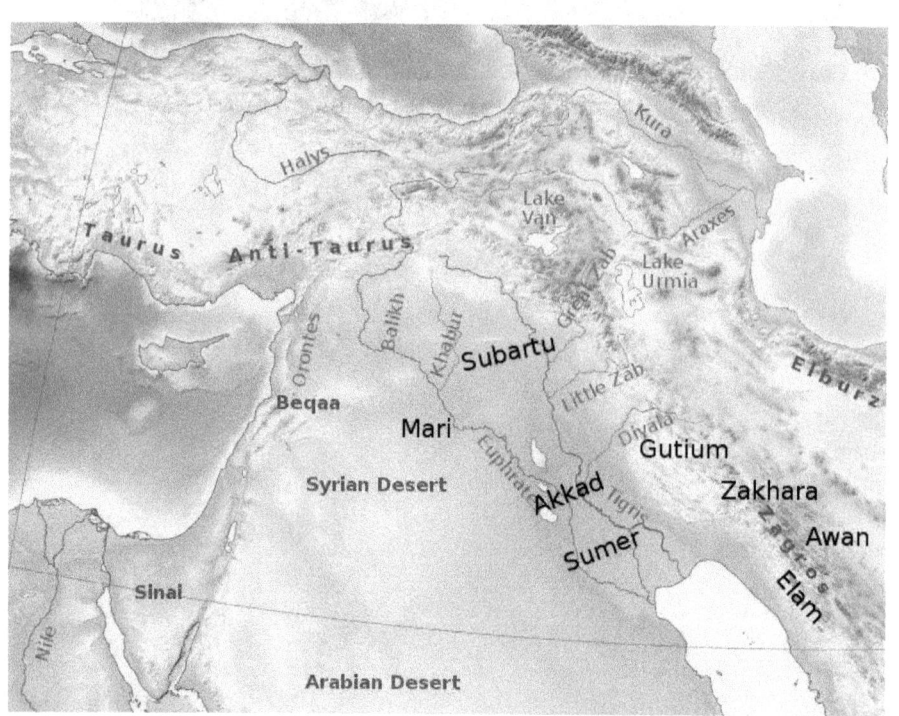

Map showing the Near East mountainous region.[11]

Where Did the Gutians Come From?

The Gutians were uncultured tribes that came from the Zagros Mountains, at least according to the Sumerians. They were in the habit of conducting quick raids into cities and towns across ancient Mesopotamia from early on. Records of the period are scarce, and much of what is available was written before and after the Gutian period. Since they were always a thorn in the side of the civilized cities of Sumer and Akkad, as well as other settled folks across much of Mesopotamia, a certain skepticism should be applied to the often-biased information in these texts.

According to the well-known Sumerologist Thorkild Jacobsen, the Gutians ruled for around one hundred years. They do not appear to have left much of an impression on Sumerian culture, language, or development. The period was described by later scribes as the "dark ages." The uneducated Gutians had no idea how to run an advanced society and were blamed for the disintegration of the irrigation systems, famine, great hardships, and the decline of the entire region.

Many of the accusations heaped upon the Gutians may, in reality, be the result of a severe drought. The earlier invasions of the Gutians consisted of quick raids to obtain whatever they wanted. They would then return to their homeland in the foothills of the Zagros Mountains. However, their pattern suddenly shifted. Their motives had changed. They came down to Sumer with no intention of leaving again. They may have been driven into Mesopotamia by other factors. Moreover, the instability of the Akkadian Empire provided them with the right momentum for a full-scale invasion.

What Was the Gutian Strategy?

The Gutian raids had turned into conquests, destroying much in their path. They now occupied the areas that they invaded and installed their own rulers.

Evidence confirms widespread, severe, and centuries-long droughts and climate change across much of the ancient Near East; no explanation has yet been established for why this took place. This could have been the instigator of the Gutian invasion—pastoralists looking for greener pastures. It is thought that climate change occurred roughly from 2200 to 1900 BCE. It is possible a large volcanic eruption took place, but no culprit has been identified. It is clear, though, that there was desertification of once-fertile areas and a significant drop in rainfall in the rest of the ancient Near East, with widespread food shortages, unrests, revolts, wars, and massive movements of people. The severe drought is confirmed by sediment samples from seabeds, riverbeds, and even ancient Egyptian records from the time of Pharaoh Pepi II.

Some of the Sumerian city-states seem to have had some amount of authority left, albeit as underlings of Gutian rulers. Thus, they went on with certain projects in their cities while acknowledging their lower status by not calling themselves kings. For example, in Umma, an inscription states the prince or governor (*patesi* in Sumerian) built a temple in the time of S'ium (or Ba-s'ium), King of the Gutians.

The Sumerian city-state of Lagash (modern Telloh) thrived around 2144 during the so-called "dark ages." Their ruler, Gudea, called himself *ensi* and believed himself to be the shepherd of his people rather than their king. Inscriptions call him the *ensi* of the god Ningirsu. He built many temples in several of the Sumerian cities, including the city-state of Lagash. The most famous of these temples is called E-ninnu in the city of Girsu, which Gudea rebuilt after having a dream of being instructed by the gods to do so. Gudea professed that he devoted his life to pleasing the gods, especially Ningirsu, the patron deity of Lagash.

During Gudea's reign, irrigation, roads, and other old Sumerian systems were repaired and used again. He had trade connections with several foreign lands, as can be seen from the materials used in temple construction and decoration, which included ebony from the Indus Valley, stone from Oman, and cedar wood from Lebanon.

The several slightly different extant Sumerian King List contains the names of twenty-one to twenty-five Gutian rulers, of which very few can be verified. It was indeed a dark age with few cultural achievements, except for those produced in semi-autonomous cities by remnants of the previous cultures. Some scholars believe the Gutians blended into the Sumerian and Akkadian cultures over time. Eventually, they worshiped the same deities and assumed Akkadian names.

The semi-autonomous city-states managed their partial freedom by paying tribute to the Gutian state. They carried on with their usual pursuits, and some localized Gutians adopted their practices. Like their predecessors—the Akkadians—the Gutians were unable to keep control over the vast geographical area that once was under the control of the Akkadian Empire.

Uruk also appeared to be thriving under a succession of its own kings, although it was a vassal state of the Gutians. It is clear that in some Sumerian city-states, power and independence were building, as the inept Gutians failed to retain control. It was only a matter of time before they would fall.

Tablet bearing an inscription of the governor of Umma declaring he erected a temple during the reign of king S'ium or Ba-s'ium of Gutium.[12]

Did the Gutians Leave Their Mark on Sumer?

As the Gutians' control declined further, a powerful king came to power in the city-state of Uruk. His name was Utu-hengal (also spelled as Utu-hegal). After making offers and supplications to the gods, he started a revolt against the Gutian rule. The Gutians gathered their forces to attack Utu-hengal, but he still triumphed. The king of the Gutians, Tirigan, fled to the Zagros Mountains. He and his family were taken prisoner by Utu-hengal's envoy. He was then returned to Utu-hengal blindfolded and with his hands in stocks.

Tirigan pleaded for mercy. Utu-hengal replied by putting his foot on Tirigan's neck. Sumerian kingship was restored to Uruk. Utu-hengal died seven years later in an accident. His son-in-law, Ur-Nammu, who was already the king of Ur, became king of Uruk as well. Thus, the next period in the history of Sumer, the Ur III Dynasty, began.

Seated King Ur-Nammu on a cylinder seal.[18]

Chapter 6: The Sumerian Renaissance

There are more than 120,000 known cuneiform tablets from the following period of Sumerian history, of which many thousands still have to be deciphered. Much of the information so far deciphered is about administrative matters, transaction records, economic matters, trade, and food.

The Reign of Ur-Nammu

Ur-Nammu became the king of Ur around 2112 BCE. After inheriting the throne of Uruk from his father-in-law, Utu-hengal, Ur-Nammu founded the Ur III Dynasty (also known as the Neo-Sumerian Empire). He amalgamated the city-states of Ur, Uruk, and Eridu and then set out to liberate the other Sumerian city-states from the Gutians. He was an enlightened ruler, and he portrayed himself as a liberator rather than a conqueror when he attacked these city-states. Consequently, the inhabitants were more than willing to join the Neo-Sumerian Empire after Ur-Nammu drove the ruling Gutians out of their cities.

He incorporated the rest of Sumer and went on to conquer the middle and north of Mesopotamia by defeating the king of Elam, Puzur-Inshushinak. This Elamite king or his father before him had taken over territories in the middle and north of Mesopotamia since the Gutians were declining in power. Ur-Nammu also brought Elamite territories like Susa under Sumerian control.

During Ur-Nammu's reign, the city-states of Sumer were united as a cohesive whole under a Sumerian ruler for the first time. They had learned from the Akkadian Empire that a centralized rule and administration could be a powerful deterrent and strong defense against enemy attacks. Ur-Nammu claimed the title of king of Sumer and Akkad, as well as king of the four corners of the world. His propaganda included a return to the old ways—the good old days of freedom before the Akkadian Empire ruled the Sumerians with an iron fist.

Ur-Nammu reinstated the use of Sumerian as the official language and promoted cultural growth in art and literature. Ancient Sumerian epics, hymns, and poems were learned and recited in public.

Ur-Nammu is the first ruler whose recorded laws and punishments are preserved in writing. His law code included both public and civil laws. To the surprise of scholars, many of the punishments included fines to compensate the victims. Serious offenses like murder and rape did carry the death penalty, though.

After ruling for eighteen years, Ur-Nammu was killed in a battle against the invading Gutians. It appears his troops deserted him. Ur-Nammu's praises were still sung, and his deeds were probably exaggerated by later generations. He was honored as a god after his death.

A poet described Ur-Nammu's death and funeral. He talked about how Ur-Nammu's body was brought back to Ur on a bier and laid in his palace while his soldiers and widow mourned. It also laments the actions of the gods, who callously let him die. Other gods could only watch and wail. According to the poet, the funeral procession included a boat being broken and sunk to take Ur-Nammu to the underworld.

King Shulgi

Ur-Nammu's son, Shulgi, became his successor. Under his reign, the Ur III Dynasty hit its peak. The government was running smoothly, and taxation on the distribution of goods and services was perfectly planned and administered. Every city was responsible for paying taxes once a year, each in a different month, to maintain the state administration, public services, and military. Taxes were paid in the form of supplies, which were delivered to a central redistribution point.

From the corpus of extant documents dating to the Ur III period, scholars learned that an entire city was built to accommodate the central administration. This city was discovered near Nippur, which was considered the religious capital of Sumer. This storage and distribution city was called Puzrish-Dagan. Archaeologists discovered a multitude of tablets there, and it appears as if every item that entered or left the city was recorded and filed.

Shulgi's military campaigns included areas north, east, and west of Sumer, although these campaigns were often a result of rebellions. These were all recorded in detail on clay tablets and in inscriptions on statues and stelae.

Local authorities administered each city according to the regulations laid down by the central government in Ur. The head or prince of a locale functioned similarly to today's prime ministers. He reported to the king in Ur.

The head of the local authority was assisted in his duties by an *ensi* or governor, as well as a general (*shagina* in Sumerian), who was the head of the local military. Each city was responsible for its own planning, budgeting, administrative functions, and distribution operations, which were all done according to the central government's instructions.

All civil servants were expected to attend a school, where they learned their jobs, which included bookkeeping, weights and measurements, the calendar, and other scribal skills.

The central authorities standardized the types and sizes of bricks and even provided building plans in some cases. Kings paid for the construction of huge ziggurats in almost every city.

Shulgi's reign was plagued by incursions and battles against neighbors, nomads, and illegal immigrants. The same could be said of almost every state in the ancient Near East. There is evidence from this period that provides clues for major droughts, food shortages, and their inevitable consequences, which included mass migrations.

There is also enough confirmation in the records to prove that trade and diplomatic relationships and treaties were forged throughout the Ur III period. Some were broken or unilaterally changed before the clay was even dry. Relationships were enhanced by marriages and other family connections.

Ur III rulers also had to suppress internal revolts. Shulgi ruled for forty-seven years before he was killed in battle. Scholars have found all the year names of Shulgi's reign, and much information can be extrapolated from that. He wrote or commissioned many praise hymns and poems about himself. From his twenty-third regnal year onward, he had a sign for divinity added in front of his name, which meant that he claimed godhood from then on.

Later accounts were not as kind to Shulgi as he was to himself. The *Weidner Chronicle*—correspondence from a later ruler of Isin to a king of Babylon—states that the Gutians triumphed over Ur III because Shulgi and his father had disrespected the Babylonian god Marduk and other deities. Shulgi did not follow the religious rites properly when placating the deities, which was a grave sin at the time. According to this chronicle, Shulgi, his father, and his son changed some religious rules, which proved offensive to the gods.

Descendants of King Shulgi

Shulgi's son, Amar-Sin, succeeded him and reigned from c. 2046 to 2037 BCE. He also claimed divine status when he was king. His name even means "immortal moon god" (Sin was the name of the moon god of Sumer).

Amar-Sin coped with the same issues and projects that his father had before him. There are extant records of all the year names of Amar-Sin. From those, it is clear that he engaged in military actions almost every year, even more than once in some years.

Amar-Sin apparently died from a foot infection or scorpion bite and was succeeded by his son, Shu-Sin. Shu-Sin reigned for nine years, all of which are known via the year names. In the fourth year of his reign, he was plagued by the Amorites. He had a wall constructed between the Euphrates and Tigris Rivers to block them from coming farther south.

Many artifacts with Shu-Sin's name or inscriptions have been unearthed. A so-called love poem referring to Shu-Sin is probably the most widely known. It was discovered in the ruins of Nippur and translated by well-known Sumerologist Samuel Noah Kramer. Scholars associate it with the ancient annual celebration of the divine marriage between Dumuzi and Inanna, where the king portrays Dumuzi as the bridegroom, and a high priestess takes the part of Inanna as the bride. Similar love poems are present across the ancient Near East, and it is also compared to the Song of Songs in the Christian Bible.

The long reign of Ibbi-Sin, the son and successor of Shu-Sin, lasted from 2028 to 2004 BCE. He was the last ruler of Ur III. The dynasty was in decline throughout most of his reign, and by the end, the empire only consisted of Ur and its surroundings.

The Unrelenting Amorites

The main culprits were the Amorites. The wall built by Shu-Sin across the divide between the Tigris and Euphrates proved totally inadequate to keep the Amorites out. The internal unrest, riots, and declarations of independence by previously conquered states were widespread across Mesopotamia and beyond. Invaders were assisted by their kin already dwelling in the lands of Sumer and Akkad.

Around 2004 BCE, the unrelenting Elamites, together with other mountain tribes from the Zagros range, attacked the city of Ur. They destroyed much of the city and took Ibbi-Sin as a prisoner back to Elam, where he later died. The demise of the city and dynasty is lamented in an elegy by an unknown composer.

Chapter 7: The Decline of Sumer

The Origin of the Amorites

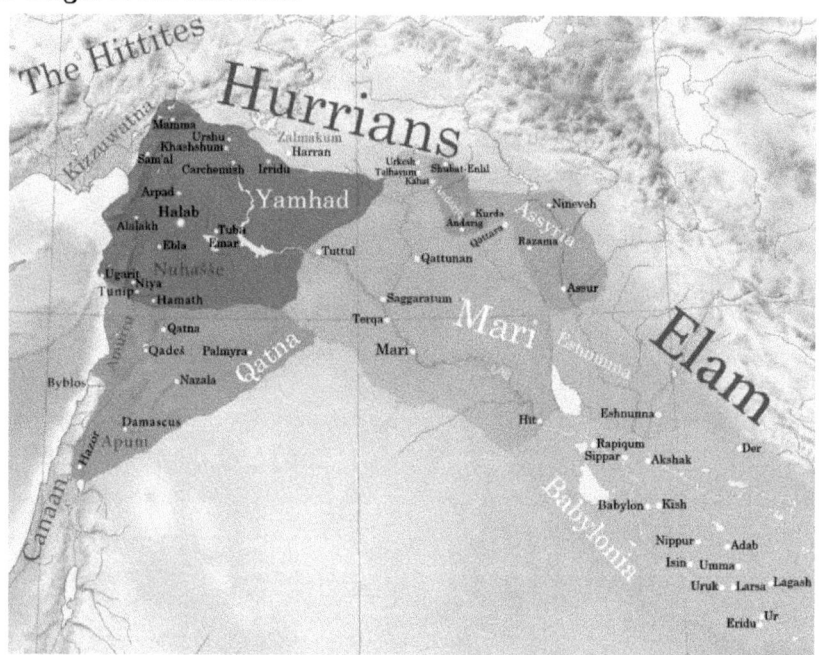

Map showing various Amorite states and Assyria, c. 1764 BCE.[14]

Scholars agree that the Amorites came from the Levant. It is further agreed that the Amorites were originally nomadic people who infiltrated communities as they traveled and posed threats to previously settled groups. These nomadic tribes were governed by chieftains who decided their routes, trade, and invasions of settlements. At some time, the name

"Amorite" was given to a specific group of Semitic people who, although nomadic and at times semi-nomadic, lived from the land and took what they wanted from settlements they came across. As this tribe grew bigger, stronger, and more adept at taking what they wanted from others, they acquired land and became a threat to the already developed city-states in the neighboring regions.

The Amorites were called "Amorites" on tablets from the northwest, such as the Ebla archives, where a transaction is recorded as being paid for with "Amorite silver." Tablets from Mari also refer to the Amorites. To the early Sumerians, all the lands to the west were known as the lands of the Martu—their name for the Amorites. The name "Amurru" was the Akkadian word used to talk about this disruptive group of people. It also denoted their geographic and linguistic origins.

At the start of the 2nd millennium, large tribal groups of the Amurru migrated from Arabia and permanently occupied Mesopotamia. They settled in small groups and took on a way of life similar to that of the Sumerians and Akkadians. Most scholars posit that this infiltration was connected to the earlier sources that describe the Amorites, while others claim that these people were Canaanites.

One of the cities that was linked to the Amorites is Mari, modern-day Tell Hariri in Syria. At this site, many clay tablets were excavated that had the same Paleo-Canaanite script that scholars attribute to the Semitic inhabitants. Some scholars even believe that Mari was part of an Amorite kingdom. According to historians, the later King Hammurabi of Babylon was a descendent of the Amorites.

Cuneiform clay tablets from the Amorite Kingdom of Mari. Dated to the beginning of the 2nd millennium BCE.[15]

The Constant Threat of the Amorites

The Amorites were known to be fierce and unwavering warriors. They were led by their chieftains and posed a threat to any settlement or city-state that they wanted to loot. This included taking lands for their herds to graze. They were said to have been a dominant force feared by the Sumerians, for they were as brave as they were violent in battle. Clay tablets in Akkadian describe the Amorites and their way of life as repugnant and revolting.

The Amorites were known across the Levant. They were called Martu by the Sumerians, Amurru by the Akkadians, and Amar by the Egyptians. They were represented in Egyptian frescoes as having light hair, fair skin, blue eyes, and pointed beards. Their facial features were dominated by a large, curved nose.

The Amorites were considered barbarians by most of the nations they came across; thus, they are usually described in negative terms, such as the following example from the Sumerians:

"The MARTU who know no grain...The MARTU who know no house nor town, the boors of the mountains...The MARTU who digs up truffles...who does not bend his knees [to cultivate the land], who eats raw meat, who has no house during his lifetime, who is not buried after death."[i]

The Amorites were a constant menace to the Akkadian and Sumerian city-states. Chieftains of the Amorite tribes established their settlements in Mari, Qatna, Yamhad, and Assur. They became urbanized while still remaining a force to be reckoned with. The Babylonians had a very famous king called Hammurabi, who is usually, although incorrectly, credited with creating the first written law code in history. (Ur-Nammu created the oldest surviving law code so far discovered.) The stele of Hammurabi found at a site in Diyarbekir claims that Hammurabi was "The King of the Amorites." Thus, scholars have concluded that Hammurabi was an Amorite who ascended the Babylonian throne after Sin-Muballit, who was also an Amorite.

The Amorites were not content with the cities they had invaded in Mesopotamia. They continued their conquest to the north of Canaan up to Kadesh. The Paleo-Semitic language of the Amorites blended well with

---

[i] *Sumerian Texts of Varied Contents*, Chiera, Edward, Published by University of Chicago Press, Chicago, 1954.

the Semitic language of the Akkadians, which became the dominant spoken and written language (lingua franca) of the ancient Near East. Akkadian was used primarily until the latter part of the 2nd millennium BCE.

Sumerian Defensive Tactics against the Amorites

King Shulgi, son of King Ur-Nammu, constructed a defensive wall at Ur to stop the invasion of the barbaric tribes known as the Martu in Sumerian (the Amurru of the Akkadians and Amorites of the later Hebrews). This wall was built along the eastern border of his kingdom to defend against the Amorites, who had already taken control of some other Sumerian city-states.

This wall was 155 miles (249.45 kilometers) long, according to the records of its construction. During Shulgi's reign, the wall kept the Elamites from invading the kingdom. This was due to extra fortifications that were added by Shulgi. Unfortunately, the design of the wall didn't include watchtowers or foot holders for defenders. (Foot holders allowed soldiers to see over the wall while still being protected.) This essentially meant that anyone could walk around at either end of the wall before they were seen.

After the death of King Shulgi, his son and heir, Amar-Sin, reevaluated the wall construction and added further fortifications. However, the wall was too long and could not be guarded efficiently. Another factor that led to Ur's eventual fall was that during Shulgi's reign, some nomadic Amorite tribes had already found their way around the wall and established settlements within the region.

Shu-Sin, the younger brother of Amar-Sin, also attempted to strengthen the defensive wall originally built by his grandfather, but the raids from both external and internal Amorite tribes made his efforts futile. Once his son, Ibbi-Sin, ascended the throne, the once-majestic kingdom was lost. The Third Dynasty of Ur was a mere glimmer of its former glory and reduced to a basic city-state.

The Weakened Sumerian Empire Attacked by the Elamites

The systematic, almost strategically planned Amorite invasion of the Sumerian Empire weakened this once-great empire to such an extent that it became ripe for attack by the Elamites.

Babylonian inscriptions confirm that the Amorites already had a strong foothold in some Syrian cities. By ransacking city after city in Sumer and conquering Babylon, which became their capital, the Amorites succeeded in bringing down a civilization that had developed over centuries. This civilization had the most innovative minds of the time and a strong character. Its people developed a complex society, religion, culture, and art, and it was conquered by uncivilized, ununified barbarians, at least according to ancient texts.

Famine Further Weakens Ur

Geologist Matt Konfrist stated at a conference of the American Geophysical Union that geological records showed an extended drought in ancient Sumer that began around 2200 BCE. He posits this drought was caused by evaporation changes from both the Red Sea and the Dead Sea, which caused lower rainfall throughout the region. The drought caused famine across the entire ancient Near East. It affected the Sumerian Empire, as the people greatly depended on irrigation from the flooding rivers—rivers that now were not filled with annual melting snow at their sources.

The Ur III Dynasty was already in a state of decline due to the widespread and persistent invasions by the Amorites. The combination of drought, famine, and invasion effectively brought this magnificent civilization to the brink of collapse.

Another factor that influenced the decline and ultimate collapse of Ur and other Sumerian city-states is that during times of drought, famine, or invasion, people living in outlying smaller cities or farmers affected severely by these factors inevitably migrated to the larger cities in search of work and food. This caused a strain on the urban economy and infrastructure.

Deciphered administrative documents from the Ur III period shows that during Ibbi Sin's seventh and eighth year of rule, the price of grain increased by 60 percent. This increase was undoubtedly caused by the combined factors of the drought and the Amorite attacks on farmers and lands.

As time went by, the architectural marvel of the 150-mile-long defensive wall fell into a state of disrepair. The once-wealthy kingdom was plagued by economic woes due to overpopulation and Amorites who usurped cities that once paid tribute to Ur in the form of money, grain, or livestock. Ur was weakened and impoverished during Ibbi-Sin's reign, making it ripe for the picking by the Elamites. Around this time, one of the king's high officials left the court and started his own small kingdom in the southern city of Isin.

The Elamites, led by Kindattu, finally attacked the city of Ur around 2004 BCE. According to some sources, the Elamites had formed a coalition with the Amorites. They ransacked the city and captured King Ibbi-Sin, the last Neo-Sumerian ruler. Records show that he was taken to the city of Elam as a prisoner. What became of him then and how he died remains unknown. On a clay tablet housed in the Louvre in Paris, the inscription states that King Ibbi-Sin would be taken to the city of Elam in fetters and that he would never return to his homeland.

The official who had started his own dynasty in Isin ruled over his tiny empire while the other cities broke off into their own city-states. The next two hundred years were a tumultuous era with constant wars between the city-states. Great lamentations were composed that bewailed the loss of support from the gods. It was believed the gods had allowed or even ordered the Elamites to destroy the great city of Ur and its prosperous empire.

The fall of Ur and the further decline of the Sumerian city-states caused the end of a civilization that is truly legendary. Today, this civilization is referred to as the "Origin of Civilization." The advancements the Sumerians made still affect our lives today—just look at your watch!

Chapter 8: Sumerian Society and Famous Rulers

The societal structure of the Sumerian civilization evolved over the centuries. It adapted and changed in regard to the environment, settlements, and city-states. The inhabitants of the lands between the Tigris and Euphrates Rivers created magnificent innovations, such as an irrigation system. This also meant that people had to work together on a large scale for these innovations to be built, maintained, and function. A governing body had to be established to ensure that canals and ditches were dug, repaired, and directed to the fields, villages, and cities in a system that apportioned the water fairly. At the same time, the rivers' flooding had to be tamed by communal efforts to ensure the safety of people and property. Thus, a government was formed, and laws were developed that needed to be enforced.

Developing a Social Hierarchy in Sumer

Farmers of early Sumer considered the land they farmed as their property and not communal lands. Subsistence farming changed to overproduction due to the successful irrigation systems, and surplus food was shared and traded. This was the beginning of barter and trade systems. Farmers who had more land and better crop yields could become wealthy through trade. In the past, a farmer's extended family was used for labor, but the people realized this could be supplemented by external labor instead of working their fields alone as a family enterprise.

Some farmers were more successful than others and had a surplus of seeds and food. Farmers with a bad crop yield would likely approach wealthier farmers to borrow seed, agreeing to repay the lender with their next harvest. If their next harvest was also unsuccessful and they could not repay their loans, they would either be forced to surrender their land or become a laborer on the lands owned by the lending farmer.

Successful and abundant food production led to the specialization of crafts, such as pottery, weaving, tool making, and other industries. These events developed a social class hierarchy, where the upper class consisted of the farmers who employed laborers and did not work their own lands, administrators of communal endeavors, priests, and successful manufacturers of essential goods. The lower class was made up of laborers, some of whom were possibly former landowners but had lost their lands and were now laborers.

Upper-class inhabitants and those who could afford it also owned slaves that worked in their households or on their lands. Slaves were prisoners of war from other city-states. They were sold and bought at markets or exchanged between households or industries.

Class Distinctions

Essentially, the hierarchy was divided into four groups: the religious class, the upper class, the lower class, and the slaves. These class distinctions formed the framework of society for the ancient Sumerians.

Religious Class - Priests and priestesses were powerful. They seemed to have had the right to do as they pleased. It was often only by currying favor with the priests that people could approach the deities for blessings, as only the priests and priestesses could commune with the gods, interpret messages, and explain omens to the people. Priests also assumed the role of doctors in ancient Sumer. If a member of the family was sick, one would call on the help of a priest. A cuneiform tablet was found depicting two priests dressed like fish. They did this to better communicate with the water god to help heal a sick boy. Priests had to shave their hair as a form of reverence to the gods they served.

The Upper Class or Elites - Upper-class men wore jewelry, particularly rings. Their hair was long, and they had mustaches and long beards. Early on, their robes were a type of kilt, but they eventually became a full dress, going from shoulder to ankle. Women often wore off-the-shoulder dresses. Their long hair was braided and sometimes piled on top of their heads. During winter, people wore cloaks made from sheep's wool to keep out the cold.

The Lower Class – Ancient Sumerians paid laborers to perform tasks, such as working in the fields or running a shop. The lower-class people lived comfortably. They had homes, wore clothing they could afford, and sported jewelry made from shells or stones. The elite, on the other hand, wore gold. No law prevented lower-class men from moving up the social ladder.

Slavery – City-states that conquered other city-states captured prisoners. They were brought back and sold as slaves to the king, the temple, the elites, or whoever could afford to keep one. Slaves were bought and sold among citizens, and records of these transactions were recorded on clay tablets. Slaves tended to cost less than donkeys or cattle.

Women in Society

Women did not have the same rights as men in ancient Sumer. An example of inequality is stated in one of the Ur-Nammu law codes, where a woman caught in an adulterous event would be killed while the man got off scot-free! However, women could trade and buy and sell goods freely at the marketplace, own property, move where they wanted, and manage legal issues. Women also had the right to start businesses. Some women had jobs running sections of the city-states and other government jobs. Upper-class women or members of the royal family could decide to become priestesses. Women in city-states that had a female patron deity were highly respected.

Sumerian women could become scribes, priestesses, doctors, and judges. The women were the prime beer brewers, which was an important job. A lady beer brewer or innkeeper named Kubaba or Ku Bau was even honored with the kingship of the important city-state of Kish.

Rulers of the City-States

Sumerian settlements developed into city-states, and each city-state had a patron deity. The temples of the city-state reflected the city's wealth. The more majestic and magnificent the temple was, the more powerful and wealthy the king would appear to others.

Clay cuneiform tablet of the Sumerian King List.[16]

The Controversial Sumerian King List

Several cuneiform clay tablets have been found across Sumerian city-states from their later periods that describe the ancient rulers as godlike humans. At some point during the last phase of the Sumerian civilization, a list of all the Sumerian kings from the beginning of the Sumerian kingship was compiled. The controversial Sumerian King List details kings that ruled for tens of thousands of years. It is considered by scholars to be a combination of reality and mythology. The Sumerian King List contains around twenty fragments of clay tablets. The main fragment was excavated in Nippur, but discoveries were made at other ancient sites, such as Susa, Adab, Sippar, and Larsa. These fragments give similar accounts of the kings and their reigns and also mention events like the Great Flood. Some texts differ, presumably due to errors from the scribes who wrote the texts.

Pre-flood kings are said to have ruled for thousands of years. Eight specific kings are named before the Great Flood. Their reign totaled 241,200 years. Time in ancient Sumer was calculated in *sars*, which equaled 3,600 years; *ners*, which equaled 600 years; and *sosses*, which equaled 60 years.

The beginning of the Sumerian King List refers to a time when "kingship first descended from heaven" over 266,000 years before the civilization emerged. According to these clay fragments, Eridu was the first city on Earth.

Verifiable rulers who are mentioned in the Sumerian King List are Gilgamesh, Mesannepada, Enmebaragesi, Elulu, Meskiagnun, Enshakushanna, and Lugal-zage-si. These seven kings lend credibility to the Sumerian King List, although the order and timeframes differ vastly from the archaeological evidence that has been found. Egyptian dynastic information has even been used to correlate these dates.

The First King of Sumer: Alulim

If you are a believer that myths and legends have a grain of truth, then you should take a look at King Alulim. According to the Sumerian King List, Alulim was the first ruler of Sumer. Over eighteen Sumerian king lists have been found throughout the region, yet they all state that Alulim was the first king. No other information regarding King Alulim is found anywhere except for the Sumerian King List. The list states that the kingship descended from heaven and was established in Eridug (ancient Eridu) and that King Alulim ruled for 28,800 years.

Two notable historians have put forward their theories about King Alulim. The late professor of Assyrian and Babylonian literature at Yale University, William Wolfgang Hallo, posited that there is a link between King Alulim and the myth of Apkallu, the demi-god created by the god Enki who taught the ancient people of Sumer how to be cultured and civilized. Hallo also noted that Apkallu was an advisor to the early kings of Sumer and was described in cuneiform texts to be one of the fish-like men that lived before the Great Flood.

Archaeologist William H. Shea from the University of Michigan linked the name Alulim to Adapa, the son of the god Enki, and postulates that the name Adapa correlates with the name Adam, the first man according to the biblical narrative of Genesis. The Adam and Alulim theory is supported by many schools of thought today.

Great Kings of Ancient Sumer: Meshkiangasher and Enmerkar

King Meshkiangasher's name is included in the Sumerian King List, yet no archaeological evidence of his existence has been found in any other sources. In some versions of the Sumerian King List, this king is known as Meshkiangasher, but even then, he remains historically untraceable. In addition, the length of his reign is impossible. The myth surrounding King Meshkiangasher states that he ruled for 324 years and was the son of the sun god Utu. The myth states that at the time of his death, he descended toward the sea and ascended to the mountains. The ancient Sumerians believed this to be the path the sun followed across the sky and that this was a suitable time to travel since it was the path of the "son of the sun god."

Enmerkar, the heir of King Meshkiangasher became the first king of Uruk, which can be verified by archaeological evidence from numerous excavations. His kingship is recorded in the Sumerian King List. Issues arise when talking about the length of his rule. According to the Sumerian King List, it was over 420 years! The historical Enmerkar reigned at the end of the 4th millennium or the beginning of the 3rd millennium BCE.

Three epics about King Enmerkar have been discovered. "Enmerkar and the Lord of Aratta" is the longest epic that has been deciphered. This particular epic gives historians a great deal of cultural and religious information. It tells of King Enmerkar's jealousy of Aratta's immense wealth of stone and metal, which were used as building materials. King Enmerkar wanted to build a temple in Eridu dedicated to the god Enki, and he required special building materials. The goddess Inanna suggested that he send the lord of Aratta a threatening message and demand the building materials. The shrewd lord of Aratta was not afraid of the king and sent a message back demanding grain as payment for them.

King Enmerkar honored the lord's request, but the lord of Aratta reneged on the deal. The epic details many messages sent between the king and the lord, but unfortunately, the text is severely damaged. The conclusion of the epic appears to end in King Enmerkar's favor.

King Gilgamesh of Uruk

King Gilgamesh wrestling two bulls.[17]

The period generally accepted by scholars for the reign of King Gilgamesh is between c. 2900 and 2350 BCE (the Early Dynastic period). According to the Sumerian King List, King Gilgamesh ruled for an impossible period of 126 years. Cuneiform texts state that Gilgamesh was the son of the priest-king Lugalbanda and the goddess Ninsun. Due to his demi-god heritage, Gilgamesh was blessed with superhuman strength and the perfect physique.

He was believed to be two-thirds god and one-third human, and the people revered him. This made him a fearful king who took what he wanted in wealth, women, and earthly possessions. His power and control were exaggerated, leading to the *Epic of Gilgamesh* and other myths and tales of wonder about his prowess as a king.

Later kings would claim him as their ancestor to gain power and respect from their subjects and kings of other regions. An example is King Shulgi of Ur, who claimed to be the brother of Gilgamesh and the son of Lugalbanda and the goddess Ninsun. Most historians consider Shulgi to have been the greatest ruler of the Ur III period.

The Infamous Female Monarch: Queen Kubaba

Kubaba, also known as Ku Bau or Kug-Baba, is the only female monarch on the Sumerian King List. What is interesting is that on the King List, she is named as the only ruler of the Third Dynasty of Kish. Textual evidence relates that she ruled around 2400 BCE for a period of one hundred years. Again, as with all the kings mentioned in the

Sumerian King List, she is said to have ruled for over a century, which is not realistic. The Sumerian King List gives her the title of *lugal*, meaning "king," not *eresh*, meaning "queen consort." Kubaba is the only female in the history of Sumer to be given the title of *lugal*.

The legend of how Kubaba became queen is unusual. It appears that she was a beer brewer and tavern keeper in ancient Kish. In the ancient world, the brewing of beer was a respected profession since beer was a daily beverage enjoyed by the ancient Sumerians. Queen Kubaba must have been a successful and independent businesswoman.

Her legendary rise to the throne is detailed in the *Weidner Chronicle*, which states that the god Marduk saw Kubaba ask a fisherman to catch a fish and offer it at the temple dedicated to Marduk in Esagila. In return, she feeds the fisherman. When the god Marduk observes this act of veneration from Kubaba, he is so impressed by her devotion that he gives Kubaba the kingship of Sumer.

King Eannatum: The Conqueror

King Eannatum was the ruler of Lagash between c. 2500 and 2400 BCE. Lagash was a city-state that also ruled over Girsu, another city-state. Both these city-states were allocated fertile lands in Gu-Edin or Guedena. To the north lay Umma, another city-state that also farmed fertile lands in Guedena. This caused adversity between the city-states, especially since Lagash and Girsu assisted each other in the form of loans when supplies were needed.

A treaty established by Mesilim, King of Kish, during the Third Dynasty kept Lagash and Girsu from warfare with Umma. This treaty was inscribed on a pillar that was placed in Guedena.

King Eannatum did not immediately break this treaty once he started conquering regions. He had a well-devised plan of action to establish an empire. He started by invading Elam, east of Sumer, in today's Iran. Elam had access to tin, which was used to make bronze. Additionally, Elam had an established trade network that brought wealth to the area.

The next city-state conquered was Urua in the fertile region of Susiana. With these two victories, Eannatum was confident enough to invade Umma. After his victory in Umma, King Eannatum had control over the fertile Guedena, access to additional soldiers, materials for weaponry, and the ambition to further expand his kingdom.

An interesting fact to note about King Eannatum is that neither his father, King Akurgal, nor his grandfather, Ur-Nanshe, appear on the

Sumerian King List. King Eannatum is the first historically verifiable king of Sumer.

Warfare in Ancient Sumer

The need for fertile land and a sufficient supply of water for farming, as well as drinking water for animals and humans, created constant conflicts between city-states.

As city-states grew and increased in population, the need for land, water, and other resources led to the development of weapons, technology, strategy, and armies for conquering neighboring city-states and surrounding regions.

The first verifiable archaeological evidence detailing a serious, strategic war was when King Eannatum of Lagash conquered the city-state of Umma in c. 2525 BCE. The famous Stele of the Vultures, housed in the Louvre, depicts vultures and lions ripping flesh from corpses on a desert plain.

The victorious King Eannatum was a master of propaganda and commanded the creation of this pictorial stele that showed him leading warriors in a chariot drawn by donkeys. This stele shows that the Sumerians fought in a phalanx formation and that warriors had body armor, copper helmets, spears, and axes. King Eannatum was struck in the eye with an arrow in the battle, which only made him more determined to win and conquer more city-states.

Stele of the Vultures, front and back view.[18]

The strategies used in this battle are well detailed on the stele and many clay tablets that talk about the victories of King Eannatum. Fighting in a phalanx formation requires training, discipline, and planning—and all of this is attributed to King Eannatum.

The technological advancement of bronze helmets denotes the development of the first defensive response in warfare. It made the mace, a weapon with a pole and a stone head, an inferior weapon on the battlefield.

King Eannatum led his army onto the battlefield in a wheeled chariot; this is considered to be a major technological innovation in warfare. Although it is referred to as a chariot, it is more accurate to call it a "battle car" since it lacked maneuverability and speed.

The Sumerians are also believed to have invented the rein-ring to better control donkeys and an axle in front of the chariot platform. This axle, in all probability, would not have been used during battles since it increased the chariot's weight and decreased stability when traveling at faster speeds.

Later developments in weaponry were javelins and axes. Bows and arrows were notably absent during these battles. Scholars posit that the sight of an opponent riding a chariot in front of the phalanx formation would scare the enemy away.

Unification of the City-States

King Etana of Kish is said to have united many of the city-states for the first time. After his death in c. 2800 BCE, these city-states broke apart again. They began to challenge and conquer each other, and the previously unified Sumer became a target for other regions, such as the Elamites and the later Akkadians.

Chapter 9: Culture and Innovation

The ancient Sumerian inventions are a testament to what the human mind is capable of in extreme and adverse conditions. The mind's ability to form original thoughts and ideas is illustrated uniquely by the Sumerian civilization. They invented systems, tools, equipment, and methods to deal with all aspects of individual and communal daily life. They adapted their lifestyles and culture to thrive in the environment in which they lived.

Inventions like the wheel, something we cannot live without today, were invented by the Sumerians. Other amazing inventions that we still use today include cosmetic sets, harps, hammers, axes, weapons, the plow, the sailboat, and a written language, among other things.

The Earliest Form of Writing

Cuneiform is believed to be the earliest form of writing. It was invented as a way to keep track of transactions, storage, and administration matters; in other words, it was an ancient form of bookkeeping. It developed from simple drawings into stylized pictographs and then into logosyllabic writing, which could be used to express concepts and thoughts.

The first discovery of cuneiform was at the archaeological site of Jemdet Nasr. This settlement dated back to the Ubaid period and lasted into the Early Dynastic period. These tablets from Jemdet Nasr are dated to the second half of the 4th millennium BCE. The script is in the proto-cuneiform or Archaic style. Proto-cuneiform is a complex script, and scholars posit that it includes both numerical and non-numerical signs.

The writings on the earliest tablets have not been deciphered yet, but it is assumed to be Sumerian.

As time passed, the script developed into the iconic wedge-shaped appearance that we now associate with cuneiform. Archives in Uruk and other excavated sites have contemporary tablets of the same proto script developing into true cuneiform, changing first into a mixture and then into logosyllabic signs.

The tablets are primarily administrative, detailing lists of animals, objects, and food that were distributed to the inhabitants, suggesting a centralized authority in charge of distribution. Clay tablets have complex calculations of the exact size of agricultural fields, which is the earliest record of this type of calculation. Other texts calculate beer, grain, and fruit distribution to traders and laborers, while other texts have a detailed accounting system for livestock.

Around 2400 BCE, cuneiform was adapted to write the Akkadian language, and it was later adapted for the Assyrian and Babylonian languages. These are Semitic languages and form the basis of today's Hebrew and Arabic scripts. Cuneiform was taken over and adapted over time to write almost all of the languages of the ancient Near East. Akkadian became the lingua franca, except, of course, for the ancient Egyptian language. But even Egyptian scribes knew cuneiform. International diplomatic correspondence discovered at the archives of Tell el-Amarna from the time of Pharaoh Akhenaten and Queen Nefertiti (c. 14th century BCE) contained a host of cuneiform letters from several ancient Near East nations.

The Sumerian language and the cuneiform script were known to scribes until the 1st century CE. Sumerian lexicons and literature with translations into other ancient Near East languages were part of scribal training. It is partly thanks to these lexicons that scholars were able to confirm the existence of the Sumerians. Modern translations of Sumerian literature in the form of myths, legends, temple hymns, and poems are mostly from these ancient scribal copies that have been found in archives across the ancient Near East.

Agricultural Innovations

The land between the lower Tigris and Euphrates Rivers was fertile because the seasonal floods deposited silt across the alluvial plains. Rainfall was scarce, so the Sumerians had either too much or too little water available for crop production. They had to come up with innovative ideas to water their crops and, at the same time, protect settlements and crops from destruction by the occasionally severe floods.

The Sumerians developed drainage and irrigation systems to ensure consistent water supplies for crops, people, and livestock throughout the year. Ancient farmers used existing natural levees created by the flooding rivers to control the water. They built new earthen levees and dikes along riverbanks to control the water during flooding. When the fields were dry, the ancient Sumerians made holes in the levees to let the water flow between the fields. Ditches were cut into the fields to carry water to the crops. The Sumerians also conserved water by building dams and reservoirs, from which canals carried water to cities and fields.

The construction of canals was not limited to agricultural use. Canals were built to divert floodwaters away from the villages and cities. These same canals could then be used to irrigate the lands during dry periods. Canals were also built to redirect water from the rivers farther inland to cultivate more crops. The larger canals were used as waterways for transporting trade goods and food.

Ancient engineers devised irrigation systems that varied in depth and design depending on the natural geography of the area. Large canals were built directly out of the rivers. They diverged into smaller canals and then into even smaller furrows or ditches that flowed directly into the fields.

The ancient Sumerians had an intricate irrigation system, and at times, aqueducts and raised canals were built to accommodate topographical issues. Further advances in the irrigation systems included mechanisms like the shaduf (shadoof), which was a pivoted pole with a bucket at one end and a weight at the other. The shaduf was used to lift water from rivers, dams, or canals onto the fields. Later, the Sumerians developed a noria. This was a wheeled device with buckets attached at the rim that moved water to irrigate lands.

Sumerians not only developed these intricate irrigation systems but also implemented administrative structures that scheduled dredging, repairs, and maintenance of these systems. This was of major importance since it ensured smooth operation and the fair distribution of water. The building of irrigation systems, their overall administration, and their scheduled maintenance were recorded on cuneiform tablets.

Clogging and silting of canals and waterways was a constant problem, especially with water from the slower moving and shallower Euphrates River that carried and deposited large amounts of silt. The heavy silt of the Euphrates contained considerable amounts of minerals, including salt. Archaeologists and other scholars of ancient history are convinced that the deep and heavy silt that covers the area today still hides many secrets yet to be discovered.

By using these innovative irrigation systems, the Sumerians successfully cultivated barley, wheat, dates, onions, cucumbers, apples, and a variety of herbs and spices.

Tools Used for Agriculture

Initially, animal horns and sticks were used to make furrows in the soil, and the seeds were sown and watered by hand. This was labor-intensive and fetched limited results. As the population increased, the Sumerians realized they had to find a way to cultivate more land to yield a bigger harvest.

Archaeologists have discovered evidence of the first plow dating back to at least the early 4th millennium BCE. The Sumerians developed a seeder plow during the beginning of the Early Dynastic period. The seeder plow enabled farmers to use oxen to till the soil and plant the seeds simultaneously. These innovations boosted harvests tremendously and provided surplus grain for export.

Sumerian Farmer's Almanac

This clay tablet containing 111 lines of cuneiform text was discovered at the Nippur site. It is a set of instructions from a father to his son detailing how the land should be prepared and at what time of the year the processes of crop planting should be undertaken. Provisions should be made for an extra ox to pull the plow—yet further evidence that the plow was in use by that time. The instruction manual also provides information on when and how to harvest.

The Invention of the Calendar

The Sumerian lunar calendar may have been invented for religious purposes and agricultural activities. The calendar allowed the Sumerians to determine which phase of agriculture they should be focusing on. It gave the Sumerians advance knowledge of the seasons and impending floods so that they could make the necessary preparations.

The lunar calendar functioned well for short periods, but the Sumerians soon realized that it was inadequate for longer periods. Their lunar calendar had a year of 354 days over twelve months, which the Sumerians rounded up to 360 days.

The Sumerian Lunisolar Calendar

By the end of the Early Dynastic period, Sumerian mathematicians, astronomers, priests, and scribes had devised a lunisolar calendar. This meant the calendar was now synchronized across the three natural cycles:

1. Day and night were divided into two twelve-hour periods

2. The lunar month was based on the monthly cycles of the moon, and a week could be based on each phase of the monthly cycle.

3. The solar cycle worked according to the changes in the sun's elevation above the horizon throughout one year.

The Sumerians calculated twelve lunar months for a year, and it took around 354.36 days to complete the cycle of a lunar year. This did not match up with the cycles of the sun. The ancient Sumerians calculated these differences and accounted for them by adding an extra month every two to three years. This was eventually done by royal decree since they were not yet measuring the precise alignments of the lunar and solar years at that time, at least as far as we know. The later Babylonians were the first to math these differences more precisely.

It is generally accepted that months, weeks, and days were first used during the Ur III period, and there are documents detailing that four weeks made up a month. The months were divided into two halves, which were based on the waxing and waning cycles of the moon.

Although the Sumerians did not calculate the calendar exactly, it is still a magnificent feat of astronomy and mathematics.

Development of a Sumerian Legal System

When humans live together in a society, there is a need for rules and regulations. As a fully developed civilization, the Sumerians naturally had laws, even before recorded history. The laws may not have been the same in each city-state, but it can be assumed that they were similar because the culture, language, and lifestyles were similar.

It was once thought that the law codes inscribed by King Hammurabi of Babylon (c. 1792-1750 BCE) were the first written laws. This is incorrect; Sumerian King Ur-Nammu had laws inscribed around 2100 BCE.

The earliest known law code was called the Code of Urukagina. He was the last king of the city-state of Lagash in the 24th century BCE. There are no extant copies of this pre-Akkadian legal code; knowledge of it only survives through references in other writings. It is said that Urukagina's law code protected widows, orphans, and the poor through tax exemptions.

The Law Code of Ur-Nammu

Tablet containing two fragments excavated in Nippur dating back to c. 2150–2050 BCE.[19]

The first text of the oldest preserved law code, the Code of Ur-Nammu, was found in Nippur. The code found in Nippur was incomplete, but later copies found at Ur enabled scholars to reconstruct most of it. It was very much an "eye-for-an-eye" kind of legal code for serious crimes, although scholars were surprised to find that many bodily crimes sometimes carried fines rather than physical punishment. An exception would be the law for a son striking his father; he was punished by having his hand chopped off. The code dealt with public and civil matters as well.

Many scholars think the laws should be attributed to King Ur-Nammu's son, Shulgi, because it seems they were distributed widely and displayed publicly during his reign.

Sumerian Housing

Social stratification seems to have been firmly entrenched by the Early Dynastic period. By that time, the early model of extended families sharing the burden of agricultural labor had long been replaced by external aid and increasing technological advances. The natural outcome of vast food production freed hands for the development of other industries, and the labor requirements could be met for monumental building projects.

The Sumerians from the Ubaid period lived in tripartite houses. This floor plan was used as the base for all buildings. As their society, culture, and religion progressed, they began to build more elaborate structures, such as temples, ziggurats, and magnificent palaces. Later upper-class houses were sometimes multi-storied. These houses still used the tripartite floor plan from the early Ubaid period.

The first city walls were built for protection against flooding. They were later built for defensive purposes. These walls also had a social element. Where one's house was located inside the city walls would indicate one's status in society. Houses were built in the suburbs, and the closer to the ziggurat a house was, the higher one's status in society was. Officials, priests, and the elites lived in the suburbs, while traders, shopkeepers, and fishermen lived on the outskirts of the city and sometimes outside the city walls.

Music

Ancient Sumerian musical instruments were found as grave goods during archaeological excavations. Musicians and their instruments are depicted in artworks. There were string, wind, and percussion instruments.

Musicians in Mesopotamia were well trained and a recognized professional class. The Sumerians must have found the music to be soothing when instruments like lyres and flutes made from bone or reeds were used. There were also discoveries of hand-held drums and rattles. We know the Sumerians loved to sing, as can be seen with the lamentations. In some of the festival halls where plates and beer jugs were excavated, musical instruments were also found.

Cylinder seal found in the tomb inscribed as Pu-A-Bi- Nin (Queen Puabi), showing her attendants playing the lyre.[20]

Musical instruments were found in the burial sites of the elites, such as in the grave of the "Lady of Puabi," also referred to as the "Queen of Puabi." This tomb was found in the royal cemetery of Ur. Her grave was given elite status, and it was posited that she may have ruled separately and without a husband. Her grave goods were utterly magnificent.

Art and Crafts

Sumerian arts and crafts were limited by the natural elements found in their geographical region. They resorted to clay or fired clay to produce pottery, plates, and statues. In comparison, the Greeks would use marble, which was readily available, to produce massive statues.

The bull's head from the lyre found in the tomb of Queen Puabi.[21]

Sumerian Art

Massive sculptures of the patron deity of each city-state have been discovered; some are even life-sized! These statues were magnificent in proportion and decorated in an effort to curry favor with the gods. They had inlays of shells, precious stones, and colorful mosaics in geometrical patterns. Depictions on clay and stone have been found showing fighting or hunting, telling us a substantial amount about the daily lives of Sumerian men.

Crafts

Intricate chairs were handcrafted using wood and reeds, and they were inlaid with shells and mosaics. Archaeologists have excavated beautiful pottery, statues, and portraits of animals created from mosaics and shells. The pottery of the ancient Sumerians was so beautiful that it was used to pay for goods traded with neighboring city-states.

Sumerian jewelry was magnificent. Craftspeople inlaid gold with lapis lazuli and other precious stones for the elite, as indicated by grave goods. Poor people also wore jewelry, but it was crafted from shells, wood, seeds, and bones.

Other intricate crafts include the inlaid helmets used by soldiers, cylinder seals, and decorated tables.

Reconstructed Sumerian headgear and necklaces found in the tomb of Puabi. This set was found on three of her attendants, and this reconstruction is housed at the British Museum.[22]

Sumerian Cloth

Sumerian clothing was made of flax or wool. Women were responsible for weaving. Weaving was an essential skill, and the Sumerians excelled at it. Reeds were abundant in the marshlands and on the riverbanks. Fresh reeds are pliable, which enabled the Sumerians to use them in multiple ways.

For instance, ancient Sumerians wore sandals made from woven reeds. They also made extremely durable baskets. These baskets were strong enough to haul clay for mudbricks from the river to the manufacturing site. Reed baskets were also used to carry grain.

Large woven baskets were put on the backs of pack animals, such as donkeys. Evidence suggests that Sumerian baskets were of excellent quality. They were exported and have been found at sites across the region. Records have been found of exported Sumerian cloth at several ancient Near Eastern sites as well.

Reed baskets that were waterproofed with bitumen were used to carry water. Bitumen-treated reeds were used to close off canals, much in the same way that we use a sluice gate today.

Houses and other buildings had woven mats from reeds that were lined with bitumen. They formed the foundations and protected the mudbricks.

Daily Life

There were times when life for all the people of ancient Sumer was comfortable and safe. They all had houses, enough food, and time for recreation. But times change. As the civilization matured, it lost its innocence. Personal wealth and power created social stratification, and greed and envy replaced an attitude of sharing.

Daily life in Sumer was hard for the workers; a workday was thought to be ten hours long. Professions included teaching, building, and farming for men, while women typically stayed home and looked after the chores at home and raised children. Wealthy families could employ tutors to homeschool their children.

The people enjoyed recreational activities, such as boxing, racing, wrestling, hunting, storytelling, dancing, and music. This is attested by some of the more than 120,000 clay tablets found at the Ashurbanipal library that was excavated in Nineveh and other major archaeological sites, such as Ur, Uruk, Nippur, and Larsa.

School

Schools were run by priests. Priests beat the boys if they did not do well at school since it was believed that a lesson could only be reinforced by a good beating; therefore, only boys were allowed to attend school. However, since most Sumerians were thought to be illiterate, it is likely only boys from the upper classes and those seeking certain positions to advance in society went to school. Typically, only girls from elite classes could have a formal education. Her parents would employ a tutor so she could learn at home.

Games and Toys

The ancient Sumerians were hard workers yet understood there must be a balance between work and home life. They made toys for their children to play with, such as spinning tops, slingshots, balls, jump ropes, rattles, and hoops. According to some sources, the girls had toys resembling dollhouses, complete with miniature furniture. Children even had miniature carts and chariots that were pulled with strings or ropes and miniature boats that floated.

Board Games

The board game found at the royal burial grounds in Ur is intricate. The board dates back to the 3rd millennium BCE and indicates that two opposing players would use strategy, time, and luck to beat the other player, much like a game of chess. Evidence of this game was found across Sumer and Mesopotamia and as far as Crete and Sri Lanka.

Sumerians invented other board games, one of which is referred to as twenty squares or fifty-eight holes. Pieces on the board were moved into the holes, but the rules and objectives of the game have not yet been discovered. Other games used dice, and some games were associated with gambling. Board games were played by all social classes.

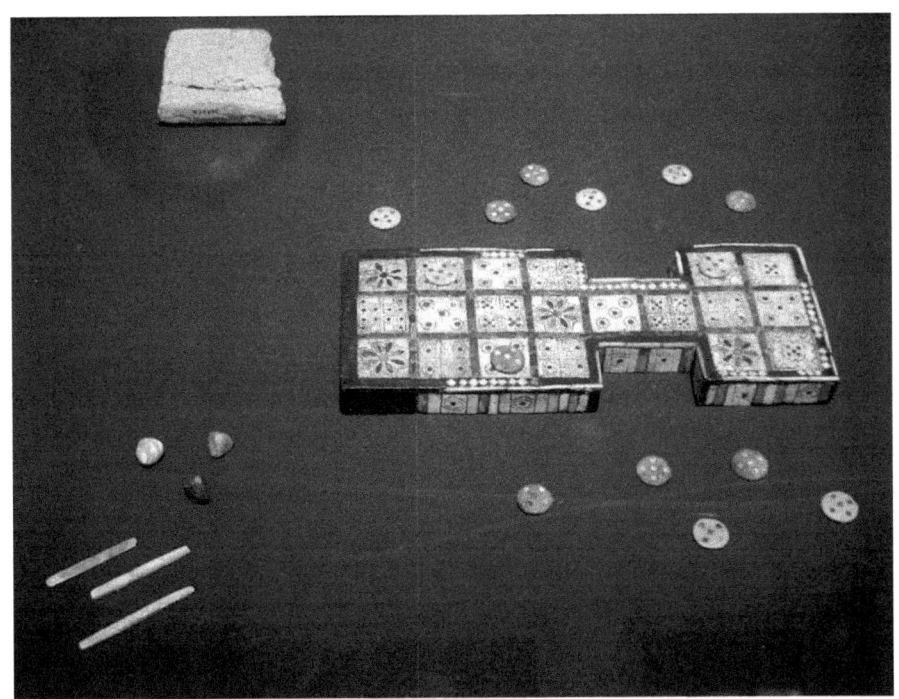

Sumerians are credited with the invention of the board game.[28]

Button Buzz

The Sumerians played a game called button buzz. To start, one needed a circle made of clay. A string or rope was tied to this circular disc. The aim of the game was to swing the disc by a piece of rope or weed as fast as possible. Once it went fast enough, it made a buzzing sound. The winner would be the person whose clay disc made the loudest sound.

Technological Advancements

There is no doubt that the Sumerians were very innovative people. When faced with a problem, they simply found a way to overcome the challenge, whether that was to sail across the water, irrigate the fields, defend themselves, or work out time and mathematical equations. They did it all. The most amazing thing is that they did it all without any assistance or prior knowledge.

Mathematics, Arithmetic, Geometry, and Astronomy

In ancient Sumer, the people soon learned that if they were going to trade with each other and other city-states, they had to develop a system that allowed them to count, take measurements of land, and pay laborers wages. Tablets dating back to 2500 BCE have detailed land measurements, accounting, and records of taxation.

Long-form division, multiplication, geometric, and algebraic calculations have been deciphered from clay tablets dating back to 2600 BCE. In addition to these calculations, tablets using mathematics were also found that depicted sky charts for navigational purposes and a detailed lunar calendar, as well as the first zodiac, which was divided into twelve sections.

Numerical System

The Sumerians created a sexagesimal numerical system. This means all calculations were worked out using the number sixty as the base number. This was already in effect in the 3rd millennium BCE. The Sumerians further progressed this numerical system into sixty seconds and sixty minutes, which became an hour. They were also the first to create the 360° circle. The first abacus was also a Sumerian invention.

Astrology

Ancient Sumerians had a polytheistic religion and worshiped a large number of human-like gods and goddesses. These deities were believed to control the sun, moon, and planets, as well as natural occurrences like wind and rain. Ancient Sumerian astronomers discovered that planets and stars moved in specific patterns around the sun and moon. To them, it seemed as if the gods were sending coded messages that they had to interpret. This was how their belief in astrology developed.

The Sumerians used their mathematical calculations to determine the cycles of the sun, moon, planets, and stars to determine things like as full moons, half moons, and the waxing and waning phases of the moon. They also calculated and predicted eclipses.

Sumerian Boats

The invention of the boat is credited to the Sumerians, as they used the Tigris and the Euphrates as trade routes. The city-state of Ur was also located on the shores of the Persian Gulf at that time. Boats were made out of reeds that were bound together and covered with animal hides. The first examples of reed-bundle boats were ceramic models of them; these were found at sites like Eridu, Uruk, and Tell el-'Oueili. The details on the ceramic models are so clear that it shows incisions, mimicking the reeds that would have been used to construct a real boat. Another example depicts a reed boat with masts and sails. Additionally, excavated pieces of reed with bitumen and barnacles have been discovered. These are pieces of an actual boat, which would make it the earliest seafaring vessel in the world.

Mesopotamian reed boats are dated back to around 5500 BCE, which is the early Neolithic Ubaid period. Ubaid ships were made from reed bundles bound together by rope and then waterproofed with bitumen. In addition, these boats often had long poles to push them down the river. Some had masts for sails. The sails would have been made from linen or flax. Ropes were used to hoist the sails up to the top of the masts. Some discoveries indicate that these reed boats had upturned bows to protect them from oncoming waves of water.

Bronze

Evidence shows that smelting copper started as early as 6000 BCE in Sumer. Archaeologists dated the making of bronze, which is made by smelting tin and copper together, to c. 3500 BCE.

The use of copper was one of the Sumerians' major innovations, and cities like Ur, Uruk, and Tell al-'Ubaid show that they made tools, such as arrowheads, harpoons, chisels, and axes, from copper and later progressed to bronze. Bronze was harder and made weapons more deadly. Copper was used for personal items like razors, jugs, and elaborate drinking vessels.

This lion-headed eagle (Imdugud or Anzu), the symbol of the god Ningirsu. The eagle grasps two deer, one on either side. This panel was found at the base of the temple of Ninhursag at Tell al-'Ubaid. It is made from copper and dates to around 3100 BCE.[24]

Weapons

The Bronze Age gave rise to stronger weapons. City-states were able to fight and invade other city-states with greater confidence due to this new harder alloy. Bronze knives, lance points, and arrowheads made weapons more durable and deadlier in battles.

The First Form of Identification

Ancient Sumerians kept written records of all their transactions, but most of them did not know how to read and write cuneiform. Sumerians who did not know how to read or write would commission a cylinder seal with unique pictograms—like a signature. This form of identification was not only for people who could not read or write. It was the preferred method of marking messages, trade goods, or any other property. Thousands of these cylinder seals have been excavated. Many of them belong to the working class, although more elaborate ones were used by the upper class.

Sumerian Seals

Stamp seals date back to 5000 BCE. These objects have simple markings to denote the number of goods sold. Archaeologists found seals on storeroom doors, baskets, and bags. In around 3500 BCE, stamp seals progressed to cylinder seals, which could be rolled over wet clay, leaving a permanent marking.

Cylinder seal of Adda.[25]

Beer-making Process

It was assumed that another interesting first for the Sumerians was the brewing of beer until the discovery of beer residue in vessels from Göbekli Tepe. It is thought beer was made at the site thousands of years before the Sumerians brewed beer. Nevertheless, evidence of a Sumerian beer recipe was found in a poem dedicated to Ninkasi dating to c. 3900 BCE. This poem dedicated to the tutelage of the goddess of beer also shows the important role women played in society since they were the primary brewers in ancient Sumer.

Archaeological evidence of Sumerian beer dates back to 3500 BCE, as chemical traces of beer were found in excavated jars. Depictions of drinking beer show that it was done using straws due to the thick consistency of the liquid. Drinking beer in this way would have prevented the people from gulping down the bitter solids left over from fermentation.

Chapter 10: Myths and Religion

Sumerian religion was as complex as the origin of its people. Ancient texts that have been deciphered tell us that each Sumerian city had a primary deity. Although humans and gods lived together, humans were only there to serve and worship the gods.

The Sumerian pantheon had hundreds of gods and goddesses and even some demons. The Sumerian deities were all related, and they were remarkably human in their behavior. They acted out of pity, kindness, rage, jealousy, betrayal, spite, and all the other emotions that humans are capable of—the good and the bad.

The main pantheon of deities were sons and mothers, sisters and brothers, or fathers and daughters that intermarried. The sun, moon, planets, animals, and plants manifested as gods and goddesses.

Scribes used clay tablets to tell stories that were once orally transmitted from generation to generation in each tribe. The archaeological discoveries of lengthy clay cuneiform tablets filled with myths and legends are considered to be the oldest myths in the world. They give scholars an understanding of the Sumerians' ideology and beliefs.

Accordingly, it was believed the deities were responsible for all things that happened in the celestial and human world.

The Development of the Pantheon

The Sumerians believed that the Earth was flat and enclosed in a dome that formed the heavens above and the underworld beneath. This was the universe over which the deities ruled. They would bless the humans with good harvests or alternately punishments if the humans were displeasing them.

Cuneiform tablets dating to the 3rd millennium BCE attribute the creation of the world to four primary deities: Enlil, Enki, Ninhursag, and An. These deities presided over daily occurrences, such as disease, health, crops, and floods. They determined wealth, poverty, and other human experiences. Generally, these gods were seen as helpful to humans, but they could be whimsical, mischievous, and malevolent. This was how the people explained events and catastrophes like earthquakes and floods.

Enlil – The Air God

Enlil, the air god, was the most important deity to the Sumerians. His breath could bring gentle winds or hurricanes, and he was the manifestation of energy, authority, and force. He was also the god of agriculture, and the people depended on him for their livelihood and wealth. One of the myths surrounding Enlil says that he was banished to the underworld after he raped his consort, Ninlil, the grain goddess. This myth was developed to explain the agricultural cycles: the fertilization of the land, ripening of the crops, harvesting, and then inactivity during the winter months.

An – Father of the Gods

An, also referred to as Anu, was the head of the Sumerian pantheon and seen as the father of the gods, the supreme ruler who maintained the entire existence of the heavens and the Earth. An is often featured in the background of myths; he was rarely the central figure.

One of the main centers of worship was Uruk, which was at times referred to as "the city of Anu." An was the father of the god Enlil and is depicted as a human wearing a horned headdress or a bull with a human head. As the primary god, An gave commands to the other gods and goddesses. In later myths, he ceded his power to his son Enlil and became more remote.

Enki – God of Wisdom and Magic

In the beginning, Earth was surrounded by an ancient saltwater sea. Fresh water came from underneath the Earth from an underworld sea called the Abzu. Enki lived in the Abzu and was known for being mischievous. According to ancient Sumerian texts, Enki was virile and embodied masculinity. His depictions often include sexual representations, particularly the life-giving characteristics of the god's semen and the fresh waters of the Abzu for agricultural purposes. In art, he is shown as a bearded, robe-wearing god with a horned cap.

Enki's sexual exploits include various goddesses, such as his daughter, Ninmu, and his granddaughter by Ninmu named Ninkurra. Enki was a son of An and had the power of wisdom, magic, and incantations. He is often linked to the city of Eridu. Beliefs surrounding Enki include exorcism. Disease and strife were believed to be the result of demonic possession or displeasing divine powers. As such, incantations were used to remove the evil presence from occupying people or places.

Depiction of the god Enki.[26]

Ninhursag – Mother Goddess

Ninhursag, known as the mother goddess, is one of the four creation deities. Evidence of a goddess figurine suggests she was worshiped during the Ubaid period around 4500 BCE. Her name means "Lady of the

Sacred Mountain." As one of the creator deities, Ninhursag is the goddess of fertility, childbirth, and growth. She is also called the mother of the Earth. Ninhursag was asked to bless unborn children and to ensure food after a child's birth.

She was the patron deity of Adab, a prominent Sumerian city-state. As the mother of the gods and the mother of men, Ninhursag is the most important female deity. All the myths of Ninhursag state that she had power over life and death. In the myth of Enki and Ninhursag, she can draw out or remove diseases and heal sickness.

Depictions of the mother goddess often show her seated in front of a mountain wearing a layered skirt, either with her hair in the style of the Greek omega symbol or with a horned headdress. Some depictions of her include ibex, deer, bison, and eagles.

The Entemena vase motif depicting Ninhursag as a stag with lions greeting her in a friendly manner.[27]

Worship and Festivities

Temples in each city-state were dedicated to its patron god or goddess. At the temples, the deities were worshiped and besieged for blessings.

Priests and priestesses lived in the temples, which allowed them to be available for daily rituals and worship. They were the only ones allowed in the ziggurats. Castraters (a person who performs castration ceremonies) and temple slaves lived in separate buildings close to the temple.

The people were expected to pray daily or bring sacrifices to the priests. These sacrifices could be votive statues or food, which the priests placed on and around the temple altar.

Temples were a central feature in the lives of the public. Singing and music were a part of daily worship, as was the consumption of beer and wine. There were also annual and monthly feasts.

Sumerians made private worship a part of their lives. Each Sumerian had a personal or family god, and they would go to the temple to wail, plead, and lament while confessing their daily sins and pleading for mercy. They would beg their family god to intervene on their behalf.

The mother goddess was venerated in festivities by ten vocalists, ten instrumentalists, and sixty-two lamentation priests during rituals in Lagash. In general, festivities included music, dancing, drinking barley beer, and eating meat and vegetables. This is evident at all the temple sites, as archaeologists have uncovered plates, cups, and vases with traces of barley beer, as well as large ovens. Great quantities of meat were cooked and consumed, as can be seen from the animal bones found at these sites.

The main festival halls contained many hearths, which confirms that festivities were held year-round, including during the cold winter months.

Annual Festivals

Dumuzi – This Sumerian festival celebrated the god Dumuzi, the god of life and death. The festivities were meant to bring Dumuzi back from the underworld to join with the goddess of life, Inanna. These celebrations were held during winter times to explain why crops and fields died during the cold.

Inanna Feast – This feast focused on the initial descent of the goddess Inanna to the underworld, where she was held captive by the goddess of death and rebirth, Ereshkigal. Inanna was a prisoner in the underworld until she agreed to call upon Dumuzi to stay in the underworld during winter.

Marriage to the Goddess – This was believed to be the most important festival in ancient Sumer. It was celebrated annually and celebrated when Dumuzi married Inanna. The current king would represent Dumuzi, and a priestess of the temple would represent Inanna. These festivities always took place around New Year's and were thought to bring prosperity to the king and all of Sumer for the year.

The Akitu Festival – During the Late Uruk period, this ritual festival had two processions: one going to the Akitu House and one returning. The processions were dedicated to the gods An and Inanna. They are described as opulent and richly decorated, and the festivities lasted for seven days. Historians posit that the festival of Akitu probably originated in Ur during the equinox since it coincided with the emergence of the moon god Nanna, which was symbolized by the waxing of the moon. During the Akitu festival in Ur, a statue of the moon god Nanna was brought into the city via a barge from the Akitu House, which was located outside the city. When other city-states adopted this festival, it was changed to revere the god or goddess of that city-state. These reenactments would occur at different times of the year to ensure they did not happen on a conflicting date with the festival of the chief moon god Nanna. This festival was the main event on Nippur's calendar, which was the religious center of the Sumerians.

Worship at the Temple of Enlil

The temple of Enlil, excavated in Dur-Kurigalzu, was a religious site where offerings of votive statues, rituals accompanied by music, and singing would be performed for the god Enlil in return for blessings. Enlil was the god of winds, storms, air, and earth, and it was believed he ensured that crops were nourished sufficiently and produced a good yield.

Temples Dedicated to the Deities

Before the first kings, the city leaders ruled in the form of a council of elders. Their duty was to ensure the patron god or goddess and the gods in general were pleased with the people's sacrifices, ceremonies, and rituals. If the gods were pleased, they would bless the people. Their health would be good, and they would be free of accidents and disease.

Temple architecture was the same throughout Sumer. The *cella*, a long central hall, ended in an altar dedicated to the god or goddess of the temple. Behind the altar was an alcove, where a statue representing the deity was placed. Small rooms used by the priests and priestesses for sleeping were built on the sides of the rectangular building. Temples were magnificently decorated with geometric mosaics and frescoes depicting animals and humans.

The White Temple – Dedicated to the God An

The father of the gods, An, was revered at the White Temple in Uruk. Uruk was a major city-state during the 4th millennium BCE and the chief god of the city. This spectacular temple was painted white and had four corners oriented in the cardinal directions.

The Temple Dedicated to the God Enki

Enki was the main deity of Eridu. Archaeological excavations at this site have found evidence dating back to the early Ubaid period, around 6500 BCE. Evidence shows that this temple was reconstructed and expanded at least eighteen times. The shrine dedicated to the god Enki had a water pool located at the main entrance. In the pool area, archaeologists have uncovered the bones of carp fish, leading to the idea that feasts were held in the temple itself. The temple was abandoned during the Persian invasion.

Temples Dedicated to the Mother Goddess, Ninhursag

Since Ninhursag was considered the mother goddess, temples were dedicated to her in many of the city-states. Before the people recognized Ninhursag as the mother goddess, some scholars posit that she was worshiped as a goddess across the region and, therefore, did not have a major temple associated with one specific city.

Temples dedicated to Ninhursag were excavated in Nippur that dated to the Ur III period. In Adab, Babylon, and Girsu, she was venerated under the regional names of Diĝirmah, Ninmah, and E-mah, respectively.

The Early Dynastic temple at Ur is dedicated to the goddess Ninhursag. It has an inscription on the temple that reads, "Aanepada King of Ur, Son of Mesanepada King of Ur, has built this for his lady Ninhursag."

Gilgamesh and the Netherworld

Gilgamesh is the well-known hero and king of ancient Mesopotamia. The collection of tablets that detail his exploits has collectively been named "the odyssey of the king who did not want to die."

Twelve clay tablets written in Akkadian at the library in Nineveh detail King Gilgamesh's quest for immortality. Also discovered at the library were five other poems with myths about the hero-king Gilgamesh. These poems had titles describing his fight with the Bull of Heaven, his death, his exploits of the netherworld, and more.

Gilgamesh was the king of Uruk. He was the first king to build a defensive wall around his city-state. King Gilgamesh wanted Uruk to be seen as powerful and wealthy, and he commanded the construction of temple towers and magnificent ziggurats. He was personally involved in the planning and layout of agricultural lands and orchards. He was known for his beautiful physique, strength, and intelligence, which makes sense since the people believed him to be two-thirds god and one-third human.

At the start of his rule, Gilgamesh was cruel and lorded over his subjects. He raped women from any class of society; it did not matter whether she was noble, a warrior's wife, or a peasant. He used slave labor and worked his slaves to the point of exhaustion.

When the gods learn of Gilgamesh's exploits and as the people cried, wailed, and lamented at the temples, they decide to create a man as magnificent as Gilgamesh. The gods called this man Enkidu, and they allowed him to grow up in the wild amongst the animals. One day, a hunter comes across Enkidu. The hunter decides to send a prostitute from the temple to tame the wild man. In ancient times, it was believed that sexual relations could calm and domesticate a man, enticing him to become a civilized person.

Enkidu became a part of civilization and was taught by the prostitute how to be a rational human being. One day, Enkidu hears gossip about King Gilgamesh's cruelty and travels to Uruk to challenge the king to become a better ruler. When he arrives in Uruk, he sees Gilgamesh about to force himself into the bedchamber of a new bride. Enkidu places himself in front of the king, blocking the door. Gilgamesh attacks Enkidu, and the two men wrestle fiercely. In the end, Gilgamesh wins. The fight results in a brotherly friendship between the two men.

The new friends decide they need to strengthen their bond by sharing adventures, and they look around for something to challenge them. Their first adventure involves stealing trees from a forest forbidden to mortals. In the cedar forest, they encounter the evil and fearsome demon Humbaba. Humbaba is devoted to the god Enlil, the god of air, wind, and earth. The two strong men wrestle with the monster, and with the help of the sun god Shamash, they defeat Humbaba. As part of their exploits, the two chop down cedar trees and make a raft. With the wood of the biggest tree, they build a huge gate, which Enkidu plans to place at the entrance of Enlil's temple.

Eventually, King Gilgamesh and his friend Enkidu sail back to Uruk. The goddess Ishtar looked lustfully upon the magnificent Gilgamesh and tried to entice him into a relationship. Gilgamesh is not interested in the goddess, though. Enraged, Ishtar asks her father, Anu, the sky god, to command the "Bull of Heaven" to descend to Earth and kill Gilgamesh. The Bull of Heaven brings seven years of famine upon the Earth, so Gilgamesh and Enkidu have to fight him to save civilization. These two strong warriors kill the bull after a gruesome fight.

However, the council of gods is angered by this and decides the two should be taught a lesson. As punishment, they inflict Enkidu with a disease. Enkidu suffers from pain and hallucinations. He tells Gilgamesh about his visions of the netherworld. Gilgamesh is devasted when Enkidu dies, and he cannot stop himself from grieving for his friend.

Enkidu's visions of the netherworld plague Gilgamesh, who starts thinking about the possibility of his own demise. He decides to discard his royal garments and wear animal skins as a tribute to Enkidu. Gilgamesh travels through the wilderness to the edge of the world to find Utnapishtim, the Mesopotamian equivalent of Noah. He had been granted eternal life after the Great Flood. Gilgamesh is determined to learn how to cheat death and never end up in the netherworld.

Upon Gilgamesh's arrival at Mashu, a mountain with two peaks, two immortal scorpion monsters confront him. After begging them for passage, they finally relent. Gilgamesh enters the dark tunnel of torments, and when he emerges, he is faced with a magnificent view of a garden and a sea.

Gilgamesh goes down the mountain pass until he meets a tavern keeper. The veiled female, Siduri, listens to King Gilgamesh and his story. She explains to him that mortality is a blessing and that his quest for immortality will amount to nothing. However, she is not able to persuade him to give up his search.

Siduri shows Gilgamesh where to find the ferryman, Urshanabi, who will take him across the "Waters of Death" to find Utnapishtim. Eventually, Gilgamesh finds Utnapishtim, who tells him about the Great Flood sent by the gods to destroy all of humanity and how he was saved.

King Gilgamesh insists that he wants to become immortal, and Utnapishtim tests him by telling him that he needs to stay awake for an entire week. Gilgamesh fails miserably. Utnapishtim is disappointed in Gilgamesh and tells him that it is foolish to think he can stay awake for eternity if he cannot even stay awake for one week.

In the end, Utnapishtim convinces Gilgamesh to put on his royal robes and become a king his people can admire. Utnapishtim's wife understands the king's plight and asks her husband to show Gilgamesh the plant that brings eternal youth. Gilgamesh takes a piece of the plant and goes back home to Uruk. Along the way, he grows tired and falls asleep under a tree. A snake notices that Gilgamesh has fallen asleep. It slithers toward him and takes the plant. When Gilgamesh awakes, he realizes the plant is gone forever. Any chance of remaining young has gone as well.

Gilgamesh knows he has traveled to the ends of the Earth to return with nothing, yet he has reconciled himself with the fact of mortality. He realizes he cannot live forever, but now his eyes are opened to the magnificence of the city he has built and the enduring achievements of the people.

King Gilgamesh is ultimately revered for his building achievements and for bringing the lost knowledge of ancient times that he learned from Utnapishtim back to Uruk. There are many variations of the *Epic of Gilgamesh*, but regardless of the exact wording, he is seen as the first hero of all time.

The Creation Story – The *Eridu Genesis*

The creation myth was found in Nippur, a city in ancient Mesopotamia that was founded around 5000 BCE. Sumerian clay tablets tell the story of how people were created. Unfortunately, many parts of the original text are missing, and scholars had to use later versions to reconstruct the missing pieces.

According to the extant texts of the creation myth, human-like gods inhabited Earth in the beginning. When they ascended down to Earth, there was a lot of work that needed to be done. The gods worked hard and made the ground habitable by mining minerals and toiling in the soil to make the land arable to produce crops. After some time, the human-like gods became aggravated by the vast amount of work that had to be done, and they complained to the father of the gods, An.

An agreed and listened to the advice of his son Enki, who proposed that they create humans who could toil the earth instead of the gods. Together, Enki and his sister Ninki killed a lesser god and mixed his blood with clay from the fertile soil of Earth to create the first human.

These new beings were unable to reproduce, but Enki and Ninki modified the new being so he could function independently without the help of the gods. They called this man Adapa. This angered Enlil, Enki's brother, as he was not consulted. A conflict between the brothers started.

Enlil became man's biggest adversary. He put humankind through suffering and hardships. Since he was the god of the air, wind, and earth, he could create drought and floods.

In the *Epic of Gilgamesh*, the gods lived in a beautiful garden, similar to the biblical Garden of Eden, between the Tigris and Euphrates Rivers. The term "Eden" is actually Sumerian and means "flat terrain."

Other versions tell of a massive flood planned by the gods to destroy humankind because their noise was bothersome. To preserve life and start a new line of humanity, some gods decided that one man should be selected to save his family. He was also told to save every kind of animal and plant. The man was instructed to build a huge boat for himself, his family, the animals, and the plants to save them from drowning in the flood.

Utnapishtim

In one version of the *Epic of Gilgamesh*, the man who was saved from the flood was named Utnapishtim.

According to this account, the god Enlil cannot sleep because of the noise the humans were making in the city of Shurrupak on the Euphrates River. Enlil confers with the other gods, and they agree with him. The constant noise is too much, so they decide to flood the Earth and destroy mankind. The gods take an oath not to warn the humans and depart, satisfied with the outcome.

However, Ea visits Utnapishtim, a pious man, in a dream and tells him to build a boat. He gives Utnapishtim exact dimensions for the boat's size and instructs him to put his family and every animal on Earth to survive the coming flood.

Utnapishtim agrees but asks what he should tell the rest of the people when they inquire why he is building such a large boat. Ea tells him to say that the god Enlil is angry with him and that he may no longer live amongst the people.

The boat is built, and just in time. Adad, the god of storms, soon unleashes a terrifying storm of such proportions that even the other gods are afraid. The queen of heaven, Ishtar, cannot believe that she agreed to this terrible event. The storm rages for six days and six nights and then abates.

Utnapishtim first releases a dove, then a swallow, but both come back, having found no place to rest. Finally, he sends out a raven. It does not return.

Utnapishtim offers a sacrifice of cedar, cane, and myrtle, which he burns in a large cauldron on top of Mount Nisir. Ishtar calls the other gods to gather around the pleasing aroma. When Enlil arrives, he is angry that Utnapishtim and his family have survived. He asks how they knew to be prepared. Ea condemns Enlil for the grand punishment he had afflicted upon the world. The punishment did not fit the crime, and Enlil understands this after talking with the other gods. He goes to Utnapishtim, blessing him and his wife with immortality.

Enki and the World Order

The Sumerian god Enki's name translates to "En," meaning "lord," and "ki," meaning earth. It is commonly accepted that he was the "lord of the earth." He was also known by the name "E-A," meaning "lord of water." Enki was the patron deity of the city-state Eridu, and the origins of his name might be linked to Abzu, not Enki (with "Ab" meaning water).

Eridu was believed by the later Sumerians to be the first city in the world. It was the place where humans were created and where law and order were taught to humans. Later, Eridu became known as the city of the first kings. As such, it remained an important cult and religious center for thousands of years. Since Enki, the god of wisdom and intellect, was the patron god of this city, it was thought that Enki originally bestowed the *meh* (the practices and institutions that will make them civilized, such as, for example, kingship, sexual intercourse, and the arts) on the Sumerians.

Enki's temple at Eridu, known as E-Abzu, House of Abzu, or House of the Subterranean Waters, had a pool at the entrance. This majestic temple was the design that most Sumerian temples followed, which helps to confirm Eridu was the first city in Sumer.

The myth of Enki and the world order is complex and based on the Sumerian texts that were preserved on old Babylonian clay tablets. These texts describe events during the 3rd millennium BCE when Enki's temple in Eridu would have been the most important.

Enki's altruism and benevolence for humans and Earth are described in great detail in this myth. Enki is described as the "lord who walks nobly on heaven and earth and is beloved and self-reliant." His father, the sky god An, and his older brother, Enlil, praise Enki for his character and goodness. He is a most beloved son and brother.

In the myth, Eridu becomes the home of Enki and is described as the noblest house, the mast of heaven and Earth, and a place of beauty and peace. Enki derives his powers of fertility from the sweet underground waters of Abzu, and he teaches the people how to serve food at the tables of gods and humans. Enki is accompanied by seven sages who teach humanity about civilization, including mathematics and computing the numbers of the stars. Enlil greatly trusts Enki, and he is given praise and authority by Enlil to organize the world for the good of the rulers and humanity as a whole.

Enlil gathers all the *meh*, the measures of power in heaven and on Earth, and places them in the hands of Enki. Enki passes the *meh* to

Eridu and then travels to all the Sumerian city-states to share the *meh* with them.

Enki establishes civilization and order on Earth. The idea behind all of this is for the deities, city-states, and neighbors of Sumer to work together as one to ensure peace and the continuation of humankind.

Conclusion

Allow your imagination to wander to the geographical area of Mesopotamia. Most of it lies in modern-day Iraq. Much of it is arid with little water, plenty of dried-up river beds, and lots of sand. It can become extremely hot in most areas. It is definitely not the perfect location for an emerging civilization to settle. So, how did this area become known as the Cradle of Civilization?

Today, it is evident from archaeological and other studies that in ancient times, some areas, especially between and around the Euphrates and Tigris Rivers, were much different. Possible seasonal settlements could have started as early as the 11th millennium BCE. Date palm remains date back to around 10,000 BCE. Oak trees, like those featured in the *Epic of Gilgamesh*, were present in antiquity and probably disappeared because of humans.

Archaeological excavations and ancient texts provide proof that the ancient people who created the world's first civilization were innovative, energetic, and brilliant. Is it perhaps due to the scarcity of some resources and the abundance of others that the people had to develop innovations? It is hard to imagine them prospering without overcoming hurdles as time passed and as the climate changed. In any event, the Sumerians thrived for millennia before they disappeared and were forgotten.

The year was 1842. Paul-Émile Botta, a naturalist, was the French consul general based in Mosul. He spent a year digging and searching mounds in Kuyunjik, only to discover some alabaster and mudbricks. Locals who worked alongside Botta on excavations told him about a mound in Khorsabad, which was a little more than twelve miles (twenty kilometers) away. He started excavating this mound, which turned out to be the ruins of the royal palace of Sargon II of the Neo Assyrian Empire. Botta found large reliefs and sculptures that referred to the town of Nineveh.

His head was in turmoil. What did he just unearth? Could this be evidence confirming the Bible? At this time, many treasure hunters and biblical scholars were searching for the lands of the biblical patriarch Abraham (Ibrahim).

The French government was jubilant over this discovery. It set in motion archaeological interest in the region, and France supplied Botta with resources and nine more archaeologists. Among them was Austen Henry Layard. Layard is best remembered for his unbelievable discovery of the Library of Ashurbanipal in ancient Nineveh, across the Tigris from Mosul in Iraq.

Sir Charles Leonard Woolley, an archaeologist who excavated the Hittite city of Carchemish between 1912 and 1914, was posted to Cairo during World War I. After the war, in the early 1920s, he and a team of archaeologists from the University of Pennsylvania and the British Museum went on a mission to uncover archaeological evidence of the ancient Sumerians.

They began to unravel the mysteries of this lost civilization in the cemeteries uncovered in and around Ur. The magnificent grave goods discovered at the cemetery, which Woolley named the Royal Cemetery of Ur, convinced archaeologists that they were dealing with a highly developed and civilized society of great importance.

Answers were found, but the answers only seemed to lead to more questions. No wonder so much of the discovered information about the Sumerian civilization is referred to as the "Sumerian Problem" in scholarly circles. There is just no consensus, and too much is based on too little factual confirmation, such as the issue of applying pottery chronology across the ancient Near East to correlate dates.

In this book, we looked at where the Sumerians came from and where they settled. We saw how their settlements became the first cities of Eridu, Uruk, Ur, and Lagash.

We learned how they developed a calendar, hydraulic irrigation, agricultural implements, and the wheel. Where would we be today without the invention of the wheel?

We were even confronted with the first evidence of urban warfare: the battle between Hamoukar and Uruk. It is sad to think about how humanity has not progressed much in that regard and that pits are still being dug for mass burials. But warfare seems to be another aspect of being human, and it is yet another thing that connects us with this ancient civilization.

We saw how the first empire was created. Sargon was a great emperor who conquered lands and people as he saw fit. Yet, his daughter, Enheduanna, was the first known poet. She was- a priestess and an adoring child who honored her father with her words. And although not all families get along, the bond of a family unit was felt thousands of years ago.

One brother usurped the throne after his father's death and was assassinated after a short but brutal rule. When his sibling, Manishtushu, took the throne, we can see the same patterns of bribery and corruption that we experience today.

It is easy to think we are set apart from people who lived long ago. But that is far from the truth. Society today has built upon the amazing advancements of ancient people, and it is always worth exploring more of ancient history to better understand how humanity has progressed through the ages. Hopefully, this book has given you a taste of that. We encourage you to learn more about the people who came before us so you can better understand the world around you today.

Part 2: The Akkadian Empire

An Enthralling Overview of the Rise and Fall of the Akkadians

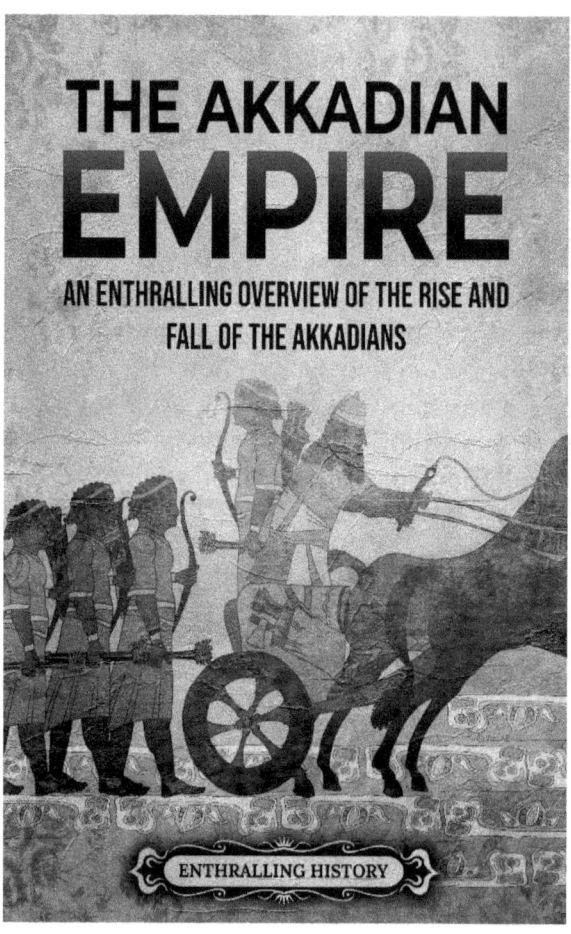

Introduction

Akki, the gardener, stretched his sun-bronzed arms and scowled at the rows of barley yet to be watered. He resolutely plodded to the river with two buckets. The sun sparkled on the river's surface, momentarily blinding Akki as he lowered one of the buckets into the water. Thump! What did the bucket hit? There! Bumping against the shore was a covered basket.

How curious! Setting the bucket aside, Akki squatted down and lifted the basket out of the water. It seemed heavy. What was inside? He noted the bitumen covering the basket; someone wanted it to be waterproof. But why? Carefully, he unlatched the top and looked inside. Something was moving under the small blanket! Akki jumped back for a moment, then heard a whimpering sound. He carefully pulled aside the blanket to find a newborn infant, whose sudden exposure to the bright sun made him horrifically wail.

"There, there, little one," he cooed. "You're all right. You're safe now." As if in a dream, Akki lifted the baby to his shoulder and began walking across the fields, never realizing he held the first king of the world's first empire.

If you mentioned the Akkadian Empire to a group of people, chances are you'd get some quizzical looks or blank stares. Most people have never heard of the world's first multi-national empire with a powerful, centralized government. Preceding the Babylonian, Assyrian, Egyptian, Chinese, and Indian empires by centuries, the Akkadian Empire rose to power in 2334 BCE to rule all of ancient Mesopotamia—and beyond!

Was there anything approaching an empire before the Akkadian Empire? In southern Mesopotamia, Sumer's city-states formed several mini-empires, with one city's king exercising "kingship" over other cities in the region. However, these were more like small countries, covering less than one hundred square miles. Everyone shared the same culture, spoke the same language, and prayed to the same gods. By contrast, the Akkadian Empire encompassed multiple ethnicities and languages: Sumerian, Akkadian, Elamite, Syrian, Canaanite, and more. At its zenith, the empire stretched from the Mediterranean Sea to the Persian Gulf, including Mesopotamia, Elam, Anatolia, Syria, Lebanon, and Canaan.

This history of the Akkadian Empire reveals many captivating mysteries of this vast realm. What civilizations existed in Mesopotamia before Akkad gained supremacy? What were the Akkadians' origins? How did they gain sovereignty over other cultures and form their vast power network? What myths drove the Akkadian culture, and what religion did they follow? How did their art and culture reflect their belief system? Who were their most famous rulers, and what made them exceptional? What were the distinctive features of their military and warfare strategies? What was everyday life like in the Akkadian Empire? Why did the Akkadian Empire collapse? How did the Akkadian culture continue to influence future Mesopotamian dynasties? This book will answer these questions and many more.

You might be wondering how this book is different from other Akkadian Empire histories. For one thing, few authors have written a comprehensive overview of this topic since the renowned archaeologist Leonard W. King published *A History of Sumer and Akkad* in 1910. Some generalized histories of Mesopotamia contain a chapter or two on the Akkadian Empire, but few are devoted solely to the Akkadian Empire.

Of the handful of books written on Akkad, most focus on specific aspects, such as Benjamin R. Foster's fascinating study of Sargonic and pre-Sargonic cuneiform texts, Melissa Eppihimer's enchanting overview of the Akkadian artistic legacy, and Alan Lenzi's enlightening introduction to Akkadian literature. This book presents a comprehensive, authoritative history drawing from the scholarly research of King, Foster, Eppihimer, Lenzi, and other Mesopotamian specialists to deliver the most recent archaeological and cultural studies. This broad overview endeavors to bring Sargon the Great and his enthralling Akkadian Empire to life in an engaging, easy-to-understand format.

Exploring past civilizations is enriching and empowering. When we understand how cultures developed, what made them extraordinary, and what led to their downfalls, we have a broader understanding of our world today. Yesterday's cultures inform our worldview and our belief systems. Comprehensive knowledge of history gives us a deeper understanding of our global state of affairs. Past victories inspire and motivate us, and past failures warn us what not to do.

Examining the spectacular rise and fall of the world's first true empire is invigorating. It's almost overwhelming to imagine how Sargon, a humble gardener, seemingly arose from nothing to conquer and rule the land between the Euphrates and Tigris Rivers (today's Iraq). Then he and his descendants pressed on to dominate the ancient territories of present-day Iran, Turkey, Syria, Lebanon, Syria, Canaan, and Oman. A keen understanding of ancient Mesopotamia gives insight into today's rich Middle Eastern cultures and turbulent political landscape.

Join us as we explore the influence of the Ubaid and Sumerian cultures that preceded the Akkadian civilization, the explosion of change wrought by the Akkadian Empire, how the empire operated, and how it continued to influence events and culture in the Middle East.

Chapter 1: The Ubaid Period

Who were the early people in southern Mesopotamia, with their lizard-lady figurines and entrancing pottery? How did they live, and what did they accomplish in the mysterious millennia before writing began? Although they formed the first true empire, the Akkadians were not the first civilization in Mesopotamia; in fact, they were relative newcomers to the scene. Before the Akkadians arrived, the Sumerians lived in central and southern Mesopotamia, sharing a common history and culture since around 3800 BCE, which later intertwined with the Akkadian culture. Before the Sumerians, although it overlaps a bit, the mysterious Ubaid civilization and several other prehistoric cultures farmed and herded livestock in Mesopotamia.

What do we know about these prehistoric cultures? By 5500 BCE, in the mid-Neolithic period, the Hassuna, Samarra, and Halaf cultures emerged in northern Mesopotamia, living in agricultural villages with baked-clay homes and circular domed temples. The Samarra culture was in central-northern Mesopotamia, where scholars believe Akkad was located. The Hassuna culture was immediately north of Samarra, and the Halaf culture was to the west. Although their distinctive pottery set them apart, these three civilizations overlapped and intermingled.

How advanced were these civilizations? All three prehistoric cultures used axes, sickles, grinding stones, baking ovens, and simple plows. They had stamp seals, which were about one inch in diameter, with a picture carved into stone that they pressed into soft clay as a sort of signature. They made cream-slip pottery painted with reddish linear designs. They grew emmer wheat, barley, and flax, and they herded sheep, goats, and cattle.

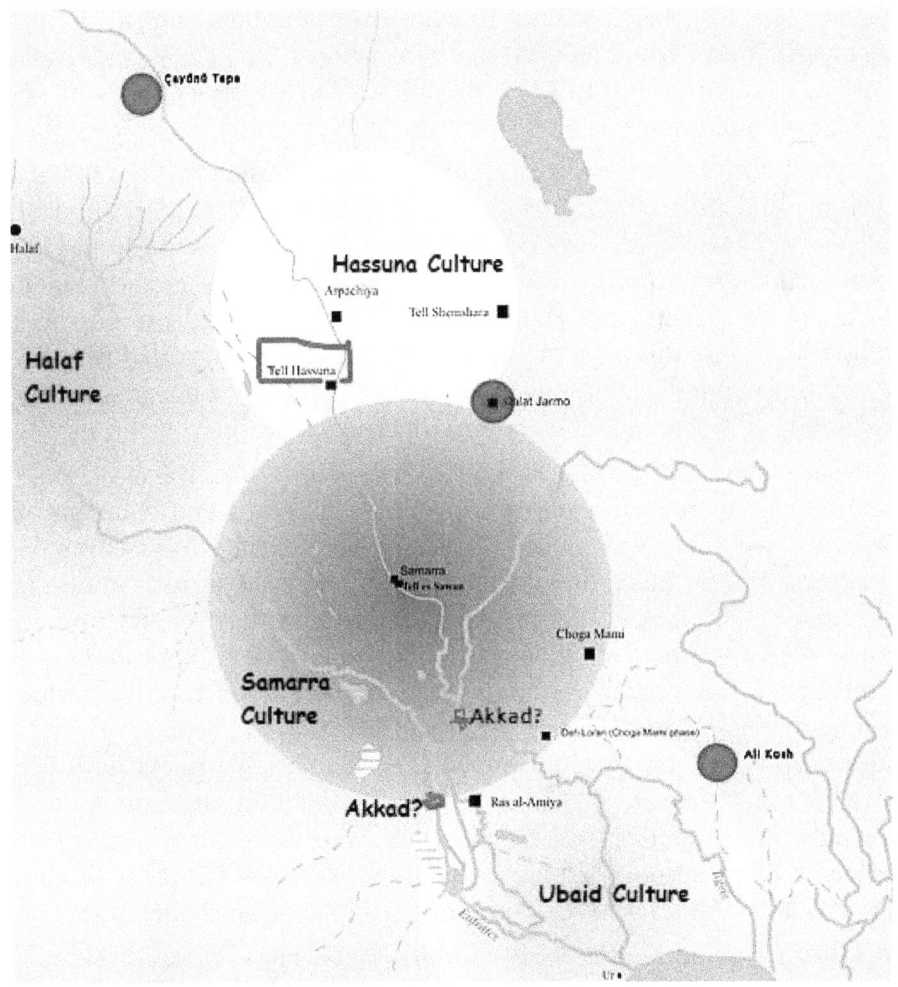

This map shows the prehistoric cultures' locations in ancient Mesopotamia prior to the Sumerian civilization and Akkadian Empire. Two possible sites of Akkad are noted in the lower map, and Tell Hassuna is circled in the upper map.[28]

In northern Iraq in 1942, a farmer was plowing the soil to plant lentils on a hill covered with wildflowers when he found some pottery shards. After closer inspection, archaeologist Sayid Fu'ād Safar determined that this hill, which was twenty-two miles southwest of today's Mosul, was actually a tell, which he named *Tell Hassuna*. A "tell" is an artificial hill or mound of accumulated, stratified debris from buildings, garbage, tombs, vegetation, and earth left by ancient generations of people who once lived there. Over the centuries—or over the millennia, in this case—buildings crumble, and nature slowly reclaims the area. In the desert and semi-arid regions like Iraq, blowing sand usually covers the tells until it's hard to distinguish them from natural land formations. In fact, the Akkadian Empire's capital of Agade (Akkad) still lies buried under the sand. No one knows quite where it is.

What did the archaeological exploration of the site reveal? Tell Hassuna and other similar tells provide valuable information about the preexisting Hassuna, Samarra, and Halaf civilizations in what would later be the Akkadian Empire region. Although the tell was in the Hassuna region, many Samarra and Halaf pottery artifacts were in the upper layers, indicating that all three cultures coexisted in the area or traded with each other. Since these cultures were preliterate, we rely on archaeological excavations for clues about these ancient civilizations.

Safar teamed up with Seton Lloyd, President of the British School of Archaeology in Iraq, to explore Tell Hassuna. Lloyd and Safar initially thought the pottery was more recent and were excited to discover they were wrong! The more they excavated, the older the artifacts they were unearthing. The Tell Hassuna's lowest and oldest level—twenty-two feet down—dated to the Neolithic Era.[i] The oldest layer appeared to be remnants of hunter/gatherers or possibly herders who used stone tools and made thick, coarse pottery. Safar and Lloyd found hearths or fire pits but no houses. They did find woven reed matting that might have been used as a covering for huts, except they didn't find any post holes or anything hinting at a support structure. Perhaps the reed matting was the remnants of baskets or sleeping mats. These Neolithic people were either tent dwellers, like today's Bedouins, or used little or no shelter at all.

Lloyd's team uncovered obsidian lanceheads and slingshot ammunition for hunting. They found stone-headed axes, which they believed may have been used to break the ground for simple farming. The archaeologists were intrigued to find a skeleton between two cooking hearths. They wondered if the person had been buried in a shallow grave or if he or she died in an abandoned settlement.

---

[i] Seton Lloyd, Fuad Safar, and Robert J. Braidwood, "Tell Hassuna Excavations by the Iraq Government Directorate General of Antiquities in 1943 and 1944," *Journal of Near Eastern Studies* 4, no. 4 (1945): 255–89. http://www.jstor.org/stable/542914.

This Hassuna redware bowl dates to about 5500 BCE.[29]

The middle layer was the Hassuna culture (5500-3800 BCE). They lived in adobe houses. At first, these were crudely constructed, one-room dwellings, but they later had several rooms. The Hassuna pottery was painted and more sophisticated than the Neolithic culture. The Hassuna culture used stone mortars and barrel-shaped clay ovens with one opening. They would light a fire inside to heat the oven, then put out the fire, sweep out the ashes, and put in the bread dough. The clay walls of the oven stayed hot long enough for the bread to bake. Near the ovens were clay disks; the archaeologists theorized these were "potboilers." The Hassuna would put them into the oven for a while, and when they were hot, they would drop them into a pot of water to heat them up.

In the Hassuna layers, Safar and Lloyd discovered sickle blades of flint and obsidian, and beneath the houses, they found grain bins, leading them to think the Hassuna were grain farmers. Animal bones at the site revealed they also herded cattle, sheep, and goats. The upper Hassuna layer displayed the sophisticated Samarra pottery and many Halaf ceramics, which indicates trade or homogeneity between the neighboring people.

Archaeologists found this circa 5000 BCE bottle-shaped jar painted with a woman's face in the Hassuna layer of Tell Hassuna, representing Samarra culture.[30]

They found the skeletal remains of infants buried in pottery jars under the houses and one complete skeleton of an older child or small adult curled into the fetal position in what appeared to be part of a room in a house sealed off by stone. Interestingly, the Assyrians, whose culture emerged in the same region about one thousand years later, also followed this custom of burying loved ones under or within their homes.

The upper layers contained remnants of Ubaid-style pottery and some artifacts from the late Ubaid and Akkadian-Assyrian cultures. The buildings in these layers were built of stone. Safar and Lloyd found no copper in any of the levels, but they did find antimony and malachite, which would have been used to make kohl eye makeup. They unearthed more adult human skeletons buried in an orderly fashion. Two skeletons, however, were flung helter-skelter into a pit. Were they the victims of foul play? Were they executed? Mysteries like this leave archaeologists scratching their heads.

The Ubaid culture (5500-3800 BCE) emerged slightly later in central and southern Mesopotamia but continued through the same period as the Halaf, Samarra, and Hassuna cultures. The Sumerian culture would later develop in the Ubaid region, and Akkad probably lay where the prehistoric Samarra and Ubaid cultures connected geographically. The name "Ubaid" derives from *Tell al-'Ubaid*—an archaeological site just west of the ancient city of Ur on what was then the Persian Gulf coast. The Persian Gulf later receded south about 155 miles due to silt deposits from the Euphrates and Tigris Rivers. Another factor for reduced sea levels was global cooling and increased ice packs on the northern and southern poles.

What does archaeology tell us about the Ubaid culture? Ubaidians used adzes (something like an ax), hoes, and knives, and they wove linen and wool, as loom weights and spindle whorls were uncovered. They made bricks to build houses and formed distinctive painted pottery and figurines. Several households shared outdoor clay bread ovens. Occupations included carpenters, farmers, fishermen, herders, potters, and weavers.

Did the Ubaidians establish the world's first city? The Ubaid culture is divided into several periods, which mainly revolve around the changes in pottery. The Ubaid I period centers around the city of Eridu in Mesopotamia's far south. Eridu was a few miles west of Ur and on the Persian Gulf at that time (now its ruins lie in a desert wasteland). Many archaeologists believe Eridu, which was first settled around 5400 BCE by the Ubaidians, is the world's oldest city. However, it didn't achieve true city status until the later Sumerian era, when it grew into a sizeable city covering one hundred acres. In the Ubaid period, it had about four thousand people, making it a large town.

How could the Ubaidians farm in semi-desert conditions? Eridu's people could grow grain despite the hot, arid conditions because the nearby Euphrates River fed Lake Hammar. The Eridu settlement sat on two shores—the Persian Gulf to the south and Lake Hammar to the west—which, at that time, was freshwater (now it's saline).[i] This proximity to the sea and a freshwater lake provided an irrigation source and an abundance of seafood.

---

[i] Carrie Hritz, et al. "Revisiting the Sealands: Report of Preliminary Ground Reconnaissance in the Hammar District, Dhi Qar and Basra Governorates, Iraq," *Iraq* 74 (2012): 37-49. http://www.jstor.org/stable/23349778.

The Ubaid culture's access to the Persian Gulf, Lake Hammar, and the Euphrates and Tigris Rivers also led to the use of boats. And not only simple canoes or rafts but sailboats! Archaeologists unearthed clay models of sailboats in the gravesites of Uruk, Eridu, and other Ubaid towns.[i] These early sailboats—the first in the world for which we have archaeological evidence—were simple yet served as a prototype for more sophisticated designs in the future.

The earliest Ubaid people in Eridu lived in reed-thatched huts and enjoyed a wide variety of food. They fished and dug shellfish from the gulf and the lake. They hunted waterfowl, gazelle, and other wild animals, and they herded goats and sheep, which provided milk, meat, and wool. They ate the wild einkorn wheat and later began cultivating it. In the Ubaid I period, they carried water to their fields, but by the mid-Ubaid period, they had learned to dig canals for irrigating larger fields, which created a surplus of grain.

As time went by, they built more permanent houses by forming bricks from the wetland mud, which provided better protection from the hot sun. The early mud-brick homes were rectangle-shaped and had several rooms with plastered floors and flat roofs constructed from beams and rushes covered by plaster. Eventually, the town covered about twenty-five acres with approximately four thousand people in an area surrounded by smaller villages.

What was the Ubaid culture's religion? A small one-room temple, first built around 5300 BCE, stood in the town's center. At one end was a sacrificial altar, and at the other end was a niche for a deity image. The question is, who did they

This reptilian-headed woman nursing a baby came from Ur, Ubaid Period (4500–4000 BCE). Figures of slim women with lizard-like heads were a common motif in the Ubaid culture.[31]

---

[i] E. Douglas Van Buren, "Discoveries at Eridu," *Orientalia* 18, no. 1 (1949): 123–24. http://www.jstor.org/stable/43072618.

worship? Multiple images of a female figure with a reptilian head have been found in Ubaid-era tells in southern Mesopotamia. Were these Ubaidian deities?

What were these lizard ladies all about? They were small, only two to six inches tall, with slanted eyes and elongated heads and noses. By comparison, ancient female figurines from the Hassuna, Samarra, and Halaf cultures were plump, seated ladies with large thighs and pendulous breasts. The Ubaid female statuettes are thin, with flat tummies and smaller breasts; they look somewhat androgynous. A few figurines are male, and some are of indeterminate gender. These figurines were often found in adult human graves but never in children's graves. The Ubaid typically buried their dead resting on their back, with their hands resting on their pelvis, which is how many reptilian figures appeared.[1] Scholars have yet to determine if they had religious significance—yet another head-scratching mystery!

Eridu was consistently inhabited through the end of the Ubaid culture, and it was abandoned around 3800 BCE, perhaps due to the same flooding that struck Ur several miles east. Ur and Uruk were two other prominent towns that emerged in southern Mesopotamia in the Ubaid I period. The Sumerians would later inhabit these two settlements, which grew into large cities dominating Sumer (southern Mesopotamia). Ur was in a strategic position, as it was about twelve miles east of Eridu, where the Euphrates River flowed into the Persian Gulf. Uruk was about forty miles north of Ur on the eastern bank of the Euphrates. Around the time that Ur and Uruk were established, the Ubaid civilization blended with northern Mesopotamia's Halaf culture, forming the Halaf-Ubaid Transitional period.

The Ubaid II period (4800–4500 BCE) is renowned for its striking Hadji Muhammed pottery and the first irrigation agriculture with canal networks. Building the irrigation canals required coordinated and collective work—a historic milestone. During this period, the Ubaid formed extensive trade networks, stretching down the Persian Gulf coast to Bahrain and Oman, west into Arabia, and into the Mediterranean. Since Eridu and Ur were coastal towns (before the Persian Gulf shrank), they likely used boats to travel along the coast. They also traded with

---

[1] R. Carter and Graham Philip, *Beyond the Ubaid: Transformation and Integration in the Late Prehistoric Societies of the Middle East*, Chicago: The Oriental Institute, University of Chicago, 2010, 149-161.

settlements in Turkey and Armenia for obsidian, which is a razor-sharp black volcanic glass used to make arrow and knife blades.

This Hadji Muhammed pottery jar dates to the Ubaid III era, circa 5300-4600 BCE.[32]

The later Ubaid period (4500-3800 BCE) is notable for progress in distinctive ceramics, including stamp seals with designs of birds, snakes, and humans. In 1990, archaeologist Andrew Moore from the Rochester Institute of Technology and British archaeologist Tony Wilkinson discovered pottery kilns in Eridu and Ur that indicated industrial-scale pottery manufacturing took place in these towns in the later Ubaid era.[i]

Around 4500 BCE, social stratification emerged in the towns, with larger houses in the town center. Likely, these people had more wealth and probably more power. Also, in the later Ubaid period, distinctions arose in the pottery between the Ubaid settlements of southern Mesopotamia and northern Mesopotamia. In their appraisal of Khanijdal East, a small, late Ubaid settlement in the Jazira plain of northern Iraq, archaeologist Tony Wilkinson and his team noted differences in the

---

[i] A. M. T. Moore, "Pottery Kiln Sites at al 'Ubaid and Eridu," *Iraq* 64 (2002): 69-77. https://doi.org/10.2307/4200519.

shape and decoration of pottery, materials used to make the pottery, and firing techniques.[i] They discovered numerous small clay figurines of sheep and goats; they believed these did not have religious significance but were children's toys. They found one in an infant's grave, along with a rattle.

Ubaid pottery was of superior quality. It was usually a buff color but sometimes yellow, yellow-green, pink, or orange. Firing at an especially hot temperature made it harder and more durable. The pottery fabric (clay characteristics) usually contained rich plant-based temper and occasionally gritty sand. (In pottery making, temper is something mixed with clay that helps prevent cracking and shrinking in the drying and firing process). The Ubaid people generally painted them with black geometric shapes or occasionally floral or animal motifs. Pottery came in all sizes and shapes: pitchers, jars, bowls (both shallow and deep), cooking pots, and cups.

This rounded-bottom Ubaid bowl, circa 5000 BCE, features a yellow-greenish color.[33]

---

[i] T. J., B. Wilkinson, H. Monahan, and D. J. Tucker, "Khanijdal East: A Small Ubaid Site in Northern Iraq," *Iraq* 58 (1996): 17–50. https://doi.org/10.2307/4200417.

A distinctive Ubaid pottery style of southern Mesopotamia is *Hadji Muhammed.* The potter used a dark-purple color wash over the ceramic, then scraped the vessel into designs to reveal the buff color underneath. Patterns included herringbone, checkerboard, and sinuous curves. This pottery type emerged in the Ubaid I period but is found in later Ubaid periods. Harriet Crawford of the McDonald Institute for Archaeological Research of the University of Cambridge theorized that the Ubaid people used specialty Hadji Muhammed ceramics for festive occasions like we might bring out the fine china for special dinners today.[i]

What happened to the Ubaidians? What caused their decline? Archaeological evidence shows that Ur and Eridu were both abandoned around 3800 BCE. An eleven-foot layer of silt at Ur indicates a significant flood covered the city at that time,[ii] which may also have affected nearby Eridu. The rapid, high amplitude climate change around 3700 BCE dramatically affected human settlements in this part of the world.

Global cooling resulted in glacier advancement and less snowmelt, which would have impacted the water levels of the Persian Gulf, the Tigris and Euphrates flowing from the Taurus Mountains, and Lake Hammar adjacent to Eridu. Most of the Near East, including southern Mesopotamia, experienced heightened aridity, which affected the available fresh water, made farming more complicated, and caused increases in sandstorms. These dramatic weather changes caused population shifts throughout the Near East.[iii] The Ubaid people might have mostly died out from harsh conditions, with the remnants migrating to other areas and assimilating into the local populations.

---

[i] Carter & Philip, "Beyond the Ubaid," 163-168.

[ii] C. Leonard Woolley, "Excavations at Ur," *Journal of the Royal Society of Arts* 82, no. 4227 (1933): 46-59. http://www.jstor.org/stable/41360003.

[iii] Joanne Clarke, et al. "Climatic Changes and Social Transformations in the Near East and North Africa during the 'Long' 4th Millennium BC: A Comparative Study of Environmental and Archaeological Evidence," *Quaternary*

Chapter 2: The Pre-Akkadian Period

Who were the Sumerians? What were their origins? Following the prehistoric Hassuna, Samarra, Halaf, and Ubaid cultures, the Mesopotamian powerhouse of the 4th and 3rd millennia BCE was Sumer, with cities along the Euphrates and Tigris Rivers and the Persian Gulf. The name Sumer meant "land of the civilized kings" in the Akkadian language. Some scholars believe they were an outgrowth and continuation of the Ubaid culture in Uruk. Others think they migrated into southern Mesopotamia and overcame and assimilated the remnants of the Ubaid culture.

Does linguistics give us a clue to their origins? Sumerians spoke a language isolate, which means it was unrelated to Semitic, Elamite, or any other known languages. Because the Ubaid culture was preliterate, we don't know if their language was a forerunner of the Sumerian language. Sumerian epic poetry alludes to a location north of Iran for the Sumerians' origins. Their language was agglutinative (stringing together multiple morphemes in one word), as are some languages in the Caspian Sea region.[i] However, the language shows complex borrowings from other languages that make it difficult to trace.[ii] Whether it was a

---

[i] Jonathan R. Ziskind, "The Sumerian Problem
[ii] Gonzalo Rubio, "On the Alleged 'Pre-Sumerian Substratum,'" *Journal of Cuneiform Studies* 51 (1999): 1-16. https://doi.org/10.2307/1359726.

continuation of the Ubaid or migrants from the northeast, Uruk's habitation flowed uninterrupted from the Ubaid era into the Sumerian period. However, around 4000 BCE, Uruk evolved into a proper city with an elaborate culture, and an explosion of innovation began.

Several Sumerian towns grew into formidable city-states independent of other cities politically and economically. Each city had its own king who ruled the urban area and the surrounding villages and rural lands. Each city-state was like its own small country. Sometimes, one city's mighty king would take "kingship" over several other cities. According to the ancient *Sumerian King List*,[i] which dates to at least the 3rd millennium BCE, this happened cyclically—before and after the Great Flood.

The *Sumerian King List* records that after the Great Flood swept over the land, the city of Kish held "kingship" or sovereignty over other cities. Then Eanna defeated Kish and took kingship, then Uruk, then Ur, and so on. The *Sumerian King List* records that the kings before the Great Flood lived tens of thousands of years, and the kings after the flood ruled for a century or more until Gilgamesh, after which the typical reign lasted thirty years or so.

Do the long reigns represent dynasties and not individual people? Or were the pre-Gilgamesh kings simply mythical? At least some kings following Gilgamesh (and one preceding him) were real people, as inscriptions with the rulers' names and other archaeological data support their existence. But 385,200 years of eight kings before the Great Flood and 28,000 years of kings after the flood and before Gilgamesh and the Early Dynastic Period (circa 2900-2350 BCE) strains credibility.

The groundbreaking Sumerians surged ahead in hydraulic engineering, constructing intricate irrigation systems for crops, along with dikes and ditches to harness the perennial flooding of the Tigris and Euphrates. They were the first to build massive city walls surrounding resplendent multi-storied temples and palaces. They created imposing ziggurat towers, majestic columns, bronze decorations, and breathtaking mosaics and mural paintings with stunningly realistic figures.

---

[i] *Sumerian King List*, Translated by Jean-Vincent Scheil, Stephen Langdon, and Thorkild Jacobsen, *Livius*. https://www.livius.org/sources/content/anet/266-the-sumerian-king-list/#Translation.

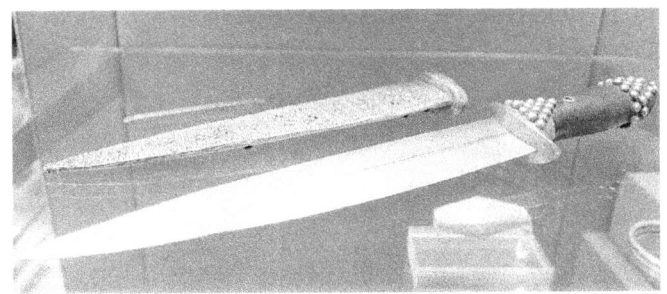

Leonard Wooley discovered this remarkable gold knife and scabbard with a lapis lazuli handle in the royal tomb of A'anepada, son of Mesannepada (circa 2550-2400 BCE).[34]

Speaking of bronze, the Sumerians were probably the first—around 3300 BCE—to blend copper and tin to usher in the Bronze Age. The strength and durability of bronze produced superior weapons and tools. Astute in metallurgy, the Sumerians also worked with gold and other precious metals in the Early Bronze Age. In Ur's royal tomb, the famed archaeologist Leonard Wooley discovered the striking "dagger of Ur," with its beautifully worked, solid-gold sheath and blade and a handle grip of gold-studded lapis lazuli of the deepest blue. Other sensational finds included a golden helmet crafted with exceptional technical excellence, a golden goblet, and lyres overlaid with silver plates.[i]

The Sumerians developed the world's first writing system, initially pictographs, around 3800 BCE. Using the end of reeds, they scratched childlike symbols into wet clay that hardened, preserving their writing for millennia. These clay tablets give us astounding insight into their culture and history. The first symbols helped track sales and administrative data but not abstract concepts. Later, these symbols evolved into the more sophisticated cuneiform in which they wrote down the first literature, including epic poetry and the first law codes.

Instead of scratching pictures into the clay, they wrote cuneiform by pressing a cut reed's end into the moist clay, making stylized, wedge-shaped impressions. By 2900 BCE, they had about six hundred symbols representing words. The Sumerians opened the first schools to teach cuneiform. It took about a dozen years to memorize the symbols and gain enough proficiency to become a scribe. Other civilizations used the Sumerian cuneiform system for their own languages over the next three millennia, including the Akkadians, Elamites, Assyrians, Babylonians, and Hittites.

---

[i] Woolley, "Excavations at Ur," 46-59.

To the left is a cylinder seal dating to 3000 BCE or older. The recent impression of this ancient seal on damp clay is on the right. The mythical creatures depicted are serpopards—lions with serpentine necks. Flying above them are eagles with lion heads.[35]

In addition to writing cuneiform on wet clay, the Sumerians used elegant cylinder seals by 3500 BCE, which were similar to the stamp seals used by the Ubaid. They rolled these four-inch cylinders into damp clay, leaving an identifying picture or inscription. The cylinders were metal or semi-precious stone, like lapis lazuli or marble, and the Sumerians wore them on a lanyard around their neck or pinned to their outer robe. All social classes used cylinder seals to certify business transactions and to "sign" letters.

The Sumerians didn't invent the wheel, but they figured out how to use it for transportation. The oldest wheel found in archaeological digs was a tournette—a basic, hand-turned potter's wheel. It was found in Iran and dated to 5200 to 4700 BCE. The Sumerians developed the tournette into a freely-spinning fast potter's wheel with an axle; one dating to 3100 BCE was unearthed in Ur. Also, in Ur, Leonard Wooley uncovered a jar with a clay seal imprinted with a crude depiction of two men in a cart or chariot drawn by a donkey. This wheeled vehicle dated to about 3750 BCE. It is the earliest evidence of a wheel used for transportation![i]

The Standard of Ur—a mosaic with a lapis lazuli background and pictures of red limestone and shell that depict early four-wheeled chariots riding over bodies of dead warriors.[36]

---

[i] Woolley, "Excavations at Ur," 46-59.

The earliest Sumerian transportation wheels were solid disks of wood horizontally cut from a tree trunk. A hole was chiseled out in the middle of the disk, and through that, they inserted a rotating axle. The first carts quickly evolved into chariots pulled by onagers (a large horse-like donkey). Mesopotamians didn't start using horses until around 2400 BCE. These early four-wheeled chariots are pictured in the Standard of Ur mosaic, which dates to about 2600 BCE.

The Sumerians were brilliantly advanced when it came to mathematics. They started by developing a counting system using both hands, but with their method, they could go much higher than ten. On the one hand, they counted up to twelve knuckles on their four fingers. Once they got to twelve, they would hold up one finger on the other hand. Then, they'd count to twelve again and hold up the second finger. Using all four fingers and the thumb, they could count up to sixty on their two hands. The Sumerians used a sexagesimal system of counting by sixty. In our counting today, we use tens—10, 20, 30—but they would do 60, 120, 180, and so on.

By the 4th millennium BCE, the Sumerians used small clay objects to represent numbers. The number one was a tiny cone, the number ten was a little ball, and the number sixty was a larger cone. They used pictographs of these objects to write numbers as they developed writing. They ingenuously created the concept of time using a sixty-second minute and a sixty-minute hour. They divided night and day into two twelve-hour sections. By 3800 BCE, they used simple measurements, and by 2600 BCE, they were multiplying and dividing, as well as using square and cubic roots and basic geometry. By 2300 BCE, they used an abacus with the sexagesimal system.

Perhaps not as important as the wheel and writing but still an intrinsic element of Sumerian culture was beer. In the *Hymn to Ninkasi*, the goddess of beer, the Sumerians recorded the world's first known recipe for brewing beer. Sumerian beer was more like a milkshake. It was very thick and often drunk with a straw, but it had a similar alcohol content to today's beer. Instead of everyone having their own mugs, Sumerian artwork often depicts several people using long reed straws to drink from one communal jar of beer.

Aside from their beer goddess, the Sumerians worshiped a pantheon of deities with human-like images and activities. Their gods got married, had children, vied for power, cheated, robbed, and killed each other.

Each city-state in Sumer—and most cultures in the rest of Mesopotamia—had a patron god or goddess. They worshiped other gods, but their patron god was the protector and champion of their city.

The primary triad of gods that ruled heaven, earth, and the underworld were An (Anu), heaven's supreme ruler; Enlil, god of the wind; and Ea (Enki), god of the earth and groundwater. Ea was the patron god of Eridu and protected humans from the Great Flood by warning a man—Utnapishtim—to build an ark to save human and animal life. Worship of these three gods pervaded most other Mesopotamian belief systems, including the Akkadians.

This cylinder seal impression pictures the god Ea (Enki).[37]

Inanna was a significant goddess throughout Mesopotamia; she was Uruk's patron deity and the goddess of beauty, love, sex, political power, and war. She later became the patron goddess of Agade, the capital of the Akkadian Empire, and she was worshiped as Ishtar by the Babylonians and Assyrians. Inanna was known for seducing human men to be her husbands, but that didn't go well for the men—one husband had to spend half the year in the underworld!

Inanna (Ishtar) was also known for repeatedly threatening to smash the gates of the underworld, getting her father (Anu) drunk, stealing the gifts of civilization for Uruk, and letting loose the Bull of Heaven because Gilgamesh spurned her marriage proposal. Ishtar figured prominently in the early life of Sargon the Great, the founder of the Akkadian Empire.

What were some key cities of Sumer, and who were their principal kings in the millennia leading up to the Akkadian Empire? Uruk and Ur were probably the second and third oldest cities. Uruk began as an Ubaid settlement around 5000 BCE and continued to exist up until the Islamic conquest around 633 CE—that is almost six thousand years! Uruk held "kingship" or dominated Sumer for about eight hundred years, beginning around 4000 BCE.

Around 3100 BCE, Uruk may have been the largest city globally with an estimated forty thousand people, plus eighty thousand more in the rural villages and smaller towns that were part of the city-state. Uruk initiated the stone construction of immense palaces and high ziggurats. In the Uruk period (4100-2900 BCE), Uruk dominated the other cities of southern Mesopotamia. It was essentially a mini-empire that served as a trade hub.

Uruk's preeminent leader in the Sumerian era was King Gilgamesh, who ruled Uruk at some point between 2800 to 2500 BCE. Although he is famous due to his myth, he was a real king. He appeared on the *Sumerian King List*, on a stone inscription in Ur, in the *Tummal Chronicle* (which says he built the Dunumunbura, Enlil's dais),[i] and on a fragment of a text found in Tell Haddad that said he was buried under the Euphrates River, which would have been temporarily diverted for his interment.

The Babylonian epic poem *Gilgamesh and Aga* has no monsters, gods, or other mythical elements; it is just an account of how Aga, King of Kish, demanded that Uruk's citizens become slaves to Kish. He wanted them to dig wells and draw water.[ii] The *Sumerian King List* reports that Kish had hegemony (supremacy) over Uruk. King Gilgamesh convinced the elders to refuse Aga's orders. King Aga and his army besieged Uruk, but Gilgamesh's friend Enkidu (who is also in the *Epic of Gilgamesh*) led

---

[i] *The Tummal Chronicle*, Livius. https://www.livius.org/sources/content/mesopotamian-chronicles-content/cm-7-tummal-chronicle/.

[ii] *Gilgamesh and Aga: Translation*, The Electronic Text Corpus of Sumerian Literature, 2000. https://etcsl.orinst.ox.ac.uk/section1/tr1811.htm

a successful attack. He captured Aga, and the war ended with peace between Aga and Gilgamesh.

While the *Epic of Gilgamesh* certainly contains fantastical elements, we should remember that historical events and people often acquire mythological qualities since the stories are retold and embellished over the centuries.[i] For instance, did George Washington really throw a silver dollar across the Potomac? No? Does that mean he wasn't the first president of the United States of America?

In this bas-relief, circa 2255 BCE, Gilgamesh slays the Bull of Heaven.[38]

---

[i] *The Epic of Gilgamesh*, Academy of Ancient Texts.
https://www.ancienttexts.org/library/mesopotamian/gilgamesh/.

What is the *Epic of Gilgamesh* all about? Gilgamesh was an immoral king, deflowering the virgins of his kingdom before they could sleep with their husbands on their wedding night. His disgruntled citizens sent a prostitute out to the wilderness to tame Enkidu, a wild man living with the beasts of the field and eating grass. After Enkidu had sex with the prostitute for days, the wild animals would have nothing more to do with him, so he agreed to go to Uruk to change the order of things.

After arriving in Uruk, Enkidu barred Gilgamesh from raping a new bride, and the two men, who were the strongest in the land, engaged in a fierce fight. Neither could overcome the other, so they kissed and became friends. Forgetting about the bride, they journeyed to Lebanon's cedar forest and killed the Humbaba monster. On their way back to Uruk, the goddess Inanna (Ishtar) fell in love with Gilgamesh, but he turned down her proposal.

Furious, Inanna demanded her father, the chief god Anu, give her the Bull of Heaven. She led it to Uruk, where it snorted and buried men in deep pits. Enkidu took the bull by the horns, and Gilgamesh killed it. However, the gods decreed that one of the men must die for killing the two divine beasts: the Humbaba monster and the Bull of Heaven. The verdict fell on Enkidu, and Gilgamesh mourned him, refusing to let him be buried until a maggot fell out of his dead friend's nose.

Confronted by his mortality, the distraught Gilgamesh then journeyed to find Utnapishtim—the Noah-like figure who built the ark to save humans and animals from the flood and became immortal. Gilgamesh failed in his quest for immortality but returned to Uruk, acknowledging his humanity and realizing the city was his destiny. Even though he would die, whatever good he would bring to Uruk would endure.

The major city of Ur was strategically situated where the Euphrates flowed into the Persian Gulf. Due to the trade from the river and the gulf, Ur was an astonishingly wealthy city. The marshland surrounding Ur provided fertile land for agriculture. A great flood ended the Ubaid settlement there around 3800 BCE, but within three centuries, the Sumerians rebuilt Ur. It grew to an estimated population of thirty-four thousand. The city of Ur was home to the Semitic forefathers of the patriarch Abraham, who probably lived near the end of the Akkadian Empire.

Ur's incredible wealth was displayed in the "death pit" discovered by Leonard Wooley in 1926. Around 2600 BCE, a great queen or priestess named Puabi was buried with over one hundred soldiers and attendants, who had been sacrificed to accompany her to the underworld. A spectacular treasure trove shared her grave. Archaeologists found a golden headdress and tableware, gold and lapis lazuli necklaces, belts, lyres, and a silver chariot.

The notable King Mesannepada of Ur overthrew Uruk's Lugal-kitun, breaking Uruk's dominance over Sumer and inaugurating Ur's First Dynasty (2500-2445 BCE). The *Sumerian King List* says he ruled for eighty years. He also ruled over the city of Kish, according to documentation in the Royal Cemetery at Ur. His son Meskiagnun was married to Queen Gan-saman, who was probably Akkadian. The bowl of Gan-Saman found in Ur had an inscription from the queen to her husband; it was written in the Akkadian language using the cuneiform script at least a century before Sargon the Great.

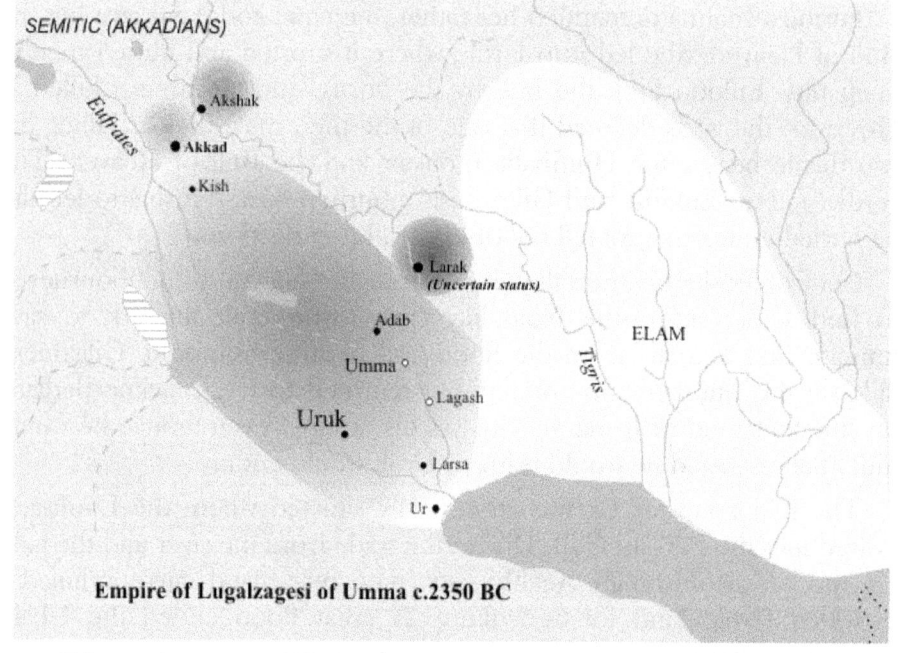

This map shows some of Mesopotamia's key cities just before the Akkadian Empire.[39]

The Sumerian city of Lagash was a key artistic center on the Tigris River about fourteen miles east of Uruk. Around 2500 BCE, in its First Dynasty, Lagash was first a tributary city to Uruk and then achieved independence until the Akkadians conquered it. King Eannatum was a sensational king who built a mini-empire. He crushed the Elamite settlements on the Persian Gulf, gained ascendency over most of Sumer's cities, and pushed his territory's borders north to Akshak, encompassing the region of Akkad.

Kish was a principal city on the Euphrates in central Mesopotamia, south of Akkad's presumed location. Sargon the Great grew up as a gardener's son in Kish and served as cupbearer to King Ur-Zababa. The *Sumerian King List* said Kish was the first city to have "kingship" following the Great Flood, and it took "kingship" back several times, once by Queen Ku-Baba, a tavern keeper. The names of its earliest monarchs hint at a Semitic-Akkadian influence from its inception. Because of its location in northern Sumer, the more powerful Sumerian kings declared they were the "King of Kish" in addition to being the king of their own city; they were making the point that their kingdom extended from the south to the northern end of Sumer.

Umma on the Tigris was an unassuming city. It was never mentioned in the *Sumerian King List* as asserting kingship over the other Sumerian cities. But then, King Lugal-zage-si came to the throne, and everything changed. Lugal-zage-si began conquering one city after another: Uruk, Lagash, Ur, Nippur, Larsa, and finally Kish. He conquered Kish with the help of Sargon, who would one day become his greatest nemesis. All of Sumer fell under his control, and according to one inscription, he may have conquered as far west as the Mediterranean Sea.

Aside from Sumer, another emerging power before the Akkadian Empire was Ashur. It was located in northern Mesopotamia, and it would later rise to form the fierce Assyrian Empire after the Akkadian Empire. Semitic Akkadian-speaking pastoral herders—probably distant relations of the Akkadians—settled Ashur by 2600 BCE. The Torah said Ashur was on the Tigris River's western banks (Genesis 2:14). It was named after its founder Ashur, who was Shem's son and Noah's grandson (Genesis 10:22). Ashur grew into a city-state before the Akkadian Empire, along with other Assyrian cities, such as Nineveh, Arbela, and Gasur. The Akkadians called this region Azubinum.

The rival city-states of Sumer and the rest of Mesopotamia incessantly fought for power, goods, and territory. They formed mini-empires and took turns dominating each other. But soon, they would face the Akkadians—a power beyond their comprehension.

Chapter 3: The Rise of the Akkadian Empire

Where did he come from? Who was this man who usurped the throne of Kish, then daringly and dramatically conquered all of Mesopotamia and beyond? Wasn't Sargon just the gardener's son? How did this obscure foundling swallow up parts of modern-day Turkey, western Iran, and Syria in an age when imperialism was a novel concept? Somehow, this seemingly insignificant young man rose to incredible power and reigned from the Persian Gulf to the Mediterranean Sea. Let's explore the unprecedented rise of the Akkadian Empire and its first king, Sargon the Great, who reigned from 2334 to 2279 BCE.

A recurring theme in ancient literature is the story of an abandoned baby in a basket floating down the river—a baby who would grow up to be a revolutionary leader of a new kingdom. Romulus and his twin Remus drifted down the Tiber to be suckled by a she-wolf and then went on to found Rome. Moses floated down the Nile to be adopted by an Egyptian princess and later led the new Israelite nation. But before Romulus, Remus, and Moses, Sargon was abandoned to the river—or at least that's what an "autobiography" probably written over one thousand years after his death says.

A clay tablet dating to 1200 BCE or later supposedly reveals Sargon's birth story in his own words. We don't know whether this was a copy of an older original or if it was a fictional account. Many scholars call it a "pseudo-autobiography." We'll discuss this story more in Chapter 9, but it says Sargon's mother was a high priestess. He never knew his father, but he somehow did know that his father's family lived in the highlands in Azupiranu (an Akkadian word for "City of Saffron") on the banks of the Euphrates.

Sargon's mother conceived and gave birth to him in secret. The story doesn't say why she had to conceal the birth; presumably, she wasn't married to the father. She put him in a reed basket and set him in the river, which carried him downstream to where a man named Akki was drawing water for irrigation. Akki took him out of the water, reared him as his adopted son, and put him to work in a date grove, where the goddess Ishtar "loved" him.

Sargon and his foster father Akki lived in Kish, and they may have tended the palace garden or sold their produce to the palace. The *Sumerian King List* said that Sargon's father was a gardener, and Sargon was a cupbearer to Ur-Zababa, King of Kish. Sargon must have been an exceptional young man to rise from a humble gardener to become the king's cupbearer. A cupbearer served the king's beverages, tasting them first to ensure the wine had no poison. A cupbearer would be in the king's presence almost all of the time. He would be a trustworthy person who would see and hear all of what happened around the king. He would likely be an informal sounding board and confidante to the king.

The Sargon and Ur-Zababa tablet tells how Sargon became King Ur-Zababa's cupbearer and what happened soon after.[i] Because the tablet was fragmented, some lines are missing, leaving one to guess what happened in some places. It begins by saying that Kish had been like a haunted town, but under its "shepherd," King Ur-Zababa, it had turned into a living settlement again. The irrigation canals flowed, the farmers' hoes tilled the land, the furnaces produced pottery and metalwork, and Kish prospered.

---

[i] "Sargon and Ur-Zababa," *The Electronic Text Corpus of Sumerian Literature,* Oxford: Faculty of Oriental Studies, University of Oxford, 2006. https://etcsl.orinst.ox.ac.uk/cgi-bin/etcsl.cgi?text=t.2.1.4#.

This mosaic from the Standard of Ur depicts a Sumerian king with his attendants.⁴⁰

However, the gods Enlil and An decided to terminate Ur-Zababa's reign and lift Sargon to the throne. One evening, Sargon brought the regular deliveries to the palace (presumably produce, as Sargon and his father were gardeners). The king was sleeping and had a disturbing dream but did not discuss it with anyone. However, following the vision, Ur-Zababa appointed Sargon to be his cupbearer, placing him in charge of the drinks' cupboard. His promotion resulted from the goddess Inanna's favor over Sargon.

After about a week, something happened that terrified King Ur-Zababa. Here, we have missing lines in the tablet, so what frightened him is a matter of speculation. We know that King Lugal-zage-si of Uruk, who had been systematically conquering all of Sumer's cities and leaving the Sumerians horror-stricken by his brutal ferocity, was headed his way. Or possibly Ur-Zababa may have been frightened about his health. The tablet says the king wet himself and that blood and pus were in his urine, suggesting a severe kidney infection.

At this point, Sargon had a horrific dream that the goddess Inanna drowned Ur-Zababa in a sea of blood. Sargon stirred in his sleep, groaning. When word that Sargon had a troubling dream reached the king's ears, King Ur-Zababa called Sargon to him. He asked him, "What did you dream?" Sargon told him, and Ur-Zababa bit his lip in fear. He understood the dream to mean that Sargon would assassinate him. The king believed he had to strike preemptively, so he plotted to kill Sargon before Sargon killed him!

King Ur-Zababa had Sargon deliver his bronze drinking vessels to the chief smith, Beliš-Tikal, apparently to melt them down. But the king had secretly ordered Beliš-Tikal to throw Sargon into the statue mold and cover him with the molten metal. Sargon would become a bronze statue! Fortunately, the goddess Inanna blocked Sargon's path to the temple where Beliš-Tikal worked. "This is a pure, holy temple! No one with blood on him can enter!"

Sargon apparently believed the goddess referred to his dream of blood, so he stopped at the gate. He called to the smith to come out to him on the street and handed over the drinking vessels, which the master smith took and melted them down to fill the mold. After about a week, Sargon returned to the king's palace—as a healthy man and not a statue—and Ur-Zababa shook with fear when he saw him. With his first plan foiled, Ur-Zababa conjured up a new plot.

People sent messages by writing on clay tablets in this era, but they weren't yet using envelopes for tablets. Later on, the "envelopes" were an outer layer of clay. The person receiving the letter broke the thin outer layer, revealing the message on the inner layer. Uruk's King Lugal-zage-si was marching north to conquer Kish, and King Ur-Zababa dispatched Sargon with a clay tablet message to Lugal-zage-si. The letter contained a plot to murder Sargon; lines of the story are missing here that might explain why Ur-Zababa asked his enemy to kill his cupbearer. Maybe Ur-Zababa was offering terms of surrender to Lugal-zage-si and warning him that Sargon would be a dangerous insurgent if allowed to live.

The tablet only has a few more lines, with gaps in between. Because it previously mentioned the message Sargon took to Lugal-zage-si not having an envelope, we can infer that Sargon read the letter. Ur-Zababa probably assumed that Sargon, the gardener's son, did not know how to read (and it took years to learn to read cuneiform), but perhaps Sargon had someone read the message to him. At any rate, it appears that Sargon somehow manipulated affairs to join forces with Lugal-zage-si against Ur-Zababa and Kish.

Knowing he was doomed if he continued to serve Ur-Zababa, Sargon likely switched alliances, offering his inside knowledge of palace affairs to

Lugal-zage-si. Somehow, Ur-Zababa was out, and Sargon became Kish's ruler, probably as a vassal ruler under Uruk and Lugal-zage-si. When Sargon usurped Kish's throne, this may be when he took the throne name "Sargon," which came from the Akkadian word *Sarru-kin*, meaning "true king." Sargon's childhood name is unknown.

At some point, probably soon after conquering Kish, the *Sumerian King List* says Sargon built the city of Agade (Akkad). But was it already there? And if so, where? And who were the Akkadians? The Akkadians were a Semitic tribe that most likely came from the Arabian Peninsula. They migrated into central and southern Mesopotamia in the early 3rd millennium or perhaps earlier. The Semitic settlement of Agade (Akkad) may have existed as early as 2900 BCE.[i] I. J. Gelb's language studies revealed that scribes with Akkadian names appeared on *southern* Mesopotamian tablets and inscriptions as early as 2700 BCE (almost four centuries before Sargon). Gelb believed the Akkadians had already populated northern Mesopotamia and gradually migrated south.[ii] The Akkadians adopted the Sumerian cuneiform script to produce the first documented written Semitic language.

The city of Agade (Akkad) rose from obscurity to such prestige that it continued to be named in royal proclamations long after the Akkadian Empire folded. In fact, it was mentioned all the way to Cyrus the Great. Despite its renown, its ruins lie under the sands somewhere in central Mesopotamia, waiting to be discovered. Some scholars believe if Akkad was where Sargon was born—and if his mother really put him in a basket in the river—Akkad would be upstream of the Euphrates from Kish. But neither premise is certain. *The Sargon Geography* said, "from Damru to Sippar is the Land of Akkad."[iii] Sippar is north of Kish, where the Euphrates and Tigris almost meet together, and from Babylonian documents, Damru appears to have been close to Kish.

Semantics scholar Christophe Wall-Romana scoured over 160 citations of Agade (Akkad) in cuneiform documents, attempting to match up geographical references to circumscribe as accurately as possible where the capital of the Akkadian Empire lay. His investigation reveals a

---

[i] D. D. Luckenbill, "Akkadian Origins," *The American Journal of Semitic Languages and Literatures* 40, no. 1 (1923): 1–13. http://www.jstor.org/stable/528139.

[ii] Jerrold S. Cooper, "Sumerian and Akkadian in Sumer and Akkad," *Orientalia* 42 (1973): 239. http://www.jstor.org/stable/43079390.

[iii] *The Sargon Geography*, Translated by Wayne Horowitz, *Mesopotamian Cosmic Geography*

location on or near the Tigris on the southeastern border of present-day Baghdad. He believed that since Sargon was a rival of Lugal-zage-si when he built Agade, he chose his capital in a region beyond Lugal-zage-si's scope of power.[i]

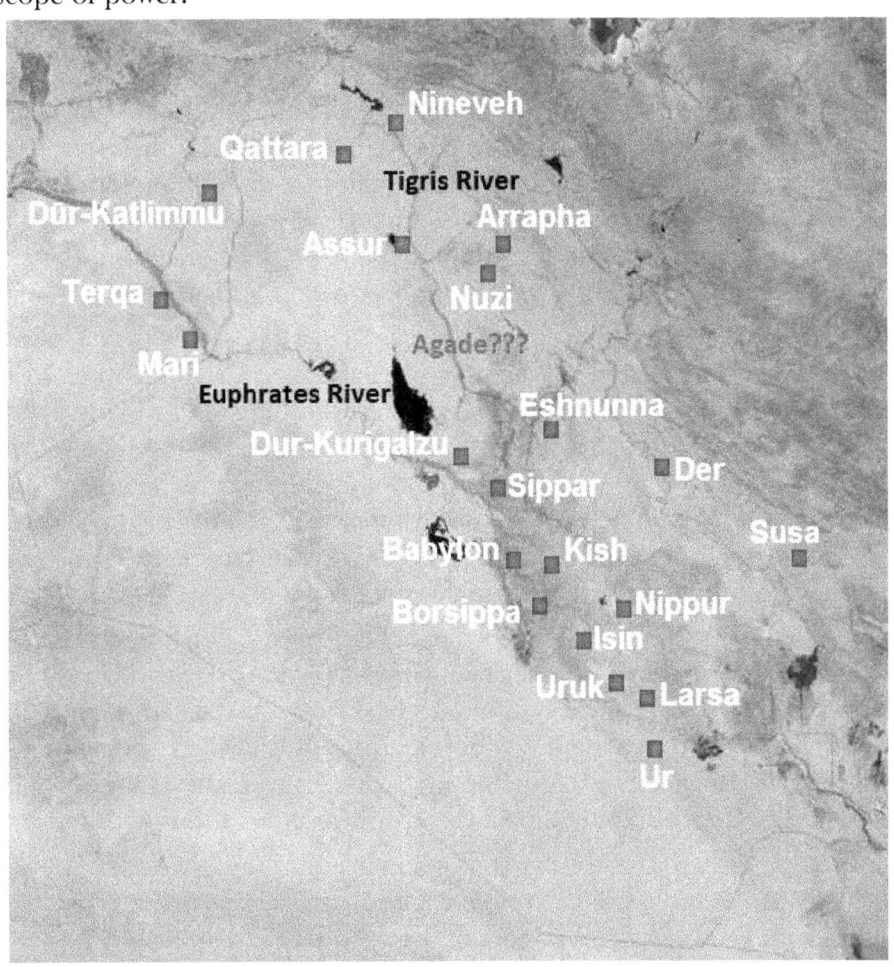

This map depicts a potential location of Agade (Akkad) on the Tigris River, between Eshnunna and Assur, southeast of present-day Baghdad.[ii]

In the Sumerian *The Curse of Agade*, which we will discuss in Chapter 5, the city of Agade (Akkad) was a busy port city. "Its harbor, where ships docked, was filled with excitement."[iii] The prologue to the Code of

---

[i] Christophe Wall-Romana, "An Areal Location of Agade," *Journal of Near Eastern Studies* 49, no. 3 (1990): 205-45. http://www.jstor.org/stable/546244.
[ii] *The Curse of Agade*, Translated by Jerrold S. Cooper, Baltimore: Johns Hopkins University

Hammurabi lists many Mesopotamian cities in geographical order, and it names Eshnunna, Agade, Ashur (Aššur or Assur), and Nineveh in sequence.[i] Since the other three cities all lay on the Tigris River going north from Eshnunna, perhaps Agade was on the Tigris between Eshnunna and Ashur, which fits with Wall-Romana's estimation.

The Akkadian civilization existed in northern and central Mesopotamia for hundreds of years before Sargon came to power, so it's possible Agade was already in place. Whether Sargon simply restored an older city, enlarged an existing town, or built a new city from the ground up, Agade became the capital city of Sargon's empire. The term *Akkad* also denotes the northern region of ancient Babylonia; thus, some scholars use the word *Agade* to mean the city and *Akkad* when speaking of the region.

Although Sargon and Lugal-zage-si collaborated in conquering Kish, they later became enemies. The clay tablet with the story of Sargon, Ur-Zababa, and Lugal-zage-si is severely damaged in this section, but it mentions Lugal-zage-si's wife apparently in reference to Sargon. Were they engaged in an affair or some sort of intrigue? It also says Lugal-zage-si received such dreadful news from an envoy that he cried, "Alas!" and plopped down in the dust. "Sargon does not yield!"

While Lugal-zage-si was consolidating his rule over the Sumerian cities in the south, Sargon had been amassing forces and power in northern Mesopotamia. He probably united the scattered Akkadian-speaking tribes. He was now marching with his army toward Uruk. Lugal-zage-si quickly gathered a massive army of fifty ensis. An ensi was a king of a city-state, so Lugal-zage-si called up all the princes of Sumer to fight Sargon.

In two heated battles, Sargon overwhelmed the Sumerian forces. Perhaps the Sumerian ensis weren't enthusiastic about fighting for their fierce overlord, Lugal-zage-si. Sargon besieged Uruk, demolished its walls, and captured Lugal-zage-si. He placed a yoke on Lugal-zage-si's neck and dragged him to Nippur, forcing him to walk in shame through Nippur's gate. Why Nippur? It was the god Enlil's sacred sanctuary, and Enlil was Lugal-zage-si's patron god. Sargon demonstrated that Lugal-zage-si had lost Enlil's patronage and was drained of his power.

Press, 1983.

[i] *The Code of Hammurabi*, Translated by L.W. King, *The Avalon Project: Documents in Law, History*

On the pedestal of Enlil's idol, Sargon inscribed:

> "Sargon, king of Akkad, overseer of Inanna, king of Kish, anointed of Anu, king of the land, governor of Enlil. He defeated the city of Uruk and tore down its walls; in the battle of Uruk, he won, took Lugal-zage-si, king of Uruk, in the course of the battle and led him in a collar to the gate of Enlil."

The land of Sumer was now free of their cruel master, Lugal-zage-si, who had laid fire to Sumer's cities, seized their precious metals and jewels, destroyed the statues of their gods, torn down their homes, and cut off the hands of anyone who defied him. The Sumerians believed the gods had judged Lugal-zage-si for his sins.[i]

This copper head—possibly of Sargon—marked a shift in the artistic expression of royalty with realistic features and precise craftsmanship.[42]

The rise of the Akkadian Empire marked a watershed moment in Mesopotamian history—not just the empire part but also the dominance of the Semitic Akkadians over the Sumerians. From this point on, the Semitic people—the Akkadians, Assyrians, and Babylonians—held

---

[i] Marvin A. Powell, "The Sin of Lugalzagesi," *Wiener Zeitschrift Für Die Kunde Des Morgenlandes* 86 (1996): 307-14. http://www.jstor.org/stable/23864744.

dominion for most of the rest of ancient Mesopotamia's history until the Persians invaded. Was Sargon's strife with Lugal-zage-si born out of a long-simmering racial feud, or was it simply two kings vying for power, as had happened throughout Sumer's history?

Most likely, it was simply a power encounter with no racial undertones. Neither king identified themselves as Sumerian or Semite, just king of the cities and the land. They ruled political units, not racial factions. The *Sumerian King List* reveals the royal families of Sumer switching from Sumerian to Semitic names and back again. Sumerians and Semites appeared to live peacefully together and assimilated each other's cultures. Sargon himself prayed to Sumerian gods.[i]

Sargon's bombastic royal inscriptions and other accounts contemporary with his lifetime are fragmentary; they were rewritten and probably altered by later scribes. The few materials available that date to Sargon's lifetime or shortly after are too few to form a composite picture. Many accounts of Sargon's life became available a century later, but by that time, they had degenerated into myth, leaving the task of comparing the tales with what Sargon said about himself and trying to trace what really happened. Perhaps when the city of Agade is finally discovered and resurrected from the desert sands, we can put more pieces of the puzzle together about Sargon and his successors.

---

[i] Thorkild Jacobsen, "The Assumed Conflict between Sumerians and Semites in Early Mesopotamian History," *Journal of the American Oriental Society*

Chapter 4: The Golden Age of the Akkadian Empire

In the centuries following Sargon's rule over the Akkadian Empire, the Mesopotamians—even those not Akkadian—called it their Golden Age. Although other rulers with Semitic names, like Ur-Zababa, had ruled Kish, Sargon transcended his predecessors. Sargon picked up where Lugal-zage-si left off: consolidating control of all Sumer, then expanding north into central and northern Mesopotamia. He conquered east of the great Euphrates and west of the Tigris and then extended the empire as far east as the Mediterranean and north into today's Turkey. Sargon established a military tradition and governmental style that served as a prototype for other Mesopotamian dynasties and empires. He left behind a strong legacy, which his sons and grandson held firm.

After Sargon, King of Kish and Agade, defeated Lugal-zage-si and took Uruk, he initiated successful campaigns against neighboring cities to expand his empire and acquire more resources. Since Lugal-zage-si had already consolidated all of Sumer under his rule, technically, Sargon would inherit his realm. But while the Sumerian city-states appreciated Sargon freeing them from Lugal-zage-si, they weren't keen on coming under the yoke of another overlord—especially an upstart with no royal lineage.

Sargon was forced to lay siege to each city-state of Sumer, one after the other, beginning with Ur, Lagash, and Umma. Conquering Ur, strategically located where the Euphrates flowed into the Persian Gulf, gave Sargon power over the river traffic and the gulf. Umma was Lugal-zage-si's home city; he had ruled there for seven years before making Uruk his center of operations. Umma and Lagash had been in constant warfare with each other for centuries, as they contended over the boundary line between the two city-states until Lugal-zage-si came to power in Umma. Now, both cities fell under Sargon's dominance, which ended Lagash's First Dynasty (2500–2300 BCE).

In Sargon's victory stele, a soldier leads Sumerian prisoners.[48]

Once Sargon gained ascendancy over all of Sumer, he turned his attention to northern Mesopotamia. For success in this endeavor, he called on a new god. Sargon had previously only mentioned the Sumerian gods in his inscriptions. He especially pointed out that Inanna had loved him as a youth and manipulated events to save him from Ur-Zababa's plots and place him on the throne. But now, he turned to the Semitic god Dagan.

Dagan is sometimes considered the Semitic version of Sumer's Enlil, the king-making god. Dagan was the father of Baal, who was worshiped in Canaan (he became a strong competitor to the Israelite god YHWH) and may be the Babylon Bel (or Marduk). Dagan was the primary Semitic god in central and northern Mesopotamia (including Agade), and the Philistines of Canaan later made him their patron god. He was the god whose head fell off when the Philistines put the stolen Israelite Ark of the Covenant in his sanctuary (Tanakh, I Samuel 5).

But that was far in the future. Sargon needed Dagan's support to conquer northern Mesopotamia and have the legitimacy to rule over the Semites. After prostrating himself before Dagan's image, Sargon tamed the Mari people east of the Euphrates and their rivals, the Ebla, to the south of Aleppo in Syria. Sargon gave Dagan credit for bestowing him the upper lands of the Euphrates, which probably included part of Anatolia (Turkey).

The "King of Battle" is an epic Akkadian story of how Akkadian merchants in Purushanda (present-day Turkey) were disputing the despotic ruler of the region, Nur-Dagan.[i] After asking Sargon to intervene, he attacked Nur-Dagan before he knew what was happening and brought that region under Akkadian control, making lucrative trade with Turkey all the easier. Sargon then headed east, raiding Canaan (Israel), Lebanon, and Syria four times. The "King of Battle" records that he sailed into the Mediterranean to "Kuppara," which is likely Cyprus or Crete.

---

[i] Joan Goodnick Westenholz, *Legends of the Kings of Akkade: The Texts*, Winona Lake: Eisenbrauns, 1997.

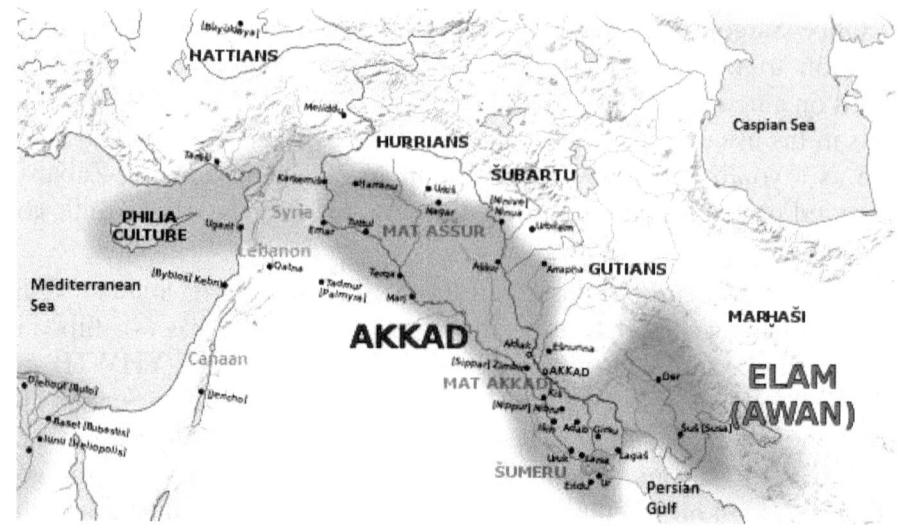

This map shows the possible extent of the Akkadian Empire under Sargon."

Sargon invaded Elam's deserts and the Zagros Mountains (in modern-day Iran) and conquered the Elamite capital of Susa in the lower Zagros Mountains. To celebrate his outstanding victory in Elam, Sargon erected a massive diorite victory stele, picturing himself and his military forces. He conquered the Awan north of Susa and asserted control over the Marhashi (possibly in the Kerman region of south-central Iran), gaining access to trade in alabaster vases and valuable stones.

In *The Legend of Sargon*—his supposed autobiography discovered in the ruins of Nineveh's Library of Ashurbanipal—Sargon recounts a rebellion while he was in his "old age."

> "In my old age of 55, all the lands revolted against me, and they besieged me in Agade [Akkad], but the old lion still had teeth and claws, I went forth to battle and defeated them: I knocked them over and destroyed their vast army. Now, any king who wants to call himself my equal, wherever I went, let him go!"

The "Reign of Sargon" details how the "old lion" fought back against the rebels.[i]

---

[i] "The Reign of Sargon," George W. Botsforth, ed., *A Source-Book of Ancient History*, New York: Macmillan, 1912. 27-28.
http://www.thelatinlibrary.com/imperialism/readings/sargontablet.html

"Afterward, in his old age, all the lands revolted against him, and they besieged him in Akkad; and Sargon went forth to battle and defeated them; he accomplished their overthrow and their wide-spreading host he destroyed.

Afterward, he attacked the land of Subartu in his might, and they submitted to his arms, and Sargon settled that revolt and defeated them; he accomplished their overthrow, and their wide-spreading host he destroyed, and he brought their possessions into Akkad. The soil from the trenches of Babylon he removed, and the boundaries of Akkad he made like those of Babylon."

Sargon and his wife, Queen Tashlultum, had at least four sons: Manishtushu, Rimush, Shu-Enlil, and Ilaba'is-takal. Sargon reigned for a total of fifty-five years. Rimush succeeded Sargon at his death, and Manishtushu succeeded Rimush. Sargon's daughter, the priestess Enheduanna, was a poetess and hymn writer. One famous hymn was the "Exaltation of Inanna," which was sung in the worship of the goddess for hundreds of years.

How well did Sargon's descendants perpetuate his legacy? Were they successful in continuing the remarkable expansion of the Akkadian Empire? Curiously, Rimush ascended the throne in 2279 BCE upon his father's death, although Manishtushu was his older brother, according to the *Sumerian King List*. Some scholars venture that Sargon passed over Manishtushu because rebellions kept cropping up, which Rimush's more ruthless nature could better manage. Rimush immediately faced a Sumerian insurrection. For five decades, they had simmered with resentment under Sargon's rule. Perhaps they could overcome the son with the "strong man" dead.

In Rimush's early years as king, six city-states revolted: Adab, Der, Kassala, Lagash, Umma, and Ur. Rimush brutally quelled the subversive cities. He bragged of obliterating massive populations, flattening cities, and even uprooting their substructures. In a series of three vicious wars in Sumer, he sent shockwaves through the land with the mass slaughter of 110,000 men, which was most of the adult male population of the six rebel cities.

He exiled another twenty-five thousand people and enslaved twenty-nine thousand, sending them to cut stone in Elam's mines. The conquered cities stood virtually empty, so he confiscated 134,000 hectares of ancestral farmland around Umma and Lagash, parceling them out to the new Akkadian landholding elite. The desolate survivors of Umma and Lagash could only remember the years they'd spent in strife over the boundary line between them; now, the land was lost to strangers.

Babylon also rebelled, and Rimush struck the city with the same merciless violence that extinguished the Sumerian insurrection. He was equally harsh against the Akkadians—his own people. One example was Kassala, which was located near Kish on the Euphrates. Kassala had resisted Sargon and reaped his vengeance. "Against Kassala he marched, and he turned Kassala into mounds and heaps of ruins; he destroyed the land and left not enough for a bird to rest thereon."[i]

The people of Kassala rebuilt their flattened city and then had the audacity to revolt against Rimush. Repeating his father's harsh reaction, he massacred twelve thousand Akkadian rebels, enslaved five thousand, and turned Kassala back into a "heaps of ruins."

Once Rimush regained his father's territories in Mesopotamia, he launched military campaigns in Elam, consolidating his father's conquests there. While he had been busy slaughtering Sumerians, the Elamites had formed a coalition under the Marhashi king to resist further expansion into their territories. Rimush successfully subdued the alliance and took Elam and its capital Susa back under Akkadian hegemony.

Although Rimush did not extend his father's empire, he recouped some areas that had attempted to regain independence. He ended his nine-year reign with approximately the same borders as in his father's day, but Akkad was much more prosperous. Rimush had brought back astonishing riches from Elam. At Enlil's sanctuary in Nippur, he dedicated massive amounts of copper and gold. He erected a statue of himself in tin, which was a rare metal in those days. His inscription on his sculpture, which stood before Enlil's image, said he counted himself among the gods.[ii]

Rimush stopped commissioning pompous inscriptions and images of himself in the year or two before he died. What happened? Did he simply take it easy after regaining his father's territory? Was he sick or depressed? Was he dealing with internal conflict? The latter may have

---

[i] "The Reign of Sargon," Botsforth, ed., pp. 27-28.
[ii] Benjamin R. Foster, *The Age of Agade: Inventing Empire in Ancient Mesopotamia*, (New York: Routledge, 2016), 6-8.

been true, as his own statesmen bludgeoned him to death with their cylinder seals. Since the seals were only three to five inches of metal or marble hanging on a lanyard, it would have been a long, merciless death for a man who showed no pity to his rivals.

This copper alloy head is probably an Akkadian king, but his identity is unknown.[45]

Why was he assassinated? If he had fallen into a state of lethargy or suffered mental or physical illness, his courtiers might have felt the empire needed a healthy, active ruler. Then, there were his atrocities. Killing off most of the male population in key Sumerian and Akkadian cities was terrible for the empire. If cities were flattened, they were not producing food and other goods necessary for the entire empire's survival.

With key civilized settlements along the Persian Gulf or the Euphrates or Tigris Rivers decimated, bandits and pirates could disrupt trade caravans and ships bringing goods to Agade. The demoralizing effect would have been horrific, especially with the cities closer to Agade like Kassala and Babylon. For all we know, some of his assassins could have been from Kassala or Babylon seeking revenge.

After Rimush was beaten to a pulp, his older brother Manishtushu succeeded him in 2279 BCE. He ruled for fourteen years. Manishtushu was an ambitious, energetic king who expanded the empire through diplomacy and military conquests, and he implemented significant internal changes. Considering his brother's assassination, Manishtushu was adamant about forming a new administrative council of men he could trust. So, he devised a land plan, building on his brother's earlier land reallocation.

He bought the ancestral farmlands of 964 men in the region of Akkad. They probably had little choice in the matter; the price they received was worth only what the farms would have produced in two years. But the fields bordered the royal lands, and Manishtushu planned to allocate this property to reward those who had served him faithfully, such as his administrators, military leaders, scribes, and priests. His devoted servants came from all points of the empire, not just Agade. He desired to establish a new Akkadian elite with undivided loyalty to him.[i]

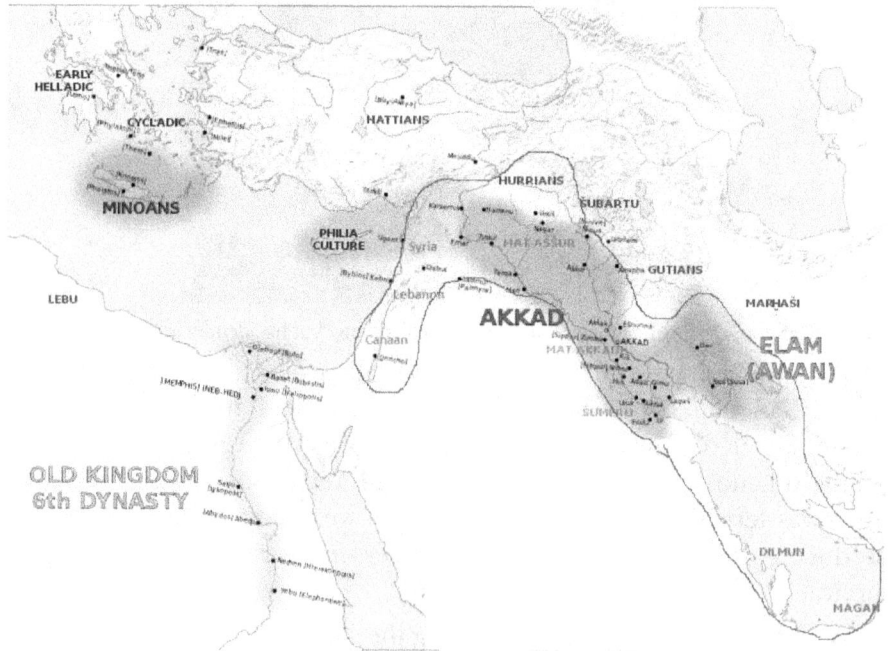

This map depicts the possible extension of the Akkadian Empire during Manishtushu's reign from where it was at the end of his father Sargon's reign.[46]

---

[i] Foster, *The Age of Agade*, 1.

Manishtushu benefited from his brother's ironfisted subjugation of rebellions within the empire. With relative peace established, Manishtushu could launch new expansion campaigns to strategic regions for trade. His first expansion involved subjugating or making shrewd alliances with thirty-two kings to control the entire Persian Gulf. He sailed from port to port, negotiating with friendly kings and conquering any who resisted, keeping the Persian Gulf waters free of invaders and pirates. Manishtushu then invaded Elam—for the third time since his father's reign—this time from the Persian Gulf. He plundered Susa's silver mines and set up Akkadian governors in key Elamite cities. He negotiated trade with thirty-seven other states up the Tigris River to its headwaters in eastern Turkey's Taurus Mountains.

As he expanded his empire, Manishtushu erected duplicate images of himself throughout his territories, with each inscription honoring the patron deity of the specific city. He was particularly proud of his Persian Gulf expedition and never missed the chance to mention it in his inscriptions. Manishtushu was a diplomatic master in recognizing his conquered city-states' gods and celebrating his foreign expansion, which brought astounding wealth to Mesopotamia. This was in stark contrast to the boastings of his father and brother of their cruel suppression of local rebellions.

Despite his diplomatic skills and military successes, Manishtushu met his brother's fate, as he was assassinated by his own officials. Naram-Sin, Manishtushu's son and Sargon's grandson, was crowned the Akkadian Empire's fourth king, and he who would elevate the empire to its grandest power. He followed in the footsteps of his father and grandfather, with triumphant conquests of the Lullubi people in the Elamite-Zagros Mountain region. He signed a treaty and married Elamite King Khita's daughter.

Naram-Sin's most significant test came early in his reign when he faced the Great Revolt of eighteen key Sumerian cities. This was led by King Iphur-Kish of Kish, and it included Uruk, Adab, Cutha, Isin, Kish, Lagash, Nippur, Sippar, Umma, and Ur. The Sumerians even joined forces with the Amorite nomads, who they usually considered a dire threat. Iphur-Kish directly attacked Agade, but Naram-Sin marshaled his forces and marched out to defend Agade. With the first battle won, he chased the remnants of the rebels to Kish, filling the Euphrates with dead bodies.

King Amar-girid of Uruk rallied the rest of the Sumerian coalition. He invited the Assyrians to the north to join in, but they held back. Naram-Sin attacked the Amorites first, then met Amar-girid's massive force and defeated them, capturing Amar-girid. Following this victory, Naram-Sin cut a swathe through Sumer and went down and around the Persian Gulf, pillaging and amassing great spoils of war. After winning nine battles in one year against the Mesopotamians, the people of Agade asked him to be their patron god of their city, making him equal to Inanna, Enlil, Enki, and the rest of the pantheon. He permitted them to build his temple in Agade, which many believed to be his downfall.

Naram-Sin continued with his brilliant military campaigns in Oman, Ebla (northern Syria), the Taurus Mountains, the Amanus (Nur) Mountains of south-central Turkey, and the Ararat region of Armenia. He followed the Tigris River north into the Taurus Mountains, tracing it to Hazer Lake, a rift lake 3,773 feet above sea level. He likewise followed the Euphrates up to the Karasu River, then to its source at Mount Dumlu.

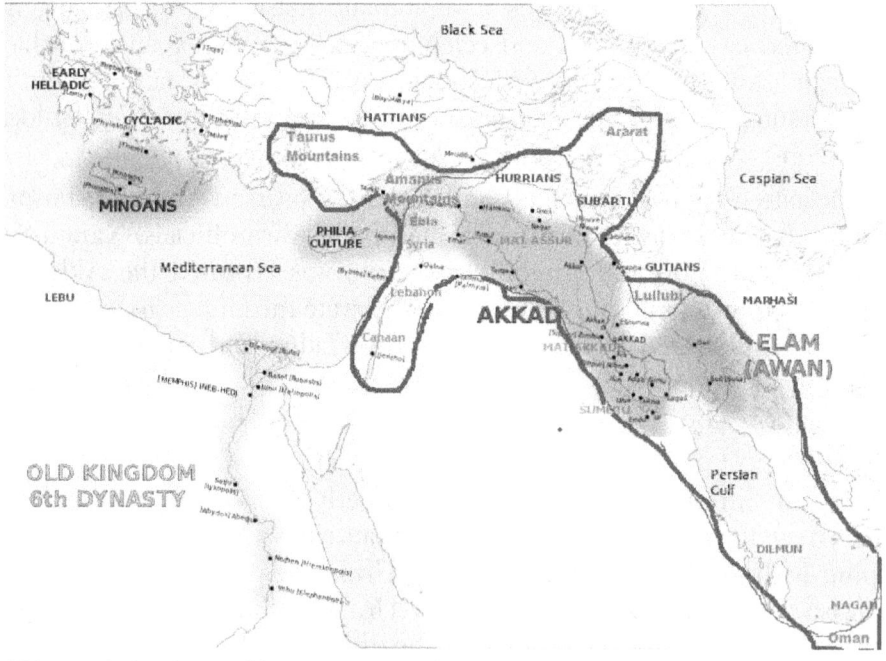

This map depicts the possible greatest extent of the Akkadian Empire under Naram-Sin. It may have considerably shrunk before he died.⁴⁷

Naram-Sin proudly called himself the "Ruler of the Four Corners of the Universe," but trouble loomed ahead. *The Curse of Agade*, which was written centuries later, said that Naram-Sin somehow incurred the wrath of the god Enlil, who retaliated by bringing famine, plague, and an invasion of the Gutian tribes to the east. Although Naram-Sin expanded the Akkadian Empire to its greatest extent, he may have lost significant portions before his death in 2217 BCE.

Sargon's conquest of all of Sumer and then all of Mesopotamia joined the Akkadians and Sumerians under one language and one government. The Akkadian Empire stretched thousands of miles at its zenith, encompassing multiple ethnic groups from the Persian Gulf to as far north as Ararat and west to the Mediterranean. He established a vision for future conquerors of what could be achieved in one lifetime. No one before him had conquered such a vast territory. He was truly the world's first emperor.

Chapter 5: The Decline and Fall of the Akkadian Empire

Naram-Sin's reign was the beginning of the end for the Akkadian Empire. Soon, it would slide into decline and ultimately crumble into oblivion. The end didn't seem near, not when Naram-Sin was winning one brilliant conquest after another. But then something happened that turned the tide, eventually closing the chapter on the Akkadian Empire after only 180 years of existence. The Mesopotamians believed Naram-Sin brought down a curse on Agade and all of Mesopotamia.

The Curse of Agade is a quasi-historical story written during Ur's Third Dynasty (2047–1750 BCE), but it is probably based on older stories. It's an example of Mesopotamian Naru literature, which portrays a king or other hero in a moralistic tale of human relationships with the divine. The *Epic of Gilgamesh* and *The Legend of Sargon* are two other examples of Naru literature.

The Curse of Agade tells how Naram-Sin offended the god Enlil and brought down devastation on all of Mesopotamia. What did Naram-Sin do to offend Enlil? The story does not divulge this information, but it could have been that he received his people's adulation as the god of Agade. It all began when several points of his extensive empire rose simultaneously in rebellion. An inscription at the base of a statue recorded Naram-Sin's victory:

> "Naram-Sin the mighty, king of Agade, when the four quarters of the earth attacked him together, through the love

of Ishtar bore him was victorious in nine battles in a single year and captured the kings whom they had raised against him."

This carving shows Naram-Sin at the top of his victory stele, standing on the bodies of conquered Lullubi warriors.[48]

Following this splendid triumph, Naram-Sin called himself the "mighty god of Agade" in an inscription, essentially claiming to be the city's patron god. However, the goddess Inanna, Sargon's patroness, had established her sanctuary in Agade, at least according to *The Curse of Agade*. It said

Inanna spent sleepless nights ensuring Agade's people had plenty to eat, good things to drink, and rejoiced together at holidays. Inanna was the city's patroness, but Naram-Sin overturned the divine order.

The Curse of Agade said Inanna even brought monkeys, elephants, and other exotic animals to amuse the citizens in the public square.[i] Inanna brought gold, silver, copper, tin, and lapis lazuli into the city, filling the granaries with precious metals and stones. She gave the old women the gift of wise counsel, the old men the gift of eloquence, the young women the gift of entertaining, the young men the gift of military might, and the children the gift of joy.

But after caring for Agade so tenderly, Inanna received disquieting news. The story doesn't say what the unsettling news was; perhaps it was some dreadful sin of the city or its king Naram-Sin. The god Enlil reduced Agade to trembling and even terrified Inanna, who abandoned her sanctuary and left Agade, carrying with her the gift of battle and handing it over to Agade's enemy. One by one, the other gods took back the blessings they had bestowed on Agade. Ninurta took back the royal crown and throne of kingship, Utu took back the city's eloquence, Enki took back its wisdom and tore away its mooring pole, and An (Anu) took away the fear the city held over others.

One night, King Naram-Sin had a vision that the god Enlil would no longer permit Agade to be a pleasant, enduring city; instead, its temples would shake, and its treasures would be scattered. The king didn't tell anyone about his dream, but he donned mourning garments and gave away his royal paraphernalia. He mourned for seven years! "Who has ever seen a king burying his head in his hands for seven years?" He performed divination on the entrails of a baby goat, trying to discover the source of Enlil's displeasure, but he received no omen, even after two tries.

Exasperated with the god Enlil, Naram-Sin mobilized his troops, marched to the holy city of Nippur, and demolished Enlil's temple. He hewed it down with axes and dug up its foundation with spades. He piled up all the temple's wood and lit a huge bonfire, and he plundered the temple's gold, silver, copper, and precious gemstones. As he pilfered and destroyed Enlil's temple, good sense and intelligence left Agade.

---

[i] *The Curse of Agade*, Trans. Jerrold S. Cooper, (Baltimore: Johns Hopkins University Press, 1983). https://etcsl.orinst.ox.ac.uk/section2/tr215.html.

Archaeologists unearthed the Nippur Temple in 1893. Naram-Sin's son Shar-Kali-Sharri rebuilt the temple, and Ur-Nammu of Ur's Third Dynasty and other kings renovated it.[49]

Now, the god Enlil was like a roaring typhoon that decimated the entire land, like a tidal wave that crushes everything before it. He gazed at the eastern mountains and called out the Gutians, "an unbridled people, with human intelligence but canine instincts and monkeys' features." The Gutians swept down into Akkad like great flocks of birds. "Nothing escaped their clutches." They drove the herds of goats and cows out of their pens and dislodged the city gates of Agade.

The region became like prehistoric times before cities were established. The fields were untended, no fish were in the neglected canals, and the orchards did not yield fruit without irrigation. The rains stopped, and no plants grew. "People were flailing themselves from hunger." They were starving and dying in their homes with no one to bury them. Roving dogs would attack and kill anyone in the street.

For seven days and nights, the cities' old men and old women raised a lament to Enlil. The other gods—the patrons of the other cities ravaged along with Agade—prayed to Enlil, cooling his heart like water. They cursed Agade and asked Enlil to pour out his wrath on that city and spare the others. And so, despite the earlier devastation of all Mesopotamia, the Akkadian Empire fell completely. This was not something that happened suddenly, but the troubles that would bring its ultimate destruction began. Within three decades, the empire would shrivel, but the Sumerian cities—Ur in particular—would rise to glory once again.

We have no other historical accounts that Naram-Sin ever attacked Nippur and destroyed its temple to Enlil. However, the recorded "Year Names" of his son Shar-Kali-Sharri report that between the fourth and tenth years of his reign, he appointed a general to oversee the building of the temple of Enlil in Nippur. He laid the foundations and cut down cedar timbers to build the temple. A temple had already been in Nippur for centuries, but this was a complete rebuilding from the foundations up. As recounted in the story, the Gutians did invade, the rains really stopped, and vast numbers of people died or were displaced throughout Mesopotamia.

The brunt of the double curse of drought and invasion fell on Naram-Sin's son, Shar-Kali-Sharri, who ascended the throne upon his father's death in 2217. He ruled for twenty-four years. He was an exemplary military strategist but was stymied by a horrific drought that led to the loss of three-quarters of the northern Mesopotamian settlements. He struggled against vicious raids by the Gutian tribes to the east until he captured their king, Sharlag. High taxes on tributary states led to rebellions, but he successfully fended off Amorite invasions.

What was this massive drought that caused a severe decline in agricultural production and weakened the empire? One of human history's most devastating climate changes—the 4.2-kiloyear BP aridification event—struck the earth around 2200 to 2000 BCE, with colder temperatures and a 30 to 50 percent reduction in rainfall in Mesopotamia, Syria, and Turkey.[i] Although the extreme drought ended in about two centuries, research on Iran's lakes and the Dead Sea demonstrates that the Middle Eastern rainfall never returned to the amounts before the drought.

Changing wind and ocean currents led to erratic weather patterns. This caused the ghastly drought, and there was also a terrible series of volcanic eruptions to the north in modern-day Turkey. Archaeological evidence and soil analysis show that the sudden climate change induced calamitous degradation of arable land. Cities and entire regions were left abandoned, leading to the collapse of the Akkadian Empire.

---

[i] Harvey Weiss, *Megadrought and Collapse*. New York: Oxford University Press, 2017, 94-183.

Leilan was a small city of twenty thousand inhabitants on the border of Syria and Iraq in the Akkadian Empire's breadbasket. Archaeological and geological investigations indicate that Leilan and two nearby cities were suddenly and completely evacuated, and a fourth city lost 80 percent of its population. Naram-Sin's fortress at Tell Brak was abandoned, with unfinished walls and floors. In Leilan, the Akkadian administrative building that had been storing, processing, and redistributing grain for a century was abruptly deserted.[i]

Nagar (Tell Brak) in northern Mesopotamia, including Naram-Sin's fortress, was abruptly deserted in the middle of a construction project around 2200 BCE.[50]

Archaeologists found a half-inch layer of volcanic ash on Tell Leilan dating to 2200 BCE, which likely came from the fallout of volcanic eruptions in Turkey. Volcanic ash and gasses can remain suspended in the atmosphere for years, blocking the sun and cooling temperatures. However, that alone could not account for the widespread drought throughout the Middle East (and beyond) that lasted for at least two centuries. Even before the volcanoes, soil analysis showed a marked contrast in sand and dust deposits, pointing to higher aridity and dust storms, while earlier eras had rich, moist soil.

Drought and global cooling not only devastated the Akkadian Empire but also affected all of the Middle East. It may have collapsed Egypt's Old Kingdom and perhaps even the Liangzhu culture of China and the Indus

---

[i] Weiss, *Megadrought and Collapse*, 94-183.

Valley civilization, although not all scientists are convinced it was a global event. Some scientists also argue that Mesopotamia experienced an enormous population growth—probably due to the relative peace and enhanced wealth brought by the Akkadian Empire—which was unsustainable in the semi-arid land even without climate change.[i]

While the empire was still expanding, vast regions in northern Mesopotamia suddenly emptied around 2200 BCE. Where did they go? The surviving populations of these cities were apparently part of a southern migration to Sumer. Why south? Didn't Sumer get hit by the drought as well? Yes, it did, but Sumer could manage deficits in rainfall.

Before the drought, northern Mesopotamia had more rainfall than southern Mesopotamia (it still does) and relied chiefly on rain for their crops. They had not developed the Sumerians' advanced irrigation system that had been used in central and southern Mesopotamia for two millennia. Sumer never relied much on rainfall for their crops. Although the Tigris and Euphrates suffered a 30 to 50 percent reduction in water flow, the Sumerians reconstructed their canal systems to adjust for the change. They continued as usual with their agricultural endeavors.

The drying up of grasslands in northern Mesopotamia and Syria displaced Amorite herders. They migrated south to the regions along the Euphrates delta, where the grass still grew. This led to the construction of a 110-mile "Amorite repelling" wall in Sumer. The Amorites never left central Mesopotamia and later formed the Babylonian Empire. This massive population shift of northern Mesopotamian agriculturalists and nomadic herders led to the Akkadian Empire's fall, the doubling of Sumer's population, and the rise of Ur's Third Dynasty.[ii]

What about the other part of the curse, the Gutian invasion? Who were the Gutians, the "fanged snake of the mountain ranges?" They were of mysterious origins and non-literate; thus, tracing these people linguistically is challenging. We only have the names of some of their kings recorded in Akkadian and Sumerian documents. They lived east of the Tigris River in the Zagros Mountains of present-day Iran, and they paid tribute to Sumerian King Lugal-Anne-Mundu of Adab before the

---

[i] D. Lawrence, A. Palmisano, and M. W. de Gruchy, "Collapse and Continuity: A Multi-proxy Reconstruction of Settlement Organization and Population Trajectories in the Northern Fertile Crescent during the 4.2kya Rapid Climate Change Event," *PLoS One.* 16 (1) (2021). https://pubmed.ncbi.nlm.nih.gov/33428648/.

[ii] Weiss, *Megadrought and Collapse*, 94-183.

Akkadian Empire era.

They were also under Sargon the Great's overlordship, but when his grandson Naram-Sin came to the throne, they were no longer docilely paying tribute. On one of his victory steles, Naram-Sin recorded a battle in which the Gutians killed one-quarter of his 360,000-man army before he finally conquered their king, Gula'an. The *Weidner Chronicle*—a Babylonian history written around 1800 BCE—said the god Marduk, Babylon's patron god, summoned the Gutians against Naram-Sin because he had attacked and demolished Babylon.[i] But the Gutians were unschooled in showing reverence to the gods and offended Marduk, so he removed them from the land.

The Gutians had been slowly filtering into Mesopotamia during Naram-Sin's reign. After his death, his son, King Shar-Kali-Sharri, fought bitterly against the Gutian hordes that suddenly increased right about when Mesopotamia fell into its two-hundred-year dry spell. The Gutians were notorious for raiding parties. They launched guerrilla attacks, devastated cities, and stripped the fields of their produce. Shar-Kali-Sharri finally captured their king, Sharlag, in the year after he finished building Enlil's temple in Nippur, which subdued the Gutians for a time.

This vase fragment depicts a prisoner of the Akkadians being pulled by a nose ring and with a distinctive braid. He may have been Gutian.[51]

Shar-Kali-Sharri spent the next three years victoriously fighting the nomadic Amorites who had suddenly migrated into the Euphrates River region

---

[i] *Weidner Chronicle (ABC 19)*, Livius, 2020. https://www.livius.org/sources/content/mesopotamian-chronicles-content/abc-19-weidner-chronicle/.

because of the drought. For two years after that, Shar-Kali-Sharri took the battle against the Gutians to their territory, fighting in Elam and bringing them "under the yoke" in his seventeenth year as king. Shar-Kali-Sharri died in 2193 BCE as the last king of the Akkadian Empire. The *Sumerian King List* summarized the anarchy following his death when four usurpers vied for power as the empire dwindled: "Then who was king? Who was not the king? Igigi, Imi, Nanum, Ilulu: four of them ruled for only three years."

The Sumerian cities, one by one, declared their independence from Akkad. They had the upper hand now. Agade was no longer the seat of a fearsome overlord. The drought wasn't affecting Sumer as much as in the north—they weren't starving and dying with no one to bury them. The region of Akkad was experiencing a precipitous drop in its population, while Sumer was growing, as it was able to sustain the people through irrigation.

During this period of instability, the marauding Gutian tribes swept back down from the mountains into Akkad and Sumer. This time, the Akkadians could not defend themselves from the catastrophic raids; the Gutian strikes on river traffic and camel caravans destroyed the trade routes. The drought had already caused lethal food shortages, and now, the Gutians stripped anything that was still growing, plunging Akkad into a gruesome famine.

The Gutians weren't the only invaders. The Elamites, Hurrians, and Lullubi formed an eastern coalition of sixteen hostile kings, taking advantage of Agade's weakness. Although initially repulsed, they attacked again, dealing the Akkadians a crushing blow. The *Cuthean Legend of Naram-Sin* also mentions the mysterious Umman-Manda people as another adversary. They possibly came from central Turkey.

Finally, in 2189 BCE, Dudu grasped Akkad's crown—but the empire was no more. It had crumbled away, leaving only Agade, Kish, and Eshnunna. Was Dudu part of the Sargonic dynasty or just another usurper? The *Sumerian King List* doesn't say who he was, only that he ruled twenty-one years. The only records available say that King Dudu campaigned against Umma and Lagash, bringing home spoils of war.

Dudu's son Shu-turul came to the throne in 2168 BCE. He was the last king of the three cities and ruled for fifteen years. After this, Akkad and much of Mesopotamia fell into the "Dark Ages" under the power of the fierce Gutians. The Gutian nomads seemed disinterested in farming except for small garden plots inside the cities. They let the sheep, goats, and cattle out of their pens to roam the land. The famine deepened in the regions they controlled, and trade came to a standstill. The canals filled with sediment, and grass covered the highways.

Meanwhile, around 2091 BCE, the "Sumerian Renaissance" arose with the Third Dynasty of Ur. Power shifted to the south as the people fled famine and invasion, emptying northern Mesopotamia. Ur would not be an empire like Akkad, but it controlled southern Mesopotamia for the next century. It restored the Sumerian language, although Akkadian continued to be used in trade and diplomacy for the next thousand years.

Climate change and invasions obliterated the Akkadian civilization, yet the empire had joined multiple cultures in its immense melting pot, sharing a common language. They showed the world what an empire looked like and set the benchmark for future empires. That legacy would endure.

Chapter 6: Akkadian Society and Daily Life

Akkad itself and all its conquered lands represented real people. What did daily life look like in the Akkadian Empire? What did the people eat and drink, what did they wear, what were their houses like, and what was their marital and social structure? This chapter will examine the literature and artifacts of the Akkadian Empire era, opening a window to the past on how people lived their lives.

The Akkadian Empire encompassed numerous nationalities and cultures. Could the conquered people preserve their cultures? Although the empire was one political unit, the conquered regions outside Mesopotamia continued with their ethnic and social traditions. Most areas within Mesopotamia continued to follow the Sumerian culture, which the Akkadians assimilated, including praying to a similar pantheon of gods. When we use the word "Akkadian" for people, it doesn't necessarily mean the Semitic ethnicity of the original Akkadian speakers. We can't even be sure if Sargon was ethnically Akkadian since his birth parents are unknown. In a broad sense, the term for Akkadian people means those from varying backgrounds who embraced the Akkadian king's worldview and culture.[i]

Speaking of Akkadian and Sumerian, did the Sumerians have to learn the Akkadian language? What language did the empire use for literature,

---

[i] Foster, *The Age of Agade,* 30-33.

administration, and governmental affairs? For centuries, the Sumerians and the Semitic Akkadians lived together in central and southern Mesopotamia. When the Akkadian Empire rose to power, most Mesopotamians were already bilingual in Sumerian and Akkadian. The two languages, although they were entirely different, borrowed from each other freely up to and through the Akkadian Empire until they became a *sprachbund*—a linguistic crossroads. The Akkadian language replaced spoken Sumerian by the end of the empire.

However, southern Mesopotamians still used Sumerian in religious ceremonies and literature for the next two thousand years, similar to Latin in more recent times. The Akkadians adopted the Sumerian cuneiform script, so their administrative and governmental affairs used spoken and written Akkadian. Following the collapse of the Akkadian Empire, the Akkadian language divided into two Semitic dialects: Assyrian (used in northern Mesopotamia) and Babylonian (used in central and southern Mesopotamia).

What about outside of Mesopotamia? The Akkadian language was similar to the Semitic languages spoken in the easternmost parts of the empire—Syria, Lebanon, and Canaan. Thus, the conquered Semitic people could quickly pick up the spoken Akkadian language. Learning the cuneiform script would have been much more difficult. The Semitic languages outside Mesopotamia were most likely preliterate, as the Proto-Sinaitic script (the earliest alphabet) did not emerge until about 1900 BCE.

When the British and French first began archaeological digs in Mesopotamia in the 1800s, they unearthed twenty-four thousand tablets in the Akkadian region of Nineveh. They discovered so many bas-reliefs (sculptures that project out slightly from a stone slab) that they would stretch almost two miles if stood side by side. These fascinating bas-reliefs recorded the great kings' wars and achievements. But to understand what these tablets and reliefs said, the archaeologists had to decipher the cuneiform script, which hadn't been done yet.[i]

So, the linguistic experts set to work, and it took them about ten years to decipher the texts. The cuneiform script contains approximately six hundred characters. Some of these represented whole words (like with

---

[i] Karen Rhea Nemet-Nejat, *Daily Life in Ancient Mesopotamia*, (Westport, Connecticut: Greenwood Press, 1998), 4.

Chinese, Korean, or Japanese today), while others represented syllables. Each character or sign could represent both a syllable and a word or even multiple words. It all depended on context.

Because each written cuneiform symbol could represent multiple values, some detractors believed it could never be translated. They scoffed at the accuracy of the early translations. To address this question, the Royal Asiatic Society sent copies of a newly discovered inscription to four well-known linguists in 1856. Each linguist had to translate the inscription without consulting any of the others. Six weeks later, the committee examined the four translations, and they were remarkably uniform![i]

The Akkadians and other Mesopotamians kept meticulous records using cuneiform script, covering the minutiae of daily life, such as sales, property information, business transactions, and even their histories. They didn't have numbered years in the Akkadian era, so they remembered dates by the years' names or a ruler's year in office. For instance, an inscription might read, "In Naram-Sin's fifth year," and notable events described different years of a king's rule, like "the year the temple's foundation was laid" or "the year Elam was put under the yoke."

A surprisingly abundant source of cuneiform family archives and letters gives us a glimpse of what family life and women's roles were like in the Akkadian Empire. Young men usually married in their twenties, but their brides were in their teens; they could have been as young as fourteen. Fathers might arrange a marriage for their daughters when they were still little girls. Thus, a girl of six or seven could be called a "wife" in an *inchoate* marriage once her father received the bride price.[ii]

An inchoate marriage meant that a couple gradually entered into the marriage in stages rather than in a single ceremony. A girl lived at home with her parents after the betrothal in the prenuptial stage, which could extend for a decade. If any other man attempted to have sexual relations with her, he could receive the death penalty as a rapist of a married woman. The Akkadian word *batultu* meant virgin, and a woman was expected to be a virgin until she began living with her husband, although kissing and intimate touching seemed to be allowed.

---

[i] Nemet-Nejat, *Daily Life*, 4-5.

[ii] M. Stol, "Women in Mesopotamia," *Journal of the Economic and Social History of the Orient* 38, no. 2 (1995): 125. http://www.jstor.org/stable/3632512.

When the young woman began living with her husband in the connubial stage, she brought a dowry. Her husband could not do anything with that money or property—they were for the woman and her future children. If she died without children, the dowry returned to her family, and the husband got his bride price back. Once a woman had a child with her husband, the marriage was complete, meaning it was no longer inchoate. If she died with children, the money was her children's inheritance; it would not go back to her birth family.

Most marriage contracts were oral, not written. Written contracts were used if the bride or groom owned considerable property or a substantial bride price or dowry was at stake. However, the bride's father and the bridegroom could negotiate issues like whether the groom could take a second wife or concubine if the wife couldn't conceive. What would be the bride's status in the home if a second wife or concubine entered the picture?[i]

Most marriages were a husband with one wife unless the wife could not conceive or had a chronic illness. Then the husband usually took a second wife, but the first wife could sometimes choose the second wife or concubine. The biblical Abraham lived in Ur, Harran (Turkey), and Canaan toward the end of the Akkadian era or soon after. His first wife Sarah could not conceive, so *she* gave him her maid as a concubine; this happened again with Abraham's grandson Jacob.

Sargon the Great was notable for protecting widows and orphans. Women were usually married to men who were about ten years older, and the Akkadian men were often called up to serve in wars. This means the empire had numerous widows and "orphans" (who usually had a living mother but no father to protect and provide for them). A woman could use her dowry to support herself and her children, but if it were not enough, she could sell herself or her children into slavery, or someone could adopt them. Boys were adopted for free labor in the fields, and girls could be adopted as household maids or became prostitutes. Cult prostitutes were associated with the goddess Inanna's temples, and some scholars believe Sargon's mother was a cult prostitute.

---

[i] Stol, "Women in Mesopotamia," 125.

This sculpture is of a young woman of Umma in the Akkadian era.[52]

How did the people of the empire dress? Most clothing was made of linen or wool. Two female sculptures from Ashur and Umma dating to the Akkadian era show young women with wavy hair combed back into a chignon at the nape of the neck and a decorative band around the head—they were simple yet elegant. The Umma woman's high-necked gown falls in layers, with each tier being about three inches. This seemed to be a Mesopotamian fashion trend for both men and women. Several Akkadian-era depictions of the goddess Inanna show her in a short-sleeved, square-necked gown that falls in layers to her ankles; sometimes, a slit on the side of the dress exposes her leg from the thigh down.

Artwork of the time shows men with long beards, which are usually elaborately braided or curled. They have long hair pulled back into a bun and sometimes wear a helmet or cap. The men are often bare-chested (because of the hot Mesopotamian climate) but sometimes wear a coat open in the front or a cape over one shoulder. They wear a simple A-line skirt to the knees or ankles. Naram-Sin's sculpture on his victory stele (see Chapter 5) portrays him wearing a helmet with horns (signifying god-likeness), a long beard, his sword on his back in a baldric (belt) that crosses his chest, and a loincloth that exposes his thighs but drops below his knees in the front and back. His bare-chested soldiers wear simple helmets and a knee-length skirt with a diagonal hemline. Shoes with turned-up toes appear in artwork beginning in Sargon's time. Male prisoners of war are pictured nude in several victory steles.

The environment defined daily life in the Akkadian Empire. The climate was primarily arid or semi-arid in Mesopotamia, with mountains, foothills, grassy steppes in the north and deserts and vast marshy regions in the southern river delta. Akkad and Sumer were extremely hot in the summer, with temperatures as high as 120°F and annual rainfall no more than ten inches, which mainly happened in the winter. The Tigris and Euphrates regularly flooded between April to June, so the Akkadians and Sumerians had hydraulic systems like dikes to regulate flooding.

This diorite statue of an Akkadian man features a long, curled beard, bare chest, and a simple, long A-line skirt.[58]

Clay was an essential natural resource in Akkad and throughout Mesopotamia. It formed the slabs for the earliest form of writing. It was also the primary material for building houses. Clay was readily available in the semi-arid land plains fed by the Euphrates and Tigris, and adobe or mud-brick houses date back to the Neolithic age in Mesopotamia. Trees were not as common, so builders usually only used wood for framing roofs or doors.

Most homes for ordinary people had one to three rooms with a courtyard for cooking and other activities. The roofs were flat and often covered with grain, fruit, or fish, which were spread out to dry. People also enjoyed sitting on their roofs in the evening breeze and even sleeping on the rooftop. Middle-class and upper-class people had larger homes centered around a courtyard.

Generally, builders used sun-dried bricks for the homes, which suffered damage from the winter rains, so they had to slab new clay layers over the houses on occasion. Palaces or temples were built from kiln-dried brick or stone (which usually had to be imported, except in northern Mesopotamia, which had gypsum). The people threw their garbage into the streets; after a while, it would mix with the sand to form a layer higher than the home thresholds, allowing rain and sewage to seep into the houses. Occasionally, the floors needed to be raised above street level.

A natural resource was bitumen, which seeped up from beds in the ground near the Euphrates. Bitumen was a black, sticky substance—something like tar—used to stick bricks together or as a waterproof covering on roofs or other objects. In Sargon's birth legend, his mother sealed his basket with bitumen before floating it down the river (as the biblical Moses's mother did).

In Akkad (and the rest of Mesopotamia), the diet was similar to today's Middle Eastern diet. They grew the native einkorn wheat, which they ground into flour and used to bake bread in clay ovens comparable to today's Middle Eastern tannour ovens. The ovens were usually in the courtyard or a central spot shared with several other neighbors. The dough was leavened or unleavened, pushed flat, and then pressed onto the inside wall of the oven to bake. It was similar to today's naan, lavash, or pita bread. The soil in Mesopotamia grew increasingly saline over time, so many areas switched from growing wheat to barley, which could tolerate the saline soil better. They used barley for bread, porridge, and a thick beer, the latter of which was consumed daily and often drunk with a straw.

They grew legumes, including chickpeas and lentils. They might have lamb or pork that would be roasted or cooked in a clay pot with seasonal vegetables on festive days. They grew fruit and vegetables like garlic, leeks, onions, cumin, cucumbers, apricots, dates, figs, grapes, melons, pomegranates, and eggplants. The Akkadians consumed eggs and meat from waterfowl and roasted or dried fish. They ate a lot of fish! They drank goat milk and made yogurt, cheese, butter, and ghee. When they weren't enduring a horrific drought, the Akkadian diet was high in protein with a wide variety of healthy produce.

The Akkadians' occupations influenced their social hierarchy. They had a five-tiered class system. At the top were the nobility: the king, his governors, and other political leaders. Many governors or others in higher administration were from the king's family. Akkadian governors were the chief administrators in the conquered territories stretching from the Mediterranean Sea to the Persian Gulf, with the Akkadian military ensuring compliance.

The second layer was the priests and priestesses, who were also often members of the royal family. The priestly caste—both men and women—usually knew how to read and write in the cuneiform script. Not only did they organize worship in the temples, but they also served as doctors and dentists in the temple courtyards. Some were astrologists, observing the movement of stars, planets, and celestial changes to predict the future and decipher omens. Sargon established a library with what may have been the first collection of astrological studies.

The upper-class citizens made up the third social stratum. These were the accountants, affluent merchants, architects, army officers, scribes, and teachers. Many people in this class were literate, as reading and writing were necessary for their trade. Otherwise, they had to hire a scribe. It took nine years to train a scribe to read and write cuneiform. The empire had schools to teach reading and writing for the middle and upper classes, and some wealthy families hired tutors.

The fourth social stratum encompassed the lower classes, who were fundamental to the empire's growth. These were the farmers, herders, and fishermen, and they labored to feed the enormous population. Mesopotamia's two most important natural resources were the twin river systems of the Euphrates and Tigris and the annual deposit of silt from these rivers that covered the land during the spring floods. With ample water and natural fertilization, farming or herding was the occupation of at least half of the Akkadian Empire's population.

Some farmers owned their land, usually around fifteen acres. Others were tenant farmers, farming about thirty acres, but they had to turn over up to two-thirds of the crop to landlords and for the "king's portion." Nevertheless, the remaining harvest was sufficient to support a family. The crop portion designated for the king was loaded on barges and shipped to Agade to feed the king's household and his army.[i]

Mesopotamians had been herders of sheep and goats long before settling into cities and growing crops. This time-honored occupation

---

[i] Foster, *The Age of Agade*, 143-46.

continued to provide wool, milk, and meat; some herders grew wealthy from the sale of wool. Raising donkeys and oxen was also a profitable occupation, as these animals pulled wagons for transport. Oxen also pulled barges up the rivers and canals.

Fishermen and fish farmers provided the most significant source of protein for the empire, as the people consumed astonishing amounts of fish, which we know from delivery documents. They netted fish in the rivers and the Persian Gulf and farmed them in ponds fed by irrigation. Ducks and geese provided eggs, feathers, and meat, and they kept small numbers of pigs for special feasts. Water buffalo appeared on Akkadian era seals and were seen there by traders. They were possibly imported from the Indus Valley.

Other lower classes included basket weavers, construction workers, craftspeople, and enlisted military men who weren't officers. Construction workers for state projects like clearing canals, making or laying bricks, or building roads received food, cooking oil, and wool rations. It was entirely possible in the Akkadian Empire to rise to higher social levels through excellent skills, work ethic, and strategic marital alliances.

Women's employment was usually at home. They ground grain into flour to make bread, wove cloth, sewed garments, tended the children, fetched water from the community well, cut reeds to weave mats, cooked, and cleaned. However, women could acquire land and manage it, which upper-class women commonly did. They also owned taverns. Women didn't have the same high status and legal protection as in the Sumerian culture, but it was higher than in the following Assyrian Empire. The most elevated position for a woman was serving as a high priestess, as Sargon's daughter Enheduanna did. Women priestesses also worked as doctors and dentists, as the medical arts involved religious practices.

The lowest class was the slaves. They were usually prisoners of war, and some were educated or highly skilled craftsmen. A few enslaved people were criminals who had received servitude as a sentence. A man with overwhelming debt could sell his children, his wife, and himself into slavery. Enslaved people were expensive to buy and maintain, so they usually did not do agricultural work. It was cheaper to allot land to tenant farmers who supported themselves and turned over at least half the harvest to the landowner.[i] Most slaves were household servants for

---

[i] Foster, *The Age of Agade*, 149.

wealthy families. Skilled or educated slaves served as accountants, craftspeople, farm administrators, scribes, and teachers.

The Akkadian Empire developed the world's first known postal service, taking advantage of the road system that spanned the empire. The "letters" delivered by postmen in those days were clay tablets with the cuneiform script. The "envelope" began with Sargon's reign; it was an outer layer of clay stamped with the sender's seal. The recipient would crack open the thin outer layer to read the message.

How did a strong empire make trade networks possible? Trade was already well established in Mesopotamia, going back to the Neolithic Age. However, the empire's road system, relative safety, strong alliances, and broader territory ignited prosperous trade with far-flung regions, pouring wealth into Agade and bringing necessary goods and luxury items from distant lands. It also speared astounding developments in mathematical understanding, metallurgy, art, and architecture, as innovations and techniques could be shared and further developed.

Where were the trade networks, and what did they trade? Mesopotamia had a shortage of trees, so they traded with Lebanon for their cedars and the Caucasus Mountains of Turkey for other lumber. Eastern Turkey (Anatolia) was also a rich silver, tin, and copper source. The Akkadian Empire didn't have flat coins, but they used silver "shekels," which were little chunks of silver that weighed about 8.4 grams. These shekels enhanced trade exponentially as an exchange medium.

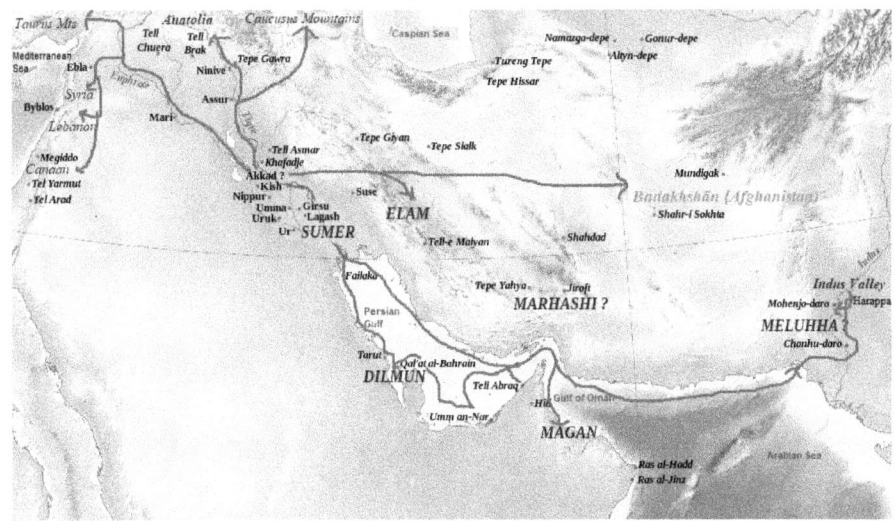

The Akkadian Empire's trade routes stretched from the Mediterranean to Anatolia in the north to the Indus Valley in the southeast and around the Persian Gulf.[54]

Sargon the Great sent ships to the Indus Valley, trading with the cities of Mohenjo-Daro and Harappa (in today's Pakistan) for cloves, unique shells, carnelian beads, ivory, timber, and cotton textiles. The Akkadian ships also sailed around the Persian Gulf, trading for copper, pearls, semi-precious stones, and linen. The Akkadians traded with Badakhshān (Afghanistan) for lapis lazuli. The Akkadians exported grain, bitumen, woolen textiles, cooking oil, dried fruit, dried fish, leather goods, pottery, and baskets.

Most of the empire's exports were necessary goods like food, while the imports, except for lumber, were luxuries, which points to the astounding wealth of the Akkadian Empire.[1] It had food in abundance (until the great drought), so trade wasn't strictly necessary; rather, it reflected the prestige and social stratification in Akkadian society and the empire's esteem and domination over the surrounding areas.

---

[1] Christopher Edens, "Dynamics of Trade in the Ancient Mesopotamian 'World System,'" *American Anthropologist* 94, no. 1 (1992): 122. http://www.jstor.org/stable/680040.

Chapter 7: Warfare and the Military

What was distinctive about the Akkadian military powerhouse? How did this martial force surge ahead to conquer like never before? Sargon the Great said he won thirty-four wars. His core force of 5,400 men was history's first standing army, and this was the first time that military campaigns involved distant regions rather than the neighboring city-states. The newly developed composite bow that used bronze arrowheads was one secret to success, as it was a weaponry revolution.

How did Sargon and other Akkadian kings recruit their soldiers? A principal way was through conquest. Conquered states usually had to do two things: pay tribute (money or goods) to Akkad and provide men for the empire's military. Most empires following the Akkadian Empire employed this conscription method. But Sargon also initiated volunteer corps called *niskum*, who received benefits for enlisting, regular fish and salt rations, and plots of land as a reward when they left service. About one in five soldiers in the Akkadian military were these loyal military professionals.

Sargon organized his full-time military into nine 600-men battalions. Whether volunteer or drafted, the empire's soldiers would soon become experienced in battle since wars of conquest and defense happened most years, along with the ongoing task of crushing sporadic rebellions of conquered states. Sargon also deployed *nim* soldiers; *nim* meant flies in Akkadian. He sent these soldiers ahead of the main body of warriors as skirmishers to harass and distract the enemy like a swarm of flies.[i]

This victory stele celebrates Naram-Sin's conquest of the Lullubi.[55]

The Akkadian king was the military's chief commander, and under him were the generals, the top field commanders of the spearmen, ax-bearers, archers, and other units. The Victory Stele of Naram-Sin shows

---

[i] "The Akkadians." *Weapons and Warfare: History and Hardware of Warfare*, 2019. https://weaponsan,dwarfare.com/2019/07/29/the-akkadians/.

him at the top, larger than life, in a horned helmet, facing the conquered Lullubi. One Lullubi soldier in front of him is dying from a spear through his neck. Behind the mortally wounded man, the Lullubi king, Satuni, begs for mercy, and below him, a Lullubi general raises his hand, pleading for himself and his men.

Under the king and his generals were *laputtum* or battalion commanders. The military appeared to use the sexagesimal system (sixties); a battalion was six hundred men, while a platoon was made of sixty men. They were led by a *waklum* or captain. Sargon had a reserve force of trained men in Agade; he mentioned mustering nine contingents from the city. They probably worked regular jobs like our present-day reserves but were trained and ready to deploy at a moment's notice.[i]

Such a large army covering thousands of miles of territory required superior organization for logistics and administration. Since the empire spread from sea to sea and the military continued to grow, Sargon desperately needed capable administrators for his army. He parceled out these bureaucratic tasks to men he trusted. They ensured the soldiers got their daily bread and beer and that supplies and siege engines were transported to the right place. These bureaucrats required a good understanding of the lands through which the military was traveling.

For instance, they needed to know what local water sources were available, how far apart they were, and how much would need to be transported. They knew precisely how long it would take to march from one point in the empire to another. Conquered cities along the way provided food for the army; documents from Umma list the provisions they supplied to the Akkadian military. Scribes traveled with the army, keeping casualty and supply records, accounts describing their adversaries, and distinctive details of the new lands. A priest accompanied the troops, and he practiced divination to determine the most auspicious tactics. Couriers carried commands and other messages from city to city.

Bas-reliefs and other artwork depict the military's arsenal, including the battle-ax, bow and arrow, javelin, lance, mace, and spear. Various corps carried specific weapons; for instance, there would be an archery platoon for long-distant assault and platoons of spearmen and ax-bearers for closer combat. Spearmen would usually also have an ax, as they would

---

[i] "Akkadian Military," *Weapons and Warfare: History and Hardware of Warfare*, 2019. https://weaponsandwarfare.com/2019/09/21/akkadian-military/.

frequently lose their spears after throwing them or impaling someone and not being able to get it back. The soldiers often tucked a slingshot or throwing club (like a boomerang) in their belts.

This rock relief at Darband-i Gawr of Qaradagh Mountain shows Naram-Sin holding a battle-ax in one hand with a bow slung over his shoulder.[56]

On his victory stele, Naram-Sin holds what appears to be a composite bow, which put the Akkadian army at a distinct advantage over its enemies. A simple "self" bow is made from one piece of wood, while a composite bow has several pieces glued together with cattle or ibex horn and animal sinew, providing increased flexibility. The compound bow's velocity was two to three times greater than a simple bow; the arrows could travel at least twice as far and pierce leather armor. Because the lethal composite bow was lighter, it was easier to shoot from horseback or a chariot.

What about armor? Most artwork from the Akkadian Empire era shows no body protection on soldiers except for helmets, sometimes with leather aventails to protect the neck. In the Victory Stele of Rimush, the soldier holding the bow is wearing what appears to be a leather garment. The soldier killing the prisoner has a sash going over his shoulder that is held in place by a belt. If the material were leather, it might have been a sort of armor. Most Akkadian artwork does not show soldiers holding shields, but the Akkadian military probably used "tower shields" like the soldiers of Lagash pictured in the Stele of Vultures.

What tactics did the Akkadian military use? Did they have a cavalry? Did they use chariots in warfare? The Sumerians used a cumbersome four-wheeled chariot pulled by one or two donkeys for centuries before Sargon, and Akkadian art depicts several types of cart vehicles in combat. Scholars initially believed horses did not appear in Mesopotamia until about five hundred years after Sargon the Great based on a lack of Akkadian and Sumerian artwork depicting a person on horseback. However, in 1992, archaeologists unearthed a clay model of a horse at Tell es-Sweyhat (Syria) on the Euphrates River dating to 2300 BCE, which would have been during Sargon's reign. Model chariots found at the same site imply that horses pulled them. Texts found in Ebla indicate that horses were in Mesopotamia even before Sargon's rule. This means the use of cavalry and horse-drawn chariots may have contributed to the Akkadian Empire's unprecedented rise.[i]

The infantrymen (foot soldiers) served in spearmen, archer, and ax-men units. The spearmen could have first deployed ammunition from slingshots before coming close enough to impale their enemies with spears. Cavalry and chariots likely supported the infantry, perhaps launching an initial charge as the two armies drew near each other. If horses and faster chariots were new to Mesopotamia and the Levant, the shock value alone could have sent the enemy packing.

This victory stele, believed to be Rimush's, portrays the massacre of unarmed foes. The soldier on the left is wielding what appears to be a composite bow.[57]

---

[i] John Noble Wilford, "Ancient Clay Horse is Found in Syria," *The New York Times*, January 3, 1993. https://www.nytimes.com/1993/01/03/world/ancient-clay-horse-is-found-in-syria.html

Nevertheless, some fighting wouldn't have lent itself to chariots or cavalry. For instance, the terrain would have been too rough and steep for chariots when the Akkadians fought in the Zagros Mountains against the Gutians, Lullubi, and Elamites. Horses might fare a little better, but the cavalry's advantage was the swift charge, which would have been difficult in hilly, forested battlefields.

Akkadian inscriptions often mention sieges, but they do not include many details of what their siege warfare involved. Sargon mentioned "pulling down" the walls of cities that resisted him but didn't say *how* he got the walls down. We know from textual evidence that Syria used battering rams (*yašibu* in the Akkadian language) in the Akkadian Empire era. Some cylinder seals depict wagons or chariots; some were pulled by horses (or donkeys), and others were propelled by people. A branch of Akkadians settled the city of Nabada in Syria (the archaeological site is Tell Beydar) about a century before Sargon the Great. During the Akkadian Empire, Nabada was an empire outpost. Cylinder seal impressions from archaeological digs at Tell Beydar show prototypes of siege engines.

One seal impression shows several four-wheeled wagons of different shapes. The vehicle in the top right (and top left) of the scene looks like a four-wheeled chariot drawn by a horse. Two carts appear at the bottom of the picture with no horses. They are both facing a tower-like structure that might represent a tall building (perhaps a city wall). The cart to the left of the elevated structure has three poles extending from it that may be a type of triple battering ram pushed from behind to knock down the structure.

This seal impression from the Akkadian city of Nabada shows what appears to be a wheeled battering ram on the left bottom and a rolling siege tower on the right bottom.[58]

To the right of the tall structure, another cart with one man in it has a tall front and back wall and is being pushed from behind by another man. This wagon's function is unclear; however, a different picture shows a cart similar to this one with sides almost as high as the walls. They appear to be siege towers on wheels to protect the soldiers and get them up high enough to shoot arrows into the structure. These pictures suggest that the Akkadian military had somewhat sophisticated battering rams and other siege engines.

What were the offensive and defensive strategies of the Akkadian military? The phalanx battle formation was used in Sumer about a century before Sargon the Great, so presumably, the Akkadian army used it. The Stele of Vultures, celebrating the victory of King Eannatum of Lagash over Umma, shows a row of eight soldiers standing shoulder to shoulder with four large shields that cover their bodies from their necks to their ankles. In a typical phalanx formation, each soldier has his own shield, but the carving seems to portray one shield for every two soldiers, which would have been possible with larger shields and double hand grips.

A phalanx formation was used both defensively and offensively. The men held the shields to touch the shields next to them; they might have even slightly overlapped. As long as the soldiers maintained intense discipline and held steady, the phalanx presented a nearly impenetrable wall of defense. The only body parts exposed were the helmeted heads and necks and the feet.

But the phalanx was also a formidable offensive tool. A typical phalanx wasn't just one row of soldiers but multiple rows, one behind the other. The rows of soldiers with shields would march steadily toward the enemy, holding pristine ranks. Meanwhile, archers shot arrows with their compound bows up in the air, over the heads of the Akkadian soldiers and into the enemy ranks. With a hail of arrows coming down on them, the enemy would begin to break rank while the phalanx steadily marched toward them.

The section from the Stele of Vultures shows a phalanx formation.⁵⁹

Once the phalanx was about thirty to fifty feet away, the soldiers would suddenly launch into a run, slamming into the enemy with their shields. The soldiers in the second, third, and other rows would push the soldiers in front of them with their shields, so it was like a giant human bulldozer plowing through the enemy ranks. In the Stele of Vultures, fallen soldiers lie at the soldiers' feet, crushed by the onslaught of shields.

Sometimes, a tight, strong phalanx could succeed in pushing through the enemy ranks. Usually, the phalanx eventually broke apart, perhaps when tripping over the bodies of the men under them or when the opposing side also had a tight phalanx. When the phalanx crumbled, the soldiers grabbed their battle-axes and maces for hand-to-hand combat. The phalanx formation worked great on a reasonably flat battlefield without trees or other obstructions in the way. But when fighting in the mountains or forested terrain, they had to implement alternate strategies. They would use smaller, rounder shields and engage more with their axes and spears.

Several steles depict naked defeated troops. Some are in chains, which means they probably faced enslavement, while others are impaled with spears or smashed over the head with an ax or mace. When they overcame the enemy, the Akkadian soldiers stripped them of their weapons and clothing. The Akkadians piled the dead enemy soldiers—sometimes in the thousands—in a large mound covered with earth. This hill of dead soldiers might have a monument stele erected at the top, celebrating the victory and posing a grim warning to other cities who might resist the Akkadian war machine.

The Akkadian king needed to be a great warrior to win his people's respect as a leader. Sargon set the standard that others had to follow. He conquered massive swathes of territories, brought in astonishing amounts of plunder, and opened new trade routes that led to unimagined wealth for Akkad. The ideal Akkadian king was fearlessly eager to leap into violent conflict to enlarge the empire's borders, protect his people against invasion, and subdue insurrections.

This concept incurred a paradigm shift in theology. Formerly, the Sumerians felt dependent on the gods for success in battle. It wasn't their fault if they lost—the gods had ordained triumph for the other side. However, especially with Naram-Sin, we see him taking credit for his victories rather than acknowledging divine intervention. When multiple disasters struck near the end of his reign, which ultimately led to the empire's downfall in the rules of his successors, the Mesopotamians latched onto the idea that his lack of piety brought a curse on Agade.

Sargon created the world's first multi-national empire with the world's first permanent army. What did that standing army do when they weren't invading new lands? The Akkadian military was often engaged in safeguarding the domains that had already been captured from internal insurrections and external invasions. Insurrections were met with the mass slaughter of populations and the flattening of cities, even Akkadian cities. The Akkadian military fiercely fought the Gutians, Elamites, and other invaders, annihilating their prisoners or enslaving them.

The full-time military also ensured peace and stability throughout the empire. Battalions were posted in the conquered provinces, discouraging rebellions and keeping the trade routes safe. This relative security led to a surge in trade, enriching the whole empire. Law and order empowered the construction of an empire-wide road system, postal system, the exciting interchange of scientific and artistic developments, and irrigation and construction advancements.

The Akkadians dealt with conflicts and wars differently than their Sumerian neighbors. Sargon and his successors had to adjust to ruling people with diverse cultures and languages. Although he generally left the indigenous religious and cultural practices in place, Sargon found that a "soft" approach was inadequate. He resorted to placing garrisons manned with Akkadian soldiers and Akkadian governors in the conquered lands.

When Akkadian garrisons and governors failed to keep a city-state in line—particularly in Sumer—Sargon and his descendants (especially Rimush) killed, enslaved, or exiled almost entire populations and resettled the land with Akkadians. The Sumerians considered this sacrilege against the gods. Once again, the Akkadian theology conflicted with the Sumerian beliefs that a patron god owned and protected each city and that kingship descended from heaven.

The Akkadians were more humanistic, believing that people owned the land and ruled the cities and that men, not the gods, determined kingship.[i] Of course, the Akkadians were religious and believed they were guided and helped by the gods; in fact, these were the same gods as the Sumerians. They certainly consulted omens at every turn, but they didn't think everything was owned or ordained by the gods.

The military played a crucial role in the success of the Akkadian Empire. The military enabled the Akkadians to unite all of Mesopotamia under one ruler and then extend the empire in all directions. The Akkadians' worldview led to a new theology of war. Competition was an essential value, as it was more important to live by one's wits and make key alliances and clever decisions than to rely on divine intervention.[ii]

Sargon believed he had a divine right to conquer. He thought that he was mirroring the heavenly pantheon by bringing all the city-states of Mesopotamia and beyond under one centralized government. He and the Akkadians believed that humans ran the universe. The Akkadians' theology of war was threefold: 1) struggle within the divine realm of the gods, 2) competition between the military forces, which depended on divine favor, and 3) order and balance brought by the human king. The military's chief role was to enable the king to bring order so that the earth's government mirrored the heavens.[iii]

---

[i] "Akkadian Military," *Weapons and Warfare*.
[ii] Foster, *The Age of Agade*, 236.
[iii] Michael Cserkits, "The Concept of War in Ancient Mesopotamia: Reshaping Carl von Clausewitz's Trinity," *Expeditions with MCUP*, United States Marine Corps University Press, (2022). https://doi.org/10.36304/ExpwMCUP.2022.01

Chapter 8: Culture and Art

What set Akkadian art and culture apart from other civilizations? Benjamin Foster, Professor of Assyriology and Babylonian Literature at Yale, summarizes Akkadian art as "a brilliant chapter in the development of iconography and technique."[i] The Akkadians took visual art to new heights. They renovated Sumerian structures into their own imposing architectural style and introduced the world's first named author of poetry, hymns, and prayers. The Akkadian civilization's innovative cultural achievements were in league with their awe-inspiring empire-building success.

Akkadian literature is enriching and fascinating, as it deals with themes like human origins, the reasons or lack of reasons for suffering, and the gods' intervention in history. The themes are reminiscent of biblical stories and poetry, mirroring humankind's struggles, frustrations, and questions. The Akkadian textual record encompasses a wide range, including mundane administrative documents, personal letters, legal contracts, recipes, "how-to" guides, mathematical tables, and medicinal prescriptions. But the jewels of Akkadian literature are the sophisticated poems, stories, and hymns that help us understand the vitality and complexity of Akkadian life.[ii]

---

[i] Foster, *The Age of Agade*, xvi.
[ii] Alan Lenzi, *An Introduction to Akkadian Literature* (University Park: The Pennsylvania State University Press, 2019), 5-6.

Naru literature was a Mesopotamian literary genre that emerged toward the end of the Akkadian Empire. They were moralistic tales involving a human hero—usually a king—and his relationship with the gods. Two predominant Naru literature examples are inscriptions written several generations after the empire's end, but they were about events in the Akkadian era: *The Legend of Sargon*, which we will discuss in Chapter 9, and *The Curse of Agade*, which was discussed in Chapter 5. These two stories blend real-life events (such as the great drought and the Gutian invasion) with the authors' interpretation of divine intervention and sometimes fanciful fiction. Naru literature isn't so much factual historical accounts as an attempt to extract meaning from history or pseudo-history.[i]

Another Naru literature example involving an Akkadian king is *The Legend of Cutha*, which featured Naram-Sin, Agade's fourth king. It is a cautionary tale about following the will of the gods rather than relying on one's own power. The story begins with Naram-Sin bemoaning the fate of Uruk's Enmerkar, who suffered the gods' wrath for no real reason, despite his attempts at divination. Naram-Sin then launches into his own story of inexplicable divine wrath brought by a massive army of 360,000 seemingly supernatural warriors suckled by Tiamat, the goddess of chaos. One by one, this diabolical army destroyed civilizations, such as Subartu, Gutium, Elam, Dilmun, and more.

Naram-Sin sent his soldier with a dagger to stab one of the warriors. If blood came out, they were human, but if not, they were fiends from the underworld. The soldier returned to report that blood came out; they were mortal. Naram-Sin then sacrificed seven lambs, and seven diviners representing seven gods forbade him from going against the army. But Naram-Sin decided to follow his own heart's counsel, saying, "Let me take responsibility for myself!"

In his first year of the military campaign against the hellish army, he sent out 120,000 men, and the entire army died at the enemy's hands. In the second year, he sent 90,000 troops, and the infernal army obliterated every man. He sent out 60,700 warriors in the third year, and no man returned alive. Naram-Sin was distraught and mystified. How could this happen? In deep anguish, he realized he was a shepherd who had failed

---

[i] Joshua J. Mark, "The Legend of Cutha," *World History Encyclopedia*, 2021. https://www.worldhistory.org/article/1869/the-legend-of-cutha/.

his people. How could he save his country?

After humbling himself before the gods, Naram-Sin captured twelve men from the abominable army and brought them back to Agade. The gods instructed him to spare these men because the god Enlil had already planned the destruction of these soldiers' city. Naram-Sin realized he needed to exercise self-control, keep himself in check, and allow the gods to act. He learned he could not save his country through his own efforts but only through divine protection.[i]

Another dominant genre of Akkadian literature is religious poetry, which was written by Sargon's daughter. Sargon strategically placed his children and other relatives in key administrative positions in Akkad and its conquered territories. He appointed his daughter Enheduanna to Ur as the high priestess of the moon god Nanna. Her royal presence would help create stability in southern Sumer. Enheduanna was a prolific writer of hymns and petitionary prayers. She is history's first literary author for whom we have a name. Enheduanna's poetry helped syncretize the Sumerian concept of deities with Akkadian theology.

Enheduanna's name was Sumerian, and it was probably a priestly title, not her birth name. It literally meant "Chief Priestess, the Ornament of Heaven." In her poem, *Queen of All Cosmic Powers*, she recounts her struggle with the king of Ur, Lugal-Anne-Mundu. He was the same king who united with the kings of Uruk and Kish in a revolt against her nephew, Naram-Sin. Sexually harassed, forced out of her position as high priestess and into exile, and feeling abandoned by Nanna, she pleaded with Nanna's daughter, the goddess Inanna:

> "Queen of all cosmic powers, bright light shining from above,
> Steadfast woman, arrayed in splendor, beloved of earth and sky...
> Yes, I took up my place in the sanctuary dwelling,
> I was high priestess, I, Enheduanna.
> Though I bore the offering basket, though I chanted the hymns,
> A death offering was ready; was I no longer living?
> ...O Moon-god Suen, is this Lugal-Anne my destiny?
> ...I am Enheduanna; let me speak to you my prayer,
> My tears are flowing like some sweet intoxicant...

---

[i] Mark, "The Legend of Cutha."

> I would have you judge the case...
> That man has defied the rites decreed by holy heaven
> He has robbed An of his very temple!
> ...He has turned that temple into a house of ill repute!
> Forcing his way in, as if he were an equal,
> He dared approach me in his lust!
> ...O precious, precious Queen, beloved of heaven,
> Your sublime will prevails; let it be for my restoration!"[i]

Enheduanna received a favorable answer to her prayers and recovered her position as the high priestess. She served over forty years and wrote at least forty-two poems about her feelings of frustration with her circumstances and devotion to Nanna and Inanna. Enheduanna's hymns and other Akkadian poetry were clearly meant for performance, meaning they were either sung or spoken. Although rhyme wasn't used, except accidentally, the meter and rhythmic patterning are pleasant to hear, with groupings of two to four lines and repetition of couplets. The works themselves often have lines like, "I will sing" or call on an audience to "hear."

However, the meter wasn't always predictable. Usually, the poems had four accentual peaks per line, but then they suddenly diverged into a different rhythm of three or five (or even more) peaks. M. L. West, a British linguistic and music scholar, theorized that Akkadian poetry was chanted, perhaps to the accompaniment of a harp or lyre, and the performers had an elastic repertoire of intonations, pauses, and inflections. In this way, the irregular rhythms could become uniform, which he felt would mesmerize the audience.[ii]

Akkadian art has various categories, bursting with innovation and energy. Sadly, the ruins of Agade still lie hidden under the sand, and they almost surely will yield a treasure in Akkadian artistic, literary, and architectural themes when discovered. But the few examples of sculptures, monuments, and other artistic achievements recovered from other sites give us insight into the ingenuity and skill of the Akkadian artists.

---

[i] Foster, *Age of Agade*, 331-336.
[ii] M. L. West, "Akkadian Poetry: Metre and Performance." *Iraq* 59 (1997): 175-87. https://doi.org/10.2307/4200442.

This cylinder seal of Kalki the Scribe (fourth from the left) shows him with the king's brother and other dignitaries and servants.[60]

One type of delicate art, which was used by scribes and administrators throughout Mesopotamia for centuries before the Akkadian Empire, was cylinder seal impressions. Because these little cylinders were so durable—hundreds have been discovered—they can still be rolled in clay to get a fresh image, giving insight into life at the time. The Akkadians seemed to prefer serpentine rock for their seals, compared to the Sumerian civilization before Sargon and the Ur Third Dynasty after.[i] Although mythological themes often prevailed, such as struggles with mythical creatures and between the gods, the scenes were more naturalistic. The sun god Shamash is frequently depicted, along with other deities, such as Ea (Enki) and Inanna (Ishtar). Human heroes display rippling muscles and thick curly hair.

The scribe Kalki's black and white diorite seal shows a picture of Ubil-Eshtar, who was probably Sargon's brother, in the center of five men. An archer in front and a bearded dignitary look back toward Ubil-Eshtar. With a shaved head and face and holding a tablet, Kalki walks immediately behind Ubil-Eshtar, followed by another bearded dignitary. Two servants, who are only half as high as the five men, denoting their lower status, carry a net and a stool in the back of the procession. The cuneiform script identifies Ubil-Eshtar as the king's brother and Kalki as his servant.

---

[i] Foster, *Age of Agade*, 202-205.

The Seal of Ibni-Sharrum, a scribe for King Shar-Kali-Sharri, displays men watering buffalo by a flowing stream.[61]

Akkadian glyphic art (cylinder seal impressions) is notable for the lifelike depiction of humans and animals, but the Akkadians also developed landscape art to new heights. Sometimes, trees, rocks, streams, and mountains form the entire composition, while other times, they are used as background or to separate scenes of men or animals. In the Seal of Ibni-Sharrum, a rivulet of water forms a border at the bottom, while the water buffaloes contentedly drink from the flowing vases.

The male figures display the typical muscular build and flowing mane of hair common to Akkadian art. They are naked, which often implies slavery, yet their elaborately curled beards and hairstyles indicate they are higher class. The Akkadian artists captured an astonishingly realistic portrayal of muscles, tendons, and bone structure. The idealized perfection of the bodies is reminiscent of the classical Greek sculptures that came about 1,500 years later.

The remnants of Akkadian sculpture that have survived through the past four thousand years show remarkable and surprisingly advanced skills for the Early to Middle Bronze Age. Akkadian artisans formed sculptures from diorite, alabaster, and copper. Metallurgy craftwork thrived in the Akkadian era. Metal was readily available from trade routes, and the kings set up workshops for artisans to ply their trade. Copper was inexpensive and abundant at the time, as it was mined in northern Mesopotamia and shipped in from Oman. Bronze, which is made from copper and tin, was used less often because tin became rarer for unknown reasons.

This exquisitely crafted copper head is an unidentified Akkadian king.[62]

The facial features on a striking copper head, perhaps representing Sargon the Great or Naram-Sin, are breathtakingly realistic, displaying haunting beauty and power. Found in Nineveh, the hollow-cast head was once part of a complete statue, and the hair, which is pulled into a bun, and elaborate beard display the male hairstyle of the day or at least of the elite. Sargon's son Manishtushu dedicated a temple to Ishtar in Nineveh, so he may have installed the head (and the rest of the statue) in the temple. In that case, it would be Manishtushu's image.

Another lifelike copper sculpture is the Bassetki Statue, named after the northern Iraqi village where it was found. The sculpture is the endearing figure of a youth. The top has broken off at his waist, so we can only imagine his face, hair, and torso. He is sitting on a flat surface with his legs bent to the side, with his left knee touching the back of his right ankle. In between his legs is a vessel that probably held a standard.

The Bassetki Statue was stolen from the Iraqi Museum in the 2003 invasion and recovered later that year, hidden in a cesspool.[63]

A cuneiform inscription in Old Akkadian at the sculpture's base says it guarded Naram-Sin's palace entrance. It says that the citizens of Agade prayed to the gods to make Naram-Sin their city's patron god and built a temple to him after he overpowered a significant rebellion. The sculpture is notable for its amazingly lifelike portrayals of the human body, once again foreshadowing the classical Greek era by well over a millennium. The inscription about making Naram-Sin a god is what later Mesopotamians believe brought down the curse of Agade.

Akkadian metallurgists produced eating, drinking, or decorative vessels but primarily crafted tools and weapons. Mesopotamia already had a sophisticated knowledge of metalworking with bronze, copper, gold, and silver before the Akkadian Empire's rise, but the Akkadians developed new shapes, such as a footed drinking goblet. The craftsmen also frequently inscribed their names or other information on the metal implements.

Most civilizations would consider stone to be useful but not especially valuable. But the Akkadians prized stone, mainly because Mesopotamia didn't have much of it other than some limestone, sandstone, and basalt in the north. When they invaded other lands like Elam or Anatolia, they would happily haul stones back as war trophies, using them for their palaces, temples, and steles. They rarely used stone for sculptures (other than bas-reliefs), but they favored imported alabaster and diorite when they did. One exquisite example is an alabaster head found in Adab (Bismaya) in southern Mesopotamia, which scholars believe represents a king or governor.

The Akkadian era is notable for steles commemorating military victories—monuments carved into large sandstone slabs or more precious stones from afar. An Akkadian stele usually had a raised bas-relief sculpture projecting from the stone with cuneiform script describing the victory. Sargon was known for setting these up in the lands he conquered, but wind, sand, vandalism, and time have eroded or covered most of what could have been hundreds of steles of the Akkadian kings. These steles were part of Sargon's propaganda campaign to legitimize his right to rule.[i]

An early Sargon stele shows him wearing a long beard almost to his waist, followed by a servant holding a parasol. Sargon's garment appears to be made of sheep hide held together with a belt and with one shoulder exposed. He holds a battle net, symbolizing captured prisoners; a row of prisoners is on the section of stele above Sargon. In the Sumerian Stele of Vultures, a god held the net of prisoners, but now Sargon has it, signifying a theological shift.[ii]

Sargon (left) carries a net of captured prisoners on this stele. A man carrying a parasol and dignitaries follow the king.[64]

---

[i] Lorenzo Nigro, "The Two Steles of Sargon: Iconology and Visual Propaganda at the Beginning of Royal Akkadian Relief," *Iraq* 60 (1998): 85. https://doi.org/10.2307/4200454.

[ii] Foster, *The Age of Agade*, 195.

Akkadian architecture implemented the Sumerian style with some new twists. The Akkadians continued the Sumerian tradition of a central courtyard surrounded by several rooms in their private homes. Since the Ubaid culture, sun-dried plano-convex bricks with a domed-shaped top—looking somewhat like a loaf of bread—had been used in construction. Akkadian builders instead used rectangular, flat-topped bricks of varying sizes.

Administrative buildings and temples were far more imposing; they were made on a grander scale and had thick walls and marked symmetry. The Akkadians built new structures and renovated older buildings to reflect the formidable, colossal style they preferred. A stunning example was the Abu Temple in Eshnunna—a city in central Mesopotamia—which is close to one potential location of Agade.

The original small shrine to the god Abu dated to around 3100 BCE. It was rebuilt into a rectangular shape and rebuilt again into a square courtyard surrounded by several rectangular structures. A horde of statuettes depicting worshipers was unearthed from this period. Finally, the Akkadians rebuilt the shrine into one massive form, known as the "Single Shrine Temple." This structure was in a long rectangular shape with walls three times as thick and twice as tall as the one it replaced. It featured a single grand entrance at one end, a platform for cult deities at the other end, and a small nook to one side with a basin for ablutions.

Naram-Sin's son Shar-Kali-Sharri oversaw the reconstruction of Ekur, Enlil's temple in the sacred city of Nippur. The temple has not survived, although later rulers rebuilt it, but records of the builders and materials have. A staggering amount of precious metal adorned the temple—tons of copper and over a thousand pounds of gold, silver, and bronze. Hundreds of craftsmen—carpenters, engravers, goldsmiths, sculptors, and woodworkers—produced exquisite ornamentation: gold-plated bison, copper and gold dragons, gold-plated statues of kings, and many more enchanting works of art.[i]

Akkadian art reflected the empire's power and ideology. The Akkadian kings' patronage of artistic workshops in metals, stones, and other elements encouraged creative brilliance. The Akkadian artists led Mesopotamia into a new era of realistic, lifelike art. Although Akkadian art and architecture reflected Sumerian influence, it was also a type of

---

[i] Foster, *The Age of Agade*, 14-16.

propaganda to communicate power and dominance. Thus, architecture tended to be formidable and large, and scenes of the kings represented their ascendency.

Chapter 9: Famous Rulers

We often think of the first four Akkadian kings as brilliant military men who invaded and conquered numerous kingdoms and squelched insurrections. But when these men weren't on military campaigns, what did they accomplish? Which leadership qualities did they display? What were their strengths and weaknesses?

What do we know about Sargon other than his conquests? Is *The Legend of Sargon* simply a fictional account of the man from nowhere? Examining Sargon's extraordinary life, his military exploits, and the Akkadian Empire's founding is like trying to put pieces of a puzzle together only to discover they come from multiple boxes! Accounts tend to be unclear and unreliable. We have a so-called autobiography, but even if Sargon wrote it himself, this man was obsessed with establishing his identity and legitimacy.

Sargon was consumed with proving his right to rule. He had no royal lineage or at least none that he could prove. His parents were obscure. He was called the gardener's son in the *Sumerian King List*, but he said he never knew his biological father in his supposed autobiography. His mother may have been a priestess of the goddess Inanna, but she abandoned him to the river. He grew up in humble circumstances, then suddenly received the honorable position of the king's cupbearer. Within weeks, out of self-preservation, he ejected the king and usurped his throne.

Sargon forcefully asserted his right to kingship, not by his parentage but by the patronage of the gods. In Sumer, he claimed the goddess

Inanna's favor and the god Enlil's support. Enlil was a part of the Sumerian triad of chief gods, believed to bestow kingship on whom he chose. A king was not legitimate without his approval. Kings would travel to his temple in Nippur to seek legitimacy, and he would bring lavish offerings. After conquering the cities of Sumer, Sargon wrote this inscription:

> "Sargon, king of Agade, emissary for Ishtar, king of the world, attendant of Anu, lord of the land, governor for Enlil, was victorious over Uruk in battle and conquered fifty governors with the mace of Ilaba and the city of and destroyed its walls and captured Lugal-zage-si, king of Uruk, and brought him to the gate of Enlil in a neck stock.
>
> Sargon, king of Agade, was victorious over Ur in battle, conquered the city and destroyed its walls.
>
> He conquered Eninmar and destroyed its walls and conquered its land and Lagash all the way to the sea. He washed his weapons in the sea.
>
> He was victorious over Umma in battle and conquered the city and destroyed its walls.
>
> Enlil gave no rival to Sargon, king of the land. Enlil indeed gave him the Upper and Lower Sea."
>
> *- Inscription of Sargon*, Old Babylonian copy from Nippur[i]

By washing his weapons in the sea, Sargon symbolized his supremacy over the "Lower Sea," the Persian Gulf. The "Upper Sea" was the Mediterranean. Sargon boasted of thirty-four successful military campaigns in his numerous inscriptions. A helpful document describing his rule's extent is *The Sargon Geography*, probably written by a Babylonian scribe in the 1st millennium BCE based on texts from the 3rd millennium. It seems to be a compilation from various ancient texts, as the author gives accounts that don't always agree.

The Sargon Geography reveals a different side of Sargon—a systematic and orderly man, carefully calculating the measurements of the conquered territories and defining their borders. For instance, he documented one land's borders as extending from "the bridge of Baza on

---

[i] Foster, *Age of Agade*, 321-22.

the edge of the road to the land Meluhha to the mountain of cedar: the Hanaean land." *The Sargon Geography* gives two locations for the land of Akkad.

1. "From Hizzat to Abul-Adad: the land Akkad."
2. "From Damru to Sippar: the land Akkad."[i]

Apparently, these two named locations of the land Akkad with different landmarks for its borders came from two original documents quoted by the author/editor of *The Sargon Geography*. Hizzat's location is unknown. Abul-Adad, or "Gate to Adad," was the name of one of Babylon's city gates (Adad was a Mesopotamian deity). We know where Sippar was—on the Euphrates in central Mesopotamia, north of Babylon and Kish, and near modern-day Baghdad. Damru's location is a mystery. But we seem to have two points defining what might be the western border of the land of Akkad (which would include the city of Agade).

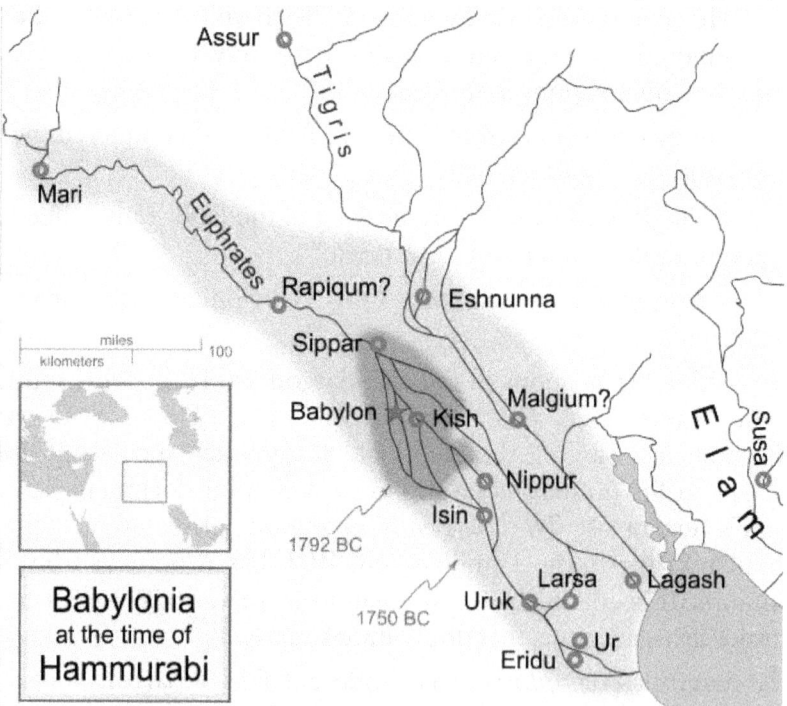

According to The Sargon Geography, Sippar and Babylon, both on the Euphrates, could be the eastern borders of the region of Akkad.[65]

---

[i] A. K. Grayson, "The Empire of Sargon of Akkad," *Archiv Für Orientforschung* 25 (1974): 56-64. http://www.jstor.org/stable/41636304.

Sargon placed Akkadian governors in his conquered lands, and Agade became fabulously rich from trade with all the subjugated territories. It was wealthy enough to feed his standing army of 5,400 men. He ruled a vast empire from the "Upper Sea" (the Mediterranean) to the "Lower Sea" (the Persian Gulf). He erected multiple self-images from Canaan to Syria and decorated his temples and palaces with booty from his conquered lands.

Was Sargon of Akkad the biblical Nimrod? The Torah speaks of Noah's descendent who established dominance over Shinar (Sumer) and then expanded to Ashur in northern Mesopotamia:

> "Cush was the father of Nimrod, who became the first powerful warrior on the earth. He was a mighty hunter before the Lord; that is why it is said, 'Like Nimrod, a mighty hunter before the Lord.' The first centers of his kingdom were Babylon, Uruk, Akkad, and Kalneh, in the land of Shinar [Sumer]. From that land, he went to Assyria [Ashur], where he built Nineveh, Rehoboth Ir, Calah, and Resen, which is between Nineveh and Calah—which is the great city." (Genesis 10:8-12)

The biblical account does seem to follow the trajectory of Sargon's conquests. He started in northern Sumer (central Mesopotamia), conquering Uruk and establishing or developing the towns of Akkad (Agade) and Babylon into prestigious cities. A tablet dating to Sargon's reign describes him laying the foundations of temples in Babylon. From central Mesopotamia, he continued to expand north into Assyrian territory.

But if he were the son of Cush, the timing wouldn't be right. Cush was Noah's grandson, so he would have lived much earlier. However, Nimrod isn't listed among the five sons of Cush in Genesis 10:7, so Cush must have been Nimrod's "father" in the sense of being his remote ancestor. The name "Nimrod" is not a Hebrew name; it may come from the Babylonian *Namra-uddu*, meaning "star-god." It could even be a pejorative nickname. An alternate meaning of Nimrod (the Hebrew צַיִד or *tsayid*), can carry the meaning of "slaughterer" with a cognate of the northern Syrian Ugaritic word *dbh*.[i] We have no stories of Sargon being a

---

[i] Douglas Petrovich, "Identifying Nimrod of Genesis 10 with Sargon of Akkad by Exegetical and Archaeological Means," *Journal of the Evangelical Theological Society* 56, no. 2 (2013): 273-305.

prolific hunter, although he certainly could have been. Naram-Sin spoke of a wild bull hunt. But Sargon was, without doubt, a great slaughterer of men.

Ancient inscriptions on cuneiform tablets provide two parts of Sargon's "autobiography." *The Legend of Sargon* tells how his mother abandoned him to the river, and a man named Akki—an irrigator or drawer of water—found him and raised him to be a gardener. Archaeologist Austen Layard discovered two partial copies of this story on three clay tablet fragments in Nineveh in 1867 CE in the Library of Ashurbanipal. Over two decades later, amateur Assyriologist George Smith found a fourth fragment in Nineveh, which helped fill in the second part of the story.

Smith believed these tablets were copies of a much older inscription going back to Sargon's time. However, no tablets of the story have been found dating to the Akkadian period and not even for the millennium following. Of course, Sargon's city of Agade, where such tablets would likely be, is still hidden under the sand. Many scholars believe the legend was written in the days of Sargon II of the Neo-Assyrian Empire, who reigned from 722 to 705 BCE. The Assyrians admired Sargon I of Akkad as an ancient hero and exemplary king; thus, Sargon II took his throne name from the ancient king.

The Sargon birth story (as shared in Chapter 3) says that his mother covered a basket with bitumen, then put the baby Sargon in it and floated him down the river. Scholars often note how this story is echoed later in the birth story of the biblical Moses, whose mother also covered a basket with bitumen and floated him down the river. But which story came first? If the Sargon story was a pseudo-autobiography written during the Neo-Assyrian Empire, the Moses story, recorded in the Torah (Exodus 1 and 2) around 1446 BCE, would predate the Sargon story by centuries.

If the Sargon birth story was written in the Neo-Assyrian era, it would have been close to the time of Rome's founding, which contains another story of a basket in the river. The legend of Rome's founder Romulus says his mother—a Vestal Virgin—gave birth to twins. Her evil uncle, who had usurped her father's throne, ordered his servant to kill the babies. Instead, the servant put Romulus and Remus in a basket, which sailed down the river to be found by a she-wolf. Twenty years later, around 753

https://www.etsjets.org/files/JETS-PDFs/56/56-2/JETS_56-2_273-305_Petrovich.pdf

BCE, Romulus established Rome.

The Sargon birth story contains several inconsistencies. How would Sargon know his mother was a priestess and put him in a basket? How did he know where he came from other than upstream from wherever Akki the gardener found him? How did he know that his father's brothers "loved the hills?" Unless he was reunited later with his birth family, which could be possible, he would know nothing other than his adoptive father found him in a basket in the river.

In the case of Moses, his sister followed the basket down the river until the Egyptian princess found it. Moses remained in contact with his biological family. Remus and Romulus later met up with their grandfather, put two and two together, and figured out their identity. But Sargon never mentions reuniting with his biological family or how he knew these details. He doesn't even explain why his mother had to give birth in secret and abandon him. If Sargon was the actual author, was he trying to establish legitimacy for an illegitimate birth? His story seems to engender more questions than it answers.

The one element of the story confirmed by the *Sumerian King List* is that his father was a gardener. Several copies of the *Sumerian King List* have survived to the present; at least one tablet's scribe signed and dated it to King Utukhegal of Uruk, placing it around 2125 BCE—less than three decades after the collapse of the Akkadian Empire. Even if *The Legend of Sargon* were a fictional story written over a thousand years later, Sargon definitely scratched his way to the top from humble beginnings. Additionally, *The Legend of Sargon* lines up with the second story, the "Sumerian Sargon Legend," which tells how Sargon rose from gardener to cupbearer to king.

Also known as the Sargon and Ur-Zababa tablet, the "Sumerian Sargon Legend" is a biography of Sargon of Akkad (shared in Chapter 3). The *Sumerian King List* confirms several story elements. Sargon was the son of a gardener and became a cupbearer to the king. He rose to "kingship" over Sumer by defeating Uruk. The *Weidner Chronicle*, which was written several centuries after the fall of the Akkadian Empire, also mentions Sargon as the cupbearer to King Ur-Zababa. Sargon's monument inscriptions record his interaction with King Lugal-zage-si of Uruk. Other historical records confirm the essential elements of the story.

Two separate manuscripts of the story have been found: a fragment of the story in Uruk and a mostly complete clay tablet from Nippur.

Interestingly, the "Sumerian Sargon Legend" is in the Sumerian language, which was dying out by the end of the Akkadian Empire. The use of Sumerian suggests that it was written during or shortly after the Akkadian Empire. Sargon may or may not have floated down the river as a baby in a basket, but he almost surely was promoted from gardener to cupbearer and then usurped the throne of Kish.

What about Sargon's successors? What do we know about their qualities and non-military achievements? Sargon's son Rimush, who succeeded him, seemed exceptionally proud. Rimush called himself "King of the World" even when he knew parts of the world, like Egypt and India, were clearly not in his domain.

Known for his bloodthirsty slaughter of a large swathe of southern Sumer's insurgent population, Rimush diligently recorded the number of people he killed, enslaved, or put into "camps." At that time, tin was a rare metal in Mesopotamia and the surrounding regions. But the prideful Rimush had a statue of himself produced in tin, which he placed in front of the idol to Enlil. He then counted himself among the gods in its inscription. Despite being in the prime of his life, Rimush seemed to decline in the last years of his reign, with few inscriptions lauding his achievements. After nine years, his courtiers cut short his rule by killing him with their cylinder seals.

These fragments from the Victory Stele of Rimush may represent Lagash's defeat.[66]

Although initially passed over for the throne, Manishtushu assumed the reign of the Akkadian Empire after his brother Rimush's assassination. Was Manishtushu involved in his brother's murder? We have no evidence that he was, but he certainly stood to benefit. Manishtushu was an astute military man, further expanding the empire's borders, but he also possessed canny diplomatic skills. These seemed to help him maintain order in Sumer and other conquered lands, as we have no records of the coordinated Sumerian uprisings that disrupted the reigns of his father, brother, and son.

Manishtushu was conscientious about honoring the Sumerian gods, which may have been part of his diplomatic strategy. Throughout Sumer and Akkad, he placed duplicate black diorite statues, which featured him standing with his hands reverently clasped. He especially seemed to target the "home cities" of the most powerful gods, such as Enlil in Nippur and Anu in Uruk. Manishtushu also focused on astral deities associated with the sun, moon, planets, and stars, such as the sun god Shamash in Sippar and the moon god Sin (or Nanna) in Ur. Of course, Inanna (Ishtar), his father Sargon's patron goddess, was highly honored in Agade.

The placement of these statues in key Sumerian cities seemed to be a way of appeasing the citizens after his brother and father had ruthlessly squelched their rebellions and decimated their populations. Manishtushu's figures weren't lauding his achievements so much as honoring the various gods of the cities, declaring his allegiance to them, and acknowledging he only had the power to rule the cities

This black diorite statue of Manishtushu, missing the upper part of his body, shows him with hands clasped in worship.[67]

through the blessing of the patron gods.[1] Unfortunately, only fragments of these statues have survived to the present day.

After Manishtushu suffered the same fate as his brother—murdered by his courtiers—his son Naram-Sin received the crown. Along with superb military triumphs, Naram-Sin revised and standardized the cuneiform script used to write the Akkadian language. Instead of reading and writing a tablet long-ways, the tablet was turned around, like we read a page today. Spelling was improved, so words were easier to read and write. Even when the Sumerians continued to write in their own language, they used the revised cuneiform script.

Like his father and grandfather, Naram-Sin achieved astounding success in conquering and expanding the empire. However, Naram-Sin did not seem to possess his father's modesty and diplomacy with conquered territories. This likely led to the Great Revolt he was forced to put down. His success in defeating the Lullubi and other peoples led him to acclaim himself a god. The Sumerians pointed to his pride and lack of piety as the reason for the empire's collapse.

---

[1] Melissa Eppihimer, "Assembling King and State: The Statues of Manishtushu and the Consolidation of Akkadian Kingship." *American Journal of Archaeology* 114, no. 3 (2010): 365-80. http://www.jstor.org/stable/25684286.

Chapter 10: Myths and Religion

What sort of religion did the Akkadians follow? Like most civilizations, the Akkadian culture included a concept of a world that transcended the tangible earthly, human realm. They had a definite idea of supernatural forces similar to yet distinct from the Sumerian religion. The Akkadian temples, rituals, prayers, and hymns were intrinsic to their lives and reflected their worldview. They were polytheistic, believing in multiple gods, but they thought certain gods were more involved in their lives.

Before the rise of the Akkadian Empire, the Akkadian people lived in Mesopotamia for centuries. Although they had a distinct belief in an all-powerful, supreme, personal god, which was shared with other Semites, they assimilated much of the Sumerian culture. By the time Sargon became king, they were worshiping the Sumerian deities and following their religion, mythology, rites, and cosmology. However, the Akkadians included their own innovations and local variations.

Ancient Mesopotamians believed the supernatural world was comprised of gods and a vast assortment of supra-human ("above" human) beings with powers exceeding human capabilities. These included demons, ghosts, protective spirits, primordial semi-divine sages, and witches. Humans could communicate with these supra-human beings through ritual speeches. Both the gods and the supra-human beings could be benevolent or malevolent to humans.[i] Usually, the same deity or supra-

---

[i] Alan Lenzi, ed., *Reading Akkadian Prayers and Hymns: An Introduction*, (Atlanta: Society of Biblical Literature, 2011), 9-10.

human being could be a combination of kindness and cruelty—even toward the same human! We see this markedly in the prayers to the goddess Inanna and in stories about her.

While the Sumerians and Akkadians worshiped many of the same gods, sometimes their concepts of individual gods differed. The Akkadians also had several gods that were not worshiped in Sumer. One example is "Il," "El," or "Ilum," the supreme god of the northern Mesopotamian Semitic people with whom one could have a personal relationship. The Semites believed Il lived in heaven, but the Sumerians believed heaven itself was the god An, who was distant and remote and had to be approached via another god. The Akkadians syncretized Ilum and An into one god—Anum (or Anu)—and made him the head of their pantheon.[i]

The Akkadian polytheistic concept was that there were thousands upon thousands of gods, just like there were thousands of humans, and each one was different. Some were ranked higher than others, and they all had specific duties. The Akkadians were flexible with their gods, as they readily accepted new ones from the Sumerians or other civilizations into their pantheon.

This gold-plated figurine from the Late Bronze Age represents El (Il), the Semitic supreme creator god.[68]

The Akkadians had three primary gods of the sky. Shamash (Sumerian Utu), the sun god, was the all-seeing, undeceivable judge. His brother Sin (Sumerian Nanna), the moon god, was a mysterious god of divination and decisions. The Akkadians introduced the gruesome

---

[i] Foster, *The Age of Agade*, 135-138.

practice of cutting open lambs and other sacrificial animals to read the omens Sin had written on their entrails to Mesopotamia. Sargon installed his daughter Enheduanna as a high priestess of Sin (Nanna to the Sumerians) in Ur. The Akkadians' third sky deity was Ishtar, goddess of the morning and evening star who blended into the Sumerian goddess Inanna. She was the goddess of war but also the goddess of familial love.

Shamash, the sun god, was a chief deity for both the Sumerians and Akkadians. In Akkadian art, size denoted status. Gods were often pictured several times larger than men, kings were larger than their dignitaries, and servants were about half the size of their masters.[69]

The mother goddess of the Akkadians and Sumerians was Mama or Mami, and she watched over childbirth and healed sickness. Ea (the Sumerian Enki) was the freshwater god, an important deity in a land that was mostly desert or semi-arid terrain. Ea was the problem-solving god, and in all Mesopotamian cultures, he was the god that saved humans from the gods' wrath during the Great Flood. Addu or Adad (Sumerian Iškur) was the storm god; in his benevolent state, he brought life-giving rain. In his malevolent persona, he brought fierce storms and floods.

Some gods introduced by the Akkadians and northern Mesopotamians that were not part of the Sumerian pantheon included

Bel and Dagan (Dagon). A deity named Ilaba seemed to be specific to Agade and faded away after the end of the Akkadian Empire. The Akkadian word *Bēlu* or Bel and the northwestern Semitic *Baal* all meant "Lord" and didn't necessarily refer to the same deity. The Babylonians used Bel as a title for their city's patron god Marduk. The Canaanites worshiped Baal as the god of rain and fertility, and the Phoenicians associated Baal with El (Ilum) or Dagan. Dagan was the Syrian father of gods, the lord of the land and prosperity. Like the Sumerian Enlil, he granted kingship; thus, Sargon bowed to him before campaigning in the Levant (Syria, Lebanon, and Canaan).

Sargon established the worship of Ilaba, "god of the fathers," god of war, and Ishtar's husband (at least one of them). A major god for the Akkadians, Ilaba carried a mace he received from Enlil. According to an inscription of Sargon's, "The god Ilaba, mighty one of the gods—the god Enlil gave to him his weapon." Another inscription referred to Ilaba as Sargon's "personal god." What was a personal god? This god was important in a person's daily life, as they took care of the person. If someone's personal god abandoned them, they were subject to dreadful calamities. A personal god accompanied a person into the afterlife, and a Rimush inscription prescribed a curse of *not* standing before one's personal god after death.[i]

Ilaba appeared to be a family god for the Sargonic dynasty, one that was passed down from father to son. One interpretation of his name is a combination of *Il* or *Ilum* (the Semitic supreme god) with *abum* (father), making him the "god of the fathers" or an ancestral god. All of Sargon's descendants mentioned Ilaba in their inscriptions. After defeating a region along the Euphrates River, Naram-Sin gave credit to Dagan for the victory yet mandated that the conquered people worship "his god," Ilaba. Naram-Sin seemed to be setting the stage for Ilaba's elevation from a family god to part of the Akkadian pantheon of gods. His son Shar-Kali-Sharri built a temple for Ilaba in Babylon. This was the first mention of Ilaba having a temple, indicating he was now part of the official pantheon.[ii]

---

[i] Stefan Nowicki, "Sargon of Akkade and His God: Comments on the Worship of the God of the Father among the Ancient Semites," *Acta Orientalia Academiae Scientiarum Hungaricae* 69, no. 1 (2016): 63–69. http://www.jstor.org/stable/43957458.

[ii] Nowicki, "Sargon of Akkade and His God," 69-71.

Akkadian prayers were not all about petitions and requests from the gods. Typically, most prayers—and certainly the hymns—were more about praising the deities, listing their benevolent actions, and speaking about their character and power. This worshipful praise taking precedence in prayer was social protocol for an inferior coming into the presence of a superior. Even petitioning prayers started with abject worship, with the petition usually tacked on at the very end in just one or two lines. However, complaints about a problem might be inserted somewhere in the middle.[i]

Nergal was the husband of Ereshkigal and the god of the underworld.[70]

---

[i] Lenzi, *Reading Akkadian Prayers*, 12-13.

This prayer to the god Nergal, who was the god of death and the underworld, is a classic example of a polite invocation and praise of the god. It includes a description of the problem, asks the god to pardon the sin and help with the issue, and promises honor when the god answers favorably:

"Mighty Lord, exalted son of Nunamnir,

foremost among the Anunnakki, lord of battle,

Offspring of Kutushar, the great queen, Nergal,

all-powerful among the gods, beloved of Ninmenna.

You are manifest in the bright heavens; your station is exalted.

You are great in the netherworld; you have no rival.

Together with Ea, your counsel is preeminent in the assembly of the gods.

Together with Sin, you observe everything in the heavens.

Enlil, your father, gave to you the black-headed ones, all living beings, [and]

The herds, the creatures, into your hands he entrusted.

I, so-and-so, son of so-and-so, your servant:

The anger of god and goddess has beset me so that

expenses and losses befall my estate [and]

giving orders but not being heard keep me awake.

Because you are sparing, my lord, I have turned toward your divinity,

Because you are compassionate, I have sought you,

Because you are merciful, I have stood before you,

Because you are favorably inclined, I have looked upon your face.

Favorably look upon me and hear my supplication,

May your furious heart become calm toward me,

Pardon my crime, my sin, and my misdeed,

May the indignation of your great divinity...be appeased for me,

May the offended, angry, and irate god and goddess be reconciled with me.

Then will I declare your wondrous deeds and sing your praise!"[i]

---

[i] Lenzi, *Reading Akkadian Prayers*, 339-348.

The Akkadians frequently spoke to their gods as if they were family members, calling them father, brother, or forefather. Rather than implore their deities based on their supernatural powers, they spoke to and of them in more human terms, such as "protector," "defender," "wise sage," or "my queen." The Akkadians prayed to their deities about any predicament or problem—even impotency! Interestingly, in prayers regarding sickness or physical problems, the Akkadians referred to their bodies as their "temples," similar to the teachings of Saint Paul in the New Testament.

Mesopotamians had a type of prayer and ritual they called *šà-zi-ga* in Sumerian and *nīš libbi* in Akkadian. It was something like an incantation against evil or sickness; it was not really a prayer to a deity, although they might invoke a supra-human creature. It either asked a benevolent one to help or commanded an evil one to leave. When they pronounced nīš libbi, the Akkadians would say, "šiptu ul yuttun," or "this incantation is not my words," meaning it was some deity speaking through them.[i]

For the Akkadians and the Mesopotamians in general, worship included much more than singing or chanting hymns and prayers. Body actions were intrinsic, such as kneeling, prostrating oneself face-down on the floor, raising both hands over one's head, clasping hands at the waist or chest level, or holding one's hand in a sort of salute in front of one's face. If in a temple, they would face the cult image or idol. If they were at home or elsewhere in the city, they would turn toward the temple of the god they were praying to; the temples usually towered over the houses and other buildings, so they could be seen from a distance. Worship also included actions such as setting up altars and offering sacrifices.

No recorded Akkadian myths have survived to the present, or at least they have yet to be unearthed.[ii] However, a macabre Babylonian creation myth—the *Enuma Elish*—may have dated back to the Akkadian era when Babylon was built. Sargon established Babylon "in front of Akkad," according to the *Weidner Chronicle*. Akkadian inscriptions mention that Shar-Kali-Sharri laid the foundations for Babylonian temples, and one Akkadian document specified Babylon as the border of the land of Akkad. Multiple cuneiform tablets with the *Enuma Elish* exist today, dating to around 1200. However, the scribes who wrote the tablets noted

---

[i] Lenzi, *Reading Akkadian Prayers*, 14-20.
[ii] Foster, *The Age of Agade*, 211.

they were copying a story from older tablets that were written centuries earlier. The first part of the myth also parallels the Sumerian flood story, the *Eridu Genesis*.

The story begins before the creation of the heavens and the earth when nothing existed except Apsu (fresh water) and Tiamat (seawater) swirling in chaos. Apsu and Tiamat created the gods by blending their waters. They immediately regretted their creation when the young gods turned out to be annoyingly loud. The youngsters' dancing and playing kept Apsu and Tiamat awake all night. They had no peace.

Apsu and Tiamat met to discuss the situation, and Apsu vowed he would kill the gods so they could have some peace. "No!" Tiamat cried, "We can't kill what we've created!" But Apsu was determined. When the young gods heard their father planned to kill them, their knees gave way, and they collapsed, howling in horror. The god Ea (Enki) was determined to stop his father. He chanted an incantation, put his father into a deep sleep, killed Apsu, and built his house in Apsu's body. Ea's wife gave birth to their son Bel (Marduk for the Babylonians) in their new home. He was a beautiful child with four ears, four eyes, and fire blazing from his mouth.

Bel killed Tiamat and defeated her demons in this bas-relief from Nineveh.[71]

Tiamat determined to avenge Apsu's death, even though it meant killing her children. Out of the chaos, she formed eleven hideous demons and sent them to massacre her offspring. Ea tried to overcome Tiamat with magic spells, but she was too powerful. The god Anu attempted to appease her but failed. The rest of the gods were too afraid of Tiamat to do anything. But then Bel charged out to confront Tiamat. He blew a cyclone into her mouth, impaled her with his spear, and broke her skull. He then overcame the demons and smashed them under his feet.

Just as his father Ea had made a home from Apsu's body, Bel decided to create one from Tiamat's body. He fileted her body like a fish, and one half became the sky and the other the earth. He appointed all the gods to their roles in the universe. The gods were ecstatic that Apsu and Tiamat were dead and that they were safe. They decided to kill Tiamat's new husband, Qingu, because he had encouraged Tiamat to kill them. The gods created humans from Qingu's blood to grow food and take care of the world so the gods could give their attention to fighting chaos. The gods celebrated their completed work by sitting down to a splendid banquet and passing around mugs of beer.

The Dynasty of Dunnum, also known as the *Harab Myth*, was found in Sippar on a single clay tablet, which was written in the Akkadian language. The tablet itself dates to the Late Babylonian period; however, its colophon (scribe's signature and notes) says it copied collated tablets from Assur and Babylon. The myth recounts the successive generations of gods who gained power by killing their fathers. The patricide is reminiscent of Ea killing his father Apsu in the *Enuma Elish*, except instead of killing their mothers, they married them! The story may have given rise to Sophocles's tragedy *Oedipus Rex* around 429 BCE.

The myth begins with Harab (or Ha'in)—the plow—marrying Earth and creating Sea in the furrows they plowed. This couple gave birth to Sakkan (Sumuqan), the god of four-legged creatures. Earth fell in love with her son and called to him, "Come here! I want to love you!" So, Sakkan killed his father and married his mother. He also married his sister, Sea, who killed their mother, Earth. Then Ewe, Sakkan's son, killed him and married his mother, Sea, who gave birth to River. Ewe also married his sister U-a-a-am. The story continues for several generations of incestual marriages and murdered parents.[i] Imagine attempting to chart a family tree!

---

[i] Marten Stol, ed., *The Theology of Dunnum*,

This Queen of the Night bas-relief may represent Ereshkigal, the goddess of the underworld.[72]

A third story is the myth of Nergal and Ereshkigal. Archaeologists first discovered the Akkadian epic myth on a tablet dating to the Middle Babylonian period, but then English archaeologist O. R. Gurney identified it on an Assyrian tablet. Ereshkigal was the queen of the underworld and Ishtar's sister, and she was a Sumerian goddess from ancient times, predating the Akkadian Empire. Nergal was a northern and central Mesopotamian god of the Akkadians, Babylonians, and Assyrians beginning in the Akkadian era.

At the beginning of the story, the gods were planning a feast and wanted to welcome their sister Ereshkigal, but the laws of the universe banned her from coming to them, although they could send messages. Anu sent a message to Ereshkigal, inviting her to send her messenger to collect food from the feast and take it down to her. So, her messenger Namtar left the underworld and climbed the stairs to heaven, but, once there, he got angry at the god Nergal. Namtar reported Nergal's offensive behavior to his mistress. Ea ordered Nergal to go to the underworld to apologize but warned him not to receive Ereshkigal's hospitality while there.[i]

Nergal descended to the underworld to apologize, but he fell in love with the beautiful Ereshkigal. He slept with her for seven nights, then returned to heaven. Ereshkigal sent a message to heaven, begging for Nergal to return to her as her husband. However, the gods had transformed Nergal into a hideous creature to disguise him from Namtar, the messenger. When Namtar reported back to Ereshkigal, she figured out what the gods had done, and she threatened to open the gates of the underworld and release the dead spirits to flood the earth if the gods didn't return Nergal to her.

Nergal arrived in the underworld, strode up to Ereshkigal, and grabbed her by the hair. He flung her off her throne; presumedly, this was rough foreplay as a prelude to another extended period of lovemaking. Anu then permitted Nergal to remain as Ereshkigal's husband and king of the underworld. Nergal and Ereshkigal worked out an arrangement where he stayed with her for six months of the year and returned to heaven for the other six months.

Although the Akkadians assimilated the culture and religion of the Sumerians, they also retained some of their earlier gods. The Akkadian theology differed from the Sumerians even when they worshiped the same gods. The Sumerians believed all fortune and calamity came from the gods; the humanistic Akkadians believed one's actions determined one's life, although the gods could guide them. The Akkadian cosmology gave them "permission" to invade the Sumerian city-states (and other regions) because they believed they reflected heaven's order by bringing all cities together under one central rule.

---

[i] O. R. Gurney, "The Sultantepe Tablets: VII. The Myth of Nergal and Ereshkigal," *Anatolian Studies* 10 (1960): 105–06. https://doi.org/10.2307/3642431.

Conclusion

What were the Akkadian Empire's contributions to ancient history and Mesopotamia's future empires? It was a watershed moment in Mesopotamian history, as civilizations moved from independent city-states to multiple states under a centralized government. Sargon picked up where Lugal-zage-si had started with unifying all of Sumer, then brought all of Mesopotamia under one political system. He continued to conquer large swathes of the known world. Sargon and his descendants set the standard for future empires in Mesopotamia and throughout the ancient world.

Benjamin Foster summarized the impact of the Akkadian Empire as a blend of innovation and maintaining tradition:

> "The Akkadian conquest, therefore, tended to replace community-based government and kinship-based oligarchy with centralized exploitation of resources, despotism, and bureaucracy. To achieve this, Sargon adopted a 'double-edged' policy of both promoting change and selectively linking with the past. He used ancient titles and restored Kish as a long-time center of political power, but founded a new capital at Agade."[i]

Consider the colossal impact of just one aspect of culture: the language and writing system. The Sargonic dynasty made Akkadian—the earliest-known Semitic language—the spoken lingua franca of all Mesopotamia

---

[i] Foster, *The Age of Agade*, 433.

and the Levant. A common language united civilizations from the Mediterranean to the Persian Gulf. This unified language sparked a tremendous increase in trade and the interchange of art techniques, military tactics, and scientific and mathematical knowledge. For the following millennia, the Babylonian and Assyrian dialects of the Akkadian language continued as the official languages of the ancient Near East.

The Akkadians also adapted the Sumerian cuneiform script to the Akkadian language, preserving the world's first writing system and spreading a common written language. The bulk of the half-million or more preserved cuneiform tablets are in the Akkadian language (although most are not yet translated). The Akkadian cuneiform writing system continued for two thousand years after the empire collapsed. It was modified by the Babylonian and Assyrians and adapted by the Hittites, Elamites, Hurrians, and other civilizations. It influenced the Old Persian and Ugaritic alphabets.

Another vital contribution of the Akkadians that shaped ancient Mesopotamia and its future empires was assuming control of the temples and their lands. In Sumer, the temples were the most powerful entity, as they controlled the kings, the economy, and the land. The humanistic-leaning Akkadians maintained old temples and built new ones, but the kings now controlled the priesthood, many of whom were royal family members. The government controlled more of the land, distributing some to private owners.

Sargon was the first king to form a standing army. In the past, able-bodied men were called up to fight their neighbors but had to return home for the planting seasons and harvests. The first professional army could fight anytime and anywhere—even a thousand miles from Agade. A full-time army could fight better, having had time to hone weaponry skills and tactics. Sargon and his successors also drafted soldiers from conquered lands. This ethnic mixture of fighting men formed an unprecedented melting pot of cultures—Akkadian, Canaanite, Elamite, Lebanese, Sumerian, and Syrian—all fighting side by side. This military model of a full-time army drawn from all corners of the empire continued through Mesopotamian history.

How did the Akkadian Empire influence our world's civilizations? Danish Assyriologist Aage Westenholz admired the intermingling of the Sumerian and Akkadian cultures, with their equivalent sharing and assimilation between north and south without one civilization blotting out the other.[i] The Akkadian Empire provided a model for future societies to successfully blend cultures, sharing their way of life, ideas, and technologies with others as equals. As cultures learn from each other, they make astounding progress in all aspects of life. Civilizations that welcome cultural blending can adapt, change, and survive.

What is the legacy of the Akkadian Empire? How did its culture, art, and empire-building model endure? The Akkadian art that has survived to the present often features victory steles and bas-reliefs extolling the kings' conquests. For Akkadian royalty, art was used for propaganda, such as celebrating divinely ordained power and expansion.[ii] The scenes in the realistic Akkadian reliefs depict a narrative, which goes to show that, since the beginning, art and architecture have been powerfully used to manipulate emotions and deliver an ideological point of view.

Elements of the Akkadian methodology of empire-building have persisted through the millennia in the Babylonian, Assyrian, Roman, Ottoman, French, Spanish, and British Empires—just to name a few. A critical component was bureaucracy. Labor and resources served the kingdom rather than individual people or cities. Enhanced road systems and trade routes provided for easier and safer travel. Taxes supported the bureaucratic administrators, military, and royal family. Scribes maintained meticulous records of accomplishments, taxes, and day-to-day affairs.

What is the legacy of the Akkadian Empire today? Numerous things we take for granted were birthed or developed extensively during the Akkadian era. Examples include a road network connecting Agade to the farthest points of the empire and the efficient water transport on the Euphrates and Tigris Rivers. We can thank the Akkadians for the first postal system, complete with envelopes; fortunately, we now use paper instead of clay! The Akkadians encouraged a common spoken and written language that unified people from diverse cultures, similar to how English, Chinese, and Spanish serve as the lingua francas for millions of people today. Most nations of the world have a professional military—Sargon's innovation—and utilize components of the Akkadian bureaucratic administrative model.

---

[i] Foster, *The Age of Agade*, 443-44.
[ii] Lorenzo Nigro, "The Two Steles of Sargon: Iconology and Visual Propaganda at the Beginning of Royal Akkadian Relief," *Iraq* 60 (1998): 85-102. https://doi.org/10.2307/4200454.

We've really only scratched the surface of the Akkadian Empire's history. Many pieces of the puzzle that would help us fully understand this great civilization and its accomplishments are still missing. More than a quarter-million unearthed Akkadian-language cuneiform tablets need translating. Unrest in the Middle East has stymied the archaeological studies that might reveal new clues. One day, someone will discover the ruins of Agade—how exciting that will be! We can only imagine the treasure troves of historical information that will finally come to light once ancient Agade has been explored.

Part 3: The Babylonian Empire

An Enthralling Overview of Babylon and the Babylonians

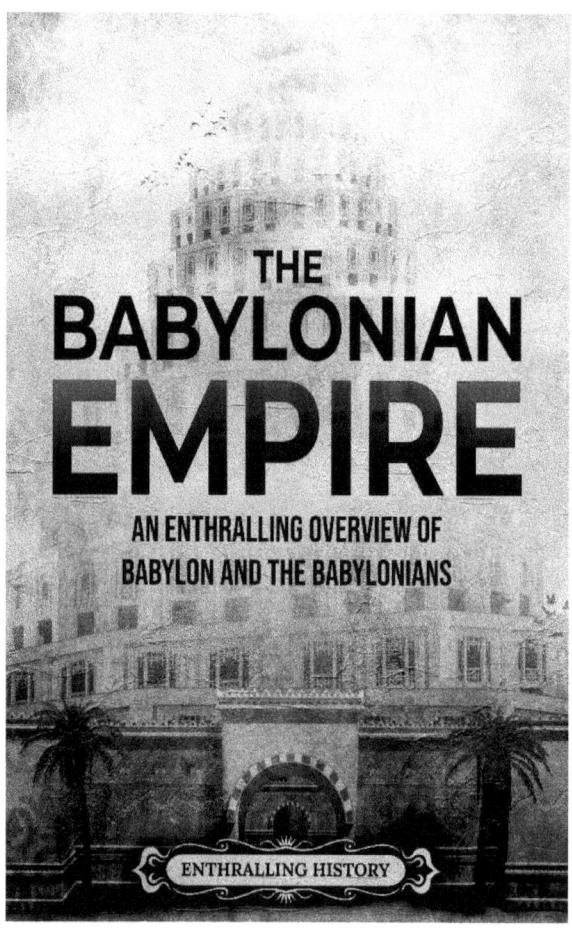

Introduction

Screams pierced the night. Within the gleaming walls of Babylon, the young king Nebuchadnezzar II lay groaning in his palace. His disturbing dream kept him from sleep, but he couldn't remember the dream. Calling his scribes, astrologers, and sorcerers, he demanded, "I must know what it means!"

"Long live the king! Tell us your dream, and we will interpret it for you."

"No!" said Nebuchadnezzar. "*You* tell *me* what I dreamed! If you can't, I'll have you torn into pieces! But if you can tell me my dream and its interpretation, I will shower you with gifts and honor."

The Chaldean astrologers looked at each other in horror. "No king on earth has ever asked such a thing! Only the gods can tell you your dream."

Furious, Nebuchadnezzar ordered the execution of all Babylon's wise scholars, astrologers, and sorcerers. The commander of the king's guard arrived at the house of Belteshazzar, one of the king's advisors, to arrest him. When Belteshazzar heard the king's order, he said, "Don't kill the wise men. Take me to the king, and I will tell him the meaning of his dream."

"Is this true?" Nebuchadnezzar asked Belteshazzar. "Can you tell me what I dreamed and interpret it?"

"God in heaven who reveals mysteries has shown you the future," Belteshazzar replied.

"In your vision, you saw a huge, shining statue of a man. The head of this frightening image was gold, its chest and arms were silver, its belly and thighs were bronze, its legs were iron, and its feet a mixture of iron and clay. Suddenly, you saw a massive boulder strike the feet of the statue, smashing them into pieces. The entire image crumbled, but the boulder grew into a magnificent mountain that covered the earth.

"Now, this is the interpretation of your dream. You are the king of kings, the head of gold. After you, an inferior kingdom will arise. Then a third kingdom of bronze will rule the earth. The fourth kingdom of iron will shatter and crush all other kingdoms. This kingdom will then be divided. As the feet of the statue were partly of iron and fired clay, it will be partly strong and partly brittle.

"The boulder that grew into a mountain covering the earth is an unshakable kingdom that will bring all other kingdoms to an end, but it will stand forever. God has told you what will happen in the future."[1]

Nebuchadnezzar nodded. It *was* his dream! He promoted Belteshazzar as ruler over the province of Babylonia and the chief of his scholarly advisors and magicians. Then he reflected on the origins of Babylon and where he would take his kingdom of gold.

While the Babylonian Empire was indisputably a formidable force on the ancient world's stage, it was much more! As a horrific drought gripped the Middle East around 2200 BCE, Semitic nomads swept into Mesopotamia, the land between the Euphrates and Tigris Rivers, seeking pasture for their flocks. They never left. Instead, these Amorite shepherds settled down, developed Babylon into a stunning city, and conquered the rest of Mesopotamia. That was only part of Babylon's metamorphosis.

After the Hittites sacked Babylon, the Kassites of mysterious origins took possession of Babylon; then, eventually, Babylonia fell under Assyrian control. Finally, the Chaldeans led Babylon into the stunning Neo-Babylonian Empire, with a rule stretching from the Persian Gulf north to Turkey and down along the entire eastern Mediterranean coastline to the Red Sea. The Chaldeans transformed Babylon into a breathtaking city, with massive walls glistening in the sun, covered with blue-glazed bricks and mosaics of dragons, bulls, and lions. A towering

---

[1] *Daniel 2*, Tanakh: Ketuvim. Jewish Virtual Library, 1997. https://www.jewishvirtuallibrary.org/the-tanakh-full-text

ziggurat rose in the city center, near the palace with its brilliant yellow and blue walls.

The Babylonians were ingenious in the sciences and mathematics. They observed the night skies, recording the movement of the planets and cataloging the constellations. They studied the Earth's rotation using mathematical models and predicted lunar and solar eclipses. The Babylonians took mathematics to astonishing heights, understanding square roots, fractions, algebra, trigonometry, and geometry and solving cubic, linear, and quadratic equations. They knew how to measure the diameter and circumference of a circle and calculated pi (π) to a value of 3.125. They used the Pythagorean theorem over a millennium before Pythagoras was born. The Babylonians were a powerhouse of innovation and scientific-mathematical development.

This book will unpack the spectacular history of Babylon and the Babylonians. What civilizations preceded them in Mesopotamia? How did Babylon rise to ascendancy? How did the Babylonian religion and worldview inform their lifestyle and achievements? What was exceptional about their renowned leaders, such as Hammurabi and Nebuchadnezzar II? How did they rise, collapse, and rise again two more times?

This history will unlock the answers to these questions and many more in a thoroughly researched, comprehensive, yet easy-to-understand narrative. Whether you are a history buff or simply curious about the Babylonian Empire, this book will bring the remarkable Babylonians to life, revealing how their story unfolded. You will gain an in-depth understanding of how Babylon left its mark on Mesopotamia's culture and history. And not just Mesopotamia, but the world!

What's the point of reading history? Learning history is fascinating: it's all about change. Examining Babylon's three-time rise and fall is truly an exploration of change. Which enterprising leaders galvanized their people into seemingly-impossible conquests? What events triggered Babylon's three cataclysmic falls? How did collaboration stimulate the explosion of mathematical and scientific knowledge? Understanding the history of change in Babylon helps us analyze how political, economic, and cultural change might happen in our own society.

Chapter 1: The Pre-Babylonian Period

What do the world's first city, first sailboats, and reptilian women statuettes have in common? These were all produced by the Neolithic-age Ubaid culture (5500–3800 BCE) that preceded the Sumerian and Akkadian civilizations. Slightly earlier than the Ubaid culture, the Samarra people settled in central and northern Mesopotamia around 6000 BCE. The Samarra and Ubaid cultures overlapped and shared innovations in pottery and simple irrigation techniques; they traded in alabaster, carnelian, copper, obsidian, and turquoise. About 3,700 years later, the city of Babylon arose approximately where the Ubaid and Samarra cultures once intersected.

The Neolithic Samarra and Ubaid were preliterate, but archaeological evidence sheds light on how these people lived. The earliest people in Mesopotamia were hunter-gatherers, hunting wild herds, harvesting fish and other food from the rivers, and gathering the wild einkorn wheat and uncultivated fruit and vegetables. Eventually, they domesticated goats, sheep, and cattle but continued a nomadic lifestyle. They either lived in tents or with no shelter at all, as nothing resembling houses appeared in the earlier Neolithic-age archaeological digs, only firepits, stone tools, and coarse pottery.

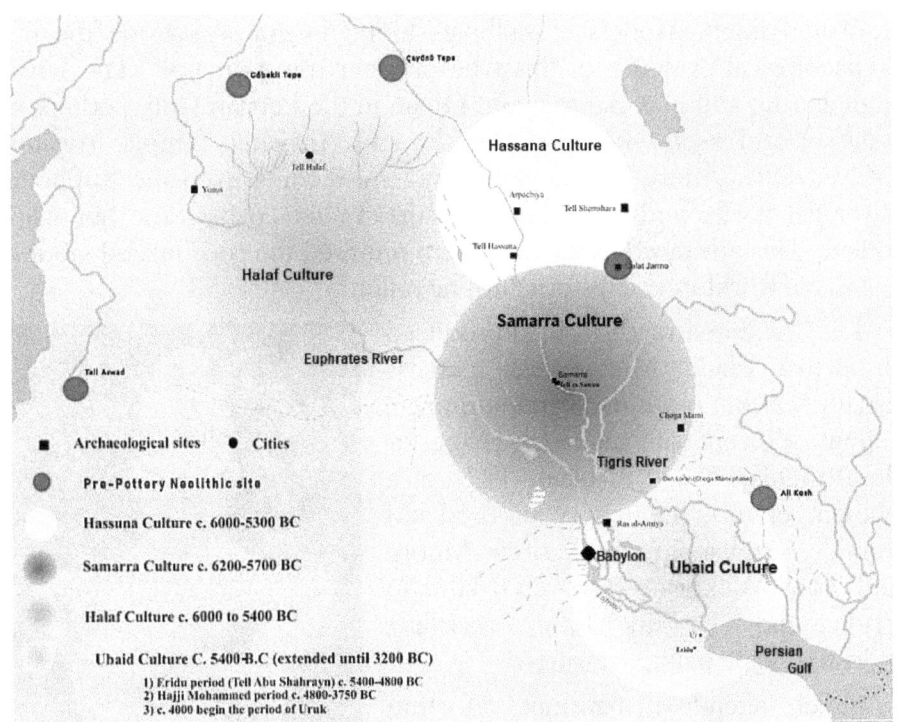

This map shows the location of the Samarra and Ubaid Cultures in the region where Babylon stood about three thousand years later.[73]

Then, around 6000 BCE, the Samarra culture emerged, with agricultural villages of clay homes; they grew barley, flax, and wheat and herded cattle, goats, and sheep. Their technology included plows, axes, sickles, clay ovens, and grinding stones. Although non-literate, they used one-inch stamp seals with a carved stone picture that left a signature when pressed into clay. They were most famous for their distinctive pottery, featuring a cream slip and reddish designs.

The Ubaid culture appeared about five centuries later than the Samarra in southern Mesopotamia, the region that would later be Sumer. They first lived in reed-thatched homes but later built clay-brick or stone houses and were the original settlers of the ancient cities of Eridu, Ur, and Uruk. Eridu (perhaps the world's oldest city) and Ur once overlooked the Persian Gulf, but over the millennia, the Gulf filled with silt from the Euphrates and Tigris Rivers, and global cooling caused the sea level to lower, leaving these cities stranded in a desert wasteland.

The Ubaid had a relatively sophisticated culture: they used sailboats for fishing and transportation, baked bread in clay-brick ovens, and wove wool and linen. Models of sailboats found in graves provide the first archaeological evidence of this type of water transportation. The Ubaid traded as far south as Bahrain and Oman in the Persian Gulf, perhaps by sailboat, and as far north as Turkey and Armenia. Simple irrigation evolved into a more intricate canal system, feeding from the Euphrates River tributaries and Lake Hammar (freshwater at that time but saline today).[i] This advanced irrigation system required the coordinated labor of a sizeable workforce: a historic turning point.

Like the Samarra, the Ubaid produced distinctive Hadji Muhammed pottery, usually buff but occasionally pink, orange, yellow, or green, with geometric shapes or floral motifs painted in black. Fired at a hot temperature, the pottery was hard and durable. Archaeologists Andrew Moore and Tony Wilkinson discovered kilns in Eridu and Ur in 1990, revealing industrial-scale manufacturing.[ii]

Small alien-like figurines of thin women with broad shoulders and reptilian faces discovered in adult graves were even more intriguing. They weren't found in the simple Ubaid temple structures, and whether they had religious meaning is a mystery. Evidence exists of infant skull-binding in Mesopotamia, Turkey, and Iran to produce elongated heads;[iii] however, that wouldn't explain the long, slanted eyes.

The significance of the reptile-woman figurines, like this one nursing a baby, is unclear.[iv]

---

[i] Carrie Hritz, et al., "Revisiting the Sealands: Report of Preliminary Ground Reconnaissance in the Hammar District, Dhi Qar and Basra Governorates, Iraq," *Iraq* 74 (2012): 37-49. http://www.jstor.org/stable/23349778.

[ii] A. M. T. Moore, "Pottery Kiln Sites at al 'Ubaid and Eridu," *Iraq* 64 (2002): 69-77. https://doi.org/10.2307/4200519

[iii] A. Deams and K. Croucher, "Artificial Cranial Modification in Prehistoric Iran: Evidence from Crania and Figurines," *Iranica Antiqua* 42 (2007):1-21.

What happened to the Ubaid culture? A massive flood covered Ur around 3800 BCE, leaving an eleven-foot silt layer. The Ubaid abandoned Eridu about the same time, as global cooling and increased aridity caused desertification, punishing sandstorms, and freshwater depletion. The Ubaid city of Uruk continued to flourish on the Euphrates' eastern shores and eventually segued into a Sumerian city. Some scholars theorize that the original Sumerians were the remnant of the Ubaid culture.

Whether or not the Sumerians were the Ubaid remnant or their conquerors, they took control of southern Mesopotamia (Sumer) around 4000 BCE. This was when Uruk experienced an explosion of population growth and incredible innovation. They spoke a non-Semitic language isolate, unrelated to any other language, and called themselves the "black-haired people."

After a flood completely submerged Ur, the Sumerians built a city on the ruins of the former Ubaid town. The new Ur grew into a powerful and fabulously wealthy city, as evidenced by the "death pit": the grave of a queen buried with phenomenal treasure and over a hundred attendants who were killed to accompany her into the afterlife. The Sumerians also rebuilt Eridu by 2900 BCE, and the new city featured a palace about the size of a football field.

Kish was another one-time Ubaid settlement that the Sumerians later occupied about 3100 BCE. Located close to the Tigris, east of where Babylon would later rise, Kish was the first city to hold "kingship," or regional dominance, after the Great Flood, according to the *Sumerian King List*.[i] This document, dating back to at least 2100 BCE, chronicled the kings of southern and central Mesopotamia before and after the "flood swept over." The earliest part of the *King List* is probably mythical, but archaeological and literary evidence supports many of the later kings. In addition to Uruk, Ur, Eridu, and Kish, about eight other large city-states sprang up in Sumer.

---

[i] *Sumerian King List,* trans. Jean-Vincent Scheil, Stephen Langdon, and Thorkild Jacobsen. Livius. https://www.livius.org/sources/content/anet/266-the-sumerian-king-list/#Translation

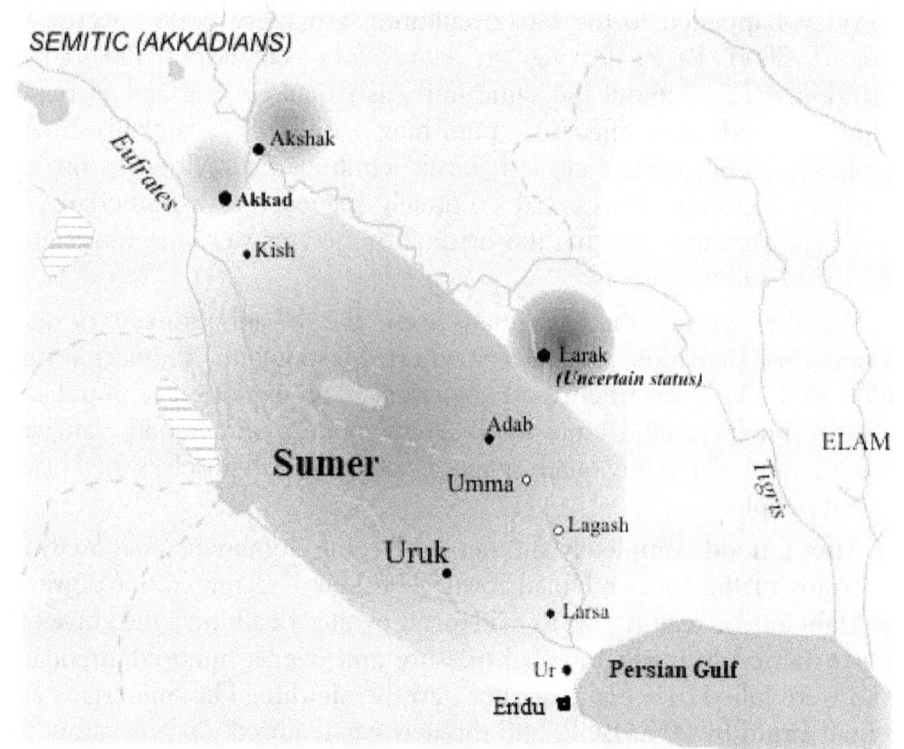

This map shows Sumer's primary cities just before the Akkadian Empire.[75]

The Sumerians were the first to build thick high walls around their cities to protect them from invaders. A city-state was the walled city itself surrounded by agricultural fields, pastures for herds, and small villages and towns. Each city-state was politically independent of the others and self-contained: able to support its population on what it could locally grow or harvest. Every so often, one city would rise to "kingship," which meant some sort of dominance over the other city-states.

The Sumerians exhibited unprecedented zeal for inventing new things, experiencing incredible breakthroughs in all aspects of civilization. By 3500 BCE, they had developed the world's first writing system, a technique using pictographs (simple drawings) scratched into soft clay, which would harden to form a durable tablet. The pictographs gradually became more stylized into cuneiform, a technique in which the end of a reed was pressed into clay to make wedge-shaped marks. This new written language provided a fascinating insight into the Mesopotamian culture once linguists figured out how to read it! Of course, a writing system required the first schools; it took twelve years to reach a scribe's proficiency level in reading and writing.

The Ubaid and Samarra used basic irrigation, but the Sumerians developed a highly sophisticated canal system for watering their crops and a dike system to control annual flooding. Despite southern Mesopotamia's arid climate, the Sumerians' advanced hydraulic engineering enabled them to produce a surplus of crops, which they could use in trade. Because they depended on the river system rather than rain for their crops, the Sumerians could survive drought conditions. They even thrived through the horrific drought that began around 2200 BCE, which nearly decimated northern Mesopotamia.

The Sumerians were the first to build multistory palaces and massive terraced ziggurats that towered over the city as part of their temple system. By 3300 BCE, they blended copper and tin to make bronze, which enabled them to produce stronger weapons and tools. The royal tomb in Ur displayed the Sumerians' astute knowledge of metallurgy, with stunning silver-plated lyres and gold goblets, daggers, helmets, and headdresses. Their colorful murals and mosaics depicted exceptionally realistic figures.

The Samarra and Ubaid had used stamp seals, but the Sumerians took this a step further by developing cylinder seals. These four-inch stone cylinders had pictures carved on them, so when rolled in damp clay, a picture would emerge, representing its owner's "signature." Hundreds of cylinder seals have survived, and even today, they can be rolled in clay to create an impression. They are invaluable for displaying the level of artistry of that age and revealing aspects of Sumerian history and culture.

This ancient lapis lazuli cylinder seal (left) produced the clay impression (right), a mythical scene of muscular heroes in hand-to-hand combat with a lion and gazelle. On each side is an example of cuneiform writing.[76]

The Sumerians invented the first transportation wheel by 3750 BCE: an ancient seal shows two men pulled in a wheeled cart by a donkey. These earliest wheels were solid wood with a hole in the middle for an axle. Basic carts quickly developed into four-wheeled chariots, pictured in the *Standard of Ur* mosaic around 2600 BCE. A large ass called an onager pulled the chariots, which were cumbersome to steer.

The Sumerians used the sexagesimal counting system, counting by sixty (60, 120, 180, etc.) rather than tens as we do. They could count up to sixty using both hands. They would count the three knuckles of each finger on one hand (excluding the thumb), which took them up to twelve. When they reached twelve, they would hold up one finger of the other hand. Once all four fingers and thumbs were held up, they reached sixty. The Sumerians also developed the sixty-minute hour and sixty-second minute and divided the day and night into twelve hours each.

The year 2334 BCE was a turning point in Mesopotamian history when the Akkadians formed the world's first multinational empire. Who were the Akkadians who led Mesopotamia's Golden Age? They were a Semitic tribe that migrated from the Arabian Peninsula into northern and central Mesopotamia by 2700 BCE, but perhaps centuries earlier: the earliest kings of Kish had Semitic names. They gradually spread into southern Mesopotamia, assimilating the Sumerian culture. Many Sumerians and Akkadians were likely bilingual, and the Akkadians adapted the cuneiform script to their own language.

The Akkadians and Sumerians shared many of the same gods, including the sun god Utu (Akkadian Shamash), the moon god Nanna (Akkadian Sin), and Inanna, the goddess of war and sexuality (Akkadian Ishtar). Later, the Babylonians would worship these gods and others of the traditional Mesopotamian pantheon. Although the Akkadians and Sumerians had different languages and ethnicities, their lifestyles were similar. They lived in flat-roofed, mud-brick homes, and most of the population labored as farmers, herders, or in the construction and maintenance of irrigation systems.

The Akkadians exploded into power under the leadership of Sargon, a man of puzzling and humble origins. Supposedly the son of a priestess who abandoned him as a newborn, a gardener rescued him from the river and raised him as his son in Kish. The king of Kish suddenly and inexplicably elevated Sargon to be his cupbearer but almost immediately began to suspect Sargon of treason and attempted to kill him. Sargon escaped the palace, gathered support, and usurped Kish's throne.

This striking copper sculpture is either Sargon or one of his descendants.[77]

Sargon's next step was to take on the mighty King Lugal-zage-si, who had already conquered all of southern Sumer. With lightning speed, the enterprising Sargon defeated the fearsome Lugal-zage-si and triumphed over Sumer's cities. Sargon then turned to northern Mesopotamia and beyond, extending the world's first empire into Syria, Turkey, Lebanon, Canaan (Israel), and the lands east of the Euphrates and west of the Tigris. Next, he turned southeast to conquer Elam (Iran). The massive swathe of territory conquered by the Akkadians opened up trade routes, pouring fabulous wealth into Agade (the capital of Akkad).

Sargon's younger son Rimush assumed the throne at his death and spent most of his years mercilessly putting down rebellions that had sprung up in Sumer. He flattened cities, killed most of southern Sumer's population, and relocated the remnant to slavery or exile. Rimush reigned only nine years before his own courtiers turned against him, beating him to death with their cylinder seals.

After Rimush's assassination, his older brother Manishtushu ascended the throne and focused on consolidating more foreign lands, bringing the entire Persian Gulf under his power. He also expanded his father's trade routes up the Tigris River to its headwaters in the Taurus Mountains. After reigning for fifteen years, Manishtushu was likewise assassinated by his men, and the throne went to his son, Naram-Sin.

Naram-Sin was a ruthless conqueror who supposedly offended the gods.[78]

Naram-Sin was another brilliant conqueror, like his grandfather Sargon, expanding the empire to its broadest scope. And yet, in popular opinion, his pride brought about the empire's eventual fall. He accepted his people's worship as a god, even building a temple for himself. Not long after, Mesopotamia was struck by the 4.2 kiloyear BP aridification event (2200 to 2000 BCE), with fifty percent less rainfall in an already semi-arid land. Northern Mesopotamia's rain-dependent agriculture couldn't survive, leading to mass starvation and an exodus south to Sumer, where advanced irrigation techniques had enabled the population to endure.[i]

To add insult to injury, the barbarian Gutian tribes from the Zagros Mountains of Elam (Iran) swept into Mesopotamia with guerilla attacks on cities, stripping the fields bare of any produce left by the drought, releasing domestic animals from their pens, and devastating the trade routes. People died of starvation with no one to bury them. The mighty Akkadian Empire fell after only a century and a half of power.

The Akkadian Empire's fall and the population shift from the drought launched Sumer's rise to power again, led by the city of Ur, in what is known as the Neo-Sumerian Empire or the Third Dynasty of Ur. It was short-lived, like the Akkadian Empire, lasting only about a century. It was renowned for its founder, Ur-Nammu, who wrote one of the world's first known law codes. In this era, Ur was also the home of the patriarch Terah, whose son Abraham later migrated to Canaan to establish the Israelite nation.

Utu-hengal, king of Uruk, finally drove the Gutians out of Mesopotamia. Ur-Nammu, who had served as a general under him, rose to power at his death, ushering in Ur's Third Dynasty (2112-2004 BCE). Ur-Nammu defeated a rival king in Lagash and united all Sumer, restoring the Sumerian language, which had almost died out. He built the Great Ziggurat of Ur and numerous other temple complexes. His written law code, preserved until today on cuneiform tablets, dealt with kidnapping, murder, premarital sex, slave rights, sorcery, and more.

Under Ur-Nammu, Ur grew to about sixty-five thousand people, the world's largest city of its day and an important trade center on the Persian Gulf and even with India. After he died, his son Shulgi claimed to have run one hundred miles in one day: from Nippur to Ur. Whether or not that really happened, Shulgi did build a 155-mile-long wall to keep the Amorite herders who had been migrating in since the great drought out of Sumer.

The wall may have kept the Amorites at bay, but the Elamites invaded Sumer from the southwest, going around the wall's eastern end. They sacked Ur and captured Ibbi-Sin, the last king of the Neo-Sumerian

---

[i] Harvey Weiss, *Megadrought and Collapse* (New York: Oxford University Press, 2017), 94-183.

dynasty, ending Ur's last dynasty. The Elamites ruled Ur and most of Sumer for the next two decades. Although Ur never again rose to dominate the political scene, it remained a wealthy, strategically-located trade city for another thousand years.

Chapter 2: The First Babylonians

When was Babylon founded? And who first built the city? The establishment of what would one day be the world's largest city is shrouded in mystery. Two curious passages about Sargon the Great and Babylon are found in the *Chronicle of Early Kings* (written around 1500 BCE) and the *Weidner Chronicle* (written around 1800 BCE). The *Chronicle of Early Kings* says this about Sargon in his old age:

> "He dug up the dirt of the pit of Babylon and made a counterpart of Babylon next to Agade. Because [of] the wrong he had done, the great lord Marduk became angry and wiped out his family by famine. From east to west, the subjects rebelled against him, and Marduk afflicted him with insomnia."[i]

The *Weidner Chronicle* expounded on the same theme of Sargon digging up Babylon (brackets and ellipses indicate damage to the tablet, making it unreadable):

> "Ur-Zababa ordered Sargon, his cupbearer, to change the wine libations of Esagila. Sargon did not change but was careful to offer [...] quickly to Esagila. Marduk, the king of the world, favored him and gave him the rule of the four corners of the world. He took care of Esagila. Everyone who sat on a throne brought his tribute to Babylon. Yet he ignored the

---

[i] *Chronicle of Early Kings (ABC 20)*, Livius. https://www.livius.org/sources/content/mesopotamian-chronicles-content/abc-20-chronicle-of-early-kings

command Bêl had given him. He dug soil from its pit, and in front of Akkad he built a city which he named Babylon. Enlil changed the order he had given, and from east to west, people opposed him. He could not sleep. Naram-Sin destroyed the people of Babylon, so twice Marduk summoned the forces of Gutium against him."[i]

Ur-Zababa was the king of Kish, under whom Sargon served as a cupbearer. The Esagila was a temple complex in Babylon, which wasn't built until centuries after Sargon, so that part of the chronicle is incorrect. These two passages make it sound as if Babylon existed even before Sargon became a mighty king (possible, but it would have been a small town) and that its temple complex was already of importance (unlikely). Apparently, Ur-Zababa's command to change the wine libations to the temple was sacrilege, and by refusing to do so, Sargon received the favor of Marduk, god of Babylon (also known as Bêl). However, Marduk was only a minor "city" god of Babylon initially, with no influence over Kish until much later.

Both accounts say Sargon "dug soil" from Babylon's pit, whatever that means, and then built a second Babylon in front of Agade (Akkad), the capital of the Akkadian Empire. Did digging soil imply that Babylon had been demolished? Or did Sargon simply take some of the soil from the sacred city? The meaning is unclear, but somehow, Sargon incurred the wrath of Enlil: the king-making god. Both passages say that Sargon suffered insomnia as a result of his sin.

The *Weidner Chronicle* says that Sargon's grandson Naram-Sin destroyed Babylon's people and received two Gutium invasions as punishment. Babylon was definitely in existence in the Akkadian Empire era, as a cuneiform tablet dating to Sargon's time mentions the city. Also, the year records of Naram-Sin's son Shar-kali-si say that he laid the foundations of the temples of the goddess Annunitum and the god Aba in Babylon in his eleventh year. In those ancient times, the Mesopotamians did not name or number their years; instead, they marked the years by identifying something the king did in that year.

The Babylonians themselves did not seem to have a story regarding Babylon's founding, but the Greeks had several versions of Babylon's

---

[i] *Weidner Chronicle (ABC 19)*, Livius. https://www.livius.org/sources/content/mesopotamian-chronicles-content/abc-19-weidner-chronicle

establishment on the Euphrates, just south of today's Baghdad. The 5th-century BCE Greek physician Ctesias said Queen Semiramis built Babylon. But Semiramis was an Assyrian queen, reigning from 811 to 806 BCE, over 1,400 years after Babylon was definitely in existence. The Greek historian Hecataeus said Babylon was an Egyptian colony founded by Belos (son of Poseidon and Libya). Abydenus and Diodorus Siculus said Belos built it, but Belos (Belus) was Mesopotamian, not Egyptian.[i] Diodorus even gave a date for Babylon's founding, 2286 BCE, and said Belus ruled there for fifty-five years. His date is plausible, as it would be toward the end of Sargon's reign. The name Belus or Belos is associated with the Babylonian chief god Marduk. However, the word "Bel" or "Baal" in Semitic languages simply means "lord."

This figure of an Amorite worshiper is from Mari in Syria, circa 2500 BCE.[79]

The Hebrew *Torah* said that Nimrod, a descendant of Cush, established his kingdom in Sumer with Babylon, Akkad, Uruk, and Calneh. Then in Assyria, he built Nineveh, Rehoboth Ir, Calah, and Resen.[ii] Several scholars believe Nimrod was Sargon the Great, and thus Sargon built Babylon. This would work chronologically and geographically. One Akkadian document listed Babylon as being a border of the land of Akkad (in existence during the Akkadian Empire), and records stated Sargon's great-grandson built temples there.

While the Akkadian Empire was in its death throes, Amorite herders speaking a Northwest Semitic dialect surged into central and southern Mesopotamia from Syria, desperate for grassland for their flocks. The Sumerians promptly built a 110-mile wall to keep them out of

---

[i] Menko Vlaardingerbroek, "The Founding of Nineveh and Babylon in Greek Historiography." *Iraq* 66 (2004): 235. https://doi.org/10.2307/4200577

[ii] *Genesis 10:10-12,* Tanakh: Torah, Book of Bereishit.

the south, but the Amorites settled along the Euphrates River delta and made Babylon their home around 1984 BCE. These Amorites worshiped a god of the mountains named Amurru or Belu Sadi. The Sumerians described the Amorites as "the powerful south wind who from the remote past have not known cities."[i]

An ancient Sumerian poem called the *Marriage of Martu* tells the story of a young Amorite man settling in a city named Inab and the discrimination he faced.[ii] Martu lived in the city but complained to his parents about the rations for the temple. The single men only had to devote a single ration to the temple, the married men gave a double ration, and the men with children gave a triple ration. However, Martu had to provide a triple ration, despite not having a wife or any children.

Martu decided if he had to pay the temple tax of a married man with children, he might as well be married. He went home to his mother and asked her to find him a wife. His mother told him he needed to choose a wife for himself, but she encouraged him to get married because his wife could help her with all the housework. At that time, Inab had a festival, and Martu and his young single friends went to enjoy the fun.

The god Numucda took part in the festival and brought his beautiful wife Namrat and his beloved daughter Adjar-kidug. As the bronze drums rumbled, the strong champions competed in wrestling matches, and the city was full of onlookers. Martu competed in the wrestling match, and the people of the city kept looking for strong fighters to challenge him, but all the most muscular men fell before Martu. Full of awe, Numucda offered Martu a reward of silver, but Martu turned it down. He offered jewels, but Martu would not accept them. "I would rather marry your daughter Adjar-kidug."

Numucda told Martu he had to bring milk cows and their calves and ewes with their lambs as a bride price, and then Numucda would give Martu his daughter. But Martu exceeded Numucda's request. He brought golden neck rings for Inab's elders and golden shawls for the old women. He even brought gifts for the slaves. While the marriage negotiations were going on, Adjar-kidug's girlfriend confronted her. Did she really want to marry this uncouth young man? She recounted all the things wrong with

---

[i] *Year Names of Ibbi-Suen*, CDLI Wiki, University of Oxford. https://cdli.ox.ac.uk/wiki/doku.php?id=year_names_ibbi-suen

[ii] *Marriage of Martu* (The Electronic Text Corpus of Sumerian Literature, Oxford: University of Oxford). https://etcsl.orinst.ox.ac.uk/section1/tr171.htm

Amorite men:

> "Their hands are destructive, and they have monkey features. He eats food forbidden by Nanna and shows no reverence. These Amorites are always roaming about; they have confused ideas and only create a disturbance. He's dressed in leather and lives in a tent, exposed to the wind and rain. He doesn't know how to recite prayers or bend the knee. He has no house, and he eats raw flesh! My girlfriend, why do you want to marry Martu?"

But the princess was adamant: "I will marry Martu!"

Ibbi-Sin, the last king of Ur's Third Dynasty, is greeted by a goddess.[80]

While the Amorites were infiltrating Mesopotamia and becoming more assertive, the Third Dynasty of Ur was beginning to crumble in the south. When the Third Dynasty of Ur was in power, governors appointed by Ur ruled Babylon, and the city paid taxes to Ur. Ibbi-Sin was the last king of Ur's Third Dynasty, and during his reign, the Sumerian cities under his control fell away, leaving only Ur. Then the Elamites attacked, navigating around the eastern end of the Amorite-repelling wall. They captured Ibbi-Sin, hauled him in fetters back to Elam, and ruled Ur for twenty-one years.

In a twist of irony, Ur's rescuers turned out to be the very people they had built a 110-mile wall to keep out. The Dynasty of Isin's Amorite king Ishbi-Erra, who was from Mari in Syria, drove out the Elamites and rebuilt Ur. His son and successor Shu-Ilishu retrieved the stolen image of the moon-god Nanna from Elam, resettling him in his temple in Ur. Shu-Ilishu quickly adopted the Sumerian culture and their gods and even fought more recent Amorite immigrants. He called himself "King of Ur," "King of Sumer and Akkad," and "Beloved of the gods Anu, Enlil, and Nanna."

The high-powered Amorite-Isin dynasty ruled part of Sumer for several generations, while more Amorite immigrants came seeking pasture for their herds. They spread throughout Sumer, maintaining a semi-nomadic herding lifestyle at first but gradually becoming more sedentary. The fifth Isin king, Lipit-Ishtar, wrote a law code over a century before the famous *Code of Hammurabi.*

But misfortune will find you, even if you try to hide! That's what one Isin king discovered, too late, when Isin's astrologers predicted an eclipse, which they thought was an omen that the king would die. King Erra-Immiti put his gardener Enlil-bani on his throne and placed his tiara on his head, hoping that the curse would fall on the gardener instead. However, the omen found the true king while he was hiding out in a corner of the palace eating porridge, and he died. The gardener kept the throne and crown and ruled for twenty-four years, beginning a new dynasty. Enlil-bani, the gardener king, wrote that he removed the heavy yoke from the people, reduced the barley tax, and kept the palace livestock from running amuck in the people's cultivated fields.

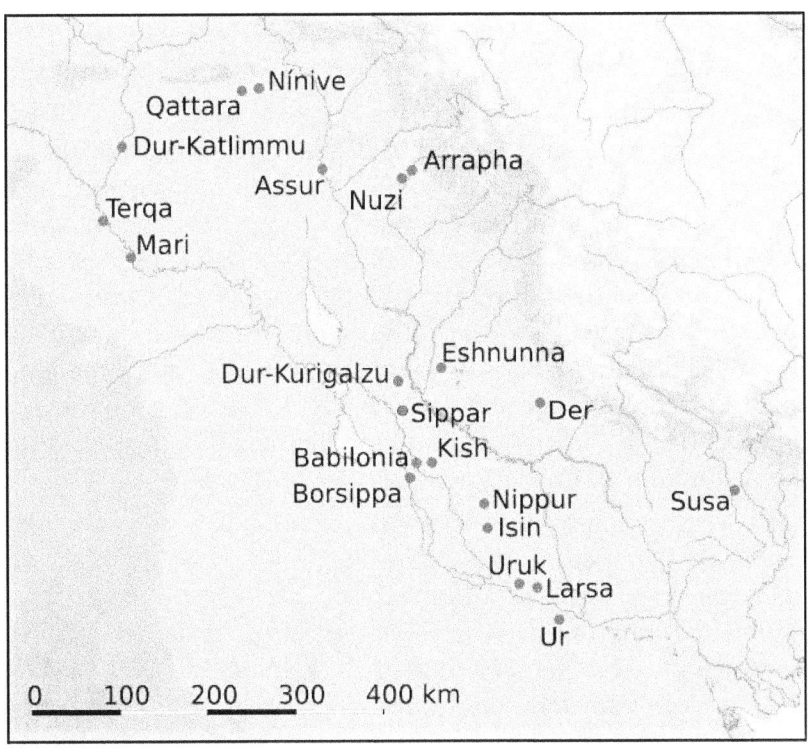

This map shows Mesopotamia's significant cities during Babylon's earliest years.[81]

By the time the gardener king was ruling Isin, the town of Babylon, called Babil by the Sumerians and Bab-ilim in Akkadian, was rising to prominence. In 1897 BCE, many of the Amorites came under the leadership of a dynamic tribal leader named Sumu-Abum (Su-abu), considered the first king of Babylon's First Dynasty. Sumu-Abum conquered Kish, Dilbat, and Elip, began the construction of a wall around Babylon, and erected temples. He also built walls for his new cities of Kish and Dilbat. Sumu-Abum worshiped a local god named Marduk or Amar, the god of thunderstorms who would become the god of domination, power, sex, and war. Marduk replaced the Sumerian god Enlil as the chief Amorite deity.

An intriguing letter written to Sumu-Abum refers to a journey of Ishtar (Annunitum) to visit Marduk's temple in Babylon. The writer wanted to carry the goddess' statue to Babylon so that Ishtar could consult with Marduk on a particular matter. The writer asked Sumu-Abum's permission to bring the goddess' statue, saying he would set off as soon as he heard from the king. He also mentioned he was concerned for the goddess' temper during the journey (Ishtar was known as a hothead).[i]

Sumu-Abum freed the Babylonians from the overlordship of Kazallu (Kassala) on the Euphrates River, which had experienced horrific history in the Akkadian Empire. Kassala had rebelled, and Sargon the Great marched to meet the insurgents. Sargon was merciless, flattening the city and even cutting down all the trees, so there was no place "for a bird to rest." When Sargon's son Rimush was king, Kassala's citizens rebuilt their city but then dared to challenge Rimush. Rimush was inhumanly cruel, killing twelve thousand Kassala citizens, enslaving five thousand, and leveling the city to the ground once again. The irrepressible people of Kassala had rebuilt their city a third time, holding the upper hand in the region until Sumu-Abum became the leader of Babylon.

Sumu-Abum's conquest of Kassala appears to be a joint effort of Babylon and Isin, as records of Erra-Immiti, the ill-omened king of Isin who died eating porridge, says he conquered Kassala at approximately the same time. Sumu-Abum triumphantly overpowered Kassala, but the city of Kish, which he had conquered, rose in rebellion, and its leader Manana forced Sumu-Abum into exile.

Sumu-Abum's vigorous successor, Sumu-la-El, ruled from 1880 to 1845 BCE. He had served as a lieutenant under Sumu-Abum and was likely his son. He sacked Kish and Kassala

This bust is probably an earlier Amorite king before Hammurabi.[82]

(again) and brought other Amorite chieftains under his command. He built defensive fortresses around the Babylonian region, completed the great city wall around Babylon his father had started, and gained temporary control of Nippur. He dug an irrigation canal called Utu-hegal and built or deepened several other canals. He erected a temple to Adad and a magnificent throne for Marduk overlaid with silver and gold.

---

[i] Rients de Boer, "Beginnings of Old Babylonian Babylon: Sumu-Abum and Sumu-La-El," *Free University of Amsterdam,* American Schools of Oriental Research, 62. https://www.jstor.org/journal/jcunestud

Sumu-la-El had a rugged ally in Uruk, whose kings had Amorite names in this era. One of his daughters, Sallurtum, married Sîn-kāšid of Uruk, "King of the Amnānum" (an Amorite tribe).[i] Sumu-la-El consolidated the northern Babylonian cities into one unified Amorite state that presented an intimidating challenge to kingdoms like Larsa or Eshnunna. He replaced the local kings with Amorite leaders loyal to him. Sumu-la-El led the "Amorite Assembly" of tribal elders loyal to him, who considered him their chieftain.

Sumu-la-El's son Sabum ruled Babylon for at least fourteen years. He was the first to build the Esagila temple to Marduk, which housed the statue of the god surrounded by idols of the cities that had fallen to Babylon. The Esagila, the "house that rises its head," was the paramount temple complex in a city considered sacred to all Babylonians, even all of Mesopotamia. He was succeeded by Apil-Sin, who ruled for seventeen years.

The industrious Apil-Sin erected a magnificent new wall for Babylon, gleaming with brilliant blue lapis lazuli stones. Like his predecessors, he dug new irrigation canals and enhanced the ones already there. After the great drought that destroyed the Akkadian Empire, the Babylonians realized the urgency of having an excellent irrigation system. Apil-Sin constructed a stupendous temple to Inanna (Ishtar) in Babylon and built or restored other temples in the city.

Apil-sin's aggressive son Sin-muballit served nineteen years as king, contending triumphantly against Larsa and taking the city of Isin captive. He relentlessly extended Babylonia's borders by vanquishing (or holding) Borsippa, Dilbat, Kassala, Kish, and Sippar. He grew in power, building up the towns and cities of south-central Mesopotamia, which had come under Babylon's rule; however, he fell ill and abdicated his throne to his famous son Hammurabi.

Most kings never see their son's accomplishments, but Sin-muballit lived through part of his son's reign. Did he live to see Hammurabi unite almost all Mesopotamia under his authority? Did he have any recommendations for his son's law code? Did he ever envision his son would be esteemed as a model ruler throughout Middle Eastern history? If he lived long enough to see just a fraction of his son's achievements, Sin-Muballit must have been extraordinarily proud.

---

[i] de Boer, "Beginnings of Old Babylonian Babylon," 67-8.

Chapter 3: The Rise of Babylon

Revered as a god in his lifetime, the exceptional conqueror and lawgiver Hammurabi elevated the modest city-state of Babylonia to astounding heights. When he ascended the throne in 1792 BCE (middle chronology), Babylon lay surrounded by four fierce kingdoms that threatened its very existence. Ancient Elam to the east, a prosperous and vigorous two-thousand-year-old kingdom located in present-day Iran, had overrun southern Sumer. Assyria, to the north, was building an immense empire that encompassed Syria, Lebanon, and Canaan and was pressing into central Mesopotamia. The ancient Sumerian city-state of Larsa guarded the southern river delta, and the Sumerian-Akkadian city-state of Eshnunna on Babylonia's northwest border controlled the upper Tigris River.

Hammurabi's father, Sin-Muballit, had already begun expanding Babylonia, bringing Kish, Sippar, and Borsippa under Babylonian jurisdiction. Hammurabi would have been relatively young when he ascended the throne, perhaps a teenager, as he ruled for forty-three years. Following in his ambitious father's footsteps, Hammurabi advanced and expanded Babylon into a thriving kingdom that swallowed up the competing kingdoms, transforming Babylon into the master of Mesopotamia.

As the sixth Amorite king to rule Babylon, Hammurabi's extraordinary reign metamorphized Babylon into one of the most dynamic and influential kingdoms in the Middle East. His first challenge arose when the Elamites of the Zagros Mountains poured into central

Mesopotamia, trouncing Babylon's neighbor Eshnunna and savagely enveloping other cities under their dominion.

This figurine of an Amorite worshipper of Amurru is from Larsa.[83]

The Elamites attempted to destabilize the region further by instigating conflict between Babylon and Larsa. Hammurabi instead allied with Larsa, and the two cities vowed to fight Elam together. However, when the time came to go to war, the Babylonians contributed the lion's share of military men, while Larsa's king held back. Although he thrashed the Elamites without much support from Larsa, Hammurabi was annoyed by Larsa's reluctance to fight.

Once he drove out the Elamites from Mesopotamia, Hammurabi subjugated Larsa by damming the Euphrates, then suddenly releasing it, covering Larsa with an epic flood. Victory over Larsa gave him mastery over Sumer, including Ur, Uruk, Isin, and Eridu, while he already held Kish, Sippar, and other Sumerian cities as his father's legacy. His triumph spelled the end of the Sumerians' sovereignty in southern Mesopotamia. The Akkadian kings had decimated the Sumerian population, but Sumer had risen to strength in the Third Dynasty of Ur. But now, the Elamite invasion and the Amorite takeover brought this revolutionary civilization to its knees. Its spoken language died out, except in religious, ceremonial, and scientific contexts.

Hammurabi had joined forces with his ancestral Amorite relatives in Syria, the Mari and Yamhad dynasties; together, they crushed Elam and annexed Sumer. However, the Mari treacherously formed a coalition army with Eshnunna against Babylon, attempting to restrict Babylon's power in the north. The attempt failed: Eshnunna fell to Hammurabi's forces, and then the Tigris River flooded, covering the city.

Once he overpowered Eshnunna, Hammurabi took his revenge against Mari. Although the people were his ancient kinsmen, he not only conquered the city but utterly obliterated it. He usually spared most of his conquered cities and even improved them once he held control, but he flattened Mari. Perhaps it was outrage at their betrayal, or he didn't want the luxurious Mari to outshine Babylon.

Next, Hammurabi turned his attention toward Assyria. Like the Akkadians and the Amorites, the Semitic-speaking Assyrians were once pastoral herders, living in tents in northern Mesopotamia but eventually becoming city-dwellers. They had fallen under Akkadian rule; when that empire crumbled, the independent Old Assyrian Empire rose to dominance in northern Mesopotamia under the powerful King Puzur-Ashur I. The usurper Shamshi-Adad expanded the Assyrian territory into northern Mesopotamia and part of today's Turkey. His son Ishme-Dagan engaged in a protracted war with Babylonia.

Although Assyria and Babylon fiercely vied for the upper hand, Hammurabi finally triumphed. He dethroned Ishme-Dagan and forced his successor Mut-Ashkur to acknowledge Babylon's overlordship;

Hammurabi allowed Mut-Ashkur to rule Assyria as a vassal king as long as he faithfully paid tribute to Babylon. Hammurabi extended his rule north into Anatolia (Turkey) and west into most of the Levant (Syria, Lebanon, and Canaan). Unlike the Akkadians, once Hammurabi initially conquered all of Mesopotamia, he maintained his control, with no significant uprisings in his lifetime.

With Mesopotamia and even part of Anatolia and the Levant conquered, Hammurabi turned to the west. The Elamites, Lullubi, and Gutians of Iran's Zagros Mountains had been persistent threats to Mesopotamia for over a century, and now the Kassites were also rising as a menacing power in the west. Hammurabi invaded Iran, subduing all of the problematic tribes.

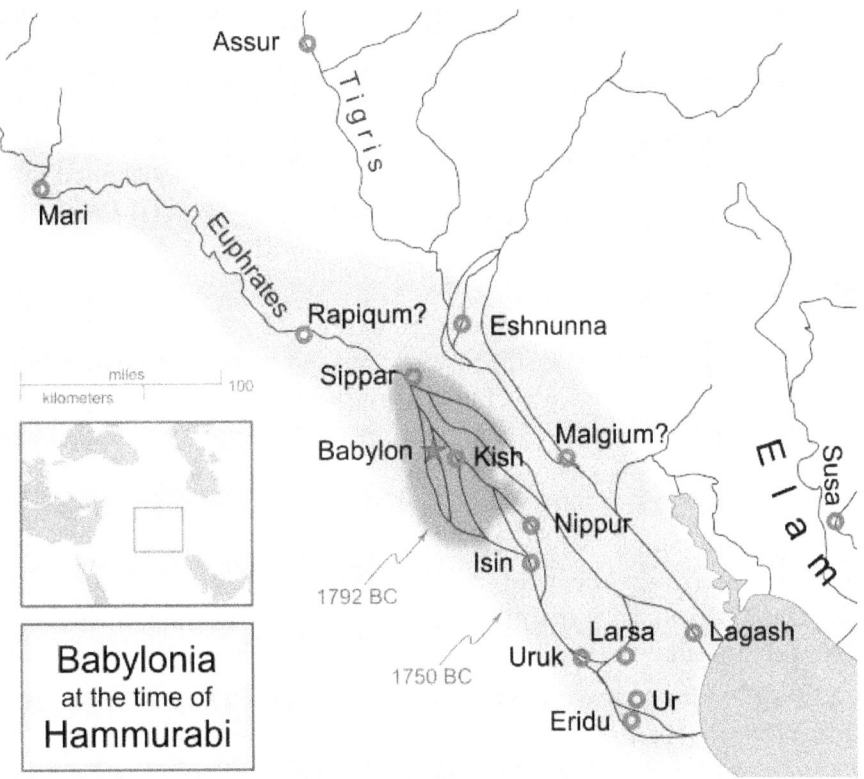

The star shows the location of Babylon. The dark shading is where the region of Babylonia was, and the light shading is the extent of the Babylonian Empire under Hammurabi, stretching from the Persian Gulf up through Syria.[84]

Although Hammurabi was a forceful conqueror, he seemed genuinely concerned for the welfare of his realm's people, with the notable exception of Mari. He was fortunate to begin his reign in a relatively peaceful era so he could focus on ambitious building projects, transforming Babylon into a dazzling city with a well-ordered, streamlined bureaucracy and strong central government.

He raised the city's walls to even higher heights and enlarged and beautified the temples. Hammurabi was a thoroughly involved leader, personally supervising flood management, changing a problematic calendar, and even overseeing the care of the city's massive livestock herds. A vast collection of his letters and administrative accounts have survived on clay tablets and portray a king engrossed in building canals, ensuring efficient food distribution, engaged in beautification projects, constructing public buildings, and fighting wars.

Hammurabi was a micromanager, but he seemed laser-focused on providing for his people's needs and ensuring justice for all. His law code illustrated his concern for ordinary people and his desire for everyone to be treated fairly and decently. Mesopotamian rulers often referred to themselves as shepherds, reflecting their pastoral roots and a desire to provide for the welfare and safety of those under their control. Although several law codes preceded Hammurabi's, his laws excelled for being so clearly written and extensive: almost three hundred laws covering varied aspects of life.

Hammurabi repeatedly formed alliances to fight formidable foes, then abruptly broke them once the danger was past and turned against his former allies. He united with Larsa against Elam, but once he defeated Elam, he formed alliances with Nippur and Lagash against Larsa and later betrayed Nippur and Lagash. He allied with his ancestral kin, Mari and Yamhad, in Syria, and once they'd helped him, he swiftly turned on them and conquered them (although Mari backstabbed him first). It never seemed to occur to the people of any of these city-states not to trust Hammurabi. Ironically, the man known for defending justice with his law code was unjust in the art of war.

Of all the Mesopotamian kings of the second millennium, Hammurabi stands out for being honored as a deity even while alive. The title *Hammurabi-ili* meant "Hammurabi is my god" and was commonly used to honor him. His subjects remembered him for being a victorious conqueror, maintaining peace in his massive kingdom, and promoting justice for all citizens.

This image of the god Marduk is from an ancient cylinder seal.⁸⁵

Hammurabi promoted the worship of Babylon's city god Marduk on a much grander scale, placing him at the head of the Mesopotamian pantheon of gods. Among his incentives for conquering vast territories was spreading the worship of Marduk; he considered his campaigns against other city-states to be a holy war: spreading the knowledge of Marduk, subduing evil, and bringing civilization to all people. A victory stele that Hammurabi installed in Ur declared:

"The people of Elam, Gutium, Subartu, and Tukrish, whose mountains are distant and whose languages are obscure, I placed into Marduk's hand. I myself continued to put straight their confused minds."[1]

Like his father, Hammurabi fell ill and could not continue with all the minutia of ruling an empire. However, given that he reigned for forty-two years, he must have been in his sixties or seventies. He increasingly delegated administrative affairs to his son Samsu-iluna, and in the last year of his life, his son was the de facto king. In less than a year after Hammurabi's death in 1750 BCE, the great empire he had built began to crumble.

Hammurabi's son Samsu-iluna ruled for thirty-eight years, but his reign was marked by the loss of control over Assyria and Elam and rebellions in other previously-conquered territories. Nine years into his reign, Larsa led a massive uprising of twenty-six cities, including Eshnunna, Isin, Ur, and Uruk. Samsu-iluna experienced immediate success against the coalition forces when he led a shattering campaign against Eshnunna and executed its King Iluni. Samsu-iluna energetically fought the rest of the rebels for four years, conquering Ur, Uruk, Isin, and finally Larsa in rapid succession, pulling down the defensive walls and sacking the cities. His triumphs ended the Sumerian rebellion temporarily.

However, the far south of Sumer wasn't ready to concede. The province of Sealand was in the marshlands of southernmost Mesopotamia, where the Tigris and Euphrates had dumped enough silt that the coastline extended out into the Persian Gulf for miles past its original shoreline. The Akkadian-speaking people of Sealand, led by Ilum-ma-ili, who claimed descent from Isin's last king, were the next to break free of the Old Babylonian Empire, forming the First Sealand Dynasty. Samsu-iluna unsuccessfully fought against the rebels, who held ascendancy in Sumer for three centuries.

---

[1] Marc Van De Mieroop, *King Hammurabi of Babylon: A Biography* (Hoboken: Blackwell Publishing, 2005), 126-7.

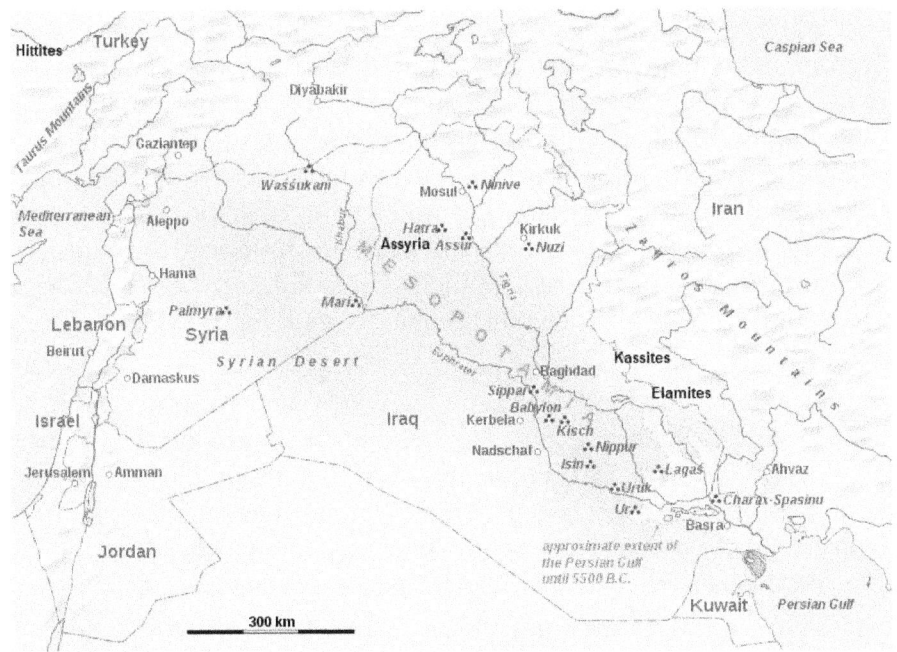

This map shows some of Babylon's rival kingdoms: the Hittites, Kassites, Elamites, and Assyrians. Map modified: names of rival kingdoms added.[86]

Twenty years into Samsu-iluna's reign, Eshnunna rebelled again, but the king triumphed once more. However, Elam and Assyria both took advantage of the chaos in Sumer. Samsu-iluna had torn down Uruk's walls, leaving the city defenseless. The Elamite king Kuturnahunte I sacked Uruk, stealing precious artifacts, including Inanna's idol; it would take over one thousand years before the statue was returned.

Next, Assyria's vice-regent, Puzar-Sin, staged a coup in Assyria, banishing its Amorite king Asinum, a vassal king to Babylonia. In the chaos, the Assyrian Ashur-dugal stole Assyria's throne, but this led to a revolution by the Assyrians against the usurper, who was a "son of a nobody, who had no title to the throne,"[i] according to the *Assyrian King List*. During his brief reign of six years, six other "sons of nobodies" also reigned, apparently fragmenting Assyria into six regions led by usurpers. No one in Assyria was paying the requisite tribute to Babylon throughout the unrest, and Samsu-iluna seemed helpless to do anything.

---

[i] *Assyrian King List,* Livius. https://www.livius.org/sources/content/anet/564-566-the-assyrian-king-list

In addition to losing large sections of the empire, Samsu-iluna had to confront new enemies. Sutean tribes from the Mediterranean were staging slave raids in the cities of Idamara and Arrapha in the northeast, compelling Samsu-iluna to pass a law forbidding Babylonians from buying enslaved people captured from Babylonian territories. In his ninth year, while simultaneously fighting the Sumerian coalition, the Kassites invaded: the first mention of this tribe in historical accounts. Of mysterious origins, the Kassites would successfully seize power 170 years later and rule Babylon for four centuries. But for now, Samsu-iluna managed to repel them.

Samsu-iluna also went on the offensive against Amorite tribes not aligned with Babylonia and annexed their territories. He killed the king of Apum in northeastern Syria and demolished the city, and in the following year, he campaigned successfully against Terqa, which was close to Mari. In his thirty-fifth year as king, Samsu-iluna was put on the defensive when he successfully ejected a coalition army of Amorites invading from Syria.

By the end of Samsu-iluna's reign, Babylonia had shrunk down to almost where it was before Hammurabi became king. He did retain control over the vital trade on the Euphrates River as far northwest as Mari. Another thing Babylon retained was its sacred status. Hammurabi had named Babylonia a "holy city," making it Mesopotamia's sacred city instead of Nippur. Despite all the loss of land, Babylonia maintained its reputation as a sacred destination.

In addition to defending Babylonia against internal revolutions and external invasions, Samsu-iluna instituted the Babylonian calendar based on a previous Sumerian calendar from the Third Dynasty of Ur. The calendar had twelve lunar months, plus an extra month to be inserted as needed. Every seventh day was a "holy day," during which citizens had to refrain from certain activities.

Samsu-iluna's son Abi-Eshuh ruled Babylonia next for twenty-eight years. He successfully repelled a second Kassite invasion in his fourth year as king, unsuccessfully attempted to capture the Sealand ruler by damming the Tigris River, and failed to repel Elamite invasions into Babylonia under King Kutir-nahhunte I. In their raids of thirty Babylonian cities, the Elamites stole the enormous diorite stone on which Hammurabi's law code was carved. They hauled it back to Susa, where it remained for over three thousand years until finally discovered in archaeological digs in 1901.

Abi-Eshuh's son Ammi-Ditana and grandson Ammisaduqa were the subsequent two Babylonian kings, blessed with long and peaceful reigns, with no war or invasions recorded. Babylonian scholars compiled the *Venus Tablet of Ammisaduqa* during King Ammisaduqa's reign: careful records of the planet Venus' risings and settings, with other astronomical observations such as eclipses.

King Samsu-Ditana then reigned as Babylon's last Amorite king. The Hittites dashed his hopes of enjoying the peaceful reigns of his father and grandfather; however, his own actions contributed to Babylonia's fall. Rather than maintaining a substantial standing army, he had permitted able-bodied men to make payments for not serving in the military.

The Hittite kingdom of Hatti lay in the far northwest, between the Mediterranean and the Black Sea. Led by King Mursili I, the Hittites first invaded Aleppo (in Syria) and brought back captives. King Mursili then marched into Mesopotamia's heartland, sacking Babylon and carrying away captives and booty, but leaving the shattered city abandoned. The Babylonians carefully noted and recorded omens, such as lunar and solar eclipses, which they believed foretold the death of a king. In this case, their superstition proved correct. Twin eclipses, first a lunar and then a solar eclipse, occurred within two weeks of each other, just before the Hittites attacked.[i]

Why did the Hittites invade from so far away and then just leave? One theory is that a massive volcanic eruption on the island of Thera disrupted weather patterns and the wheat harvests in the Hittite homeland. The Hittites might have been raiding a distant land for wheat.[ii]

Perhaps most devastating of all for the remnant of Babylonian civilization was that the Hittites stole the image of the god Marduk. Marduk was Babylon's patron god, but Hammurabi had also been promoting him as the new leader of the Mesopotamian pantheon. People made pilgrimages to Babylon from all over Mesopotamia just to worship Marduk in the sacred city and seek omens from him. The ancient Mesopotamians believed the god inhabited his image. How could Babylon ever hope to revive without Marduk? What no one knew at the

---

[i] Peter J. Huber, *Astronomical Dating of Babylon I and Ur III*. (Cambridge: Harvard University, 1982).

[ii] William J. Broad, "It Swallowed a Civilization," *New York Times*, October 21, 2003. https://www.nytimes.com/2003/10/21/science/it-swallowed-a-civilization.html

time was that this was just one of many journeys Marduk would take as his image was stolen, returned, and stolen again. An epic poem was even written about Marduk's wanderings from his own perspective.

The Hittite invasion left the city mostly uninhabited, ending the Amorite political reign in Mesopotamia forever. It also spelled the end of the Amorites in Mesopotamia as a distinct ethnic group, and within four hundred years, the Amorites disappeared from history altogether. However, Hammurabi's influence lived on through his example as a leader and through his law code, which the succeeding Kassite Dynasty adopted, and which influenced other Middle Eastern laws.

In a hymn apparently written by Hammurabi, he extolls himself:

"I am the king, the brace that grasps wrongdoers, which makes people of one mind,

I am the great dragon among kings who throws their counsel in disarray

I am the net that is stretched over the enemy,

I am the fear-inspiring, who, when lifting his fierce eyes, gives the disobedient the death sentence,

I am the great net that covers evil intent,

I am the young lion, who breaks nets and scepters,

I am the battle net that catches him who offends me.

I am Hammurabi, the king of justice."[i]

---

[i] Van De Mieroop, *King Hammurabi of Babylon*, 127.

Chapter 4: The Kassite Dynasty

"Fallen, fallen is Babylon! All the images of her gods lie shattered on the ground!"[i]

For twenty-five years, Babylon was a ghost town. The Hittites had hauled off the grain stores, temple treasures, and thousands of captives. They had leveled nearly all the buildings, and most survivors fled. Perhaps a few straggled back from where they had hidden and huddled in the few remaining structures. Possibly they gleaned a small harvest from the remnants left in the fields and rounded up some of the stray goats and sheep. They may have been able to plant a few fields and live off the proceeds.

And then, after twenty-five years, the Kassites marched into town and assumed residence in the abandoned city. Twice they had tried to take possession of Babylon: during the reigns of Hammurabi's son Samsu-iluna and grandson Abi-Eshuh. Both times, the Babylonians had repelled the Kassites. But now, Babylon had no king and just a minuscule population struggling to survive.

---

[i] *Isaiah 21:1*, Tanakh: Navi: The Book of Yeshayahu.

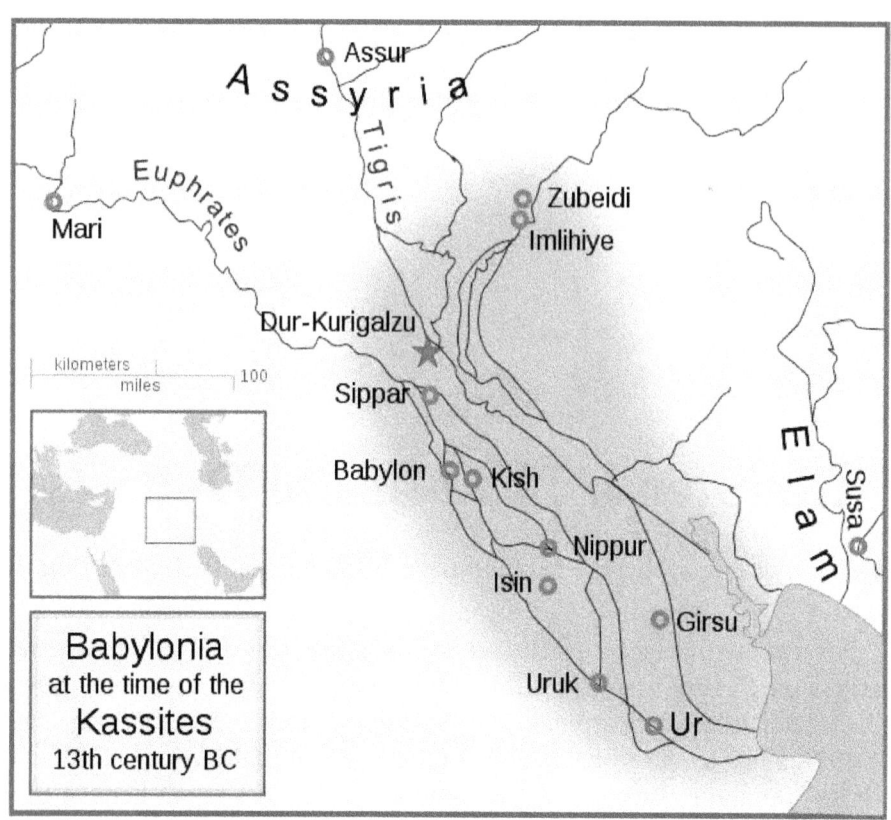

Babylonia's territory during the Kassite rule stretched from the Persian Gulf to the border of Assyria.[87]

Who were the Kassites, and from where did they come? They may have come from the Zagros Mountains of Iran, but even that is uncertain, based on where they fled when they were eventually driven out of Babylon centuries later. They spoke a non-Semitic language isolate, unrelated to the languages of the Elamites, Gutians, or other Iranian people. They were not mentioned in any Middle Eastern histories before their failed attacks on Babylon.

If they were from the Zagros Mountains, they must have only lived there for two or three centuries. They were never mentioned during the many military campaigns the Akkadian Empire waged in the region. They may have had an Indo-European heritage or lived near Indo-Europeans, as their gods were similar to the Vedic pantheon (the ancestors of the Hindu gods and Zoroastrian demi-gods).

Kassite names began to pop up in the city of Larsa during Hammurabi's reign, and records with names of Kassite people indicated they infiltrated Babylonia during the reigns of Hammurabi's descendants. They appeared to have served as military mercenaries for the Babylonians and were known for breeding horses and manufacturing swift war chariots. While the Kassite direct invasions failed, Kassites slowly worked their way into Babylonian society.

Some scholars suggest that the Kassites were in alliance with the Hittites, possibly even related, as the Hittites were Indo-European and used horses and speedy war chariots. Geography makes both theories unlikely. The Hittite homeland of Hatti was a thousand miles from Babylonia and even further from Iran's Zagros Mountains. What's more, the Kassites did not immediately take possession of Babylon after the Hittites left; they waited twenty-five years, which strains the credibility of a link between the two cultures.

This Kassite cylinder seal impression features a male worshiper, a dog, and a prayer in cuneiform script.[88]

Wherever they were from, the Kassites took possession of Babylon and held it for four hundred years! Intriguingly, their first king, Agum

Kakrîme (Agum II), marched one thousand miles northwest to the Hittite kingdom, crushed the Hittites, and stole back Marduk's statue. He returned Marduk to Babylon, rebuilt the Esagila (Esangil) temple, purified it by a snake charmer, built protective demons to guard the door, and installed Marduk's image in its rightful place. A scribe documented all of this in what is known as the *Agum Kakrîme Inscription*.

Some scholars question the authenticity of the *Agum Kakrîme Inscription*. Its two existing copies, unearthed in Nineveh, were written after the Kassite era but based on an original inscription. The copies were written in Akkadian (the written language of the Babylonian Amorites and the Kassites) with the Neo-Assyrian cuneiform script (used after 900 BCE) but following a more ancient style. The main point of the inscription is Agum's legitimacy to rule Babylon and how he was the tender, attentive shepherd of all Babylon's people, regardless of ethnicity. He also asserts his dominance over the Alman, Gutians, and Padan: all tribes from the Zagros Mountains, which helps support that region as the Kassite home territory.

If the inscription is authentic, it says much about Agum's character and the Kassites. Traveling a two-thousand-mile round trip to retrieve the god of the previous civilization and return it to its restored temple reflects the profound respect of the Kassites for the vanquished Amorite-Babylonians. It also puts to rest the speculation that the Hittites and Kassites were in league.

Rescuing Marduk may have been a way for Agum to assert his legitimacy. Babylon was a holy city, and the Amorites had championed Marduk as the new head god of Mesopotamia's pantheon. Agum showed respect for the sacred temples and images. Marduk had replaced Enlil as the "king-making" god, so bringing Marduk "home" would win favor with Marduk and his followers. In addition to rebuilding Babylon, Agum also rebuilt Nippur, the most sacred city of the Sumerians from ancient times, and replicated all Nippur's temples that had fallen into ruin. Agum and the rest of the Kassite kings worshiped the Amorite god Marduk, the Sumerian gods such as Enlil, and their own chief deities, Šuqamuna and his wife, Šumaliya.

The "Dark Age" of Mesopotamia took place in the interim period after Babylon fell to the Hittites. This age marked political and cultural regress, with drastic changes to society and the Mesopotamian way of life. Before about 1400 BCE, we have sparse documentation of what happened in the earliest days of Kassite rule in Babylon, including no documentation in the Kassite language and almost nothing in any other language.

Were the Kassites literate when they took possession of Babylon? Since no inscriptions or cuneiform tablets have been found in the Kassite language, they presumably had no written language of their own. They adopted the Babylonian-Akkadian dialect for legal documents and used the virtually extinct Sumerian language for some monuments. This may have been a way to honor the preceding civilizations, as the Kassites seemed determined to do, perhaps as a way to preserve their legitimacy. Some Kassites lived in Babylonia and Sumer before rising to power; they may have already used the Babylonian and Sumerian written languages.

The lack of documentation for this age may stem from a loss of literacy in the ruling classes. It may also relate to the destruction of documents, either by rival kings' invasions or environmental conditions. Babylon's underground water table is quite near the surface. While the cuneiform tablets and other artifacts of Mesopotamia fared well in other places with desert conditions, they disintegrated in the lower levels of Babylon's ruins, aided by several significant floods of Babylon through the millennia. Even if they still survive in the watery depths under Babylon, getting to them is a challenge.

The data we have for the earliest Kassite era in Babylon come from several contemporary sources, including the *Assyrian King List*, which has a few notations of interactions with Kassite-ruled Babylonia. Another contemporary Assyrian document is the *Synchronistic History (ABC)*, which records two treaties between the Assyrian and Kassite kings. The *Chronicles of the Early Kings* was written later, in the Neo-Babylonian age, but provides information on the Kassite kings. However, the further back in time one goes in this document, the more dubious the information becomes.

Only three important artifacts have been unearthed from the Dark Age of the early Kassite period in Babylon. These were a mace head and a stone frog, both with inscriptions to Ula-burarias, son of King Burna-burarias of Sealand. The mace head was found in a more recent Parthian-period house in Babylon, and the frog was found in the Ararat plain of Armenia.[i] Although King Burna-burarias is called the king of Sealand in

---

[i] Frans van Koppen, "The Old to Middle Babylonian Transition: History and Chronology of the

both inscriptions, he was also the second king of Babylon. Twenty tablets excavated from the island of Bahrain in the Persian Gulf named King Agum the first Kassite king of Babylonia. He succeeded where the Amorites had failed by conquering the Sealand Dynasty and also gaining control of Bahrain, which had been under Sealand's domination.

The early Kassite kings of Babylonia conquered Sumer within their first sixty-five years of rule. Sumer was no longer a network of combative city-states but one large, unified province. The Kassites then began pressing north into what is present-day Baghdad. Expanding north brought them into conflict with the Assyrians, so Agum's successor Burna-burarias I negotiated a treaty with Assyria regarding the border between Babylonia and Assyria.

The Ziggurat of Dur-Kurigalzu once stood in the Kassite capital.[89]

Mesopotamian Dark Age." *Ägypten Und Levante / Egypt and the Levant* 20 (2010): 455. http://www.jstor.org/stable/23789952

As the Kassite kingdom of Babylonia grew in territory and control of profitable trade routes, its exponential wealth led King Kurigalzu I to construct a splendid new 560-acre royal city, Dur-Kurigalzu, with gleaming palaces and temples. The ruins of the Ziggurat of Dur-Kurigalzu still tower over the desert close to Baghdad. Babylonia now stretched almost a thousand miles from Bahrain (Dilmun) in the south to the border of Assyria in the north. Babylon was also enjoying unprecedented and lengthy stability and peace, with rewarding trade with neighbors such as the Assyrians and Mitanni of northern Mesopotamia and Elam to the east.

Kurigalzu and his descendants also corresponded regularly and traded with more distant kingdoms like Egypt, Anatolia, the Hittite Empire, Greece, and Armenia. The *Amarna Letters*, a collection of cuneiform tablets found in Egypt, include correspondence between the Egyptian pharaohs and the Kassite kings, fourteen letters where they affectionately called each other "brother," exchanged gifts, and arranged royal marriages. The Kassite royalty intermarried with the royal families of Egypt, Elam, Assyria, and Hatti (western Turkey). These other powerful kingdoms recognized Babylon as an equal.

The Kassites were master assimilators, so much so that they left little of their own cultural trace behind. They thoughtfully followed the Mesopotamian customs and practices, yet they did leave their unique stamp in the arts. One innovation was glazing bricks, which became a hallmark of Babylonian artwork on their city walls, gates, palaces, and temples through the Neo-Babylonian and Achaemenid periods.

Babylonia's wide-reaching trade and friendship with far-flung lands brought in lapis lazuli and other brilliantly-colored semiprecious stones. The Kassites used these beautiful stones in their artwork with cylinder seals, which featured tall, thin figures, exquisitely engraved prayers, and gold caps at the end of the cylinders. The Kassites also devoted careful attention to restoring ancient temples, following the exact model of what had once stood there. Curiously, they often used the Sumerian language for inscriptions on cornerstones and victory steles, even though the language had barely been used for centuries. They considered themselves stewards of the past Sumerian, Akkadian, and Babylonian civilizations, meticulously preserving ancient documents, literature, and religious artifacts.

One type of monument the Kassites innovated was *kudurrus*: polished stones gracing the inside of temples with inscriptions of pivotal real estate transactions. They decorated the kudurrus stones with Mesopotamian and Kassite deities. The kudurrus were a Kassite legacy that endured long after their reign in Babylon ended.

On this Kassite kudurra, King Meli-Shipak II presents his daughter to the deity Ḫunnubat-Nanaya.[90]

Murder and mayhem struck the Kassite palace in 1333 BCE. Shortly after Kara-hardas ascended Babylon's throne, a military coup d'état overthrew his government. The rebels killed the young king and installed the usurper Nazi-Bugash on the throne. The murder infuriated the Assyrian king Assur-uballit. His daughter Muballitat-Serua was married to the previous Kassite king, and the renegades had killed his grandson, Kara-hardas.

A vengeful Assur-uballit marched his Assyrian army south, invaded Babylonia, executed the usurper, and installed Kurigalzu II, another grandson and the slain Kara-hardas' brother, as Babylonia's new king. The boy-king was essentially a vassal to his grandfather. Despite the blood ties between Assyria and Babylonia, acrimony grew as the young king matured. After his grandfather died and his uncle Enlil-nīrāri ascended the throne, Kurigalzu II went to war against Assyria and lost the battle. He also lost territory as the boundary lines between the two kingdoms were adjusted in Assyria's favor.

After several more years of intermittent battles between the Assyrians and Kassites, they declared a truce so Assyria could deal with the Mitanni and Hittites. King Shalmaneser I successfully defeated the coalition Mitanni and Hittite forces and gouged out one eye from each of his 14,400 war prisoners. While Assyria was at war with other enemies, the Kassites enjoyed peace, with Nippur especially flourishing.

The Kassites' brief peace came crashing to an end when Tukulti-Ninurta I ascended Assyria's throne. After trouncing the Hittites, he marched south to deal with the Babylonians, who had been disrespecting the boundary lines with Assyria while he'd been busy with the Hittites. He flattened Babylon's walls, massacred the Kassites, and stole Marduk's statue. He hauled the naked and chained Kassite king and his harem back to Assyria as prisoners and ruled over Babylonia himself for eight years, from 1235 to 1227 BCE. Two decades later, Tukulti-Ninurta's own sons staged a coup and stabbed him to death. In the chaos, the Babylonians somehow managed to get Marduk back, perhaps voluntarily returned by the Assyrians!

Around 1200 BCE, the Bronze Age Collapse struck the Middle East, North Africa, Greece, and Turkey. A series of environmental events, including drought, earthquakes, tsunamis, and volcanic eruptions, disrupted civilizations, leading to population shifts and the sudden decline of once-great political powers. The "Sea People" of unknown origin besieged the Mediterranean coastal areas, violently destroying cities in Canaan, Lebanon, Syria, and Turkey. During this era, the stately cities of Mycenean Greece lay abandoned, and the Hittite Empire crumbled. In Mesopotamia, Assyria survived—even thrived—but the Kassite Dynasty declined.

Meanwhile, the Elamites began stirring up trouble. The Elamite and Kassite royal families had been intermarrying for generations, and the Elamites claimed their blood ties to Babylonia as justification for invading and claiming their "rightful throne" in 1150 BCE. They captured Enlil-nadin-ahi, Babylonia's last Kassite king, and took him as a prisoner to Susa. They also stole Marduk's idol and carried him away: the third time Marduk was stolen!

After the Elamites successfully took Babylon, the fleeing Kassites rallied at Isin. With Isin's assistance, they launched a counterattack, drove the Elamites out of Babylonia, and ruled in Dynasty IV of Babylon (1153-1022 BCE). By this time, all of Mesopotamia was feeling the effects of the prolonged drought and other factors of the Bronze Age Collapse. Most cities emptied, except Babylon, Ur, and Isin.

A century of chaos followed when the Arameans invaded, ending Kassite rule in Babylonia forever. Most of the Kassites retreated to the Lorestan region of the Zagros Mountains in Iran, where centuries later, the Assyrian King Sennacherib fought them in 702 BCE. However, some Kassites remained in Babylonia and held important positions in later dynasties. During their own reign, the Kassites had honored the previous Amorite, Sumerian, and Akkadian civilizations, and the later rulers of Babylon likewise esteemed the Kassites.

Chapter 5: The Assyrian Rule

Babylonia existed south of its neighbor Assyria, usually in an uneasy truce. The royal families intermarried and allied against common enemies, yet peace was tenuous. Babylon and Assyria exercised dominance over one other in a constantly shifting power play in which the fierce Assyrians usually had the upper hand.

The Assyrians struck fear into their neighbors for two millennia, even terrorizing nations a thousand miles away. They created the largest empire in the world at that time and, like Babylon, passed through several eras of extensive sovereignty in the Middle East, followed by horrendous falls. Who were the Assyrians? The *Torah* said the Semitic shepherds living by the Tigris River were the descendants of Ashur, the son of Shem and grandson of Noah.[i] They spoke an Akkadian dialect, and their original city was Assur (Ashur).

Sargon the Great conquered the fledgling town of Assur and probably founded Babylon around the same time. After the Akkadian Empire fell, Assur (although not the northern Assyrian settlements like Nineveh) and Babylon came under the Third Dynasty of Ur's dominance. Then, under King Puzur-Ashur I, around 2025 BCE, Assyria grew into a modest, independent city-state with approximately ten thousand people. Babylon gained independence about two centuries later under the Amorite king Sumu-Abum.

---

[i] *Genesis 10:22,* Tanakh: Torah: Bereishit.

In 1808 BCE, an Amorite usurper, Shamshi-Adad, grabbed power in Assyria and expanded the unassuming group of city-states into an empire that stretched northwest into Turkey and Syria. But toward the end of Shamshi-Adad's reign, Hammurabi ascended the Babylonian throne and rapidly transformed Babylon into a dominant kingdom over Assyria and Sumer. Under Hammurabi's long reign, Assyria's subsequent three kings were vassals to Babylon.

Assyria regained independence after Hammurabi died, although it entered chaotic self-rule with multiple usurpers for several years until the Adaside Dynasty gained power in Assyria and held it for almost one thousand years. The Hittites bypassed Assyria to invade and plunder Babylon, after which it fell under Kassite rule. Meanwhile, Assyria endured a couple of decades of dominance by the Mitanni.

When the Assyrians shook off the Mitanni, they made a treaty with the Kassite Babylonians, rebuilt Assur, and reestablished their advanced trade system. Shortly after, in 1392 BCE, King Eriba-Adad I ascended the Assyrian throne, which marked the beginning of the Middle Assyrian Empire (1392–1056). At this point, Babylon was in its Kassite era (Middle Babylon). Assyria rebounded phenomenally, seizing most of the western Turkey homeland of its bitter rivals, the Hittites, and northern Mesopotamia, Syria, Lebanon, and Canaan.

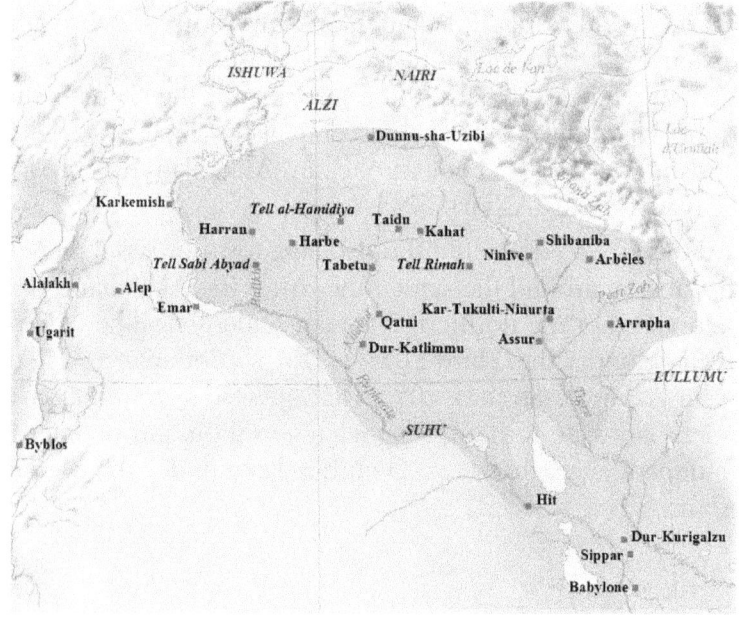

This map shows the location of the Middle Assyrian Dynasty.[91]

In a desperate attempt to regain control, the Hittites unsuccessfully allied with Babylon against Assyria. In the 1245 BCE Battle of Nihriya, Tukulti-Ninurta decimated the Hittites, capturing and enslaving 28,800 prisoners. He then wreaked his revenge on Babylon by flattening its walls, massacring the population, and plundering its temples in what both the Babylonians and Assyrians considered a frightful act of sacrilege. However, Tukulti-Ninurta justified his actions in the *Tukulti-Ninurta Epic*, claiming the Babylonians offended the gods by breaking oaths and disregarding their treaty with Assyria.

The Assyrians, however, were aghast at Tukulti-Ninurta's desecration of the sacred city, and especially of his stealing Marduk from Babylon. They trembled in fear of what Marduk might do to them. When Tukulti-Ninurta's sons murdered him, the Assyrians nodded to themselves: he'd brought disaster down by his impiety. Tukulti-Ninurta's death prompted Babylonia, which had been a tribute-paying vassal kingdom, to declare independence.

Mesopotamia had entered into the Bronze Age Collapse by this point, but it wasn't as devastated by environmental catastrophes and invasions by displaced people as the Mediterranean region. Nevertheless, the Kassites fell to the Elamites in the twelfth century. Babylon fell under Assyria's domination, with new populations of Arameans and Suteans moving into Babylonia, fleeing the drought and Sea People invasions along the Mediterranean. Assyria began weakening with internecine conflict, holding tenuous control over Babylon.

In 1121 BCE, King Nebuchadnezzar I of Isin took possession of Babylon and ruled for twenty-two years (not to be confused with the more-famous Nebuchadnezzar II of the Neo-Babylonian era and biblical fame). King Nebuchadnezzar made a failed attempt at invading Elam, interrupted when the plague hit and routed his troops. His second try was an insane surprise attack in the heat of the desert summer, tramping over scorching roads with dried-up water holes and their metal weapons burning like fire in their hands. His madness paid off: the Elamites were unprepared and never recovered from the attack. The best part of the raid was that he recovered Marduk, whom the Elamites had stolen from Babylon three decades earlier.

This kudurru stone tells of Nebuchadnezzar's rescue of Marduk from the Elamites.[92]

Flushed with victory over the Elamites, Nebuchadnezzar I set his sights on Assyria. He had initially existed harmoniously with Assyria's King Ashur-resh-ishi I (1133–1116 BCE). However, Nebuchadnezzar I later broke his treaty and besieged two Assyrian cities, a dismal failure. He was no match for the forceful and brilliant military tactics of Ashur-resh-ishi, who chased him out of Assyria.

Ashur-resh-ishi's son Tiglath-Pileser I was even more invincible than his father. He transformed Assyria's military into the Middle East's preeminent power in his forty-one-year reign. After overcoming the Arameans in Syria, he charged through Phoenicia's maritime cities, conquering Byblos, Berytus (Beirut), Tyre, and Sidon along the Mediterranean. After rebuilding and restoring Assyria's neglected temples, he dedicated them through the human sacrifice of "precious victims."

While Tiglath-Pileser was off fighting in foreign lands, Nebuchadnezzar I daringly attempted raids in Assyria. When Tiglath-Pileser heard of Nebuchadnezzar's audacity, he charged back to Mesopotamia, lay siege to Babylonia's cities, and destroyed Nebuchadnezzar's palace in Babylon—but left the city's temples untouched. He would not repeat Tukulti-Ninurta's mistake of incurring the gods' wrath.

Tiglath-Pileser's son Ashur-bel-Kala received a friendly visit from Babylon's King Marduk-šāpik-zēri at his coronation, and they allied against their common enemy: the Arameans. Five years later, Marduk-šāpik-zēri died, and Ashur-bel-Kala put a puppet king on Babylon's throne. The last king of the Middle Assyrian Empire, Ashur-bel-Kala, was forced to defend his realm against a usurper: Tukulti-Mer. He finally gave the pretender the boot, but the Hittites and Arameans took Phoenicia and Syria while he was distracted by internal affairs. This loss began a one-century Assyrian slump, during which it lost Babylonia and all territory except the original Assyrian cities.

The Assyrians' skilled horsemanship led to victory in war and the hunt.[98]

Assyria recovered from its nosedive when Adad-nirari II (911–891 BCE) ascended the throne as the first king of the Neo-Assyrian period. For three centuries, the Neo-Assyrian Empire exponentially expanded, overpowering all of Mesopotamia and the eastern Mediterranean coastline from Turkey to Egypt. One component of their success was their advanced siege engines that struck terror into the hearts of rival cities huddled behind their city walls.

The Assyrians' revolutionary use of iron weapons and war chariots also contributed to a nearly indomitable army. The Mesopotamians, Egyptians, and Hittites had been using iron found in meteorites for two millennia, but around 1300 BCE, the cultures of the Near East began developing iron smelting and smithing technology. Iron weapons and chariots were of a higher caliber than bronze, which had to be cast, making it more brittle. The stronger iron weapons were made from hammering heated iron ore, which was readily available. Bronze was cast from copper and tin; although copper was available in Mesopotamia (but not as common as iron ore), tin deposits were rare and usually imported.

Because iron ore was five hundred times more common than copper in Mesopotamia, once the Assyrians developed iron smelting, cold forging, and tempering technologies, they could afford to outfit entire massive armies with iron weapons. Coupled with formidable siege engines, logistical capabilities, and strategic tactics, the Assyrian iron chariots and weapons made it the most advanced military of the day.

Beginning with the astute leadership of King Adad-Nirari II, Assyria's incredible conquering force took one nation after another. City by city, the Assyrians used wheeled siege towers, battering rams, mobile ladders, and earthen ramps to breach city walls. They even dug tunnels under the walls! Adad-Nirari led two campaigns into Babylonia, capturing extensive territory north of the Diyala River and forming a treaty with Babylon that ensured peace for several generations. However, his successors destroyed and reconquered Babylon multiple times.

Adad-Nirari's grandson, the diabolically cruel Ashurnasirpal II, aggressively extended the empire, beginning in the Armenian highlands. From there, he marched on Syria, overcame the Neo-Hittites and Aramaeans, and then entered into diplomatic relations with Phoenicia and Israel. He continued the diplomatic ties with Babylon that his grandfather established, for which they were no doubt grateful, considering his treatment of other regions.

Ashurnasirpal II's palace stood in Nimrud for three millennia before ISIL bulldozed it in 2015.

Whenever a city revolted against Ashurnasirpal's harsh rule and heavy tribute requirements, they would receive his horrific retribution, beginning the shock and terror methods that Assyrians would use for the next few centuries. When the city of Tela in Syria resisted him,

Ashurnasirpal cruelly crushed the citizens with actions he would repeatedly use to squash rebellion:

> "I built a pillar over against the city gate, and I flayed all the chiefs who had revolted, and I covered the pillar with their skins. Some I impaled upon the pillar on stakes, and others I bound to stakes around the pillar. I cut the limbs off the officers who had rebelled. Many captives I burned with fire, and many I took as living captives. From some, I cut off their noses, their ears, and their fingers; of many, I put out their eyes. I made one pillar of the living and another of heads, and I bound their heads to tree trunks round about the city. Their young men and maidens I consumed with fire. The rest of their warriors I consumed with thirst in the desert of the Euphrates."[i]

Ashurnasirpal's son, Shalmaneser III, led a 70,000-man force with 4,000 chariots and 1,200 horsemen. Large cavalry forces were a novelty and probably used mercenaries from Turkey and the Zagros Mountains. The Assyrian military grew to 200,000 soldiers in the next few generations, the largest army in the Middle East up to that point. Although most of their military were farmers called up for duty, the Assyrians began training specialized forces, engineers, and spies.

Shalmaneser III continued the peace treaty with Babylon that Adad-Nirari had established. However, Babylonia experienced a coup d'état when King Marduk-zakir-shumi's younger brother Marduk-bel-usate tried to usurp the throne. Shalmaneser marched to Babylonia to defend his ally, and the rebel brother fled to the mountains, where Shalmaneser pursued him and cut him down with his sword.

Shalmaneser also encountered a palace coup when his son Assur-danin-pal attempted to steal his throne, grasping power over twenty-seven Assyrian cities and allying with the Babylonian king Marduk-balassu-iqbi. Another son of Shalmaneser, Shamshi-Adad V, defended Shalmaneser (who died after two years) and continued with a four-year power struggle against his brother, which he finally won, although with a much-weakened Assyria.

---

[i] Joshua J. Mark, "Ashurnasirpal II," *World History Encyclopedia*. https://www.worldhistory.org/Ashurnasirpal_II/

Shamshi-Adad then led two revenge campaigns against Babylon. In his first campaign, after taking time out for a lion hunt (a favorite Assyrian pastime), he wreaked havoc on northern Babylonia until the coalition forces of Babylonians, Chaldeans, Elamites, Arameans, and Kassites fought him off. In his second campaign against Babylon, Shamshi-Adad captured King Marduk-balāssu-iqbi and dragged him to Assyria in chains.

Tiglath-Pileser III became the joint king of Assyria and Babylon.[95]

For sixty-five years, Assyria struggled to recover from the impact of its civil war. In 745 BCE, Tiglath-Pileser III received the Assyrian crown and immediately set to work restoring Assyria to power, recovering the breakaway provinces, including Israel, and engaging in population-relocation programs to ward off any further rebellion:

> "King Pul of Assyria (also known as Tiglath-Pileser) invaded the land and took the people of Reuben, Gad, and the half-tribe of Manasseh as captives. The Assyrians exiled them to Halah, Habor, Hara, and the Gozan River, where they remain to this day."[i]

> "In the days of Pekah, king of Israel, came Tiglath-Pileser king of Assyria and took Ijon, Abel-beth-maacah, Janoah, and Kedesh, and Hazor, and Gilead, and Galilee, all the land of Naphtali; and he carried them captive to Assyria."[ii]

Tiglath-Pileser then turned his attention to Babylonia. Like Assyria, Babylonia had been experiencing a period of stagnation, lacking the military power that Assyria had built up. It engaged in ongoing power struggles with the Chaldeans who had migrated into Mesopotamia from the Levant (Syria, Lebanon, Israel) beginning in the tenth century BCE and were settling in southeastern Babylonia. The Chaldeans spoke a western Semitic language, similar to Aramaean.

In the 8th century BCE, three Chaldean tribal leaders, apparently unrelated, gained ascendency over Babylonia, ruling as kings during the power vacuum created by conflict with Assyria. One of these Chaldean kings, Erība-Marduk, helped restore order to Babylonia after a prolonged period of instability. He reverenced Babylon's god Marduk by restoring his throne in the Esagila temple.

Two years after Tiglath-Pileser III ascended Assyria's throne, Nabonassar deposed a Chaldean ruler and became king of Babylonia. Two years later, in 745 BCE, Tiglath-Pileser invaded Babylonia, pillaging the cities of Hamranu and Rabbilu and stealing their gods. He destroyed the major Chaldean city of Bit-Shilani, skewered its ruler, and subdued the Aramaeans and Chaldeans. Tiglath-Pileser did not bother Nabonassar; in fact, the Babylonian king may have invited Tiglath-Pileser's assistance—he certainly benefited from the Assyrian king

---

[i] *1 Chronicles 5:26,* Tanakh: Book of Divrei HaYamim I.
[ii] *2 Kings 15:29,* Tanakh: Book of Malachim II.

trouncing his rivals.

The next few years in Babylonia's history featured insurrection, dynastic overthrow, and usurpation. Another Chaldean, Nabu-mukin-zeri, crowned himself king in 731 BCE, much to Tiglath-Pileser's annoyance. Nabu-mukin-zeri immediately set about mediating the differences between the various Babylonian ethnic and political groups. Tiglath-Pileser preferred Babylonia to be disconnected and at odds so it could not rival Assyria.

Tiglath-Pileser set out to overthrow Nabu-mukin-zeri, first installing a blockade to the east to prevent Elam from getting involved. He then conquered several Aramean and Chaldean tribes. In 730 BCE, he sent his envoys to urge the city of Babylon to surrender, promising tax privileges, but to no avail. In 729 BCE, Tiglath-Pileser lay siege and took Babylon, declaring himself king of both Assyria and Babylonia, although Nabu-mukin-zeri continued to resist for several years. Tiglath-Pileser kept all of Babylonia, which comprised most of central and southern Mesopotamia, as one united vassal kingdom to Assyria. He honored the Babylonian deities, temples, and culture, attending religious festivals in Babylon.

Tiglath-Pileser's son Shalmaneser V spent most of his short, five-year reign (727-722 BCE) campaigning in Israel. He dealt with unruly kingdoms by implementing the population-relocation programs used by his father. He evacuated the Samarian province of northern Israel and resettled them in Assyria and Babylonia. He then exiled some of the troublesome tribal groups in Assyria and Babylonia to Samaria.[i] This created a wholly different Mesopotamian ethnicity and religion in Samaria, at odds with the rest of Israel even in Jesus's day centuries later. It also meant that a large Jewish population lived in Babylon (from this and other population-relocation endeavors), and some rose to positions of power and influence with the Babylonian kings.

Sargon II ruled Assyria next, probably usurping the throne from his brother. Despite Shalmaneser's population relocations, the Babylonian king Marduk-apla-iddina proved insubordinate to Assyrian rule, forcing Sargon II to reconquer the kingdom. Before a military invasion, Sargon astutely used secret negotiations with the northern Babylonian tribes and cities to forge alliances. He then marched along the Tigris River to

---

[i] *2 Kings 17:24-41*, Tanakh: Malachim II.

southern Babylonia to conquer Dur-Abi-hara. He successfully negotiated again to win over the southern Babylonians from that stronghold.

Marduk-apla-iddina fled to Elam, and the cheering people of Babylon opened their city gates to Sargon II. Fortunately for the Babylonians, Sargon was not as savage as his predecessors: he did not punish the rebels as harshly and even extended the rights of Assyrian citizenship in a relationship in which Assyria was considered the husband and Babylonia the wife. He lived in Babylon for the next three years, engaging in the traditional religious ceremonies and improving the infrastructure.

Sargon II died in battle in Anatolia, and his body disappeared; in the chaos, his men could not recover it. Many perceived the lack of proper funeral rites as a bad omen, and rebellions sprung up around the Assyrian Empire, which Sargon's son Sennacherib struggled to subdue. Babylonia refused to be a submissive "wife": the people felt he'd disrespected Marduk by refusing to "take the hand" of the god.

Sennacherib subdued the rebellion and installed a vassal king, Bel-ibni: a Babylonian who had grown up in his palace. That didn't go well; the young king almost immediately began conspiring with the Chaldeans and Elamites, so Sennacherib exiled him to Assyria. He put his son, Ashur-nadin-shumi, on Babylonia's throne, but that didn't go well either. The Elamites invaded, killed the young king, and, once again, stole Marduk.

Another son of Sennacherib, Esarhaddon, became king of Assyria and Babylon. He retrieved Marduk from the Elamites and rebuilt the Esagila temple and the city of Babylon, living in Babylon part of the time. After Esarhaddon died, his oldest son Shamash-shum-ukin ruled Babylon while a younger son Ashurbanipal ruled Assyria from Nineveh. The brothers fell into a civil war, with the Elamites, Persians, Chaldeans, Canaanites, and Arabs supporting Shamash-shum-ukin. Despite the massive coalition forces, Ashurbanipal won the war.

Ashurbanipal laid siege to Babylon, and when the starving and disease-ridden population surrendered, he killed his brother by burning him to death, then appointed an Assyrian as governor of Babylonia. He dismembered his brother's concubines and officials and fed their body parts to the vultures and dogs. Ashurbanipal also took many of Babylon's ancient texts to Nineveh, where he installed them in his massive library, preserving them for history. He was the last of Assyria's great kings; the empire crumbled shortly after his death.

While Assyria was deteriorating, Babylonia was rising in power once again. Of uncertain origins, calling himself the "son of nobody," Nabopolassar took advantage of Assyria's weakness to stage a revolt. Nabopolassar's first strikes were against Nippur and Babylon, which he swiftly conquered. The Assyrians wasted no time in counterattacking, taking Nippur back. However, they found Nabopolassar too strong when they attacked Babylon and Uruk. He crowned himself king in 626 BCE, freeing Babylonia from centuries of vassalage under Assyrian rule.

Chapter 6: A New Empire – The Neo-Babylonians

A phenomenal power shift rocked Assyria when Nabopolassar seized power over Babylon in 626 BCE. This marked the beginning of the short-lived but dynamic Neo-Babylonian Empire, known for its scientific and mathematic breakthroughs, brilliant architecture, and interactions with Judah, Tyre, and Egypt, as recorded in the Hebrew Tanakh (Old Testament). While the sensational Neo-Babylonian exploded unto the Middle Eastern scene, the Neo-Assyrian Empire drifted into its twilight years, to eventually be snuffed out altogether.

The Assyrian king Sinsharishkun desperately attempted to regain dominance over Babylonia in 625-623 BCE. His counteroffensives in northern Babylonia were initially successful: he conquered Sippar and held Nippur from Nabopolassar's assaults. However, trouble loomed to the east. Elam had been a vassal to Assyria but now threw off its shackles, cut off tribute payments, and joined forces with Nabopolassar. Sinsharishkun responded by amassing a gigantic army to meet the new threat and spectacularly retook Uruk.

Just when Sinsharishkun thought that triumph over Babylon was in his hand, he received disturbing news. One of his own generals from the western provinces had revolted and was marching on Assyria's capital city of Nineveh. With most of Assyria's military in the far south, Nineveh's small army did not even try to defend the city. The unnamed usurper crowned himself Assyria's new king, forcing Sinsharishkun to abandon his campaign in Babylonia and rush home to confront his challenger.

After several months of brutal civil war, Sinsharishkun ejected the interloper, but the Babylonians took advantage of his absence to lay siege to Uruk and Nippur. Desperate for food, the Assyrians finally surrendered the cities, but not before some citizens made the agonizing choice between selling their children into slavery or watching them starve. Nabopolassar then wreaked havoc on the remaining Assyrian garrisons in the south; they all capitulated by 620 BCE. After chasing out the Assyrians, Nabopolassar now securely held all Babylonia.

While the Assyrians and Babylonians had been experiencing coup d'états and viciously struggling for control of Babylonia, new powers were rising to the east. The Medes, a tribe in today's northwestern Iran, were taking advantage of Elam's weakness to expand their territory. As the Assyrian Empire unraveled, the Medes stopped the tribute they'd paid Assyria for centuries.

To avenge his father's death by the Assyrians, King Cyaxares of Media staged a frontal assault on Assyria's capital of Nineveh. In the midst of their barrage on Nineveh, the Scythians launched a surprise attack on the Medes' rear, led by King Madyas. Who were the Scythians? They were fierce nomadic shepherds from the Eurasian steppes north of the Black Sea in today's Kazakhstan, Russia, and Ukraine. These bloodthirsty, expert horsemen were staging savage raids on northern Mesopotamia but had allied with Assyria.

This Greek vase features a Scythian archer painted by Epiktetos, 520-500 BCE.[96]

The Scythians pummeled the Medes, forcing them to bow to their overlordship. For a few years, the Medes had no choice but to pay tribute to the Scythians and leave Assyria unmolested. But in 625 BCE, Cyaxares schemed to break the Scythian yoke. He invited the Scythian nobility to a grand feast, serving them full-strength wine while the Medes drank watered-down wine. When the Scythian lords were roaring drunk, the Medes attacked and killed them all. With their leadership wiped out, the Scythians pragmatically joined forces with the Medes. Together, they launched another siege on Nineveh and took the city.

Nine years later, having consolidated all of Babylonia, Nabopolassar dared to invade Assyrian territory in 616 BCE. Following the Euphrates north into Syria, he took Assyrian cities up to the Khabur River. The Assyrians called on their ally, Egypt's Pharoah Psamtik I, who preferred having the Assyrians controlling the Levant, providing safer borders for Egypt with its northern neighbors. Psamtik marched north to merge his mammoth military with Assyria's.

Babylonia had not been much of a threat to other empires for centuries, so it came as a shock when the coalition Assyrian-Egyptian forces lost the first battle to the Babylonian upstarts. Disconcerted, the Egyptians backed off, forcing Assyria to withdraw and leaving Babylonia in control of the middle Euphrates. This gave Babylonia unlimited access to the prosperous trade routes and provided a buffer zone against an Assyrian attack on Babylonia. With that accomplished, Nabopolassar halted any further invasion of Assyria for the time being.

Before plotting his next step against Assyria, Nabopolassar needed to negotiate strategic alliances. He already had Chaldean support, and in 616 BCE, he allied with Cyaxares, king of the Medes and great-grandfather of Cyrus the Great. As part of the treaty, Nabopolassar's son, Nebuchadnezzar II, married Cyaxares' daughter, Princess Amytis, and Cyaxares married Nabopolassar's daughter. The Medes brought the Scythians with them to the Babylonian side.

Nabopolassar then marched into Assyria's heartland, attacking Assur, the Assyrian's first city, one-time capital, and sacred home of their principal god Ashur. Sinsharishkun hurriedly mustered his forces, marched to Assur, and forced Nabopolassar into retreat. But then King Cyaxares led the Medes into Assyria in 614 BCE and launched a horrific attack on Assur. He brutally conquered the city, massacring the citizens and pillaging the sacred temples. Nabopolassar arrived after the city was taken, appalled by Cyaxares' ruthlessness and disregard for the holy sites.

As dreadful as the sacking of Assur was for the Assyrians, the horror had only begun. In 612 BCE, a staggering coalition force of Babylonians, Chaldeans, Cimmerians, Medes, Persians, Sagartians, and Scythians launched a full-scale invasion of Assyria. The Cimmerians were from southwest Asia and had assimilated with the Scythians, while the Sagartians were from the Iranian plateau. After laying siege to Nineveh for three months, the united forces ground its walls to dust, killed the Assyrian king Sinsharishkun, and destroyed the city, carrying off immense treasure from the palace and temples. Nahum, the prophet, described the desolation:

> "Your enemy is coming to crush you, Nineveh. Man the ramparts! Watch the roads! Prepare your defenses! Call out your forces!
>
> Shields flash red in the sunlight! See the scarlet uniforms of the valiant troops! Watch as their glittering chariots move into position, with a forest of spears waving above them. The chariots race recklessly along the streets and rush wildly through the squares. They flash like firelight and move as swiftly as lightning.
>
> The king shouts to his officers; they stumble in their haste, rushing to the walls to set up their defenses. The river gates have been torn open! The palace is about to collapse! Nineveh's exile has been decreed, and all the servant girls mourn its capture. They moan like doves and beat their breasts in sorrow. Nineveh is like a leaking water reservoir! The people are slipping away. 'Stop, stop!' someone shouts, but no one even looks back.
>
> Loot the silver! Plunder the gold! There's no end to Nineveh's treasures—its vast, uncounted wealth. Soon the city is plundered, empty, and ruined. Hearts melt, and knees shake. The people stand aghast, their faces pale and trembling."[i]

The Cimmerians, Medes, and Scythians stormed the rest of the Assyrian heartland, flattening the cities and defiling the temples. Nabopolassar and the Babylonians shared many of the same deities with

---

[i] *Nahum 2,* Tanakh: Navi: Trei Assar.

Assyria and found the sacrilege disturbing. The merciless attack on Assyria's homeland left only a minuscule remnant of a once-thriving population. The Cimmerians, Medes, and Scythians then charged into the Levant, laying waste to Turkey, Judah, and Israel, all the way south to Egypt's coastline.

THE BATTLE OF CARCHEMISH.

The Babylonians utterly defeated the Assyrians and Egyptians in the Battle of Carchemish.[97]

The surviving Assyrian nobility escaped to Harran in Turkey, where they holed out, desperately seeking the aid of Egypt's Pharoah, Necho II. After consolidating their victory in Assyria, the Babylonian-Median forces marched on Harran in 610 BCE. As they approached, the Assyrians fled into Syria's desert. Necho II marched north from Egypt to rescue the Assyrian remnant, but Judah's King Josiah refused to let him pass through his country. Necho killed Josiah in the Battle of Megiddo, but the delay doomed the Assyrians.

The Babylonian coalition forces conquered Harran before Necho got there. When Necho arrived, the Babylonian crown prince Nebuchadnezzar led the Babylonian army in a lethal assault on Necho II and the few remaining Assyrians, wiping out the Egyptian military to the last man. Assyria had fallen, and Egypt was brought to its knees, but the formidable Neo-Babylonian Empire rose as Mesopotamia's new shining star.

Shortly after the staggering victory against Egypt, Nabopolassar died, and Nebuchadnezzar II returned home as the war hero to ascend Babylon's throne in 605 BCE. He ruled for forty-three years as the Neo-Babylonian Empire's greatest king. Babylonia now held power over Assyria and all Mesopotamia, and Nebuchadnezzar would eventually subjugate western Saudi Arabia, Syria, Lebanon, Israel, Jordan, southern Turkey, and eastern Iran.

Nabopolassar's legacy to his son was stability in central and southern Mesopotamia, with the entire region under Babylonian control. Nebuchadnezzar swiftly consolidated the Assyrian heartland, subduing any remaining resistance and bringing all Mesopotamia under one throne. Nebuchadnezzar took advantage of this peace to expand and enhance his military and initiate stunning building projects around Babylonia, especially in the city of Babylon.

One nagging issue for Nebuchadnezzar II was the insubordinate kingdom of Judea. Over a century earlier, Shalmaneser V of Assyria had soundly defeated Judah's sister kingdom Israel, relocated most of its population to Assyria and Babylon, and resettled Israel with Mesopotamians. Judah remained independent until the Egyptian Pharoah Necho II killed King Josiah, making Judah a vassal to Egypt. But after Nebuchadnezzar destroyed Necho's army, he took control of Judah as a vassal kingdom while still crown prince.

Josiah's son Jehoiakim rebelled after three years of paying tribute, and Nebuchadnezzar, now Babylon's new king, marched to Judah to suppress the vassal king's rebellion. He defeated Jehoiakim and took some of the young men of Judah's royal family back to Babylon. These youths received Babylonian names, trained in the Babylonian language and literature for three years, then entered royal service. Four of these youths were Daniel (Belteshazzar), Hananiah (Shadrach), Mishael (Meshach), and Azariah (Abednego). Daniel served as an advisor and dream interpreter to the Babylonian kings throughout the Neo-Babylonian Empire and briefly under Persian rule. Nebuchadnezzar appointed Daniel's three friends as leaders over the Babylonian provinces.[i]

After several years, the new king of Judah decided to throw off the yoke. In the eighth year of his reign, Nebuchadnezzar invaded Judah and

---

[i] *Daniel 2,* Tanakh: Ketuvim: Book of Daniel.

took the young King Jehoiachin prisoner with his wives and the queen mother. He stripped the royal palace and the Jewish temple of the treasures of silver and gold accumulated centuries earlier by King Solomon. In what is known as the Babylonian Captivity, Nebuchadnezzar took ten thousand people of Jerusalem as captives back to Babylon—the military commanders, skilled soldiers, craftsmen, and artisans—leaving only the poorest people in the land. He installed Jehoiachin's uncle Zedekiah as a vassal king over Judah:[i]

> "By the rivers of Babylon, there we sat down, yea, we wept, when we remembered Zion. There on the willows, we hung our harps. For there our captors demanded of us songs, and our tormentors, jubilation, saying, 'Sing for us one of the songs of Zion!'"[ii]

Despite the disastrous consequences his predecessors experienced when they rebelled, it wasn't long before Zedekiah, in league with Egypt and King Ithobaal III of Tyre, revolted. King Nebuchadnezzar laid siege to Jerusalem for two years as the people starved. Finally, King Zedekiah chanced a daring nighttime escape that ended in tragedy. The Babylonians captured him, forced him to watch his sons' executions, then gouged out his eyes and dragged him to Babylon in chains.[iii]

Under Babylonian rule, the ancient city of Tyre on Lebanon's coast had enjoyed a few years of independence, except for paying tribute. The seaside Phoenician city had suffered under Assyrian rule, but under Nebuchadnezzar's more benevolent reign, it had been rebuilding its legendary wealth as a key trade center and harbor. Then Tyre's king joined forces with Egypt and Judah against Babylon: a foolhardy move. While laying siege to Judah, Nebuchadnezzar also besieged Tyre for thirteen long years, the last holdout in consolidating his empire. When Tyre finally surrendered, Nebuchadnezzar was amazingly merciful, allowing the city to continue as before with vassal kings. He astutely determined that the vast tribute he would receive from the city's affluent trade would enrich his empire.

---

[i] *2 Kings 24,* Tanakh: Navi: Book of Malachim II.
[ii] *Psalm 137:1-3,* Tanakh: Ketuvim: Book of Tehillim.
[iii] *2 Kings 25.*

Germany's Pergamon Museum displays this reproduction of the Ishtar Gate.[98]

Once Nebuchadnezzar II had expanded and consolidated his empire's borders, he focused on ambitious building projects: completely reconstructing thirteen cities. His primary focus was the city of Babylon, which he transformed into a stunning religious and political center. He restored the Esagila temple of Marduk into an exquisite pilgrimage destination and finished the construction of the towering Etemenanki ziggurat in front of the Esagila.

The Processional Way was a majestic seventy-foot-wide road that began at the gleaming and imposing Ishtar Gate and led through the city to the central temple complex. Fifty-foot walls lined the Processional Way with glistening, blue-glazed bricks and 120 bas-relief images of bulls, dragons, and lions in gold. The Ishtar Gate gleamed in the sun and honored the goddess Ishtar (Inanna). On each side of the cedar and bronze gates, high towers in vibrant blue featured bas-relief depictions of the gods Adad, Ishtar, and Marduk. Marduk's image was a dragon-like creature with a snake head and tail, a scaled lion-like body, and frightful talons on its rear feet.

The dragon-like mušḫuššu represented Marduk.[99]

In addition to constructing stunning cities, Nebuchadnezzar also initiated the excavation of the Royal Canal, or Nebuchadnezzar's Canal, which linked the Euphrates to the Tigris. It was not completed until the end of the Neo-Babylonian era, but it dramatically transformed the region's agriculture.

After ruling the Babylonian Empire for forty-three years, Nebuchadnezzar died in 562 BCE. For unclear reasons, Nebuchadnezzar had chosen one of his younger sons, Amel-Marduk (Evil-Merodach), as the crown prince but later regretted his decision. He believed Amel-Marduk was conspiring against him, disrespectful to the temples, and exploiting the people. When Nebuchadnezzar was absent from Babylon, the nobles declared Amel-Marduk king.

This was odd. Why would the nobles stage a coup against their renowned king and military hero? Was he mentally ill, as Belteshazzar (Daniel) recorded? We will discuss this possibility further in chapter eight. When Nebuchadnezzar returned to Babylon, he locked his son up in the palace dungeon, where Amel-Marduk befriended Judah's King Jehoiachin, whom Nebuchadnezzar had imprisoned thirty-seven years earlier. While Nebuchadnezzar was in the process of appointing a different crown prince, he died suddenly.

When Amel-Marduk ascended the throne, he brought his new friend King Jehoiachin out of prison, and the Judean royal dined at the Babylonian king's table for the rest of his life.[i] Nebuchadnezzar had exiled a number of kings and other royalty to Babylon who retained some sort of status; in the Tanakh, the books of 2 Kings and Jeremiah mention that Amel-Marduk elevated Jehoiachin above the other kings in Babylon.

In his short reign, inscriptions say that Amel-Marduk "ruled capriciously and had no regard for the laws."[ii] He was consumed with worshiping Marduk to the point of neglecting his family and royal duties and offending his courtiers, who refused to obey him. At least, that's what the inscriptions said, but they may have been attempting to justify regicide. After only two years as king, his brother-in-law Neriglissar formed a conspiracy against him, murdered him, and usurped the throne.

Who was Neriglissar? He was one of Nebuchadnezzar's leading generals who had won Nebuchadnezzar's admiration and the hand of the king's daughter. As an astute military leader, he successfully conquered Lydia and Turkey. When King Appuasu of Pirindu assembled a mammoth force to raid Syria, Neriglissar charged out to defend the Babylonian territory. Although Appuasu set an ambush for Neriglissar, the Babylonian king evaded it and trounced Appuasu's army.

---

[i] *2 Kings 25,* Tanakh, Book of Malachim II.

[ii] Frauke Weiershäuser and Jamie Novotny, *The Royal Inscriptions of Amēl-Marduk (561–560 BC), Neriglissar (559–556 BC), and Nabonidus (555–539 BC), Kings of Babylon* (PDF). (Winona Lake: Eisenbrauns, 2020), 1.

After capturing many of Appuasu's men and horses, Neriglissar pursued the Pirindu king for a full day through treacherous mountain passes until he caught up with him and took him prisoner. He then captured Appuasu's royal capital city of Kirsi and burned it down. Following this astounding victory, Neriglissar launched a fleet of ships into the Mediterranean with six thousand troops, defeated the land of Pitusu (probably Crete) in the middle of the sea, flattened the city, and enslaved the people.[i]

After ruling only several years, he fell ill and died. His young son Labashi-Marduk ascended the throne for a brief reign before conspirators beat him to death in another palace coup led by Belshazzar, son of Nabonidus. Nabonidus was surprised to be named king by his son and the other conspirators, as he was not from the Babylonian ruling family. His mother was from the family of Ashurbanipal, the last king of Assyria.

Oddly, after completing a successful military endeavor in Arabia, Nabonidus spent ten of his seventeen years as king in self-imposed exile there. He left his son Belteshazzar to run the empire as regent. In the decade that Nabonidus was away from Babylonia, Cyrus the Great was building his great Persian kingdom in Iran. Nabonidus' neglect of his kingdom left it vulnerable to the imminent threat from the east. Combined with the failure of Nebuchadnezzar's descendants to match his strength and vitality and a series of palace coups, the empire gradually crumbled.

---

[i] *The Chronicle Concerning Year Three of Neriglissar (ABC 6)*, Livius, 2006.
https://www.livius.org/sources/content/mesopotamian-chronicles-content/abc-6-neriglissar-chronicle

Chapter 7: The Decline and Fall of Babylon

Babylon's decline had begun. Nabonidus had no preparation for ruling an empire. Unrelated to the current Chaldean-Babylonian dynasty, he wasn't even Babylonian; his parents were Assyrian and Aramaean from Harran in Syria. His mother, Adagoppe, daughter of Ashurbanipal, the last Assyrian king, was a priestess to Sin, the moon god. Nabonidus was her only child. Nabonidus referred to his father as "a prince," suggesting he was an Aramaean chieftain or held a prominent position in Harran's government.

Adagoppe's life was upended in 610 BCE when the Babylonians, led by their crown-prince Nebuchadnezzar, conquered Harran and sacked the city. The Babylonians took Adagoppe and her small child Nabonidus as captives; presumably, her husband died in the fighting. As an Assyrian princess, she was treated with the same honor the Babylonians extended to other captured royals. Adagoppe wrote that she introduced Nabonidus to King Nebuchadnezzar II and King Neriglissar, and he was educated and served them in the royal court.[i]

---

[i] Paul-Alain Beaulieu, *Reign of Nabonidus, King of Babylon (556-539 BC)* (New Haven: Yale University Press, 1989), 69.

Nabonidus prays to the moon god Sin, Ishtar, and the sun god on the Harran Stele.[100]

The Babylonian historian Berossus wrote that Nabonidus was a priest of Marduk, so his service to the royals was likely in a religious context. Although he participated in the coup d'état orchestrated by his son Belteshazzar, he never expected to be thrust to the throne. In one of his inscriptions, Nabonidus wryly noted, "In my mind, there was no thought of kingship."[i] Yet, there he was at an advanced age in 556 BCE, wearing

---

[i] Beaulieu, *Reign of Nabonidus*, 67.

the crown, responsible for hundreds of thousands of people of numerous ethnicities and languages spread over thousands of miles.

But Nabonidus' interests lay elsewhere. Intrigued by the ancient histories of Mesopotamia, he wanted to learn more. He is called the world's first archaeologist, as he studied and attempted to interpret the artifacts discovered when the foundations of ancient temples were unearthed to build new ones. He uncovered a statue of Sargon the Great and had it restored, along with Inanna's temple in Agade.[i]

As a priest and the son of a priestess, Nabonidus' primary concern was religion. He rebuilt the temple of the god Sin in Harran, where his mother once served. He renovated Uruk's Eanna temple and changed the order of sacrifices to include offerings that had stopped under King Neriglissar.

Of course, one couldn't be a Mesopotamian king without being a great warrior. Nabonidus excelled in military exploits, leading successful campaigns in Cilicia and Arabia. Mysteriously, after conquering Tayma in Arabia, Nabonidus remained there for about a decade while his son Belteshazzar ran the kingdom as his regent.

Belteshazzar was an inept diplomat, and his citizens were appalled that he failed to celebrate the New Year's religious festival, an ancient Babylonian tradition. Yet, they were even more disgruntled with Nabonidus' long absence and his attempts to force what they considered strange religious reforms.

Why did Nabonidus stay at the isolated desert outpost of Tayma? Why did he conquer the city to begin with, as the Arabians were not a threat to the Babylonians? The answer to the second question was to control the prosperous trade that crossed the deserts. But once he had Tayma under control, he rebuilt the city's walls, erected a new palace for himself, and constructed an elaborate irrigation system: all signs he intended to stay.

Nabonidus deeply wanted to reform the Babylonian religion, but Babylon's priests and his son Belteshazzar staunchly resisted his efforts. Although he had been a priest to Marduk (probably assigned to the position) before becoming king, he desired to elevate Sin over Marduk as the primary god of the Babylonian pantheon. Since Babylon's inception, Marduk had been its chief god, and the Babylonians considered

---

[i] Beaulieu, *Reign of Nabonidus*, 138.

Nabonidus' efforts to supplant Marduk an unholy abomination. Nabonidus wrote in inscriptions that he remained in Tayma because of the "impiety of the Babylonians."[i]

While Nabonidus was in Arabia, he seemed oblivious to the threat of Cyrus the Great, who was building the astounding Persian Empire, surrounding the Babylonian Empire to the east, north, and west. Decades earlier, the Medes had allied with the Persians, sealing their alliance by the marriage of King Cambyses of Persia to Mandane, the daughter of King Astyages of Media and granddaughter of Cyaxares the Great. Cyrus II (Cyrus the Great) was the child of this marriage.

One legend said that when Cyrus was born, King Astyages dreamed that Cyrus would overthrow him one day. He sent his general Harpagus to kill his grandson, but instead, Harpagus gave the baby to a shepherd, who raised him as his own. Ten years later, Cyrus' true identity came to light. Astyages punished Harpagus by killing his son and serving his body to Harpagus at a banquet; however, he permitted Cyrus to return to his biological parents.

At the beginning of Nabonidus' reign, Cyrus was king of Persia, and Astyages ruled the Medes. Cyrus engaged in a power struggle with Astyages and broke off his grandfather's overlordship with the help of General Harpagus, who was eager to avenge his son. Harpagus convinced the Median military to abandon Astyages and join with Cyrus. After Astyages' death, his son Cyaxares II (with the throne name Darius) became the king of the Medes in a subservient position to his nephew Cyrus. When the Medes joined with the Persians, they held power over Bactria (Tajikistan and Uzbekistan), Parthia (northeastern Iran), and the Saka nomads, who roamed the Eurasian Steppe and into what is now China's Xinjiang province.

While Nabonidus was in Arabia, not paying attention, the Medes and Persians conquered kingdoms to the north and northwest of Babylonia. They took Lydia in 547 BCE and then shocked the Greek world by defeating the twelve Greek colonies in Ionia, important city-states and trade centers. Cyrus permitted Asia Minor's city-states to continue under self-rule as long as they paid tribute and supplied men for his massive army.

---

[i] Beaulieu, *Reign of Nabonidus*, 184.

Cyrus put his camels in the front line at the Battle of Thymbra, sending the Lydian horses, which had never seen or smelled camels, into a panic.[101]

Cyrus then targeted the Sogdian nomads to the north of Bactria and successfully defeated them. For the next 150 years, they paid a tribute of carnelian, lapis lazuli, and other semiprecious stones. The Medes and Persians also took control of the rest of the Anatolian peninsula (today's western Turkey). Nabonidus' seeming indifference spurred Babylonia's citizens into an increasing malcontent. However, the regent Belshazzar fully understood the Persian peril and reinforced defenses in critical areas.

The Persians' next move was south, down the Mediterranean coastline. The Phoenician cities overlooking the sea, including ancient Tyre, Sidon, Byblos, and Tripoli, did not resist them, aware of Cyrus' track record of mercy toward conquered regions. Cyrus permitted them to carry on as usual with an annual tribute of 350 talents. This was the Persians' first incursion into Babylonian territory, and it finally jolted Nabonidus out of his stupor. Springing into action, Nabonidus returned to Babylon.

Cyrus' next move against the Babylonian Empire was conquering its vassal territory of Elam and its capital Susa, to the southwest of the Babylonian heartland. This impelled Nabonidus to call for the principal statues of the gods and goddesses to be brought from Babylonia's cities and stored in Babylon for safekeeping.[i] Nabonidus then marched north with his troops to defend Sippar and Opis on opposite ends of the Median Wall. Nebuchadnezzar had built the wall to protect against invasions by the Medes, and it stretched from Opis on the Tigris River to Sippar on the Euphrates. Thus, the rivers on both sides and the north wall protected Babylonia.

Cyrus approached with Gubaru (Gobryas), a cunning general whose innovative military tactics were pivotal to Cyrus' invasion of Babylonia. Some scholars believe Gubaru was Cyaxares II, king of the Medes, also known as Darius the Mede. If not, King Darius was also part of the coalition forces. At the end of September 539 BCE, Cyrus' Persian troops and the Medes led by Gubaru approached Opis in the season when the Mesopotamian rivers were at their lowest levels. By overcoming Opis on the eastern shore of the Tigris, Cyrus could ford the river and outflank the Median Wall.

The coalition army of Cyrus and Gubaru launched their assault on Opis, crushing the Babylonian forces, plundering the city, and slaughtering the citizens. Herodotus wrote that Cyrus' engineers diverted the Tigris into several canals, lowering the river level even further, enabling his troops to wade across. Cyrus then divided his army. He led part of his military west to Sippar and sent Gubaru to attack Babylon.

When Cyrus approached Sippar, the city surrendered on October 10 without a battle. The military leaders defending Sippar were unsupportive of King Nabonidus, who had spent over half his reign outside the country and disrespected their god Marduk. They also may have doubted their ability to defend Sippar, realizing that Cyrus must have already conquered Opis to the east. When Sippar surrendered to Cyrus, Nabonidus fled south.

Oblivious to the catastrophe in the north, the city of Babylon was celebrating the festival of the moon god Sin, which had been on hold all the years Nabonidus was away.[ii] They had no inkling that Cyrus had crossed the Tigris, defeated Opis, breached the Median Wall sixty miles north of Babylon, and taken Sippar. With little resistance from the Babylonians between Sippar and Babylon, Gubaru reached Babylon with

---

[i] *The Chronicle Concerning the Reign of Nabonidus (ABC 7)*, Livius, 2020. https://www.livius.org/sources/content/mesopotamian-chronicles-content/abc-7-nabonidus-chronicle/

[ii] *Reign of Nabonidus (ABC 7)*.

lightning speed in only two days.

Unaware of the Persian coalition forces rapidly closing in, the co-regent Belshazzar hosted an elaborate dinner for a thousand of his noblemen on the religious holiday. After tasting the wine, Belshazzar commanded that the gold and silver goblets that Nebuchadnezzar had taken from Jerusalem's temple be brought to the palace so his princes, wives, and concubines could drink from them.

Then, suddenly, Belteshazzar looked up. All the color drained from his face, and his legs gave way under him as he saw the disembodied fingers of a human hand inscribing something on the wall! The co-regent shouted for his astrologers and enchanters to read the writing and tell its meaning, but no one could do it. Hearing the clamor, the queen (Nabonidus' wife) hurried into the banquet hall, telling her son not to be so pale and frightened:

> "There is a man in your kingdom in whom is the spirit of the holy gods, whom the king Nebuchadnezzar made master of the magicians, astrologers, Chaldeans, and soothsayers. Knowledge, understanding, and interpreting of dreams were found in the same Daniel, whom the king named Belteshazzar. Call for Daniel, and he will tell you what the writing means."[i]

By this time, Daniel was an old man in his eighties, brought as a captive to Babylon about sixty-five years earlier. Belshazzar promised to give him a purple robe, a gold chain around his neck, and make him third in the kingdom if he interpreted the writing on the wall. Daniel answered:

> "Keep your gifts! Or give them to someone else. You have not honored the God who gives you the breath of life and controls your destiny!
>
> This is what the writing on the wall says: 'MENE, MENE, TEKEL, UPHARSIN.'
>
> This is the interpretation: God has numbered the days of your kingdom and ended it. You are weighed in the balances and found wanting. Your kingdom is divided and given to the Medes and Persians."[ii]

---

[i] *Daniel 5*, Tanakh: Ketuvim: Book of Daniel.
[ii] *Daniel 5*, Tanakh: Ketuvim: Book of Daniel.

That night, the Persian forces arrived on the eastern side of the Euphrates, while the Babylonians were drinking and partying in the streets, celebrating the holiday, unaware of their impending doom. Usually, the depth of the Euphrates was about twelve feet deep at that location, but, once again, the Persian engineers diverted the river into a canal, dropping the water level so the Medes and Persians could wade across. They broke through the Enlil Gate, launching a surprise attack on Babylon.

> "Thereupon they entered, and of those they met, some were struck down and slain, and others fled into their houses, and some raised the hue and cry, but Gubaru and his friends covered the cry with their shouts, as though they were revelers themselves. And thus, making their way by the quickest route, they soon found themselves before the king's palace.
>
> Here the detachment found the gates closed, but the men appointed to attack the guards rushed on them as they lay drinking around a blazing fire and closed with them then and there. As the din grew louder and louder, those within became aware of the tumult, till, the king bidding them see what it meant, some of them opened the gates and ran out. Gubaru and his men, seeing the gates swing wide, darted in, hard on the heels of the others who fled back again, and they chased them at the sword's point into the king's presence.
>
> They found him on his feet with his drawn scimitar. They overwhelmed him by sheer weight of numbers: and not one of his retinue escaped; they were all cut down, some flying, others snatching up anything to serve as a shield and defending themselves as best they could."[i]

The "king" killed by Gubaru's men was the regent Belshazzar, not his father King Nabonidus, according to Belteshazzar (Daniel), an eyewitness to the events: "That very night Belshazzar was killed, and Darius the Mede took over the kingdom at the age of sixty-two."[ii]

The Babylonian historian Berossus said Darius the Mede was the Median king Cyaxares II, Cyrus' uncle. Gubaru may have been the same

---

[i] Xenophon, *Cyropaedia: The Education of Cyrus,* trans. Henry Graham Dakyns. (Project Gutenberg E-book). https://www.gutenberg.org/files/2085/2085-h/2085-h.htm

[ii] *Daniel 5,* Tanakh: Ketuvim: Book of Daniel.

person, but more likely, he was of lesser status. Daniel called Darius a king, saying he divided the realm into 120 provinces and appointed satraps (governors); this implies Darius ruled over the whole empire temporarily, not just Babylonia.[i] The *Nabonidus Chronicle* says Gubaru appointed the district officers of Babylonia as the appointed satrap of Babylonia.[ii] Cyrus may have designated his uncle, King Darius of the Medes, as regent over the empire while he finished consolidating the Levant.

What happened to Nabonidus? The *Nabonidus Chronicle (ABC 7)* recorded that Nabonidus initially fled following Sippar's surrender to Cyrus, but the Persians captured him after Cyrus conquered Babylon. Cyrus treated him kindly and sent him to live in Carmania (Iran).[iii]

Cyrus arrived with great fanfare about two weeks later. Persian inscriptions said the people of Babylon threw open the gates and welcomed Cyrus as their deliverer with peace, joy, and jubilation. This propaganda likely whitewashed the invasion; however, the Babylonians were clearly unhappy with their absentee king and his despotic regent. Cyrus' reputation of considerate treatment of submissive conquered cities preceded him, and few Babylonians resisted the Persian takeover.

The Medes and Persians treated the religious sites and temples with the utmost respect and encouraged the priests to continue the worship rituals. Cyrus offered the Magi the first pick of the spoils of war to consecrate to the gods. He returned all the cult images of the Babylonian deities that Nabonidus had gathered into Babylon and publicly worshiped Marduk, endearing himself to the Babylonians.

Cyrus took the title "King of Babylon, Sumer, and Akkad. King of the four corners of the earth." Once he consolidated Mesopotamia under his rule, he swiftly conquered northern Arabia, Israel, and Syria. Cyrus reversed the population-relocation program the Babylonians and Assyrians used against rebel provinces. He permitted the Jews and other exiles to return home in the first year of his reign, although Daniel and many others remained in Babylonia in leadership positions. Cyrus ordered the rebuilding of Jerusalem's temple:

---

[i] *Daniel 6.*
[ii] *Reign of Nabonidus (ABC 7).*
[iii] Beaulieu, *Reign of Nabonidus,* 231.

"Concerning the house of God at Jerusalem, let the temple, where sacrifices are offered, be rebuilt. Let its foundations be retained, its height being sixty cubits and its width sixty cubits, with three layers of huge stones and one layer of timbers. And let the cost be paid from the royal treasury. Also, let the gold and silver utensils of the house of God, which Nebuchadnezzar took from the temple in Jerusalem and brought to Babylon, be returned and brought to their places in the temple in Jerusalem; you shall put them in the house of God."[i]

Cyrus' vast Achaemenid Empire reached from Asia Minor to the Indus River by the end of his life. He won the hearts of his new subjects through extraordinary humanity and respect for their cultures. He governed Babylonia and his other vast territories through a centralized administration, with a governor (satrap) over each province. Under Persian rule, Babylon became a center of scientific and mathematic knowledge. A year before he died in 530 BCE, Cyrus appointed his son Cambyses II as Babylon's king, while he continued as the empire's king.

A Greek painting of Darius the Great.[102]

---

[i] *Ezra 6.* Tanakh: Ketuvim, Book of Ezra.

After the short reigns of Cyrus' sons, Darius I (the Great) seized control of the Persian Empire. Taking advantage of the chaos, Babylonia declared independence in 521 BCE under King Nebuchadnezzar III, who ruled for about a year. Darius led an enormous army against Babylon, where the citizens jeered him from the walls, "You'll capture Babylon when mules have foals!" Typically, mules are sterile, but a mule gave birth after an unsuccessful twenty-month siege of Babylon! This miraculous event galvanized the Persians to take Babylon successfully. Darius did not show the Babylonians the mercy they had received under Cyrus. He impaled three thousand leading citizens and pulled down the city's massive gates and defenses.[i]

Over the next two centuries, as Persia's vassal kingdom, Babylonia declined. High taxes and warfare led to the neglect of the elegant temples and canal systems necessary for adequate agriculture. Two other rebellions sprung up, but Persia quickly suppressed the renegades. When Alexander the Great conquered the Persian Empire in 331 BCE, Babylon became his home and center of operations when he wasn't leading military expeditions. He adopted the Babylonian dress, reverenced the temples, and the city flourished in his brief stay. He planned to restore Babylon's ziggurat but unexpectedly died in Babylon before he could see it through.

Babylon maintained its urban life through two centuries of warfare between Alexander's successors, but it was no longer an administrative or economic hub. Alexandria in Egypt took over as the center of science and mathematics for the known world. Babylon's Esagila temple remained a religious center and pilgrimage destination, but gradually, Babylon deteriorated. When the Muslims invaded Babylonia in the mid-seventh century CE, Babylon had dwindled to only a village. The ruins of the once majestic city were a source of bricks for construction elsewhere.

---

[i] Herodotus, *Capture of Babylon*. Livius. https://www.livius.org/articles/person/darius-the-great/sources/capture-of-babylon-herodotus

Chapter 8: Babylonian Society and Famous Rulers

Babylonia was a majestic empire, pivotal to ancient Middle Eastern history, but history is always the story of people. From those who lived in palaces to the commoners of shops and farms, Babylonia's people were consequential to its three-time rise and fall. We've already discussed the exploits of many of its leaders, but what about its ordinary citizens? What was their social structure, and how did they live their everyday lives? How did the Babylonians develop military technology? What more can we learn about their famous leaders? Aside from great conquests, what were they like as people?

Hammurabi's law code, which we will discuss more extensively in chapter nine, gives a fascinating insight into Babylonian family life and women's legal status.[1] For instance, if a wife were caught in adultery, she and her lover would be drowned in the river unless her husband pardoned her. If someone accused a woman of adultery, but with no proof, she could "jump into the river": if she drowned, she was guilty, but if she survived, she was innocent.

If a man violated a virgin girl betrothed to another man, the rapist would receive the death penalty, but the girl would be considered

---

[1] *The Code of Hammurabi*, trans. L.W. King (The Avalon Project: Documents in Law, History, and Diplomacy. Yale Law School: Lillian Goldman Law Library).
https://avalon.law.yale.edu/ancient/hamframe.asp

innocent. If a man abandoned his wife and she moved in with another man, the husband could not reclaim his wife if he returned.

This bas-relief of a man and woman dates to the Old Babylonian era.[108]

When a woman married, her husband paid a "bride price" to her father, and her father gave her a dowry. Her husband had no claim to the dowry for his own use: it was for her children. If a man separated from the mother of his children, he had to return her dowry and give her the benefit of part of his field and garden to support the children. Once their children grew up, he had to provide her with a payment, and then she could marry "the man of her heart." If a couple had no children, the husband simply needed to return her dowry to divorce her. The only time a man could divorce his wife without returning her dowry was if she were a substandard wife, running up debts and neglecting her husband and home.

A man could take a second wife if his first wife could not conceive, but the first wife would hold higher status over the second. If a wife became chronically ill, the husband could take a second wife, but he had to permit his first wife to live in his home and care for her as long as she lived. She could leave if she wanted to, but he had to return her dowry. A man could have a wife and also have sexual relations with a maidservant in his home. If he acknowledged the maid's children as his own, both his legitimate sons and his sons by the maid would receive equal portions of his estate. A man was expected to provide a dowry and arrange a marriage for his daughter by a concubine.

What if a man had several sons and arranged marriages for them (paying their bride prices) but died before negotiating a union for the youngest son? In that case, the older brothers had to set aside money for their younger brother's bride price before dividing up the property among them; they also had to arrange a marriage for their brother.

The Babylonian social hierarchy had five principal layers: nobility, middle class, landowning farmers, tenant farmers, and enslaved people. The elite *awilum* or *mar bane* (nobility and upper class) were "freemen" of the royal family, chief administrators, high-ranking military, high-ranking priests and priestesses (often members of the royal family), and owners of large estates.

The term *muškenum* in Hammurabi's code appeared to refer to anyone in the middle status between the *awilum* elite class and the *wardum*, or slaves. This middle class comprised scribes, lower-ranking priests and priestesses, merchants, skilled artisans, and farmers. The regular farmers were owners of smaller plots, and they often performed double duty: serving in the lower military ranks and coming home in time for planting and harvesting. Tenant farmers worked the large estates' fields. The landowner usually provided housing, and the tenant's harvest would be split three ways: part for taxes, part for the landowner, and part for the tenant farmer.

Slaves (*wardum*) ranked lowest in Babylonian society, and a person could become enslaved in two ways. One was being captured in war, but usually, the Babylonians only brought back scribes and highly-skilled artisans. If a man had a debt he could not pay, he could sell himself, his wife, or his children into slavery. They would work for three years for the person who bought them and go free in the fourth year.

Giving shelter to a runaway slave meant the death penalty, but if a man returned a runaway slave to his owner, the owner had to pay two shekels. If an enslaved man married a free woman, their children would be free. If a slave married to a free woman later died, she had to give half her dowry and any accumulated wealth from the marriage to her husband's owner. If an enslaved person was accidentally killed or seriously injured, the penalty for the offender was less than for a free person.

Throughout its history, trade was intrinsic to the Babylonian economy. The population relocations of rebellious conquered people into Babylonia, first by the Assyrians and later by Nebuchadnezzar II, created ethnic groups of Babylonians with solid ties to their lands of origin. They were integrated into the social and commercial Babylonian milieu but maintained contact with their homelands, with the language knowledge and valuable contacts intrinsic to trade.

Even before the massive population shifts, the Mesopotamian people traded with the Eastern Mediterranean, Armenia, Elam, and points along the Persian Gulf. The fertile Mesopotamian river system provided surplus food, which the Babylonians traded for wood, metal, and luxuries like precious and semiprecious stones, dyes, and incense. The courtyards of the Babylonian temples served as a marketplace, and the priests and priestesses were among the chief buyers of luxury items for adorning the temples.

Thousands of clay tablets with cuneiform script and the Aramaic alphabet illustrate the Babylonians' literacy level. Written communication included letters, hymns, prayers, inscriptions on monuments, sales records and inventory, history annals, law codes, property transactions, and legal documents. A portion of Babylon's society knew how to read and write, and everyone else hired scribes. Young people from wealthier families were tutored at home or attended privately-run schools, often in the temples.

In the Neo-Babylonian Empire, scribes had to learn both cuneiform and Aramaic script and be fluent in several languages. They practiced by copying older tablets and transcribing their teachers' dictations. One scribal duty was preserving the ancient literature of the Sumerians, Akkadians, Assyrians, and earlier Babylonians; the scribes would translate and copy these history annals, myths, prayers, and other literature.

What language did the Babylonians speak? The Akkadian, Assyrian, Babylonian, Arabic, and Hebrew languages were all from the Semitic language family. However, the written Assyrian and Babylonian languages were so close to Akkadian that most linguists classify them as dialects of Akkadian, although the spoken languages may have been more distinct. Throughout Babylonia's history, the people would have spoken Babylonian-Akkadian; they probably also spoke Sumerian in the First Babylonian dynasty. We don't know what language the Kassite-era Babylonians spoke, but they wrote in the Sumerian and Akkadian languages.

Aramaic, another Semitic language initially spoken in Syria, gradually took precedence. The Neo-Assyrians used Aramaic as their second official language, and it eventually replaced Akkadian, becoming the Neo-Babylonian Empire's standard spoken and written language. The Aramaic alphabet was far easier to read and write than the ancient cuneiform, which required a distinctive character for every word. One had to memorize at least six hundred characters for basic literacy in cuneiform, but written Aramaic used only twenty-two letters, all consonants.

The Chaldean King Marduk-apla-iddina (722–710 BCE) and his attendant wear ankle-length skirts with long sashes. The king is wearing a conical hat.[104]

What did the Babylonians wear? Both men and women wore long tunics or skirts that often fell in tiers. Sometimes, a gown would come up over one shoulder like a toga and be trimmed with fringe. In summer or when doing heavy work, men would wear a simple knee-length skirt and go bare-chested. Men often wore conical or bowl-shaped hats and long beards, elaborately braided or curled if they were upper-class. They wore their hair down to their shoulders, also often braided or curled.

Women also wore curled or braided shoulder-length hair. The tops of their tunics covered their breasts and sometimes were bandeau-style, with one or both shoulders bare but more often with a modest, rounded neckline. Their gowns might have short or long sleeves or be sleeveless. Both men and women wore earrings, headbands, bracelets, and necklaces of gold and precious metals.

Babylonia's military assimilated some of the tactics used by the Sumerians, Akkadians, and Assyrians but often added its own twists. Generally speaking, Babylonia's kings and military commanders were not as cruel as some of the notorious Assyrian kings and Akkad's King Rimush. They usually did not torture conquered or rebellious populations or wipe out large populations. The exception was when they allied with the Scythians, Medes, and Parthians for Assyria's final defeat.

This woman holding a baby from the Old Babylonian period wears a full-length, tiered tunic and elaborately-braided shoulder-length hair.[105]

Interestingly, on two occasions when they allied with these tribes, they arrived late for the battle, after their allies had broken the city's defenses and were plundering the temples and palaces. Perhaps the Babylonians were slow to muster their troops. But maybe they were canny: why endanger their own men and horses when their partners were eager to do the dangerous part of eliminating their enemies?

A common tactic used by the Babylonian military was diverting rivers into existing irrigation canals or new canals they dug themselves. This enabled them to cross even large rivers like the Tigris and Euphrates. A well-used strategy for conquering a city was to flood it in two ways: damming and suddenly releasing the river's water or diverting the river to flow into the city. On more than one occasion, they defended themselves against invading Assyrians by redirecting the river and canal system to form a lake around their own forces!

Aside from their innovative military tactics, what more can we know about Babylonia's famous rulers? Hammurabi, the famous conqueror of the Old Babylonian Empire, wrote one of the world's earliest and most complex law codes, but he also engaged in outstanding building projects that put Babylon on the map. He transformed Babylon by promoting the god Marduk and constructing majestic temples, palaces, and city walls. What was once a humble and unremarkable small town grew into a breathtaking metropolis that usurped Nippur's position as Mesopotamia's "holy city" and became the political capital of Sumer and Akkad.

Hammurabi ruled from 1792 to 1750 BCE (middle chronology).[106]

Hammurabi's promotion of Marduk from an obscure city god to the supreme deity of the pantheon proved problematic for the god: he was constantly being stolen. That is, his cult image (idol) was stolen, but the Mesopotamians believed their gods inhabited the statues. If someone removed a god's cult image from the city, it meant the god had left the city, which would bring all sorts of misfortune. Even though he was a god, Marduk couldn't get back on his own. He had to wait for months or even years before someone brought him back to Babylon.

Rescuing Marduk was one of the things for which King Nebuchadnezzar I was famous. Although not as well-known as his Neo-Babylonian namesake Nebuchadnezzar II, the first Nebuchadnezzar was a king of Isin who conquered and ruled Babylon from 1121 to 1100 BCE. His rescue of Marduk, stolen earlier by the Elamites, is immortalized in the *Epic of Nabu-kudurri-uṣur I*.[i] The *Marduk Prophecy* also tells of Marduk's journeys to different points outside Babylon.[ii] Although Marduk enjoyed his stay with the Hittites and Assyrians, he found Elam distasteful. He prophesied his return to Babylon through a zealous king who would avenge the sacking of Babylon and Marduk's theft, and that king turned out to be Nebuchadnezzar I.

Nabopolassar, the "Avenger of Akkad," is known chiefly for crushing Assyria for all time and initiating the Neo-Babylonian Empire in 626 BCE. But the Babylonians and even the Greeks remembered Nabopolassar for his piety, fair-mindedness, and integrity. He rose to power from obscurity, crediting Marduk's patronage and the support of Babylonia's priests and noblemen. The Babylonians, Hellenists, and even the Jewish historian Josephus portrayed him as a just king who deeply revered Marduk. The Babylonians and Nabopolassar himself concluded that his devoutness elevated him to kingship, enabling him to liberate Babylonia and conquer the Assyrians when previous kings had failed:

> "Šazu perceived my intentions, and he placed me, the insignificant one who was not even noticed among the people, in the highest position in my native country. He called me to

---

[i] *Cuneiform Texts from Babylonian Tablets in the British Museum: Part XIII* (Piccadilly: Longmans and Co., 1901), 54. https://www.yumpu.com/en/document/read/18926135/babylonian-tablets-c

[ii] Joshua J. Mark, "The Marduk Prophecy," *World History Encyclopedia* (2016). https://www.worldhistory.org/article/990/the-marduk-prophecy

the lordship over land and people."[i]

Nabopolassar's son Nebuchadnezzar II was Neo-Babylonia's shining star, yet he did not always display his father's humility. Daniel's account in the Tanakh tells how he paid the price for his pride and impiety:

> "One night, I had a dream that terrified me. When all the magicians, enchanters, astrologers, and fortune-tellers came in, I told them the dream, but they could not tell me what it meant. At last, Daniel came in before me, and I told him the dream. (He was named Belteshazzar after my god, and the spirit of the holy gods is in him.)"[ii]

Nebuchadnezzar told Belteshazzar his dream of a great tree reaching to heaven, loaded with fruit for the entire world and providing shade and protection to all. But then he heard a voice from heaven saying to cut down the tree but leave the stump. When Belteshazzar heard Nebuchadnezzar's dream, he was horror-stricken:

> "I wish the events foreshadowed in this dream would happen to your enemies, my lord, and not to you! That tree, Your Majesty, is you. You have grown strong, and your greatness reaches up to heaven and your rule to the ends of the earth.
>
> This is what the dream means, Your Majesty, and what the Most High has declared will happen to my lord the king. You will be driven from human society and live in the fields with the wild animals. You will eat grass like a cow, and you will be drenched with the dew of heaven.
>
> Seven periods of time will pass while you live this way until you learn that the Most High rules over the kingdoms of the world and gives them to anyone he chooses. But the stump and tree roots were left in the ground, and this means that you will receive your kingdom back again when you have learned that heaven rules."[iii]

---

[i] Rocío Da Riva, "The Figure of Nabopolassar in Late Achaemenid and Hellenistic Historiographic Tradition: BM 34793 and CUA 90," *Journal of Near Eastern Studies* 76, no.1. https://www.journals.uchicago.edu/doi/full/10.1086/690464

[ii] *Daniel 4.* Tanakh, Navi, Book of Daniel.

[iii] *Daniel 4,* Tanakh, Navi, Book of Daniel.

William Blake's relief etching depicts Nebuchadnezzar's madness as told by Daniel.[107]

The dream came true twelve months later, as Nebuchadnezzar was pridefully gazing at Babylon from the roof of his palace, boasting of his power, the beautiful city he had built, and his majestic splendor. He lost his sanity and crawled about in the fields, eating grass like an animal "until his hair was as long as eagles' feathers and his nails were like birds' claws." Finally, when his reason returned, Nebuchadnezzar acknowledged and praised God, who restored him as head of the kingdom.

Many scholars dismiss Belteshazzar's account in the *Tanakh* due to the lack of other Babylonian records corroborating Nebuchadnezzar's madness or a seven-month (or seven-year) period of absence from Babylon. Some historians believe the story actually refers to Nabonidus, the last king of the Neo-Babylonians, who spent ten years in exile in Tayma, Arabia. The *Verse Account of Nabonidus* alludes to mental illness.[i] The *Prayer of Nabonidus*, found in the Dead Sea Scrolls, stated, "I was afflicted for seven years...and an exorcist pardoned my sins. He was a Jew from among the children of the exile of Judah."[ii]

---

[i] *Verse Account of Nabonidus*, trans A. Leo Oppenheim. Livius. https://www.livius.org/sources/content/anet/verse-account-of-nabonidus/

[ii] *Prayer of Nabonidus (4Q242)*. Livius. https://www.livius.org/sources/content/dss/4q242-prayer-of-

Belteshazzar (Daniel) was an exile from Judah, he was alive in Nabonidus' day, and he may have been the one who ministered to Nabonidus. However, a badly-damaged cuneiform text in the British Museum implies Nebuchadnezzar experienced a mental break. He no longer valued his life, gave confusing orders, neglected his children and family, and lost interest in the Esagila temple and Babylon's affairs.

The text said that the Babylonians gave "bad counsel" to Evil-Merodach (Amel-Marduk, Nebuchadnezzar's son).[i] Nebuchadnezzar's son Nabû-šuma-ukīn (believed to be Amel-Marduk) took part in a coup against Nebuchadnezzar and was thrown into prison.[ii] Why would his son and nobles seek to supplant Nebuchadnezzar? Where was Nebuchadnezzar while this was happening? What destabilized Babylon in this latter part of Nebuchadnezzar's reign? Only four inscriptions have survived that document Nebuchadnezzar's activities in this period, compared to over fifty in his first ten years.

If nothing else, Babylonia's well-known kings were complex, multifaceted individuals who struggled with humility and mental soundness. They were propelled to greatness by their ability to think differently and innovatively. Sometimes, they experienced dramatic successes; other times, people thought they were experiencing mental breaks, and perhaps some were. When a king achieved astounding triumphs, and everyone dropped to the floor in worship when he entered the room, staying grounded in reality would be challenging.

---

nabonidus/

[i] A. K. Grayson, *Babylonian Historical-Literary Texts: Toronto Semitic Texts and Studies, 3* (Toronto: University of Toronto Press, 1975), 87-92.

[ii] Irving Finkel, "The Lament of Nabû-šuma-ukîn." in *Focus Mesopotamischer Geschichte, Wiege früher Gelehrtsamkeit, Mythos in der Moderne.* (Saaerbrücken, 1999), 323-341.

Chapter 9: Culture and Innovation

The Babylonian powerhouse generated astounding advances in the arts, sciences, and law. Their libraries held impressive literature collections from throughout the Middle East, and their mosaics and distinctive architecture were unparalleled. They made unimaginable leaps in the knowledge of medicine, mathematics, astronomy, and concepts of time. Their legal codes served as prototypes for generations to come.

Babylonia hosted the world's first known libraries. However, the Assyrians quickly imitated their southern neighbors, with copies of Babylonian literature stored in Ashurbanipal's palace library in Nineveh. One impressive Babylonian collection of seventy tablets on astronomy and astrology dates to 2000 BCE and discusses the movements of comets, the north star (Polaris), and Venus. Other noteworthy collections included mathematical formulas, such as cube roots. The libraries contained fascinating historical chronicles and famous literature: poems, hymns, and epic tales.

Excavation of a temple at Sippar uncovered fifty thousand clay tablets, mostly cataloging business transactions, administrative affairs, and private correspondence. However, it also included a respectable literary collection with a narrative of the Great Flood and vital religious texts, including incantations, hymns, and prayers. Evidence from the documents showed that the temple had a school that taught reading, writing, and mathematics. Archaeologists uncovered similar collections in a temple in Nippur.

One of the most acclaimed Babylonian literary works, and possibly the world's oldest, is the *Epic of Gilgamesh*. The oldest full copy of the epic dates to around 1800 BCE, but five Sumerian poems from about 2100 BCE tell part of the story, and it likely had an oral history that went back even further. The captivating epic is about King Gilgamesh, a real-life king of Uruk (based on ancient inscriptions and the *Sumerian King List*), yet the story contains fantastical elements.

Gilgamesh was part human and part divine in the legend, with unmatched strength and beauty. Yet, he had a dark side: he claimed the "right of the first night," forcing himself on Uruk's virgin brides on their wedding day. When Uruk's people complained of this injustice to the gods, the gods created Enkidu, a hairy wild man as strong as Gilgamesh. He roamed the plains with the wild herds, eating grass.

A trapper saw Enkidu shoving his way through the animals at the watering hole. Frightened, he hurried home to tell his father about the wild man; no doubt he was the one who had been setting the animals free from his traps! His father told him to get Shamhat, the prostitute, to tame this feral creature. Then they could use him as their champion against their hated king Gilgamesh.

Shamhat agreed to the plan and went out to the watering hole; when Enkidu showed up, she opened her gown. One look at Shamhat's beautiful figure and Enkidu forgot everything but having sexual relations with her for the next seven days. But now, his animal friends ran away when they saw him. Shamhat taught Enkidu how to eat human food, and he especially enjoyed his first rounds of beer!

Shamhat invited Enkidu to come with her to Uruk, telling him they needed help overthrowing their wicked king. She told him a wedding was taking place that night, and King Gilgamesh would force himself on the bride. Enkidu marched into Uruk to defend the bride and stationed himself outside her door, refusing to let Gilgamesh in. The two men lunged at each other and brawled ferociously, but they were equally strong, and neither could overcome the other. They stepped back, exhausted, looked at each other, then kissed and became friends.

They grew so excited about what they could do with their combined strength that they forgot all about the bride and plotted to kill the Humbaba monster, guardian of Lebanon's cedar forest. They quickly marched toward Lebanon, and when they arrived, Humbaba sneered at them, "I will feed your bodies to the shrieking vultures!"

But the two mighty men killed Humbaba, cutting off his head. They built a raft and sailed back to Uruk, but the goddess Ishtar saw Gilgamesh bathing just before he arrived in Uruk. When he shook out his long curls, she was stirred to lust and called out, "Gilgamesh! Come, be my husband!"

Gilgamesh laughed, "Where are all your other bridegrooms? Where's Tammuz, your shepherd? You send him to Hades for half of every year!"

Infuriated, Ishtar flew up to her father Anu in heaven. "Father! Gilgamesh mocked me repeatedly! Give me the Bull of Heaven, or I'll rip open the gates of the underworld, and the zombies will come out to eat the living people!"

Anu gave her the Bull of Heaven, and Ishtar led it to Uruk. The Bull snorted, the ground opened, and one hundred men fell into an abyss. A second time, the Bull snorted, and two hundred men fell into a second hole. The third time the Bull snorted, Enkidu began to fall but quickly grabbed the Bull's horns. "Quick, Gilgamesh! Stab the Bull!"

Gilgamesh kills the Bull of Heaven.[108]

When Ishtar saw her Bull was dead, she screeched curses from Uruk's wall, but Enkidu flung the Bull's hindquarter at her. The horrified gods conferred and determined they had to execute one of the men; they were getting out of control and killing the divine animals! Although Gilgamesh had been the one to kill both Humbaba and the Bull of Heaven, the gods sentenced Enkidu to death.

With tears flowing, Gilgamesh mourned Enkidu for six days and seven nights, not letting anyone bury his friend until a maggot fell out of Enkidu's nose. Horrified, Gilgamesh considered his own mortality: he would be lying dead like Enkidu one day! He set off to find Utnapishtim, who had built the ark to save people and animals from the Great Flood. Utnapishtim was still alive after all these centuries, and Gilgamesh wanted to learn the key to immortality.

Gilgamesh hiked to the highest peak, Mount Mashu, then tunneled through twelve terrifying leagues of utter darkness. He emerged into brilliant light and sailed through the Waters of Death until he reached Utnapishtim's land. "Why do you look so devastated?" the patriarch asked.

"How could I not despair?" Gilgamesh asked. "My best friend died! I can't be silent. Won't I meet the same fate? I must know, how did you discover immortality?"

Utnapishtim told his story, "When Anu planned to flood the whole earth, the god Ea spoke to me through the wall of my reed house. He told me to build a boat and bring all the animals inside. After I built the boat and covered it with bitumen, the rain started falling. It rained for six days and seven nights, covering the people and even the mountains. Finally, the wind and rain stopped, and the ark rested on Mount Nimush.

"After seven days, I released a dove, who flew around but came back to me, unable to find a place to land. Later, I released a swallow, but it came back. Finally, I released a raven, and it flew away, never to return. I let the animals out of the ark and sacrificed a sheep to the gods. At that point, the god Enlil gifted my wife and me with immortality."

Utnapishtim told Gilgamesh about a unique plant growing under the sea that gave eternal life. Tying rocks to his feet, Gilgamesh sank into the sea, discovered the magical plant, cut it, then untied the stones and swam up to the surface. But traveling home with the plant of eternity, he stopped to bathe in a spring, and a snake stole his plant! Gilgamesh collapsed to the ground, weeping. Finally, he traveled home to Uruk, realizing that his legacy would continue through his city even though he would die.

In addition to its remarkable literature, the Neo-Babylonian Empire sparked a cultural renaissance of exquisite art and stunning architecture, featuring majestic temples with brightly-colored walls. The Greek historian Herodotus said Babylon was the most breathtaking city of its day, with city walls so wide that chariots could ride on top. The three palaces and temples gleamed with bricks glazed in yellow and blue, adorned with bright mosaics of lions, dragons, and horses.

Towering over the rest of the city stood the ninety-one-meter high Etemenanki ziggurat, the "foundation of heaven on earth." The Mesopotamian ziggurats were tall and massive terraced structures that were part of their cities' temple complexes. The Etemenanki had a shrine to Marduk at its top and stood next to the Esagila temple. The Etemenanki would have been one of the world's highest structures in its day, with its terraced sides appearing as steps up to heaven.

Was the Etemenanki ziggurat the Tower of Babel?[109]

The Amorites probably built the original ziggurat during the Old Babylonian Period (1894-1595 BCE), when Babylon was likely the largest city in the world. Like other Mesopotamian ziggurats, it was probably remodeled and rebuilt several times over the centuries. The Assyrian king Sennacherib bragged of destroying it in 689 BCE. Nebuchadnezzar II completed the final structure after forty-three years of work during the Neo-Babylonian Empire when Babylon was likely once again the world's largest city. Nebuchadnezzar II reported that he and two of his sons even took part in the construction project (at least ritually):

> "I rolled up my garment, my kingly robe, and carried on my head bricks and earth. I had soil-baskets made of gold and silver and made Nebuchadnezzar, my firstborn son, beloved of my heart, carry alongside my workmen earth mixed with

wine, oil, and resin chips. I made Nabûsumilisir, his brother, a boy, issue of my body, my darling younger son, take up mattock and spade. I burdened him with a soil-basket of gold and silver and bestowed him on my lord Marduk as a gift. I constructed the building, the replica of E-Sarra, in joy and jubilation and raised its top as high as a mountain."[i]

Many scholars believe the earlier Etemenanki ziggurat was the Tower of Babel, which the Torah said was built following the Great Flood:

"As the people migrated to the east, they found a plain in the land of Shinar (Babylonia) and settled there. They said to each other, 'Let's make bricks and harden them with fire.'

Then they said, 'Come, let's build a great city for ourselves with a tower that reaches into the sky. This will make us famous and keep us from being scattered all over the world.'

But the LORD came down to look at the city and the tower the people were building. 'Look!' he said. 'The people are united, and they all speak the same language. After this, nothing they set out to do will be impossible for them! Come, let's go down and confuse the people with different languages. Then they won't be able to understand each other.'

In that way, the LORD scattered them all over the world, and they stopped building the city. That is why the city was called Babel because that is where the LORD confused the people with different languages. In this way, he scattered them all over the world."[ii]

Nebuchadnezzar II built not only the Etemenanki ziggurat but also the Hanging Gardens of Babylon. Philo of Byzantium lauded the gardens in an ancient Greek tour guide, *On the Seven Wonders*, written in 225 BCE. Other historians who spoke of seeing the Hanging Gardens included Callimachus of Cyrene (310-340 BCE), Berossus of Babylon (third century BCE), Antipater of Sidon (second century BCE), and Diodorus Siculus (first century BCE).

---

[i] Andrew George, "The Tower of Babel: Archaeology, History and Cuneiform Texts," *Archiv für Orientforschung* 51 (2005/2006): 75-95.
https://eprints.soas.ac.uk/3858/2/TowerOfBabel.AfO.pdf

[ii] *Genesis 11,* Tanakh: Torah: Book of Bereishit.

They described the gardens as ingeniously laid out on a trellis of reeds over palm tree beams supported by stone columns. All sorts of flowers and trees grew high in the air in ascending tiers and were irrigated by a pump system bringing water up from the river. Although archaeologists haven't yet discovered the remains of the gardens, the literary evidence with detailed descriptions advocates for the garden's existence, not only in the Neo-Babylonian era but also in the subsequent Persian era.

Berossus wrote that Nebuchadnezzar II built Babylon's Hanging Gardens to please his wife Amytis, who missed the mountains of her Iranian homeland.[110]

Babylonians matched their artistic genius with astonishing advances in medicine, astronomy, and mathematics. The Babylonians produced medical texts as early as the original Amorite dynasty (1894–1595 BCE). Esagil-kin-apli, the chief scholar of king Adad-apla-iddina (1067–1046 BCE), wrote the forty-tablet *Sakikkū* or the *Diagnostic Handbook*, introducing concepts of diagnosis, prognosis, etiology, therapy, and prescriptions. A Babylonian pharmacy inventoried about five hundred medicines around 1000 BCE.

The *Diagnostic Handbook* took a supernatural approach to medicine, including omens a physician might encounter. He recorded symptoms and treatment of neurological issues believed to be associated with demonic forces requiring exorcism, such as basal ganglia disorders, brain tumors and trauma, epilepsy, motor impairments, tetanus, and stroke. Esagil-kin-apli also wrote on skin problems, fever, gynecological care, pregnancy, childbirth, and childhood illnesses.

Physicians refined their surgery techniques and knowledge of wound care throughout Babylonian history. Although they didn't have hospitals for multiple patients, doctors did treat patients in smaller clinics, with beds for those requiring overnight care. Surgeries included relieving pleural effusion in the lungs, setting bones, excising wounds, draining abscesses, and castrating boys who were to become eunuchs. Their instruments included scalpels and bronze lancets.

Doctors had specific guidelines in *The Code of Hammurabi*. They had to charge fees on a sliding scale: the highest for those of the noble class, one-half the amount for the middle class, and one-fifth the amount for enslaved people. If a doctor's malpractice resulted in a patient's death, his hands would be chopped off unless the dead person were a slave. In that case, the physician had to give the owner the purchase price for a replacement slave.

From their earliest history, Babylonians were keenly interested in astronomy and time. They recorded the length of daylight on each day of the solar year and employed mathematics to study the earth's rotation. They developed our twelve-month calendar with each month having four seven-day weeks, except they didn't add in the extra days as we do. They occasionally added a thirteenth month to keep their lunar calendar in sync with the solar-determined seasons. Each day had twelve *kaspus* (two hours) marking each time the sun traveled thirty degrees.

For the Babylonians, astronomy and astrology went hand in hand. They believed celestial phenomena affected their earthly lives. Thus, they observed and documented Venus' risings for twenty-one years straight in the *Enuma Anu Enlil* tablets, along with the movements of other planets and principal stars. They knew when and where certain stars would appear just before sunrise (helical risings) and, stunningly, could predict when planets would come into alignment.

The Chaldean Neo-Babylonians chronicled the moon's phases and observed retrograde planet movement. (As the orbiting Earth passes other planets in their orbits, it appears some planets are moving backward). By 721 BCE, the Babylonians predicted and recorded lunar and solar eclipses; they thought eclipses were associated with a king's death or some other calamity. But their eclipse records have come in handy for today's historians to figure out when certain historical events occurred. They are also helpful for scientists analyzing the lunar orbit's long-term variations.

The Babylonian contribution to mathematics included the concepts of zero and place value. They counted by sixties rather than tens and could calculate reciprocal pairs equaling sixty when multiplied. As early as 1800 BCE, the Babylonians used algebra and fractions and solved cubic, linear, and quadratic equations. They could determine a circle's circumference and diameter, and a tablet dating to at least 1680 BCE showed they calculated pi (π) to a value of 3.125. Their understanding of trigonometry included using the Pythagorean theorem over a millennium before Pythagoras' birth, as recently discovered in 2021 through an analysis of the *Plimpton 322* tablet dating back to about 1800 BCE.[i]

Another brilliant contribution of the Babylonians was the *Code of Hammurabi,* a legal treatise written by the king in the eighteenth century BCE. Other law codes preceded his legal system, but Hammurabi's stood out for its detailed extensiveness. Its 282 laws covered legal issues related to marriage and family, commerce, wages, property, slavery, medical malpractice, and crimes including rape, theft, assault, incest, and kidnapping. His code even regulated barbers, construction workers, shipbuilders, doctors, and veterinarians in their trades. His stated purpose was "to prevent the strong from oppressing the weak and to see that justice is done to widows and orphans, so that I should enlighten the land, to further the well-being of mankind."

Hammurabi had his law code carved into a finger-shaped stone pillar of black diorite more than seven feet high.

Hammurabi's Law Code (circa 1770 BCE) is etched into this black diorite pillar.[ii]

---

[i] D. F. Mansfield, "Plimpton 322: A Study of Rectangles," *Foundations of Science* 26 (2021): 977-1005. https://doi.org/10.1007/s10699-021-09806-0

Archaeologists discovered it 250 miles from Babylon in the Elamite capital of Susa, where the Elamites had taken it after raiding Babylon and stealing it. Moving the four-ton monument that far, presumably by oxcart, was a noteworthy feat! The hard diorite stone kept it well-preserved over the millennia. At the top is a carving of Hammurabi receiving the law from Shamash, god of the sun and justice. The rest of the monument has the 282 laws chiseled into its sides in cuneiform script.

Hammurabi harshly punished false accusations and false testimony with the death penalty; however, it was generally in the case of murder, adultery, or other crimes punishable by death. He also expected the judges to expend due diligence in determining guilt or innocence. If a judge carelessly gave a guilty verdict and collected a fine, and then later the defendant was proven innocent, the judge had to pay the defendant twelve times the fine and be permanently removed from the court.

Parts of *Hammurabi's Code* are strikingly similar to the *Law of Moses* written three centuries later in the *Torah*. For instance, the *Law of Moses* stated if someone hurt another person, the punishment must match the injury: a life for a life, an eye for an eye, and so on (Exodus 21). *Hammurabi's Code* said the same thing, except one could pay money in lieu of losing an eye or having one's teeth knocked out, and the amount of money depended on the social status of the injured person.

Moses and Hammurabi had similar civil laws, but *Hammurabi's Code* included many regulations regarding one's occupation, which the *Torah* did not. The *Torah* dealt a lot with religion: instructions on how to build the tabernacle, what the priests should wear, how to offer sacrifices, how to celebrate festivals, and warnings not to worship any other gods. Hammurabi's code barely mentioned religion, except stealing from temples, which got the death penalty.

Hammurabi's Code monument shows him standing before Shamash, the god of justice, and receiving the law.[112]

Hammurabi's Law Code penalties were severe and heavy-handed, like cutting off an offender's hand, tongue, ear, or breast, or worse yet, execution. However, he led the way in legal views such as presuming innocence until proven guilty, determining whether an offender intended to cause harm, and considering mitigating circumstances influencing a crime. In these areas, he was a pioneer, as the Babylonians were in so many ways.

Chapter 10: Myths and Religion

Spirituality was paramount to the Babylonians, but what did they believe? What were their temples and festivals like, and how did they worship their gods? What do their myths tell us about their understanding of creation, the afterlife, and the character of their deities? This chapter will unpack the answers to these questions, exploring their macabre creation story and other captivating myths.

The Sumerians and Babylonians worshiped many of the same gods, but usually with different names. The *Enuma Elish* creation myth is about the younger gods staging a revolution, killing off the oldest gods, and establishing a new spiritual regime with Marduk as its head. The tale paralleled the reorganizing of religion when Babylon gained preeminence. The Sumerians had never worshipped Marduk, but Hammurabi elevated him from an obscure city god to Babylonia's supreme god, their nation's patron.

Ishtar (Inanna), the goddess of war and sexuality, remained popular in Babylonia, but a distant second to Marduk, although they did name the main gate of Babylon after her. Babylonian myths portrayed her in a somewhat unfavorable light; the *Epic of Gilgamesh* and *The Descent of Ishtar to the Underworld* (which we will dive into later in this chapter) characterize her as mercurial, spiteful, shameless, and grasping. She's not mentioned at all in the *Enuma Elish*. The Babylonians tended to be more patriarchal and favored male gods.

Adad, the storm god, could send life-giving rain or deadly storms.[118]

According to the *Enuma Elish* myth, the Babylonians worshiped six hundred gods who answered to Marduk after he prevailed over Tiamat, the primordial goddess of chaos. Anu (An) was the Sumerian's chief god, and in Babylonia, he was Marduk's grandfather but less powerful than Marduk. One of Anu's sons, Adad, was originally a Semitic god (Hadad). The Babylonians worshiped Adad as the god of storms and portrayed him holding a lightning bolt or hammer, like the Greek Zeus or the Germanic Thor. The popular Sumerian god Enki (Ea) was Marduk's father, beloved by the Babylonians because he warned Utnapishtim to build the ark to save mankind and animals from the Great Flood. Ea was an auspicious god for incantations, magic, and exorcisms.

Babylon's most important temple was the Esagila, Marduk's sanctuary, but it also housed shrines to numerous other gods. Forty-three other temples stood in Babylon and fifty-five shrines of Marduk. Unlike the Assyrians and other nearby civilizations, the Babylonians constructed their imposing and exquisite architecture to please the gods rather than

extol their military conquests.[i]

Festivities and worship connected the Babylonians with their gods, who erratically shifted from malevolence to kindheartedness. Failure to keep the gods contented through proper rituals could result in catastrophes like drought, disease, or military disaster. Thus, the priesthood and sorcerers organized worship ceremonies and festivals, fed the gods, adorned them with beautiful clothing and jewelry, chanted hymns and prayers, and offered sacrifices. Although Hammurabi ordered the death penalty for sorcery, by the Neo-Babylonian era, sorcerers were commonplace, needed to protect from evil spirits and interpret omens.

Religion and government were closely intertwined. The Babylonian New Year fell in the spring, in the month of Nissan, when it was time to cultivate the fields. Babylonians celebrated the New Year with the Akitu Festival, the year's most celebrated gala, lasting eleven days. An important ritual was the king taking the hand of Marduk's statue, giving legitimacy to the king and displaying Marduk's supremacy over the earthly monarchs.

At the beginning of the Akitu Festival, the priests carried the statue of Marduk and other gods in a grand parade. They marched down the Processional Way with its towering fifty-foot walls covered with gleaming, blue-glazed tiles featuring golden mosaics of lions, bulls, and dragons. Proceeding out the Ishtar Gate, the priests ceremoniously placed Marduk and his entourage of lesser gods in the Akitu temple, where they rested for the next few days.

Mosaic lions adorned the blue-glazed bricks of the Processional Way.[114]

---

[i] Andrew George, "Ancient Descriptions: The Babylonian Topographical Texts," in *Babylon*, ed. I. L. Finkel and M. J. Seymour. (New York: Oxford University Press, 2008), 161-5.

The priests led the people in prayer for eleven days at the temples, telling the Enuma Elish creation story and acting out parts of it. The king would visit the Akitu Temple and strip off his royal robes, kneeling before Marduk and the other gods in humility. Marduk would mysteriously disappear on the seventh day, symbolizing he had left to fight Tiamat, goddess of chaos; his image would reappear the next day. On the tenth day, Marduk returned to the city with great pomp and dancing in the streets, blessing the upcoming planting season and ensuring the coming year's prosperity.

Marduk's presence within Babylon was critical to the city's well-being. If enemies stole his statue (which they did, repeatedly), Babylonians suffered calamities, as the Mesopotamians believed their gods inhabited the cult images. The *Marduk Prophecy* is a somewhat humorous account of Marduk's "travels" to Hatti, Assyria, and Elam, after enemies invaded and sacked Babylon, carrying Marduk off with their spoils of war.

Although Marduk couldn't resist capture or get himself back to Babylon without assistance, he actively participated in his travels. The narrative of the two tablets containing the *Marduk Prophecy* is in the first person; Marduk himself is telling the story. In it, Marduk describes his travels to Hatti and Assyria as if they were his idea and relates how the Hittites and Assyrians received him kindly.

The other gods followed Marduk to Elam on his third trip out of Babylon, leaving Babylon desolate. That trip wasn't as pleasant as the earlier ones; Marduk disliked his treatment by the Elamites. In the tablet found just behind the *Marduk Prophecy* tablet, known as the *Prophecy of Šulgi*, Marduk foretold that a brilliant new king of Babylon would trample Elam and rescue Marduk. The prophecy was likely propaganda written after the fact during Nebuchadnezzar I's reign, following his retrieval of Marduk.

The *Marduk Prophecy* doesn't list people's names or dates, but Marduk's journey to Hatti would have been in 1595 BCE when the Hittite king Mursili I laid waste to Babylon. He stole Marduk and ended the Amorite dynasty. The Kassites retrieved Marduk and ruled Babylon, but then the Assyrian king Tukulti-Ninurta I plundered Babylon, stealing Marduk again. The Assyrians themselves returned Marduk, fearing his retribution. Marduk's third "visit" was to Elam, after the Elamites conquered and ended the Kassite state in 1155 BCE.

The *Seven Tablets of Creation* (the *Enuma Elish*) was Babylonia's gruesome creation myth, explaining how Marduk gained preeminence over the other gods, created the earth and sky, appointed each of the six hundred gods to their duties, and oversaw the creation of humans. The oldest preserved tablets of the disturbing tale date back to about 1200 BCE, with notations that the scribes copied them from earlier tablets written before the Early Babylonian Era.

Although the story includes many Sumerian deities, Marduk rises above all the other gods as the grand champion over chaos. It begins as a bizarre retelling of the Sumerian *Eridu Genesis* (the Flood myth). In both tales, the oldest gods can't sleep because of the noisy youngsters. In the *Eridu Genesis,* the rambunctious humans keep the older gods awake, so the gods send the Great Flood. But Ea (Enki) intervenes and tells Utnapishtim to build the ark.

The god Enki (Ea) warned of the Great Flood.[115]

The *Enuma Elish* takes a different twist; it wasn't the humans being noisy, as they hadn't yet been created. It was the escapades of the unruly younger gods that were annoying the very first god Apsu (the begetter) and his wife Tiamat, goddess of chaos. Apsu represented fresh water, and Tiamat was the swirling, tumultuous ocean. When the two waters mingled, they created the other gods.

Almost immediately, Apsu and Tiamat regretted bringing the new life into being, as now they could not sleep with all the uproar from their children. But neither Apsu nor Tiamat reprimanded the younger gods for all their riotous dancing and clamor through the night. Finally, they couldn't bear it anymore, and they met to discuss the problem. Apsu declared: "Their behavior is infuriating! Night or day, I can't sleep! I'm going to kill them!"

"No!" Tiamat raged and wailed. "We can't murder our children. I know their behavior is deplorable, but can't we give them a chance? Let's scold them, punish their obnoxious behavior, and see if they will change."

Apsu's vizier Mummu interjected, "Father! Get rid of these rioters, and then you can sleep!"

Apsu grinned, happy that Mummu supported his plan to kill the unruly gods. Mummu curled up in Apsu's lap and kissed him. Tiamat fumed and cursed but could not persuade Apsu to let the young gods live. When the young gods heard that Apsu planned to kill them all, they were undone. Falling to the ground, they wailed in despair.

But the young god Enki, son of Anu, decided to act. Speaking an enchantment over Apsu, his magical powers put Apsu into a deep sleep. Overwrought, Mummu gasped but was powerless against Enki. Enki killed Apsu and, from his body, formed a house to live in: the Chamber of Destinies. He brought his bride Damkina into their magnificent new home, and they conceived a child, Marduk, who had four eyes, four ears, and fire exploding from his mouth. Anu gave his grandson Marduk the four winds: "Send them spinning and blowing, my child. Make a hurricane!"

Meanwhile, Tiamat was beside herself. She had tried to spare her offspring, but now they had killed her husband. Some of the gods were scolding her for letting it happen; she must retaliate! Tiamat joined forces with a new and powerful husband, Qingu. After Marduk's hurricane flooded her with a tidal wave, Tiamat conjured all her chaotic superpowers, producing new offspring with Qingu: eleven ghastly fanged demons with toxic blood and indomitable weapons. These fiendish creations would kill off the younger gods!

Enki approached his grandmother Tiamat, hoping to put her into an enchanted spell, as he'd done with Apsu. But Tiamat was ready for him, with earsplitting shrieks and incantations. Realizing he was outpowered, Enki stole away. Next, his father, Anu, tried to pacify Tiamat, but her spine-chilling screeches, sorceries, and demonic forces paralyzed Anu with fear. The rest of the gods bit their lips, powerless to do anything to defend themselves.

But then Marduk burst out in his chariot pulled by four mighty stallions: Trampler, Demolisher, Malevolent, and Speed. He summoned the seven winds to assault Tiamat's bowels. Qingu's witchcraft unnerved him, but he held his ground, raging at Tiamat, "You! Our mother! Why don't you defend your own children? Why do you despise us?"

But Tiamat was out of her mind with feverish fury, howling hexes and witchery as Marduk captured her in his battle net. He sent his hurricane into her gaping mouth, blowing up her body. Then he impaled her heart with his lance, crushed her skull, and eviscerated her. He captured and tied up Qingu, then trampled the eleven demons under his feet. Exhausted, Marduk sat down and inspected Tiamat's mangled body.

This bas-relief from Nineveh may depict the battle between Tiamat and Marduk.[116]

His father Enki had made his house from Apsu's body, and Marduk would do the same with what was left of Tiamat! His new home would parallel Enki's. As one would filet a fish, Marduk split Tiamat into two halves, which became the sky and the earth. He formed the Euphrates and Tigris from the tears flowing out of her eyes. Marduk then created the moon and the stars to mark the passage of time and appointed the six hundred gods to their duties.

The gods gathered around their new leader with great applause, kissing his feet and acknowledging Marduk as their king. Marduk and Enki executed Qingu because he'd incited Tiamat to war against the gods. Enki used Qingu's blood to form the first man: Lullu. The humans would be useful in taking care of all the practical details of regular life so the gods could focus on running the universe.

The ecstatic gods cheered these new events and set to work building a stellar new city: Babylon. This magnificent place would be the home of Marduk and the chief gods. The gods built the Esagil temple for Marduk, then built temples for themselves. They happily sat down to a lavish feast when they finally finished all the construction, passing around the beer mugs and toasting their new king Marduk.

Another Babylonian myth, the *Epic of Erra*,[i] deals with Marduk's multiple "journeys" away from Babylon when he was "godnapped." Nergal (Erra), the god of war, was bored, so he decided to stir things up. It was no fun being the god of war when Babylonia was enjoying peace, and, for heaven's sake, he needed to ensure mankind would continue to worship him. "They hold me in contempt," he muttered repeatedly.

Nergal used enchantments to trick Marduk into taking a trip away from Babylon, as his statue was in dire need of refurbishing. He promised Marduk he'd look after things in his absence. With Marduk gone, Nergal began implementing his plot to instigate war, but Marduk returned early, and Nergal had to put his plans on hold. Nergal bided his time, and eventually, Marduk left on another journey. Nergal took advantage of the chaos during Marduk's absence to stir up a horrific war in Nippur, receiving the praise of his vizier Ishum:

"Heaven's at your disposal, Hell's in your hands,

you have charge of Babylon; give orders to Esagil:

---

[i] Andrew George, "The Poem of Erra and Ishum: A Babylonian Poet's View of War," in *Warfare and Poetry in the Middle East*, ed. Hugh Kennedy (London: I. B. Tauris, 2013), 39-71.

You're master of all the cosmic powers; even the gods are in terror of you...
is there warfare without you?"[i]

The war god Nergal almost destroyed the cosmic order in Marduk's absence.[117]

Gleefully feeding off the incomparable misery he caused by his indiscriminate violence and destruction, Nergal even made megalomaniac plans to upend the universe. He would unseat the cosmic government until every nation, city, family, and man annihilated each other. Aghast, his vizier Ishum created a distraction, launching a war on Mount Sharshar in Lebanon, the homeland of the fierce nomads that threatened Babylonia. Ishum flattened Mount Sharshar, felled the cedars of Lebanon, and created a tidal wave that swept over the land.

Ishum's violence somehow brought Nergal back to his senses. Nergal finally realized that if he destroyed all mankind, there would not be anyone to feed and serve the gods and take care of all the menial tasks that the gods created the humans to do:

---

[i] George, "The Poem of Erra," 54.

"Without Ishum, my vanguard, what now would exist?

Where is your provisioner, where are your high priests?

Where are your food-offerings? You would smell no incense!"[i]

The Descent of Ishtar to the Underworld [ii] is another bizarre Babylonian myth. Ishtar (Inanna), the goddess of sexuality and war, plotted a takeover of the underworld, where her sister Ereshkigal reigned as queen over the land of darkness. Ishtar arrived at the gate of the Land of No Return and rattled it. "Gatekeeper, ho! Open the gate! Let me enter! I'll break the lock, smash the door-posts, and force the gate open if you don't. Then I'll bring up the dead to eat the living!"

The gatekeeper called back, "Stop! Oh lady, do not destroy it! I will go and announce your name to my queen Ereshkigal."

When the gatekeeper informed Queen Ereshkigal that her sister Ishtar had arrived, Ereshkigal trembled like a reed. "What has possessed her? Does she want to live here like me, eating clay as food and drinking dust as wine? Will she weep, like me, for the men here who are cut off from their families? For the wives torn from their husbands' embrace? For the little ones cut off before their time?"

"Go, gatekeeper, open the gate. Deal with her according to the ancient decree."

The gatekeeper passed up to the first gate, opening it. But as Ishtar passed through the gate, he removed her crown from her head. "Why did you remove my crown?" Ishtar asked.

"It is the ancient decree," the gatekeeper replied.

At the second gate, he removed her earrings. At the third, he removed her necklace. At the fourth, he removed her breast ornaments. At the fifth gate, he removed her girdle studded with semiprecious stones. At the sixth gate, he removed her bracelets and anklets. At the seventh and last gate, he removed her loincloth.

When Ishtar entered the Land of No Return, Ereshkigal bristled with anger when she saw her. Ishtar threw herself at Ereshkigal without a second thought, but Ereshkigal called to her vizier: "Namtar, throw her into the dungeon! Inflict her with sixty diseases as punishment: eye

---

[i] George, "The Poem of Erra," 59.

[ii] "Descent of the Goddess Ishtar into the Lower World," in *The Civilization of Babylonia and Assyria*, Morris Jastrow, Jr. (1915). https://www.sacred-texts.com/ane/ishtar.htm

disease, heart disease, brain ailment; send disease against her entire body."

Meanwhile, in the Land of the Living, trouble was afoot. Ishtar was the goddess of sexuality; when she left the world, the bulls stopped mounting the cows, all the animals stopped mating, the men stopped approaching the young women in the street, and everyone slept alone. No animals or humans were reproducing. If this continued, all life would be gone! Shamash, the sun god, went weeping to Enki. With tears flowing, he told him that Ishtar had gone into the underworld, and all life would soon end.

Enki sent a messenger to the underworld, requesting that Ereshkigal release her sister and sprinkle her with the water of life. When Ereshkigal heard this, she bit her finger and cursed the messenger. "May the dregs from the city's gutters be your food! May the drunkards strike you on the cheek!"

Nevertheless, Ereshkigal obeyed Enki. She released Ishtar, sprinkled her with the water of life, then sent her out of the underworld, up through the seven gates. Ishtar retrieved her clothing and jewelry as she passed through the gates.

But for Ishtar to leave, someone had to replace her in the underworld. She looked up into the Land of the Living and saw her human husband, Tammuz, the shepherd. Instead of weeping for her, he was wearing festive garments and prancing about with his sister, playing a lapis lazuli flute! Indignant, Ishtar chose Tammuz to replace her in the underworld for six months of the year, and she returned for the other six months when the fields lay fallow.

While the Babylonian myths would probably give little children nightmares, they provide a fascinating insight into the Babylonian culture, beliefs, and values. They inform us about the Babylonian perception of cosmic order and the character of their deities. More than anything else, Babylon was a highly-respected religious center for Mesopotamia, a holy city. In the Babylonian mind, it was the center of the world.

Conclusion

The Babylonians sprang from humble origins as nomadic herders to build a stunningly beautiful city with up to 200,000 people at its peak, the largest city in the world for over two hundred years. They built massive city walls adorned with gleaming mosaics, elaborate temples, and a towering ziggurat that could be seen from twenty miles away. Their elegant hanging gardens were so impressive in beauty and engineering that the Greeks listed them as one of the seven wonders of the ancient world.

After the Assyrian Empire fell, the Neo-Babylonians rose to become the world's most powerful empire of the time, covering nearly 200,000 square miles with multiple ethnicities and languages. It encompassed modern-day Iraq, large swathes of Iran, Kuwait, Syria, Arabia, and Jordan, and stretched down the Mediterranean to include Lebanon, Israel, and Palestine. The multicultural milieu encouraged novel advances in the arts, architecture, and sciences.

The Babylonians were not monocultural; in Babylonia's three dominant eras, the Amorites first ruled, then the Kassites, and lastly, a mixture of Chaldeans and other ethnicities. In all three periods, Babylon was regarded as a holy city, the center of the world. Throughout its history, Babylon perpetuated the worship of Marduk and a distinctive culture dedicated to exploring new knowledge about the universe, medicine, and mathematics.

What are our key takeaways from Babylonia's history? What lessons can we learn from its civilization and the events that shaped it into a nation? Awe-inspiring cultures had shaped Mesopotamia before the

Babylonians rose to power: the Ubaid, the Sumerians, and the Akkadians. Master assimilators, the Babylonians borrowed freely from these previous cultures and their greatest rival, the Assyrians.

Through absorbing the knowledge, culture, and technologies of other civilizations, the cosmopolitan Babylonians helped preserve the ancient cultures while forging ahead with a blend of adaptability and innovation. When we learn from our own histories and the people and cultures around us, we remain relevant and adaptable, able to adjust to an ever-changing world and grow in creative energy and success.

To survive and thrive, the Babylonians had to build brilliant alliances with their neighbors and far-distant tribes. They even had to form alliances with their chief rival Assyria throughout their earlier history. These alliances were a definitive element in preserving their existence and eventually growing their empire to startling heights. Collaboration and cooperation often decide whether our endeavors succeed or fail, no matter what we hope to accomplish.

What are Babylonia's connections to modern society? How has this ancient civilization contributed to our global heritage? Where do we begin? The Babylonians gave us our seven-day week, four-week month, and twelve-month year. The Babylonian's astute studies of astronomy and their phenomenal breakthroughs in mathematics formed the underlying foundations of modern astrophysics, trigonometry, numerical analysis, and countless other applications in math and science. Today's medical science owes much to the Babylonians' development of diagnosis, medicines, surgical techniques, and wound care. Hammurabi's law code influenced our modern legal system's concepts of intent, mitigating circumstances affecting a crime, and presumption of innocence until proven guilty.

Babylon's revolutionary legacy lives on. We continue to benefit from Babylon's groundbreaking advances in so many areas of life. This exceptional and creative civilization still reaches through time to influence our everyday lives, even our calendars. Echoes of Babylon resound in our criminal justice system, scientific and mathematical understanding, art, architecture, and more. The city may have sunk into the sand over the past millennia, but its contributions to today's world persevere.

Part 4: The Assyrian Empire

An Enthralling Overview of the History of Assyria, the Assyrians, and Their Role in Ancient Mesopotamia

Introduction

Assyria was one of the world's first great powers. It was based in northern Mesopotamia—the area between the rivers Tigris and Euphrates in modern Iraq. Assyria started out as one of a number of Middle Eastern states, but it rapidly became one of the most influential. Eventually, after a series of conquests, it became one of the world's first empires. It included not just its heartland in modern Iraq but also parts of Syria, Turkey, Lebanon, Iran, Israel, and Jordan.

It's fascinating to find out how the process of state formation worked in ancient times. It's even more fascinating that when this empire failed, it failed catastrophically and quickly. It went from riches to rags in a single generation.

However, until fairly recently, Assyria was hardly known at all, apart from a few biblical references. It was only in the mid-19th century that archaeologists started discovering the early civilizations of Mesopotamia.

Austen Henry Layard was the first to start excavations, concentrating on Nineveh, King Sennacherib's capital. He also worked at Nimrud (ancient Kalhu) and later on Babylonian sites in the south of Mesopotamia. He published the first works on Assyria and sent a large number of antiquities to the British Museum. As well as uncovering splendid palaces, massive sculptures, and delicate friezes, he also found an amazing resource, the Library of Ashurbanipal. This consisted of twenty-two thousand inscribed clay tablets dating from around 668 to 627 BCE and covered the history of Assyria and earlier cultures, going back two thousand years from Ashurbanipal's time.

However, Layard did not excavate at Ashur, the original Assyrian capital. This excavation had to wait until 1903 for German archaeologist Walter Andrae, who spent eleven years excavating the site. He was a more systematic archaeologist than Layard. Andrae dug trenches across the entire site to understand the life and layout of the city, including small houses, temples, and palaces.

Assyria was not the first civilization in the Middle East. The Sumerians ruled for several centuries before the rise of Assyria. The Sumerian culture was preserved as a "classical" culture by the Assyrians. And from the very beginning of Assyria, there was a deep rivalry with Babylon, which was based in the more fertile lands farther south.

Although Assyria was not the first empire, it lasted much longer than the Akkadian Empire. And thanks to the preservation of its libraries, we know a lot about it. We know how production was centralized and controlled, what happened in the temples, what omens were considered good (and what was unlikely), and what food was considered a particular delicacy (locusts).

This book will cover Assyrian history from the very beginning to the end of the empire. First, it will introduce the Sumerians, who developed many of the technologies and ideologies the Assyrians used to create their state, and the Akkadians, who were the first real military power in Mesopotamia. The Assyrians knew their history, as some Assyrian kings even took Akkadian kings' names, perhaps stressing their desire to emulate Akkadian success in war.

The Assyrians had a reputation for being a particularly aggressive nation. This was partly because they were, for centuries, known only through the Bible, where they were shown as warlike aggressors. The poet Lord Byron certainly saw them this way:

"The Assyrian came down like a wolf on the fold,

And his cohorts were gleaming in purple and gold;

And the sheen of their spears was like stars on the sea,

When the blue wave rolls nightly on deep Galilee." - Lord Byron[1]

Of course, there was more to Assyrian expansion than just military prowess. Little by little, the Assyrians built an empire rather than just an assemblage of conquered states. To do that, they had to innovate

---

[1] Lord Byron, "The Destruction of Sennacherib" lines 1-4, from *Hebrew Melodies*, 1815.

economically and create a highly structured administration and infrastructure, such as roads and a post office.

There are a few difficulties in writing Assyrian history. Some early kings (not listed in the timeline below) are only known from lists of Assyrian kings that were written much later; they may be mythical. Dating is not reliable for the Old and Middle Assyrian periods. For the early era, most of the data historians can use is known through royal inscriptions in temples, which were intended to show the king as an ideal ruler, building cities and temples, defeating enemies, and producing plenty of sacrifices for the gods. They are, obviously, biased. The Neo-Assyrian Empire has detailed correspondence that allows for a clearer assessment of rulers as individuals, and even then, it is sometimes not quite clear why certain things happened or exactly what happened.

Correspondence between merchants and traders exists from earlier periods that give us a fascinating view of the life of the middle classes at the time. Many of these letters were found in the houses of the individuals concerned in the letter, so the archaeological and written evidence complement each other in an unusual and very satisfying way.

Understanding the Assyrians just in terms of names and dates doesn't give the whole picture. That's why this book includes chapters on the languages they used, their art and superb monumental architecture, and their religion. While, in some ways, the Assyrians can seem quite close to us (they loved their beer, for instance), in other ways, their culture was very different (for instance, they lived on top of their ancestors' tombs or used oracles to decide military strategy).

An impression of what Nineveh might have looked like at its height. [118]

Assyria might not have been where you'd want to live. It certainly wasn't an empire you would want to fight. Nevertheless, it left some magnificent remains behind, and for many Assyrians, including subject peoples, life was good, not least because one of the avowed tasks of any Assyrian king was to look after his people's well-being.

It's well worth studying the Assyrians since their idea of how to put a state together became incredibly influential over the next several hundred years. Without Assyria, there would have been no Persian Empire, no Alexander the Great, and no Roman Empire. And without the Romans, Western history would have looked very different.

Timeline

Old Assyrian Period	
Puzur-Ashur I	C2025 BCE
Shalim-ahum	uncertain
Ilu-Shuma	uncertain
Erishum I	1974-1935 BCE
Ikunum	1934-1921
Sargon I	1920-1881
Puzur-Ashur II	1880-1873
Naram-Sin	1872-1819
Erishum II	1818-1809
Shamsi-Adad	
Shamshi-Adad I	1808-1776

Ishme-Dagan I	1775-1765
Mut-Ashkur	uncertain
Rimush	uncertain
Asinum	uncertain
Usurpers 1735-1701	
Puzur-Sin	
Ashur-dugul	
Ashur-apla-idi	
Nasir-Sin	
Sin-namir	
Ipqi-Ishtar	
Adad-Salulu	
Adasi	
Adasides	
Bel-bani	1700-1691
Libaya	1690-1674
Sharma-Adad I	1673-1662
Iptar-Sin	1661-1650

Bazaya	1649-1622
Lullaya	1621-1616
Shu-Ninua	1615-1602
Sharma-Adad II	1601-1599
Erishum III	1598-1586
Shamshi-Adad II	1585-1580
Ishme-Dagan II	1579-1564
Shamshi-Adad III	1563-1548
Ashur-nirari I	1547-1522
Puzur-Ashur III	1521-1498
Enlil-nasir I	1497-1485
Nur-ili	1484-1473
Ashur-shaduni	1473
Ashur-rabi I	1472-1453
Ashur-nadin-ahhe I	1452-1431
Enlil-nasir II	1430-1425
Ashur-nirari II	1424-1418
Ashur-bel-nisheshu	1417-1409

Ashur-rim-nisheshu	1408-1401
Ashur-nadin-ahhe II	1400-1391
Eriba-Adad I	1390-1364
Middle Assyrian Period	
Ashur-uballit I	1363-1328
Enlil-nirari	1327-1318
Arik-den-ili	1317-1306
Adad-nirari I	1305-1274
Shalmaneser I	1273-1244
Tukulti-Ninurta I	1243-1207
Ashur-nadin-apli	1206-1203
Ashur-nirari III	1202-1197
Enlil-kudurri-usur	1196-1192
Ninurta-apal-Ekur	1191-1179
Ashur-Dan I	1178-1133
Ninurta-tukulti-Ashur	1132
Mutakkil-Nusku	1132
Ashur-resh-ishi I	1132-1115

Tiglath-Pileser I	1114-1076
Asharid-apal-Ekur	1075-1074
Ashur-bel-kala	1073-1056
Eriba-Adad II	1055-1054
Shamshi-Adad IV	1053-1050
Ashurnasirpal I	1049-1031
Shalmaneser II	1030-1019
Ashur-nirari IV	1018-1013
Ashur-rabi II	1012-972
Ashur-resh-ishi II	971-967
Tiglath-Pileser II	966-935
Ashur-Dan II	934-912
Neo-Assyrian Empire	
Adad-nirari II	911-891
Tukulti-Ninurta II	890-884
Ashurnasirpal II	883-859
Shalmaneser III	859-824
Shamshi-Adad V	824-811

Adad-nirari III	811-783
Shalmaneser IV	783-773
Ashur-Dan III	773-755
Ashur-nirari V	755-745
Tiglath-Pileser III	745-727
Shalmaneser V	727-722
Sargonids	
Sargon II	722-705
Sennacherib	705-681
Esarhaddon	681-669
Ashurbanipal	669-631
Ashur-etil-ilani	631-627
Sin-sumu-lisir	626
Sinsharishkun	627-612
Ashur-uballit II	612-609

Note: All of these regnal years are approximate dates; it is impossible to know for sure when all these kings ruled. Also, the Mesopotamian practice was to date a king's rule from his first full year in office rather than from his accession. That's why the dates for many kings in the earlier periods look too neat. For the later part of the Neo-Assyrian Empire, more detailed information allows for more precise dating.

Chapter 1: North Mesopotamia Before the Assyrians

Mesopotamia is known as the land "between the rivers" (that's what the name means in Greek). The rivers in question were the Euphrates and the Tigris, which ran down through what is now Iraq toward the Persian Gulf.

Mesopotamia was mainly flat land, steppes, plains, and marshland. Particularly toward the south, there was a lot of fertile soil with a lot of silt and clay. However, the conditions were arid, and toward the sea, the land is very marshy, so a certain amount of hard work was required to make the land productive.

Civilization emerged first in Mesopotamia, even before it did in Egypt, the Indus Valley, or China. The first people in the area were the Proto-Euphrateans or Ubaid people, Stone Age agriculturalists living in small villages whose settlements have since been excavated at al-Ubaid, near Ur. However, it wasn't until the Sumerians arrived, possibly from somewhere near the Caspian Sea, that an urban culture was first created.

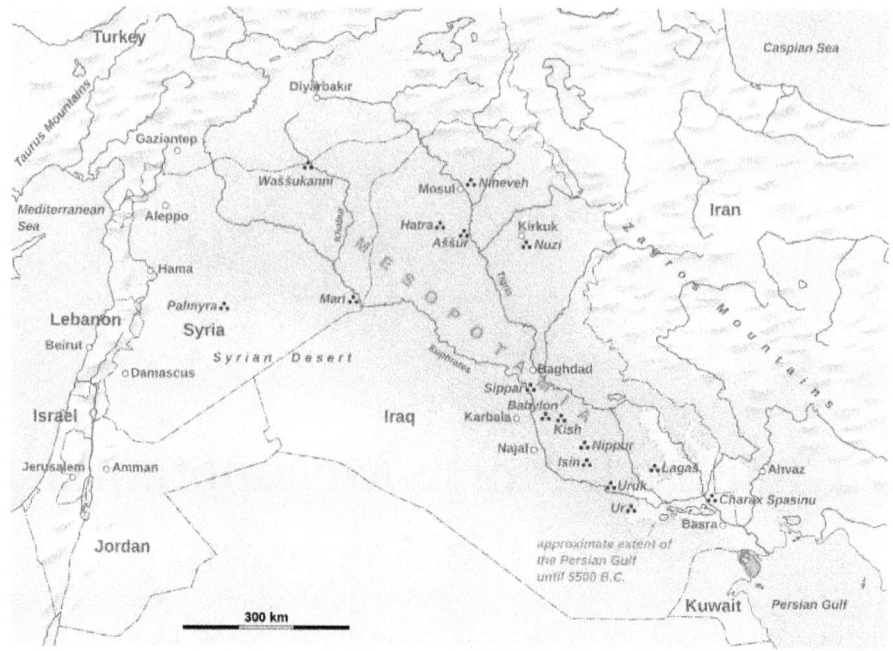

A map of Mesopotamia showing some of the early settlement sites.[119]

The Sumerians made huge advances. They advanced from the Stone Age (Chalcolithic, to be precise) into the Bronze Age and vastly increased agricultural productivity through irrigation. They also invented the seeder plow, which had a funnel to place the seed immediately after the furrow had been turned. This was much more efficient than simply throwing the seed (known as broadcast sowing) and might have increased yields by as much as 50 percent.

Sumer didn't just have a singular water god. The main water god's name was Enki, who is often shown with the two great rivers falling from his shoulders like watery wings. There was also a canal god, Ennugi. Everything in Sumer came from the rivers. The rivers gave them water for agriculture, fish, clay for pottery, bundles of reeds tied together for the earliest buildings, and clay for mudbricks.

The Sumerians also told the story of a great flood, similar to that of Noah's flood. Both the Tigris and the Euphrates overflowed frequently but also unpredictably, and the myth reflects that reality. This flooding made Mesopotamia a different place from Egypt, where the overflowing of the Nile was predictable; the Egyptian civilization developed in a very different way because of that.

There's another link to the Great Flood too. The Bible sets out the way in which Noah was the patriarch of all the people of the Middle East. According to the Bible, Noah's three sons each began a family of nations. Shem, for instance, was the father of the Hebrews, but his sons also included Elam, founder of the Iranian city-state of Elam, and Ashur, founder of the city of Ashur and the Assyrian nation. Ham's family founded Egypt and the Canaanite culture. Ham's grandson, Nimrod, was later traditionally identified as the builder of the Tower of Babel.

However, the Bible obviously doesn't mention the fact that Ashur was not a king but a deity, and Nimrod is not attested in any of the king lists of Babylon.

The first writing and mathematics are found in Sumer. Writing started as rough pictographs, originating around 3000 BCE. It soon developed into a more abstract script written on clay found in the river basin. Writing enabled the Sumerians to write down a code of law for the first time in human history. Written law played a big part in Sumerian society; for example, deeds of sale have been found dating from 2700 BCE onward.

For arithmetic, Sumerians used base six as well as base ten. The need to account for agricultural surpluses might have motivated the development of both math and writing. The transition to a money economy also happened at an early date. (It's interesting that Egypt didn't develop a money economy for two millennia; it developed a centralized economy rather than a commercial one.) Perhaps it's significant that math questions for pupils reflected their concern with water resources and agriculture. "If a cistern measures this wide and this deep, and it's full, how much land can it irrigate?" seems to have been a typical way of exercising young students' minds.

Reliance on irrigation also meant that Sumer needed a method of organizing its population and land holdings to enable large irrigation systems to be set up. In other words, the need to irrigate forced the state to evolve. Urban living also required a more complex system of governance than pastoralism, which led to increasing specialization of crafts. Rather than living in small settlements, Sumerians set up cities, which were walled very early on.

There was one major problem, though. Mesopotamia had rivers, silt, and clay. What it didn't have a lot of was metal, stone, and wood. There were no major metal resources in the region, and trees didn't grow well there. This forced Sumer to trade its agricultural surplus for everything it required. By the time the Sumerian civilization had matured, the Sumerian cities were trading as far afield as India, the Horn of Africa, and the Caspian and Mediterranean Seas.

Yet, for a very long time, all trace of Sumer was lost. It was even better hidden than Assyria since it wasn't mentioned in the Bible. Although first Old Persian, Assyrian, and Babylonian cuneiform texts had been deciphered, Sumerian took longer. It wasn't until 1869 that French Assyriologist Jules Oppert named the writers of the early cuneiform as Sumerians. The excavation of Sumerian Lagash in 1877 and the excavation of Nippur vastly expanded the number of texts in Sumerian available to scholars.

Sir Leonard Woolley made the next big advances in the 1920s and 1930s when he excavated Uruk and then Ur. At Ur, he found the tomb of Queen Pu-Abi, an untouched royal tomb containing a cylindrical seal with her name on it, a golden headdress, a chariot, and a harp. He also discovered a number of other tombs and death pits containing the bodies of retainers who appear to have been sacrificed.

These excavations, together with the use of Sumerian written texts, enable archaeological stratigraphy (dating artifacts by the layers, or strata, of the earth in which they are found) to be cross-checked against Sumerian records. The dating of Sumerian history is based on archaeologists' discoveries in Uruk, where a twenty-meter-deep test pit enabled archaeologists to determine the stratigraphy from the first settlement on the site to about 2500 BCE, by which time the Sumerians were already using writing.

Around one thousand "historical" inscriptions from Sumer survive, but date formulas used in administrative and commercial documents can also be used to help date events. Years were not numbered; rather, they were named after particularly important events that occurred, and lists were then created of the year names for each king's reign.

The Sumerian King List, of which sixteen versions (mostly incomplete) survive, runs from the line "after the kingship descended from heaven, the kingship was in the city of Eridu" to the historical Isin dynasty. The history of Sumer probably began between 4500 and 4000 BCE when the first settlements were established. The Sumerian culture lasted nearly three thousand years from this date.

The king list is based on the idea that "kingship" was invested in one city at a time. After the Great Flood, first Kish, then Uruk, and then Ur are mentioned as sites of kingship, giving the impression that each succeeded the other. In fact, these dynasties overlapped, with all three cities competing for dominance. Other cities that are noted in the king list are Akshak, Mari, Adab, and Lagash.

There were around a dozen city-states in Sumer. Each was a walled city and had a ziggurat—Sumer's biggest contribution to architecture. A ziggurat is a sort of stepped pyramid, which perhaps began as a square plinth or mound under a temple building. More terraces were added around this; the center was made of relatively soft, unfired mudbricks, which was then surrounded by retaining walls made of fired (harder) mudbricks. (The Ziggurat in West Sacramento, California, is an excellent model; the SIS Building in London, England, is a flashier update.)

The Great Ziggurat of Ur[120]

The earliest ziggurat dates from around 4000 BCE, but its precursors were raised platforms or mounds dating from as far back as the Ubaid period in the 6th millennium BCE. The ziggurat was seen as a means of connecting heaven and earth. Babylon's ziggurat was called Etemenanki, "House of the Foundation of Heaven and Earth" in Sumerian.

On flat land, builders made an artificial mountain on top of which the city's deity was thought to live. Ziggurats were part of a sacred complex that included other buildings, and they were the tallest buildings in each city. According to Herodotus, there was a shrine at the top of each ziggurat. None have ever been found, but the advanced state of ruination of most extant ziggurats may account for that. Ziggurats were not public places; they were the dwelling places of the gods. Only priests would have had access in order to provide the gods with food and drink and otherwise care for them.

Every city had its own god, something that became very important once Assyria started to build an empire. Babylon's god was Marduk, Uruk's deity was the goddess Inanna, and Enlil, the earth god, was the patron of Nippur.

It seems that Sumerian cities were not initially ruled by kings but run by an *ensi*, or governor, in cooperation with a council. Kingship probably grew out of the need for military leadership once the city-states started to compete with each other.

It's intriguing that in most Sumerian cities, there is a distinct separation between the temple and the palace. Both are placed at the edge of the city, but they are distant from each other. However, the temple always seems to have dominated the skyline.

One thing that was very important to the Sumerians was beer; this was a Mesopotamian passion that continued under the Assyrians and Babylonians. In fact, the Sumerians probably invented beer. They gave it a goddess, Ninkasi, whose name means "mistress of beer." Beer was usually drunk through a long straw so several people could drink from the same pot at once, which was a great way to promote friendship and cooperation among the people.

You may not think beer is historically important, but one of the very few inscriptions that mention King Enannatum II of Lagash is an inscription on the door socket of Nigirsu's brewery, telling how Enannatum, son of Entemena, ensi of Lagash, restored the brewery for the warrior god Nigursu. Without that brewery, it might not have been possible to distinguish him from Enannatum I, and history would look just a tiny bit different.

Uruk was the first great city. It is called Erech in the Bible or Warka in Arabic. Its first king was Meskiaggasher, and he was followed by his son Enmerkar. Then, his companion, Lugalbanda, took the throne, and

Dumuzi followed him. Dumuzi became the focus of a sacred marriage rite and formal mourning once he died. These rites were still being celebrated in the 6th century BCE). The next king, according to the Sumerian King List, was Gilgamesh, who became the Sumerian hero par excellence. He ruled Uruk between 2900 and 2350 BCE during the Early Dynastic period.

The *Epic of Gilgamesh* was one of the texts discovered in the Library of Ashurbanipal. It tells how the hero Gilgamesh befriends the wild man Enkidu, how together they defeat Humbaba, and how Gilgamesh rejects the goddess Ishtar and defeats the Bull of Heaven, which she sends to punish him for his rejection. Then, Enkidu dies, and Gilgamesh, afraid of death, tries to find immortality. He fails in his quest, but he returns to Uruk, understanding that he, too, will die (not the most upbeat of endings, it has to be said, but it does pack an emotional punch that even modern-day humans can understand).

Although the *Epic of Gilgamesh* is written in Akkadian and was probably written between 1600 and 1100 BCE, long after the end of Sumerian rule, the Akkadian text conflated several different Sumerian texts, which still exist, each telling a different episode of the story. Gilgamesh is also attested by more prosaic inscriptions as a historical figure. A very early inscription states, "Gilgamesh is the one selected by Utu [the sun god]," and the Tummal Inscription, which dates to around 1950 BCE, credits him with rebuilding the walls of Uruk, which were nearly six miles long.

Uruk was a key cult center for the goddess Ishtar or Inanna. In fact, the development of the city might have been driven by its priesthood rather than its kings. The temple seems to have been built before any palaces. The king's relationship to the gods was crucial. It was believed that the gods chose the king, giving him divine approval, but the king needed to continue to ensure the gods' support by enriching the temples. Unlike in ancient Egypt, the king himself was not seen as divine—hence Gilgamesh's struggles with mortality.

Uruk was a sizable city. At its prime, it might have had as many as 100,000 people, not far off from the population of Albany, New York, or Wichita Falls, Texas, today.

Ashur, the city that lent its name to the Assyrians, was probably founded around 2600 BCE, by which time Uruk was already a mature and highly populated city. During its early years, Ashur was sometimes independent. At other times, it was subject to Akkad or Ur.

Ashur was situated just at the edge of the fertile zone, where there would have been enough rainfall for agriculture. Even so, agriculture around Ashur was marginal, with low yields compared to the south. Agriculture here was fed by rain. In Babylonia, to the south, the rivers delivered most of the water through irrigation canals. Since it was hard to grow enough agriculture to feed the inhabitants of Ashur, trade became a pressing concern. Tin, a necessary ingredient for making bronze, came from central Asia, while copper came from Anatolia. Silver, which was the main currency of the Middle East at the time (not gold), also came from Anatolia. Throughout Assyria's history, securing supplies of timber and metal drove expansionist policies. In its earliest days, Ashur became a major commercial center.

Why build a city in a less fertile area? The answer is likely the fact that the site controlled a ford on the Tigris, which opened up trade routes to Syria, Anatolia, and central Asia. The site also had a huge rock outcrop above the river, which made it defensible. On open land with no clear natural boundaries, cities were open to attack by nomads coming down from the highlands, so Ashur's craggy site was a key strategic advantage.

Ashur was a liminal spot, the threshold between the fertile land and the arid land to the west, where nomadic herdsmen relied on pastoralism as a way of life. The heartlands of Assyria were always to the east of Ashur, roughly in a triangle between the cities of Nineveh, Arbela, and Ashur.

Tin, a necessary ingredient for making bronze, came from Central Asia, while copper came from Anatolia, as did silver, which was the main currency of the Middle East at the time (not gold).

Ashur was situated on a tight bend of the Tigris River, where a forty-meter rocky outcrop now called Qal'at Sherqat soars above the river. This rock was the site of Ashur's temple, and it's likely that the rock itself was originally seen as embodying the deity. The god and the city would have been one and the same thing to the Assyrians. At various times, this temple was given different names in the Sumerian language:

- Eamkurkurra - the house of the wild bull of the lands
- Ehursagkurkurra - the house of the mountain of the lands
- Esharra - the house of the universe.

The Sumerian economy was a mixed model. The temples controlled a good deal of the wealth, as did the nobility, but there was also a middle class to which many of the merchants belonged. Slavery existed. Most slaves were prisoners of war, but debtors could also be enslaved by their creditors, and some parents sold their children in time of need. However, slaves could buy their freedom, and any child who had a free father was born free.

Monogamy was the usual practice unless the first wife had no children. Male and female spheres became sharply defined over time. There might have been female rulers very early on (probably priestesses ruling a temple-led culture), but by the later period, kings were exclusively male. However, women could run their own businesses. They could also buy and sell land and slaves. They were often bakers, brewers, and weavers.

Kingship "descended from heaven," as it says in the Sumerian King List. The king was the representative of the gods. He was responsible for "feeding" the gods, protecting the city against its enemies, and establishing justice. Images of the king frequently show him as a provider, sacrificing to a god, building a temple, making a libation (pouring out beer on the ground), or hosting a banquet. (The word "banquet," by the way, is literally "pouring out beer" in Sumerian.)

Kings are also shown as protectors. For instance, there are scenes of kings fighting or killing lions, which became a prevalent image in the area from the Sumerians all the way to the end of the Assyrian Empire. The king is often seen in triumph, driving his chariot, reviewing prisoners of war, or presenting his captives to the gods, but there is no equivalent to the "smiting scene" in Egyptian culture, which shows the pharaoh grabbing enemies by the hair and raising his mace to smash their heads.

Kings in Sumer were often called the "beloved of Inanna." However, scholars have disagreed on how to interpret the concept of sacred marriage. Royal hymns of Ur-Namma from the Neo-Sumerian period refer to a sexual union between Inanna and the ruler. Some have suggested that the king was initiated by a priestess of Inanna's temple, while others believe the image was simply a metaphor. The scene of the king watering a tiny palm tree in a pot might have been a sophisticated metaphor for the sacred marriage (water and semen are referred to by the same word in Sumerian, "a").

Sumerian culture was highly literate, not just in terms of being able to read and write but also in terms of reverence for the written word. Every building had a foundation tablet inscribed and buried. Words were a form of magic; it was as if writing something down could make it happen. When a king rebuilt a temple, he would try to find the foundation tablets that the first builder and any subsequent restorers had deposited. He would make sacrifices, oil the tablets, and then place them with a new tablet that recorded the restoration. The tablets were, in a way, sacred objects, preserving the lineage of the royal family and the history of the temple.

There is a great deal of continuity between the Sumerians and the civilizations that succeeded them. However, there was also a major break in history, as new people speaking a different language arrived in Mesopotamia and set up their own civilization. That is the subject of the next chapter.

Chapter 2: The Early Period and the Akkadian Empire

Around 2800 BCE or a little later, a number of new people started to arrive in Mesopotamia. Unlike the Sumerians, they spoke a Semitic language, an ancestor of modern Arabic. (Nineteenth-century archaeologists saw the racial question as highly important, and they contrasted Sumer and the Semitic "races" of Babylon and Assyria. In fact, Mesopotamia appears to have been a highly unified, multi-lingual culture. The Sumerian language survived and was used alongside the Semitic languages of Babylonian and Assyrian. Sumerian-language texts were sometimes signed by scribes with Akkadian names. Much of Sumerian religion and social organization survived in the later cultures too.)

While the names of the kings of Kish were Akkadian from 2800 BCE onward, the first ruler who is well attested is Sargon the Great, the first ruler of the Akkadian Empire and the founder of the Old Akkadian dynasty, which ruled for a century after his death. Sargon (Sharru-ukin in Akkadian, meaning "the king is established") came to power around 2334 BCE and brought with him a new concept of kingship and the territorial state.

During this period, there was tension between the Sumerian idea of the city-state, as new concepts of territorial states could include a number of cities. The Sumerian city-states sometimes came together and sometimes separated; their relations were often fluid. Sargon was hellbent on conquest, though. The regnal year names for his reign show the nature of his rule. They include "Year in which he destroyed Elam" and "Year in which Mari was destroyed."

Sargon's capital, Akkad or Agade, has not yet been identified. It was most likely in the area of Baghdad. Sargon himself is something of a mystery; even his name might be just his title as king rather than his birthname or adoptive name. The Sumerian King List says that he was the son of a gardener and a cup-bearer to King Ur-Zababa of Kish. The *Legend of Sargon of Akkad*, a Sumerian text, says that when Ur-Zababa heard that Sargon had dreamed of the goddess Inanna's favor, he tried to have Sargon killed. He sent Sargon to the chief smith with a bronze mirror. Ur-Zababa told the smith to throw both the mirror and Sargon into the crucible. However, Inanna warned Sargon to hand over the mirror and not to enter the workshop. So, Sargon was saved.

An Akkadian text from around 2300 BCE (contemporary with Sargon) tells how Sargon's mother put him in a basket of rushes and cast him into the river. Akki, the drawer of water, found him and decided to look after him. Sargon was Akki's gardener when the goddess Ishtar granted him her love, and he became king. (This is remarkably similar to the story of Moses, though not quite the same. Moses, after all, was brought up by the pharaoh's daughter.)

In Neo-Assyrian literature, Sargon appears as an almost legendary figure. Perhaps he could be compared to King Arthur, who might have been based on a real ruler but developed a whole mythical narrative, including the Lady of the Lake who gives Arthur a sword, an episode quite close to the narrative of Ishtar's favor and also includes water. Arthur is said to have been conceived when King Uther Pendragon disguises himself as Igraine's husband and lies with her. Sargon, on the other hand, is born of a "changeling" mother; his father is unknown. However, while historians generally don't believe Arthur existed in reality, we know that Sargon did.

Sargon's story fascinated the Assyrians. Some Assyrian rulers even adopted the Akkadian names Sargon and Naram-sin (Sargon's grandson), hoping to emulate the Sargonid dynasty's achievements.

Sargon was a military genius, but he was also a savvy administrator. He used archers and light troops rather than heavy infantry. Unlike the Sumerian states, he maintained a permanent army rather than raising levies when needed. He took Uruk and Mari, conquered Ur and Umma, and raided Elam. Under Sargon, Sumer became unified into a single state. He conquered lands in the Levant as far north as Lebanon, which meant the Akkadian Empire stretched from the Mediterranean to the Persian Gulf. He also made Akkadian the official language.

Sargon's inscriptions and those of his sons, Rimush and Manishtushu, survive, albeit only in the form of copies made some centuries later. He was known as "Sargon, king of Akkad, overseer of Inanna, king of Kish, anointed of Anu, king of the land [Mesopotamia], governor [ensi] of Enlil." Sargon boasted that 5,400 men ate bread daily before him as members of his household. This was his administrative and military team.

With Sargon, the idea of being king changed. Sumerian kings represented themselves as *primus inter pares*, "first among equals." Gudea, ruler of Lagash, for instance, made many almost life-size statues of himself, but he appears as an ordinary man in a robe. His inscriptions don't talk about his victories. Instead, they detail his pious acts. Sargon, on the other hand, stresses his aggression and military prowess in his inscriptions. He set himself apart from other men. He certainly saw himself as the first in a line of heroic rulers.

The Mask of Sargon, now thought to represent Naram-Sin of Akkad.[121]

Manishtushu, Sargon's son, was succeeded by Naram-Sin of Akkad. He ruled between 2254 and 2218. Naram-Sin appears to have centralized the administration, increasing royal control of the various city-states. However, this set off a major uprising. The rulers of Kish and Uruk led the revolt, together with numerous other city-states. Then, the Gutians from the mountainous region to the east of Mesopotamia invaded, briefly conquering the whole of Sumer. Naram-Sin appears to have successfully put down the first rebellions, but later in his reign, he lost control of much of the empire.

Shar-Kali-Sharri, Naram-Sin's son, took over Akkad, but the fact that he didn't use the title "king of the four quarters" like his predecessors suggests that he realized his dominion was much less extensive than his father's. He might have been the last Akkadian king to control more than just the city of Akkad.

In 2193, the Gutians invaded again. Not much is known about the Gutians, but they threw Akkad into chaos. The Sumerian King List describes this period with the question, "Then who was king? Who was not king?" There were a number of rivals who took the throne for short periods. In 2189, the dynasty was reestablished under Dudu, who was probably the son of Shar-Kali-Sharri. Dudu's son, Shu-turul (c. 2168-2154), was the last king of Akkad. After this, Uruk regained preeminence.

Sargon's Akkadian Empire lasted less than two hundred years. This gave rise to the idea of the "Curse of Akkad." A Sumerian literary composition called *The Frown of Enlil* asserted that Akkad had fallen out of favor because its later kings disrespected the gods. Whatever happened, the Akkadian Empire retained its hold on the imaginations and ambitions of later kings. For instance, Ur-Nammu, who founded the Neo-Sumerian Empire, called himself "king of Sumer and Akkad." Assyrian kings also used the title when they held control of Babylon.

After the fall of Akkad and after some years of Gutian rule, a number of Sumerian cities were able to reassert their independence, including Ur, Uruk, Lagash, and Umma.

Gudea of Lagash, who ruled between 2080 and 2060 BCE, might have been the impetus behind this movement. He claimed several conquests, but most of his inscriptions record the creation of irrigation channels and temples. This represents a return to the Sumerian style of kingship rather than the military imperialism of Akkadian rulers.

Under Gudea, Lagash traded with Oman, northern Arabia, Lebanon, Sinai, and even India. His title was *ensi*, town leader or governor, rather than *lugal* (Sumerian) or *sharrum* (Assyrian), or king. Gudea is well known from the numerous statues he had made of himself. He is often shown with the drafts of a temple plan in his lap. He ruled for two decades, and he was later deified.

Gudea of Lagash, a statue in the Louvre. Note the writing on his apron. By the way, this is the only image of a ruler in this book that shows a non-bearded man. Both the Akkadians and the Assyrians had long hair and beards. Some Sumerians were also bearded. It may be that Gudea had to shave his beard and head because he was a priest and needed to be in a state of ritual purity.[122]

Another major ruler, Ur-Nammu, came to power in Ur at a time shortly before Gudea's reign in Lagash. He probably ruled from 2212 to 2094 and founded the Third Dynasty of Ur, which is also sometimes known as the Neo-Sumerian Empire. Ur came out ahead in a major power struggle after the Gutian invasion and extended its rule farther north.

He defeated Lagash and Uruk and was crowned at Nippur. He eventually came to rule Eridu and Susa. He was a state-builder, but he was also a ziggurat-builder, creating the Great Ziggurat of Ur. He also created a law code, the Code of Ur-Nammu, which is the first known unitary code, and standardized weights and measures.[i] But unlike the Akkadians, he was not particularly interested in conquering the north of Mesopotamia. He preferred diplomacy so that towns like Nineveh, Mari, and Ebla remained independent but were friendly to Ur.

A set of weights from Shalmaneser V's reign.[123]

Like Gudea, Ur-Nammu emphasized civil works in his inscriptions. Draining the marshes was a particularly important aspect of his work, creating more and richer farmland to feed a growing population. By this time, Ur had 200,000 people.

The Neo-Sumerian Empire also included Ashur. Several documents from Ur mention individuals with names including Ashur, so this was clearly not a Sumerian ethnic state; it included people of Akkadian and Assyrian origin.

---

[i] A set of sixteen different weights from the time of Shalmaneser V was found at Nimrud. They were all roaring lions that could be lifted by their curved-over tails.

Ur-Nammu was succeeded as ruler of Ur by Shulgi (2094-2046), who standardized not just the calendar but also the tax system and administration. He captured Susa, the capital of Elam (western Iran), which had long been a potent enemy of the Mesopotamian powers. Ur-Nammu created a major empire, stretching from modern Turkey to the Persian Gulf. However, under Shulgi's three successors, the territory receded. The Elamites invaded, sacked Ur in 2004, and made King Ibbi-Sin their captive.

The destruction of cities was a perpetual feature of Middle Eastern history. In some ways, the sack of Ur was the end of Sumer, which was quickly absorbed into Babylon. However, the Sumerian language remained, like Latin after the end of the Roman Empire.

The Elamites only lasted a couple of decades in Mesopotamia, though. There were other forces at play, both in Babylon to the south and in Ashur.

Chapter 3: The Old Assyrian Empire and Babylon

The first attested kings of Ashur emerged around 2025 BCE. These kings of the Old Assyrian period took advantage of the increasing precarity of Ur to set up their own kingdom. Ashur (the god) gave his name to the city, which, in turn, gave its name to the Assyrian people and the Assyrian nation (which included many people who were not ethnic Assyrians).

The Assyrian king lists include nearly thirty rulers who are otherwise unattested; nothing of them survives but their name. Among them is Ushpia, who is said to have built the temple of Ashur in the late 3rd millennium BCE. The king list includes "kings who lived in tents" and "kings who were ancestors," but it seems likely that they were added to the list later, possibly during Shamsi-Adad I's rule to incorporate his Amorite ancestors.

Ashur must have had governors under the rule of Ur, and it's likely that these governors simply claimed their independence after Ur fell to Elam and became kings. Possibly the first was Sulili, who might be the Ilaba-siululi mentioned as the governor of Ashur in a text from Ur. His seal is interesting, as it features the motto "Ashur is king." This shows a theocratic understanding of kingship, with the ruler acting as a steward for the god.

This was not a divine monarchy, like the pharaohs of ancient Egypt who were seen as incarnations of the god Horus (when alive) or Osiris (after death). Instead, it was a monarchy mandated by the god Ashur. In the early days of Ashur, the monarchy probably was a form of what we now call a constitutional monarchy, in which the hereditary leader ruled together with a popular assembly. These kings called themselves overseers, princes, or stewards.

The city assembly (*alum*) might have included all free adult men or consisted mainly of nobles.[i] Ot met near the Step Gate, by which a stele was erected detailing the city's laws, including commercial laws. The city hall (*bet alim*) was in charge of the treasury; it was not until later in Ashur's history that the king became the head of city hall (a position known as *limmum*). Years in Ashur were named after the *limmum*, not the king, unlike societies in the south of Mesopotamia.

The first line of kings that can be verified is the Puzur-Ashur dynasty or Old Assyrian dynasty. The style of kingship was perhaps not very different from what was going on in Babylon; however, the priesthood in Ashur was not nearly as strong as it was in Babylon. The king of Ashur (the city) effectively acted as the high priest of Ashur (the god).

Puzur-Ashur claimed Assyria's independence around 2025 BCE, though it is possible that he continued the lineage of earlier rulers. The succession was then unbroken from son to son for eight generations, with each becoming Ishiak Ashur, or vice-regent of Ashur. Under Puzur-Ashur's son Shalim-ahum, Ashur's trading network greatly increased, and under Erishum I (Shalim-ahum's grandson), the *karum* system of trading enclaves in Anatolian towns began.

A tablet from Kanesh, one of these enclaves, contains the invocation, "Ashur is king! Erishum is Ashur's Steward! He who tells a lie in the Step Gate, the demon of the ruins will smash his head like a pot that breaks."[ii]

There were *karum* trading posts in Kanesh, Hattusha, and Ankuwa, among other cities, where Assyrian merchants traded textiles, tin, iron, copper, wool, grain, gold, and silver. These *karum* weren't ruled by Assyria; rather, Assyrian merchants enjoyed special rights in each city and governed their own extra-territorial enclave. Local rulers had an incentive to set up a *karum* since they profited from the trade and enjoyed privileged access to scarce goods.

---

[i] Only about 50 percent of men were free; the rest were chattel slaves or debt slaves.

[ii] Frahm, Eckart. *Assyria: The Rise and Fall of the World's First Empire*. Basic Books, New York, 2023.

Not all towns bought into the system, though. A letter found at Kanesh suggests traders on their way to the *karum* should hide tin in their underwear to avoid paying tolls on these goods at a less friendly town en route.[i]

Assyrians who traded and lived away from Ashur could take a wife in the place where they were living. Their wife in Ashur was considered the main wife, while the other was seen as a temporary arrangement. A secondary wife would likely see the marriage as beneficial. She would enjoy a good lifestyle while her husband was there, and when he went back to Ashur, she would get an amicable divorce, retaining the house and receiving a good payoff. She would also be able to remarry. This is an intriguing adaptation of the generally monogamous mores of Assyrians.

Women had a less privileged position in Assyrian society than they did in Sumer or Babylon. High-born women wore veils, and their contacts were highly controlled. Adultery was punished by death (though this was even-handed for both parties; there was no double standard). Women were dependent on their male relations.

During the latter part of the Puzur-Ashur dynasty, Assyria came under increasing pressure from the Amorites, who had already overrun the south of Mesopotamia. Erishum II was deposed, and the throne was taken by Shamshi-Adad I.

It is uncertain exactly who Shamshi-Adad was. He might have been an Amorite usurper, but the king list asserts that he was of the royal house of Ashur, descended from Ushpia. In that case, he might have been a cousin or another relation of the royal house who took power after Erishum proved unable to resist the Amorite threat. On the other hand, the mention of the house of Ushpia might be a later attempt to "legitimize" Shamshi-Adad and give the Assyrian monarchs a completely unbroken lineage from the earliest days. It is also possible that Shamshi-Adad was a member of the same extended family as Hammurabi, another expansionary ruler of the time.

Whichever is the case, Shamshi-Adad claimed the title of "king of the universe" and "unifier of the land between the two rivers." His rule was clearly expansionist. For instance, he took the city of Mari to the west. Ashur was the religious center of his realm. He rebuilt the god's temple in

---

[i] Frahm, Eckart. *Assyria: The Rise and Fall of the World's First Empire.* Basic Books, New York, 2023.

Ashur and added a ziggurat. He also appears to have been the first king to build a palace in Ashur. However, his capital was Shubat-Enlil in northeastern Syria, which was situated in a much more fertile region.

As the name of Shubat-Enlil ("Enlil's residence") suggests, the god to whom Shamshi-Adad gave particular worship was not Ashur but Enlil, the Sumerian storm god and creator. It must have been around this time that Enlil became identified with Ashur. While Ashur originally had been a single god with no family, this identification with Enlil gave him a wife, Enlil's wife Ninlil (Mullissu), and a son, Ninurta. The Assyrian pantheon was growing.

Shamshi-Adad reigned for thirty-three years, and one of the things we know about him is that he required a good stock of beer to be maintained for the palace. This was probably not just because he liked a drink or two. Beer was used in temple rituals. In fact, the entire brewing process was a ritual. The importance of ensuring that beer was correctly brewed can be seen by the fact that the Babylonian Code of Hammurabi required the death penalty for those guilty of watering down the beer they brewed or sold.

Brewing Assyrian Beer

This recipe is based on the Hymn to Ninkasi, a Sumerian text from around 1800 BCE that actually describes the brewing process as the goddess brews her beer.

On the first day, wheat grain is soaked in water. On the second day, the wheat is drained, put in a bowl, and covered. It is left until it begins to sprout. On the same day, bappir or beer bread is started. One would mix yeast, barley flour, and water and then set the mixture aside in a covered bowl for two days.

On the fourth day, the bappir is baked for ten minutes until just the crust is cooked, leaving the inside of the loaf raw. The wheat is also baked (nowadays, we would say "malted") in the same oven but for longer.

The next day, the wheat is crushed in a mortar, and the bappir is torn into pieces and placed in a pot with water. Dates and yeast are added to it (the Sumerians might have relied on wild yeasts). The pot is then covered and left to ferment for two days. In the high temperatures of Mesopotamia, fermentation would have occurred easily.

Finally, the beer is filtered.

The Sumerians would have brewed on a large scale, but it's probably best if you just try for a couple of quarts. You'll need half a cup of wheat, a cup and a half of barley flour, half a cup of chopped dates, half a cup of honey, a couple of tablespoon of dried yeast, and two quarts of water.

This was a time when state formation was occurring in a number of different centers. Kanesh became an Anatolian power and eventually transformed into the center of the Hittite Empire, while Assyria began to expand beyond the Tigris to the Zagros Mountains.

Shamsi-Adad shared power with his two sons. Ishme-Dagan was made viceroy of Ekallatum, just north of Ashur, while Yasmah-Adad was given Mari. However, Yasmah-Adad was incompetent and often drunk, at least if his father's letters to him are to be believed. In one letter to Yasmah-Adad that was found at Mari, Shamsi-Adad compared Ishme-Dagan's military prowess with the way Yasmah-Adad lazed at ease with women. The message was clear: turn your life around!

Shamsi-Adad died in 1776 BCE at a time when Assyria was under attack. Yasmah-Adad had turned a deaf ear to his father's advice, as Mari was lost a few years after Shamsi-Adad's death. But Ishme-Dagan was made of sterner stuff. He created a joint enterprise with Dadusha, king of Eshnunna, which was located farther south. He was able to conquer the cities of Nineveh and Arbela with this support. Dadusha took the plunder, while Ishme-Dagan consolidated Nineveh into the Assyrian heartland. This was the first time that the core of the Assyrian Empire was united.

However, Ishme-Dagan's victories didn't last. Perhaps the king of Eshnunna realized that Ishme-Dagan had got the best out of the deal. Whatever the reason, Eshnunna turned into an implacable foe. Its people attacked Ishme-Dagan at Ashur and drove him into exile in Babylon.

The house of Shamsi-Adad failed after five monarchs. Puzur-Sin rose to power. This king portrayed himself as returning to the "true" line of Assyria, destroying the "evil" of his predecessors. However, by the time of Shalmaneser I in the Middle Assyrian Empire, Shamsi-Adad was thought of as a true Assyrian king and Puzur-Sin as the usurper.

At this point in the history of Mesopotamia, a new power arrived on the scene. The Amorites had migrated to Assyria and the south, bringing their Semitic language, Akkadian, with them. As well as taking over Ur and Lagash, an Amorite dynasty took over the previously unimportant city of Babylon. The first king of Babylon was Sumu-Abum, who reigned from around 1894 to 1881 BCE. He was followed by Sumu-la-El, who conquered the city of Kish.

The fifth king, Sin-Muballit, was the first to declare himself king of Babylon and expanded his territory by taking the cities of Isin, Borsippa, and Sippar. However, it was his son Hammurabi who built Babylon into a major power, as he took over most of southern Mesopotamia.

Hammurabi came to the throne around 1792 BCE while his father was still alive; Sin-Muballit had abdicated due to ill health. Hammurabi began his reign with a program of public works, including expansions to temples and improving the city walls. However, the Elamites' move into the plains, taking Eshnunna and other cities, forced Hammurabi to take a more active part in the region's military affairs. By allying himself with Larsa, he was able to send the Elamites packing.

However, relations with Larsa turned sour. Hammurabi took that city, Eshnunna, and other northern cities, including Mari. This gave him control of the entire southern part of Mesopotamia, bringing him up against Ashur in the north. (His destruction of the palace in Mari in 1759 BCE was a godsend to later archaeologists, as it left behind a huge number of easily dated, well-fired clay tablets. This archive included shopping lists, tax documents, legal cases, and personal letters.)

At first, Ishme-Dagan of Ashur allied with Hammurabi. Ashur was weak at the time, and Ishme-Dagan might have seen Babylon, a rising power, as a protector against the ever-threatening Elamites. However, this uneasy alliance did not hold, and eventually, Hammurabi took both Ashur and Nineveh. Ishme-Dagan I appears to have been forced to live in Babylon as a client king. His successor, Mut-Ashkur, was forced to pay tribute to Hammurabi.

The creation of this Babylonian superstate took Hammurabi twenty years, at the end of which he was truly entitled to call himself "king of Sumer and Akkad."

As king, Hammurabi had three tasks: to build, which he had done; to protect the state militarily, which he had done; and to preserve justice. The latter he did by issuing the Code of Hammurabi, known from the stele that is now in the Louvre in Paris, France. The top of the stele shows Hammurabi receiving the code from the god Shamash, and the inscription states the law was meant to protect the weak, orphans, and widows. In an empire where military might was often seen as right, the law offered recourse to those without power.

Law codes had been written before. For the first time, though, the law was written in Akkadian, not Sumerian. It covered a broad range of areas; for instance, it talked about the warranties on the sale of slaves, giving purchasers a form of consumer protection. It specified wage rates for craftsmen and seasonal laborers and rates of hire for boats. The code covered family law, inheritance, property title, and legal process. Rules for indemnities in the case of trespassing cattle were set (this was evidently a frequent problem), and merchants were indemnified if trading agents lost their cash. Reading the law code gives a good idea of how society was structured and how developed the Babylonian economy had become.

The stele on which Hammurabi's Code is written.[124]

The 3rd millennium BCE was a period of experimentation, with power shifting from city to city. But Shamsi-Adad and Hammurabi created a new idea, the idea of the territorial city, moving from the city-state to a state that included a number of cities. At the same time, the original idea of a hereditary civic leader ruling with a council was replaced by a monarchical ideal—the king who ruled in glorious isolation as the military leader and law-maker. That idea would prove to be very influential.

Hammurabi believed he had brought peace to Mesopotamia. He died around 1750 BCE, still believing that. However, peace did not survive for long after the accession of his son, Samsu-iluna. The kingdom of Sumer and Akkad began to fall apart. Puzur-Sin reclaimed Ashur, and in the south, the Sealand dynasty broke free, looking back to Sumerian times by using pseudo-Sumerian king names even though they spoke Akkadian.

Even so, from Hammurabi's reign onward, Assyria was highly influenced by trends and events in Babylon. Babylonia and Assyria were two separate, though related, empires, but it can sometimes be difficult to disentangle their two histories.

Middle Eastern Chronologies

Because there are few definite sources for dates in the earlier part of Mesopotamian history, historians have to base their datings on relative chronology. Dendrochronology, radiocarbon dating, and astronomical records have failed to fix dates closely enough to be certain.

A key source for chronology is the Venus Tablet of Ammisaduqa. This cuneiform text dates from the mid-17th century BCE and gives the time that Venus rises and sets on lunar dates for over twenty-one years. However, because Venus's visibility varies on an eight-year cycle, the start of the observations noted in the tablet could have taken place in 1702, 1646, 1638, 1582, or 1550 BCE. Dating systems based on these dates are referred to as the Long, Middle, Middle Low, Short, and Ultra Short chronologies.

For later periods, comparisons with the dates of Egyptian pharaohs and lunar observation dates can be used to give absolute dating. For instance, Ramesses II came to the throne in 1279 BCE, giving us a firm date to work with.

In 1595 BCE, Babylon was ruled by Hammurabi's great-great-grandson, Samsu-Ditana. The kingdom had shrunk, but it still was quite large, even including the city of Mari. Sealand continually threatened the Babylonians from the south, though.

However, events far to the north, in the Hittite capital of Hattusha (near modern Ankara), were responsible for Babylon's end. Mursili I conquered Aleppo in Syria, a prize that had eluded his predecessor. He decided Babylon, which was more than five hundred miles south, would be his next target. Mursili made his way down the Euphrates, plundering cities as he went. Goods and captives were sent back to Hattusha, leading to widespread depopulation. Perhaps realizing that it would be difficult to hold together a state that extended so far south, Mursili decided not to stay, instead simply taking his loot back with him. But it was too late for Babylon. He had put an end to Samsu-Ditana's rule, and Babylon was abandoned for some years.

(As a side note, Mursili might have made a mistake in returning to Hattusha, as he was assassinated soon after his return due to the Hittite royal family's infighting.)

It wasn't until 1530 BCE that Burnaburiash I, a Kassite, was able to take over Babylon and kickstart the city again. His son, Ulamburiash, conquered Sealand, putting Babylon back in control of the south. Around this time, Babylon adopted Marduk as its patron god, a decision that was crucial to later Babylonian religion and ideology. The new Kassite dynasty ruled Babylon for the next five hundred years.

Most of the historical sources from this period are commercial and private in nature. At the trading station in Kanesh, a huge number of dockets, bills, IOUs, and letters from one merchant to another have been found. The house of the merchant Usur-sha-Ishtar yielded more than two thousand separate documents. On the other hand, for the early kings of Assyria, there are very limited sources, which is a sharp contrast to the Neo-Assyrian Empire, where a very high proportion of extant documents come from royal holdings and are focused on the king.

Chapter 4: Restoration and Fall to the Mitanni

Babylon had been destroyed, and Ashur had fallen. Assyria entered a dark age for several centuries. While a king list exists for the period, there is little historical evidence about what happened in Assyria.

During this period, Assyria continued to change, moving ever further away from the status of a city-state. It became more of a larger entity governed by hereditary rulers. However, following the details of this change is extraordinarily difficult, owing to the lack of inscriptions and even archaeological data. One result of this black hole in data is that the book will have to fast-forward a couple of centuries.

Following Ishme-Dagan and Mut-Ashkur, who is not included in some versions of the king list, there appeared to have been fairly short reigns of eight different kings, lasting from 1765 to 1745. However, it is also possible that some of the names might be those of *limmum* who gave their names to the years of another king's reign. The last of these kings was Adasi, whose son, Bel-bani, succeeded him as king, founding the Adaside dynasty.

It is possible that the people of Assyria did not see this as a dark age. It is also possible that the lack of information is simply due to the fact that archaeologists have not excavated a source of documentation for this period that can deliver enough information. However, historians tend to think it was a dark age because Assyria was not involved in the events happening in the Middle East during this period. Events to the west and north of Ashur would have the biggest impact on Mesopotamia during the next few centuries.

For once, there were the Hittites to be reckoned with. Mursili had bypassed Ashur on his way to Babylon, but the Hittites had already destroyed Assyria's trading system. Hittite King Zuzzu destroyed Kanesh around 1710 BCE, and the rest of the system did not survive for long. And while the success of the Hittites did not last, it galvanized another people group, the Hurrians, to create their own state.

There were a number of small Hurrian principalities clustered in northwestern Syria and farther east in the mountains at the headwaters of the Tigris and Euphrates. These states started to coalesce into what would become Mitanni (Hanigalbat in Assyrian). Mitanni was established around 1600 BCE and became increasingly powerful in Mesopotamia.

At the same time, Egypt became an expansionary power and, for the first time, was looking beyond the Nile Valley. This brought Egypt and Mitanni into contact with each other, and they appeared to have enjoyed excellent diplomatic relations, even forming a pact against the Hittites.

Thutmose I became pharaoh around 1506, and early in his reign, he made an expedition to the north into Syria. He made his way as far as the Euphrates, setting up a stele on the banks of the river. (The Euphrates confused the Egyptians, who, living on the Nile, had never seen a river that flowed from north to south. They called the Euphrates the "backwards river.") However, this was purely a short-term punitive mission, as Thutmose did not expand the Egyptian kingdom into the Levant on a permanent basis.

Later, during the Eighteenth Dynasty of Egypt, Thutmose III, the grandson of Thutmose I (r. 1479-1425 BCE), led another campaign into Syria and then copied his grandfather's example by heading south to reach the Euphrates. Like Thutmose I, he erected a stele there. His main targets were a resurgent Hittite Empire and the Mitanni, both of which he pillaged extensively.

Thutmose III changed the balance of power. Egypt was now a force in the Middle East, not just in the Nile Valley, and Thutmose III received tribute from Assyria and Babylon, as well as from the Hittites. The Assyrian king who paid him tribute is not named in Thutmose's otherwise prolific inscriptions, but it was probably Ashur-nadin-ahhe I. Inevitably, the presence of both Mitanni and Egypt put pressure on Assyria, whose northern borders were at risk.

Few of these historical events appear in the Assyrian record. Assyria seems to have been something of a backwater, though the Adaside dynasty continued to rule and build. Between 1563 and 1548, for instance, Shamshi-Adad III rebuilt the temples and the city wall in Ashur. His successor, Ashur-nirari I, built a new palace in Ashur, and his son, Puzur-Ashur III, increased the city's size, adding a large suburb to the south. Puzur-Ashur is also said to have made a treaty with King Burnaburiash of Babylon, though the only evidence for this comes from a much later date.

However, the threat from Mitanni continued, and in 1465, the city of Ashur was sacked. The king of Mitanni, Shaushtatar, carried away a silver and gold door from the citadel, which was taken back to Ashur many years later, as well as other plunder and captives. Fortunately for Ashur, like the Hittites, the Mitanni had no desire to make Assyria a permanent part of their territory. When the Mitanni started to falter, Assyria was ready to pick up the pieces, creating the Middle Assyrian Empire, the subject of our next chapter.

Chapter 5: The Middle Assyrian Empire

Ashur-uballit I took power in Assyria just as the Mitanni was losing influence. The Mitanni were engaged in a civil war. Tushratta, the king of Mitanni, and a rival, Artatama, were fighting for control. Tushratta was eventually assassinated, and the Mitanni Empire was unstable for some time afterward, giving Ashur-uballit his chance to reestablish Assyria as a major power. It appears that Ashur-uballit's father, Eriba-Adad, might have made use of this instability by playing off different sides to create a pro-Assyrian faction in Mitanni. Ashur-uballit went a step further, defeating the Mitanni and securing tribute from its king.

Ashur-uballit ("Ashur-has-kept-alive") also expanded Assyria to the south. By the end of his reign, Assyria ruled Nineveh and probably also Arbela. These states were agriculturally richer than Ashur, and communication via the Tigris River were easier. Ashur-uballit also destroyed the Hurrian city of Arrapha (probably modern Kirkuk in northeastern Iraq) and divided its territories with Babylon.

Ashur-uballit was the first Assyrian ruler to use the title of king. Previously, rulers asserted that "Ashur is king and I am the representative of Ashur." Ashur-uballit I, on the other hand, used the title shar mat Ashur, "king of Ashur," instead of issi'ak Ashur, "governor of Ashur." Clearly, there had been a change in expectations of what a king was. There had also been a change in the vision of what Assyria ought to be. It was no longer seen as a small state based on a single city; rather, it was seen as a major power.

Ashur-uballit corresponded with Pharaoh Akhenaten. This correspondence survived in Akhenaten's capital, along with other diplomatic correspondence written in Akkadian, which was the diplomatic language of the time. Early in his reign, Ashur-uballit sent a lump of lapis lazuli, a chariot, and two horses with his first letter. He sent two chariots, more lapis lazuli, and a request for twenty talents of gold with his second letter. He was building a new palace, he said, and wanted Akhenaten to send enough gold to decorate it. Neither letter seems to have been written with great elegance or much tact.

What's particularly interesting is that Ashur-uballit signed his letter as not just "king" but "great king." In doing so, he was putting himself on the same level as the big players—Egypt, Babylon, the Hittites, and the Mitanni.

Ashur-uballit also maintained good relations with Babylon. With the Mitanni still potentially a threat on the northern borders, it made sense to have diplomatic ties to the south. He married his daughter, Muballitat-Sherua, to Burnaburiash II of Babylon. Their son Karahardash became king of Babylon. Evidently, Ashur-uballit's objective was to bring the two states of Ashur and Babylon into the same family and perhaps even under the same rule.

However, things did not work out quite as he had planned. Events took an unexpected turn. Karahardash was executed by an anti-Assyrian faction, which replaced him on the throne by the non-royal Nazibugash. Those Babylonians who didn't want an Assyrian on the throne would be disappointed, though. Karahardash's fate gave Ashur-uballit the excuse he needed to invade Babylon. He defeated the usurper and installed another of his grandsons, Kurigalzu II, on the Babylonian throne.

This worked for a while. But Kurigalzu, who had been brought up in Babylon even if his mother was an Assyrian princess, seemed to have eventually come to resent the Assyrian influence in his kingdom and invaded Assyria. A battle took place at Sugagu, which is only a day's journey south of Ashur. There are two accounts of this battle. One reports a Babylonian victory, while the other says Assyria, under Ashur-uballit's son Enlil-nirari won the day.

Whatever happened at Sugagu, Assyria was headed toward creating an empire. Ashur had become the capital of an expansionary state that relied on its military might to increase its territories. "Assyrian" now meant being a subject of the empire, not a person from the city of Ashur. Popular representation in the city council appeared to have ended, and the monarchy became the sole authority in Assyria.

The rise of kingly power necessitated the creation of an Assyrian court, which included eunuchs (who were barred from becoming kings, making them "safe" servants and ministers) and a harem.[i] Bureaucratic documents ceased to be the affairs of the city and instead became the affairs of the king.

Archaeologist Bleda Düring sees the Middle Assyrian Empire as the first lasting empire of the age. Earlier imperial states had managed to last for no more than a century, and most of them were short-lived empires based on conquests that fell apart once the founder's impetus had disappeared. Assyria survived the Bronze Age collapse, and its empire lasted for seven hundred years. This, Düring emphasizes, was a major achievement that has rarely been matched in history.

Although Assyria defeated the Babylonians, there was a good deal of Babylonian influence in Assyria at this time, particularly in regards to religion. Many of the Babylonian gods appeared in Assyrian religion. They were sometimes given new names. The city of Babylon's god, Marduk, was now worshiped in Ashur.

Ashur-uballit's great-grandson Adad-nirari I (r. 1305-1274) and his son Shalmaneser I (r. 1273-1244) continued the expansion of Assyria. Adad-nirari called himself "pacifier of all enemies above and below," fighting the Kassite dynasty of Babylon to the south and the Mitanni and Hittites to the north. (By this point, the Mitanni had been reduced to a vassal state of the Hittite Empire.)

Adad-nirari fought his way along the Khabur River in northeastern Syria, a region that was both fertile and densely populated. He made the king of Mitanni pay him tribute. When payments stopped coming, he sacked the capital, Washukanni, and kidnapped the royal family. After this, he started calling himself "king of the universe" (the same title used by Shamshi-Adad I), putting other kingdoms on notice that his ambitions were limitless.

---

[i] A harem from a later period was found in the palace at Nimrud and was excavated from 1988 into the 1990s. Because of subsequent wars in Iraq, the discovery has not been properly assessed or published. Intriguingly, archaeologist Muzahim Mahmoud Hussein found four tombs of royal wives under the floors of the harem; the women of the harem lived with their predecessors buried directly underfoot.

However, it was Adad-nirari's successor, Shalmaneser I, who ended the Mitanni Empire for good. Despite the Hittites' assistance, Shattuara II of Mitanni could not stand against the might of Assyria. Shalmaneser integrated the new territory into Assyria by appointing his younger brother, Ibashshi-ili, as chancellor of Assyria in the newly built city of Dur-Katlimmu. The chancellor was given the title "king of Hanigalbat" ("king of Mitanni"), but it was only a courtesy title; he was clearly responsible to Shalmaneser. A temple was built at Dur-Katlimmu to the god associated with the royal family, Salmanu. (Shalmaneser means "Salmanu is eminent.")

Shalmaneser was probably the first king to use wholesale deportations as a means of building his empire. From this time onward, it became a regular method of Assyrian imperialism. Deporting people allowed Assyria to take possession of craftsmen or professional laborers by bringing them to the capital or sending them to cities that needed assistance. For instance, farmers might be reassigned to an area where fertility was low to improve agricultural methods. (The experience of Ashur's traders, who often lived in Kanesh and other cities for years on end, might have made this feel quite normal to the Assyrians, though it doesn't to us.)

Additionally, reassigning populations to new areas would help create "Assyrians" by reducing feelings of local identities. It also deprived conquered areas of potential leaders who might rebel against Assyrian rule.

Throughout the history of Assyria, there are a few "sweet spots" where three or four great rulers appeared in a row. Tukulti-Ninurta I was the successor to Shalmaneser. He came to the throne in 1244 BCE and reigned for around thirty-seven years, during which he both consolidated the northwest of Assyria and reasserted Assyrian rule over Babylon.

Tukulti-Ninurta I justified the invasion by asserting that the Babylonian king, Kashtiliash IV, had broken his agreements with Assyria. Kashtiliash was captured. Tukulti-Ninurta ritually trod on Kashtiliash's neck, using him as a footstool, and brought him to Ashur. He then installed a series of puppet rulers in Babylon. The first two proved useless and were rapidly replaced. Tukulti-Ninurta called himself ruler of "Sumer and Akkad" as the Babylonian kings had before him; by that point, it was an archaism, but it enshrined his claim to power over southern Mesopotamia as well as Assyria. The third puppet ruler, Adad-shuma-iddina, lasted six years before Tukulti-Ninurta deposed him, sacking Babylon and taking the statue of Marduk, Babylon's god, to Ashur. Tukulti-Ninurta called himself ruler of Sumer and Akkad as the Babylonian kings had before him; by then, it was an archaic title, but it enshrined his claim to power over southern Mesopotamia as well as Assyria.

Tukulti-Ninurta brought a huge number of texts from Babylon. These included works on divination, medical texts, prayers and liturgies, literary works, lists of gods, and Sumerian word lists. Scribes in Assyria could use old Babylonian cuneiform and the even older Sumerian language for their own writing.

Assyrian kings were expected to be builders and warriors, and Tukulti-Ninurta did not disappoint. He built a new temple to Ishtar in Ashur and also created a new trade town, Kar-Tukulti-Ninurta, which was just upstream on the Tigris from Ashur. This town had a new palace, a temple to Ashur, and a ziggurat.

Pride always comes before a fall. No temple to Ashur had ever been erected outside the god's own city, and the creation of Kar-Tukulti-Ninurta might have been unpopular with the people in Ashur. Worse, Babylon turned against Tukulti-Ninurta again later in his reign. This time, the Babylonian revolt, led by Adad-shuma-usur (possibly a son of the deposed Kashtiliash), was successful. The Assyrian army had become overextended and was struggling to hold on to all the territories that had been gained since Adad-nirari I's accession.

Tukulti-Ninurta was becoming increasingly unpopular at home since his string of military successes had come to an end. His move to the new city, together with his plundering of temples in Babylon, were seen as tempting the gods to punish Assyria. In 1207 BCE, a coup d'etat took place. Tukulti-Ninurta was assassinated by his sons. Assyria's fortunes were no longer headed upward; the wheel of fortune had turned.

Chapter 6: Assyria during the Bronze Age Collapse

While Assyria was focused on its rivalry with Babylon, the world around it had been changing dramatically. First, around 1200 BCE, the Sea Peoples arrived, attacking the coasts of the eastern Mediterranean. Their origins remain a mystery, but they clearly posed a formidable threat to settled civilizations in the Levant and Egypt.

In 1177, Pharaoh Ramesses III was able to defeat them on the Egyptian coast. However, Egypt was greatly weakened by the need to fight them off and eventually lost its eastern colonies. Nevertheless, Egypt survived. Other states were not so lucky. Mycenaean Greece was almost completely destroyed. Greece saw its population decline, with people migrating to Cyprus and the Levant. However, Athens survived to take its place later in history.

The Hittite state had already been damaged by Tukulti-Ninurta's attacks. The Sea Peoples put further pressure on the Hittites, taking Cilicia, Cyprus, and most of Canaan. This cut off the Hittites from their trade routes and left them vulnerable to attacks both from the Mediterranean and from Assyria to the south. A few Hittite city-states survived, such as Carchemish and Melid, but Assyria made them tributary states and later incorporated them fully into the Neo-Assyrian Empire.

Babylon's Kassite dynasty fell in 1155 after being conquered by Elam. In fact, Elam had overrun most of Babylonia by 1158 BCE. Assyria was able to take a good deal of Babylonian territory when the last Kassite king of Babylon, Enlil-nadin-ahi, was defeated and taken captive. The next dynasty was based in the city of Isin before Itti-Marduk-balatu managed to retake Babylon in the 1130s.

In the Levant, a number of states fell. Ugarit, an important port on the Syrian coast with trade links to Egypt, was destroyed around 1200 BCE; it was never rebuilt. Other Amorite states, such as Qatna and Alalakh, had already been abandoned by 1300, and the survivors, such as Amurru, collapsed or were destroyed during the Bronze Age collapse. There was a decline in trade in the eastern Mediterranean since most economies were stagnating.

Egypt suffered too despite Ramesses's victory over the Sea Peoples. Egypt slowly declined until 1078 when the New Kingdom came to an end with the death of Ramesses XI and the Third Intermediate Period started, during which the country was divided between the rule of Tanis in the Nile Delta and Thebes, which ruled Middle and Upper Egypt.

There are numerous theories as to why the Bronze Age collapse happened; it was probably a combination of causes. Climate change caused some of the migrations, which put pressure on established states once those new people arrived. The Hekla 3 eruption in Iceland might have led to widespread air pollution, disrupting agriculture. In the Near East, there were a number of droughts; in some areas, yields fell to such an extent that the land ceased to be cultivated.

The beginning of ironmaking also created technological turbulence, which must have changed the competitive nature among states. Egypt, for instance, was very late to adopt ironworking and relied on external supplies of the metal, putting it at a disadvantage despite its impressive military power.

Politically, the Bronze Age collapse virtually wiped out the "palace states." New groups were less hierarchical and often based on ethnicity, such as the Philistines, Arabs, and Aramaeans. The Bronze Age collapse also wiped out the use of cuneiform script in the Mediterranean. From this point onward, alphabetic scripts began to be used in the Levant. Cuneiform was restricted to use in Mesopotamia and Persia.

The Bronze Age collapse appears to have started in the Mediterranean Basin, so it took time for the effects to be seen in Mesopotamia. Initially, Assyria seemed to have benefited from the distress of many of its westerly rivals.

Tiglath-Pileser I (r. 1114-1076) was one of Assyria's greatest kings. He made Assyria the leading power of the Middle East, which it remained so for the next five hundred years. He led an expedition into Anatolia, Cappadocia, and Syria, expanding Assyrian dominions far to the north and west and as far as the Mediterranean. He took tribute from the cities of Sidon and Byblos in modern Lebanon.

However, these victories were difficult to consolidate. The mountainous territory, which was very different from the Mesopotamian plains, allowed Assyria's enemies to operate a guerrilla resistance and prevent Assyria from setting up a lasting administration in these areas. Perhaps as a result of these difficulties, Tiglath-Pileser started the custom of taking royal princes as hostages, ensuring their fathers' obedience. The princes would be educated as Assyrian princes, giving them a strong sense of Assyrian culture and ideology. The idea was to eventually make them into vassal kings.

Tiglath-Pileser also planted foreign trees in Ashur. Mesopotamia had few trees of its own, so the Assyrians were fascinated by the trees they saw elsewhere. Although what remains of the Assyrian kings is their buildings, they also created huge gardens.

Tiglath-Pileser's conquests did not last. By the time of Ashurnasirpal I (r. 1049-1031), Assyria had shrunk back to its heartlands and was under attack by Aramaean raiders. After his reign, there are no records of any military campaigns led by Assyria for almost a century. Under his younger son and third successor, Ashur-Rabi II (r. 1012-972), Assyria even managed to lose its cities on the Euphrates.

However, Ashur itself was never conquered, and power remained in the hands of the Adaside dynasty. This would give Assyria an important advantage when things began to change.

Chapter 7: The Neo-Assyrian Empire

If the Bronze Age collapse was at least partly caused by climatic change, so, too, was the rebirth of the empire. However, in this case, it was not because of widespread drought. Increasing rainfall improved agricultural productivity in Mesopotamia, kickstarting local economies and creating new agricultural surpluses that could be invested in building, improving irrigation, or (the Assyrians' choice) creating an army for taking over neighboring states.

The Aramaeans were no longer a potent threat. Many had settled in the Near East, and those who had moved into Assyria had become naturalized. Large-scale migration, which had been part of the Bronze Age collapse, was no longer occurring, so fighting off incursions was no longer the top need.

This gave Assyria a huge opportunity, and its rulers seized it with both hands. Assyria came out of the starting block fast, taking advantage of its rivals' weaknesses. Assyrian rulers had a single objective: to restore Assyria to its greatest extent. Many of the kings of this period were named after earlier great rulers, harkening back to the Middle Assyrian period as the "classical" age of Assyrian culture and aiming to emulate their achievements.

Late in the Neo-Assyrian Empire, King Esarhaddon wrote, "Before me, cities; behind me, ruins," a phrase that encapsulates the hunger and aggression of Assyrian rulers during this period.[i]

However, this was no longer an empire based on opportunistic military adventures. Innovations in government administration, together with the new ideology of absolute kingship, made it the first of the great world empires. Egypt, which was shut away in the Nile Valley anyway, was slightly apart from the rest of the world, so it was behind technologically, putting it out of competition. Greece was still in the early stages of its development. It was divided into a mass of small city-states in much the way Mesopotamia had been during early Sumerian times.

Ashur-Dan II (r. 934–912 BCE) is usually considered the first ruler of the Neo-Assyrian Empire since he reconquered much of Assyria's lost territory. In particular, he aimed at ensuring the trade routes into Anatolia were free from danger and retook land to the west that had come under Aramaean rule.

Assyrian warfare could be brutal. When Ashur-Dan II took Kadmuhu in the northwest, he executed the ruler and had his flayed skin displayed on the walls of Arbela. However, Ashur-Dan also resettled indigent Assyrians in fertile areas and started a program of land reclamation.

His son, Adad-nirari II (r. 911–891 BCE), expanded the empire further, though he appears to have had to fight off some opportunistic rebellions when he succeeded his father. In particular, he turned his sights south, twice defeating Babylon and pushing Assyrian rule downriver. He also created vassal states in the Khabur area in Syria.

However, he was able to use diplomacy wisely, concluding an advantageous peace treaty with Babylon. He and the king of Babylon, Nabu-shuma-ukin, married each other's daughters. (Though the Babylonian Chronicles are fragmentary, it might have been the next Assyrian ruler, Tukulti-Ninurta II, who swapped daughters.)

With Adad-nirari II, Assyrian history arrives at a very important point. From the first year of his reign, 911 BCE, there is a full record for every year of every Assyrian ruler, which allows for more precise dating of events from this time onward.

Tukulti-Ninurta II (r. 890–884 BCE) took the name of an illustrious predecessor like his father and grandfather. He campaigned along both the Euphrates and the Upper Tigris, consolidating his father's gains. He

---

[i] Frahm, Eckart. *Assyria: The Rise and Fall of the World's First Empire.* Basic Books, New York, 2023.

took tribute, including horses for his army. The amount of tribute taken each time might have been small, but everything was added to the central treasury, which enabled a prolific building program at Ashur and Nineveh.

One of Tukulti-Ninurta's inscriptions sums up the priorities of his reign: "to her lands I added land, and to her people, I added people."

Ashurnasirpal II succeeded his father in 883 BCE. Four years later, he made a momentous decision and moved the capital of the Assyrian state from Ashur to Kalhu (today known as Nimrud). Until that point, Kalhu had been a small provincial capital. Ashurnasirpal also undertook an extensive rebuilding program in Ashur and continued to use the vaults under Ashur's Old Palace as the mausoleum of the Assyrian monarchs. He clearly knew the story of Tukulti-Ninurta I's fated move of the capital to Kar-Tukulti-Ninurta and his assassination by his sons. He was determined to keep the priesthood and nobles in Ashur on his side.

He also kept on the good side of Tukulti-Ninurta's master scholar, Gabbu-ilani-eresh. This was a more important post than it sounds; it would be equivalent to a chief of staff or head of strategy today. A number of later master scholars (ummanu or tupshar sharri, "king's scribe") traced their descent to Gabbu-ilani-eresh, so it seems that the post was hereditary.

Kalhu was a good choice since it was a central region in Assyria; Ashur was peripheral, located to the south and west of the center of the state. Kalhu also had space to expand, while Ashur was limited by the curve of the river on which it was built.

A lamassu guards the gate of Ashurnasirpal's palace in Kalhu.[125]

The move also gave Ashurnasirpal the chance to refresh his administration. He kept the master scholar but handpicked the other officials he wanted to take with him. This weakened the power of the nobility, who were left behind in the now peripheral cities of Ashur, Nineveh, and Arbela. Ashurnasirpal brought more eunuchs into his bureaucracy. They could not aspire to be king since a king had to be perfect in body. Reliefs show more and more clean-shaven men; almost all of these men would have been eunuchs.

Ashurnasirpal changed the balance of power within Assyria in favor of the king and to the detriment of high-ranking families and temple priesthoods. He also changed the nature of the Assyrian state. Unlike earlier rulers of the Neo-Assyrian Empire, he assimilated his conquests into the Assyrian kingdom rather than leaving them as vassal states. Assyria moved from needing tribute to rebuild its cities and armies to having enough resources to invest in administering new territories.

Kalhu (Nimrud) was created at least partly by craftsmen who had been resettled from elsewhere in the empire. It had nine temples and a northwest palace. The palace marked a major departure from city-planning norms since it dominated the entire city. At Ashur and elsewhere, the building that dominated the skyline had always been the city god's temple or ziggurat; now, the kingship was asserting itself much more strongly.

The palace was a masterpiece. It was also an ideological assertion of Ashurnasirpal's control of his universe. Human-headed winged bulls (*lamassu*) up to sixteen feet high guarded the gates as protection, and alabaster reliefs celebrated the king's achievements. One scene shows Ashurnasirpal raising his hand in worship to a god in a winged sun disk. A protective spirit stands behind the king, guarding him. In the center is the "sacred tree" motif, a symbol of fertility and prosperity. Clearly, Ashurnasirpal's reign was mandated by the gods, according to this and other similar scenes. These scenes were copied again and again, not just in the palace but also on royal seals.

Ashurnasirpal raises his hand toward the symbol of Ashur.[125]

The palace had three courtyards: one for state business, one for the administration, and one for the royal family. Each room had glazed brick or painted walls above the stone reliefs and a ceiling made of Lebanese cedar beams. The themes of the reliefs are varied. They included military campaigns, hunting parties, rituals, and protective deities. Ashurnasirpal's palace was probably the first use of such extensive reliefs in Assyrian history; they became a precedent for every later Assyrian ruler's building works.

Ashurnasirpal channeled the Zab River to irrigate pleasure gardens full of exotic plants. These gardens might have been the ancestors of the much later Persian and Mughal *charbagh*, which was known for its lush vegetation and central water channels.

Ashurnasirpal's Banquet Stele gives the menu he served his guests at a huge ten-day "palace-warming" feast: one thousand oxen, one thousand calves, ten thousand sheep, fifteen thousand lambs, five hundred stags, five hundred gazelles, one thousand ducks, five hundred geese, ten thousand doves, ten thousand fish, and ten thousand loaves of bread. This was all washed down with ten thousand jars of beer. Snacks included nuts, salted seeds, pistachios, and olives.

Ashurnasirpal was not prone to understatement. An inscription at the temple of Ninurta claims, "I am king, I am lord, I am praiseworthy, I am exalted, I am important, I am magnificent, I am foremost, I am a hero, I am a warrior, I am a lion, and I am a man."[i]

---

[i] Frahm, Eckart. *Assyria: The Rise and Fall of the World's First Empire*. Basic Books, New York, 2023.

Several other things changed besides the idea of the monarchy. For instance, while the Code of Hammurabi was still known, it was used as a statement of ideal justice rather than as a practical legal text. There was no separate judiciary. Either state officials or temple personnel adjudicated; the king generally only became involved in cases of treason. The king might also be called in if people stole from temples. Since the gods were responsible for protecting the king and the state, theft from temples jeopardized the empire and was taken extremely seriously.

Messenger services were being developed, along with royal roads. This helped the empire to improve, as it increased the distance over which direct government was effective.

Though beer remained the staple drink in Mesopotamia, as more wine-producing territories entered the empire, drinking imported wine became an affordable luxury for the wealthier Assyrians. Some of those Assyrians probably became even wealthier by importing it!

Although it was Ashurnasirpal II who moved the court to Kalhu, it was his son, Shalmaneser III, who built it into a major imperial center. By this point, Assyria was the major power in the region. It was much larger than any of the states around it. The old settlement mound at Kalhu became the citadel, and the rest of the city was surrounded by a four-mile-long wall, with a second citadel in a corner to provide further protection. This became the pattern for later capitals, including Nineveh and Dur-Sharrukin (present-day Khorsabad). There was no temple for Ashur, who remained only the god of his own city. Ishtar and other deities had temples at Kalhu, though.

Kalhu was excavated by Max Mallowan from 1949 to 1957. He found a huge number of documents in the palace, including letters that throw light on Assyrian campaigns against Babylon, as well as royal building projects. (Mallowan is an archaeologist who is not quite as well known as his wife, who also came on the dig at Nimrud. Who was she? Well, she was the famous murder mystery writer Agatha Christie.)

Ashurnasirpal had fully restored the borders of the empire; Shalmaneser wanted to go further. He led more than thirty military campaigns during his thirty-five-year reign. Heading west, he took Bit-Adini and renamed its capital Kar-Shulmanu-ashared, "Shalmaneser's trading post." He then relocated native Assyrians to Kar- Shulmanu-ashared, probably to transfer Assyrian government and commercial norms, as well as to ensure the city's loyalty.

The borders of Assyria had previously ebbed and flowed with time since the army was based in the capital and could not always arrive in time to resist pressure from enemies or rebellious vassals. The army was also based on temporary levies, which meant raising an army took time.

Shalmaneser took action to make the empire bulletproof. He established a standing army and stationed units in the four border marches. The official in charge of each army was entrusted with great power, which could become a problem should any of them decide to rebel. However, the fact that they could act quickly and on their own initiative enabled Assyria to react rapidly to any outside threats. In many cases, eunuchs were chosen for the border march "field marshal" positions.

Shalmaneser also created a strong cavalry division. Chariots were good vehicles for the steppes and plains, but they were not useful in the mountains. Extending army operations outside Mesopotamia required a more flexible response. (Chariots had to be taken apart, carried through mountain passes, and then put together again before engaging the enemy. So, while they remained high-status vehicles, they were a strategic weakness.)

Shalmaneser raided far outside the borders of the empire. In the Levant, he created a number of client states, including Judah. He eventually occupied most of Syria and Arabia.[i]

However, one thing Shalmaneser did not do was invade Babylon. Instead, he made it a firm ally. When he led a campaign into Babylon, it was to save Marduk-zakir-shumi I, the rightful king, from a rebellion led by his younger brother. After two campaigns, Shalmaneser finally managed to run the rebel to ground and killed him. Shalmaneser's throne dais shows the two kings grasping each other's hands in friendship.

In old age, Shalmaneser had to hand over the leadership of military campaigns to his commander in chief, Dayyan-Assur. This ordinarily would not be worthy of notice, but Shalmaneser's Black Obelisk mentioned Dayyan-Assur. This was the first time a royal inscription had ever ascribed a victory to anyone other than the king.

The end of Shalmaneser's reign saw a threat to the succession. Shalmaneser had made his younger son, Shamshi-Adad, crown prince,

---

[i] Ahab, King of Israel, together with Hadadezer of Damascus, fought against Shalmaneser at the Orontes River. Jehu later brought fought against Shalmaneser tribute.

but his elder son, Ashur-dain-aplu, rebelled. This rebellion was eventually crushed, but in order to do so, Assyria had to rely on Babylonian help. Marduk-zakir-shumi was happy to return the favor Shalmaneser had done him, and Shamshi-Adad V inherited the throne in 824 BCE.

The succession struggle had weakened Assyria, and nobles who had seen Dayyan-Assur's magnificent conquests wanted a piece of the Assyrian pie for themselves. So, Shamshi-Adad started with a disadvantage. Several client kingdoms attempted to withhold tribute, spotting potential weakness. Shamshi-Adad appeared to have struggled for about a decade before finding his feet. He also appeared to have resented the fact that during the earlier part of his reign, Babylon held the upper hand.

So, despite his father's friendship with Marduk-zakir-shumi, Shalmaneser took his troops south and ended up getting a treaty with Marduk-zakir-shumi that was in his favor. Later, he campaigned twice against the succeeding king, Marduk-balassu-iqbi, who might have been his brother-in-law. After making his way to the east of the Tigris, Shalmaneser was able to avoid the Babylonian fort at Zaddi and head for the center of Babylonia. He boasted of taking more than thirty thousand captives during his second campaign. Shamshi-Adad later fought against the next Babylonian king, Baba-aha-iddina, taking him captive too.

Babylonia was in disarray. There is no record of a king in Babylon for at least a decade after Baba-aha-iddina. The empire was ripe for the picking. But when Shamsi-Adad died in 811, his successor, Adad-nirari III, was probably too young to exercise his rule effectively. His mother, Shammuramat, might have acted as regent. She was the only Assyrian queen to have retained her title after her husband's death, making her a rare feminine figure in what is an almost exclusively male narrative. She had a stele erected in her honor in Ashur (another exception to the men's club rules) and even accompanied Adad-nirari on a campaign.

Adad-nirari III was never a strong king. The eunuch Palil-eresh governed the western half of Assyria and appeared to have done so semi-independently. This might have worried Adad-nirari; a few years before his death, he installed a new general, Shamshi-ilu. Shamshi-ilu quickly consolidated his power over the army and over the western half of the empire. On one of his steles, Shamshi-ilu omitted the king's name and took all the credit himself. This was unprecedented.

During these four decades, Assyria was strong economically. It saw the increased production of good and an increase in the population that gave it a sturdy base; the empire simply had an internal focus, not an external one, and no strong leadership. Plagues occurred during this period, and consequent quarantines and lockdowns interfered with trade, but the underlying economy was strong.

Tiglath-Pileser III (r. 745-727) was able to launch a new expansion campaign. The circumstances under which he came to the throne are not clear, nor is his parentage; he might have been a son of his predecessor, Ashur-nirari V, or of Adad-nirari III (in which case he took the throne from his brother). It is possible he came to power as the result of a coup d'etat.

Tiglath-Pileser transformed Assyria into a true empire, doubling its size despite his relatively short reign of eighteen years. He centralized authority, bringing new men into the administration and cutting back the power of the nobles. He ensured that each noble's land holdings were widely dispersed across the empire so that no individual could accumulate a strong position in any single province.

A mural from Tiglath-Pileser III's palace in Til Barsip showing him giving an audience.[127]

Unlike Shamshi-Adad V, Tiglath-Pileser hit the ground running. He had no sooner acceded to the throne than he invaded north and eastern Babylon. In the same year, he took action to suppress restive Aramaean tribes near the Assyrian borders.

In 743, he defeated Urartu. In 740, he conquered Arpad and made northern Syria into a new province. Later, he consolidated his dominion over modern Lebanon and made Judah, Moab, and Edom into tributary states. He even reached the Egyptian border. By 734, he had annexed Damascus and had made Hoshea his puppet king in Israel.

By Tiglath-Pileser's time, chariots had become larger. Three men drove them rather than only two. The driver and the archer had a third man tasked with protecting them. The chariots were also heavier due to having more armor.

Tiglath-Pileser III in his chariot with the royal parasol held over him.[128]

Babylon was a prize that two Assyrian kings had left untouched. Tiglath-Pileser bided his time for more than a decade. But finally, he found conditions had moved in his favor. In 734, Babylonian King Nabonassar died. His son, Nabu-nadin-zeri, succeeded him, but he only lasted a little more than a year before he was killed by one of his provincial governors, Nabu-shuma-ukin. This usurper lasted just a month before a Chaldean (southern Babylonian), Nabu-mukin-zeri, put down the rebellion and took the throne himself. This left Babylon looking ripe for the picking, and Tiglath-Pileser took full advantage. In 729, he invaded Babylon and proclaimed himself king of Babylon.

Tiglath-Pileser united the two kingdoms under his personal rule. This was not a political union. Babylon remained a separate kingdom and was not brought into the Assyrian system of government.

Tiglath-Pileser's son, Shalmaneser V, continued the expansion and brought Israel's independence to an end by annexing Samaria. However, his reign was brief, lasting just five years, from 727 to 722 BCE.

He was succeeded by Sargon II (r. 722–705 BCE). Evidence is hard to find, but Sargon might have led a palace coup in 722 that put Shalmaneser out of power after just five years of rule. On the other hand, the Babylonian Chronicles simply say, "Shalmaneser died." Sargon's name was a reference to the Akkadian Empire and its greatest king; perhaps, ironically, the name Sargon, or Sharrukin in Assyrian, means "the legitimate king."

Sargon II was probably a younger son of Tiglath-Pileser, but he is generally regarded as the founder of a new dynasty. Babylonian inscriptions assign him to the dynasty of Hanigalbat rather than that of Baltil, the Assyrian main line. This suggests he might have been from a lateral branch of the family or perhaps was a son of the monarch's younger brother.

Sargon was a decisive leader, using both military action and spectacle to achieve his aims. He had a highly developed sense of *realpolitik* and how to get his way with both allies and enemies. Sargon had to put down a rebellion in Palestine almost immediately, but he also needed a strategy to hold back a resurgent Elamite kingdom. His solution was neatly calculated; he made peace with Elam and put down the rebellions by Ilu-bi'di and Hanunu, flaying one and blinding the other. Harsh punishment and clemency were weapons; he could play "good cop" or "bad cop" and often aimed to achieve a balance of the two to encourage others to do what he wanted.

His earlier conquests included Carchemish, which he conquered in 717. He looted the treasury, taking an immense amount of silver. In 714, he conquered Urartu and made a surprise attack on Musashir with a small raiding party after having made his way through very difficult mountain territory. Musashir was a rich city, and its contents were accounted for by Sargon II's scribes. The Assyrians took silver and gold from the temple, over twenty-five thousand bronze shields, and hundreds of thousands of bronze daggers.

Sargon increased the size of his army by taking charioteers (and presumably other forces) from conquered peoples. For instance, he acquired fifty chariot teams from Samaria, two hundred from Hamath, and fifty from Carchemish. A chariot was an expensive asset, so the owners of these teams were probably rich men or nobility. By taking them into his army, he killed two birds with one stone, turning these opinion-makers into loyal subjects and increasing his military resources.

The result of this recruitment can clearly be seen from the fact that a fifth of his army had non-Assyrian names. The army, as well as the empire, was becoming increasingly ethnically diverse.

In 710 BCE, he turned his attention to the reconquest of Babylonia. By now, Sargon had a seasoned army full of campaign veterans. Babylon, on the other hand, was divided between the urban population and semi-independent tribes in the marshes. The succession of a new king in Elam had put Babylon's ability to access help from the Elamites in question. Marduk-apla-Iddina II was tactically clever and avoided battles where he could, but Assyria was winning supporters among the governors and the tribes. Several cities defected to Sargon's side.

The Assyrian forces were getting ever closer to the capital, and when Elam explicitly stated that it would not help Babylon, Marduk-apla-iddina fled to the marshes in the south. Cleverly, Sargon consolidated his control of the north of Babylon before heading south for a final confrontation with Marduk-apla-Iddina, who was hiding out in his home city, Dur-Yakin. Marduk-apla-iddina flooded the fields around Dur-Yakin, breaking down all the bridges and causeways to impede Sargon's approach. Marduk-apla-iddina was partly successful, as the city managed to withstand Sargon's blockade for a year before finally negotiating a treaty. Marduk-apla-Iddina was exiled to Elam—an example of Sargon's occasional and usually well-judged clemency.

The priests of Babylon, who appeared to have been more powerful than the priests of Ashur, took matters into their own hands and invited Sargon into the city and then into the temple to grasp Marduk's hand at the New Year festival, making him king. He stayed in Babylon until 707.

When Sargon II returned to Assyria, he moved the capital to Dur-Sharrukin, "Sargon's Fort" (modern-day Khorsabad). It took him ten years to build. Moving the capital might not have been a simple whim; by creating a new capital, Sargon was expanding the economy, opening new land to cultivation, and improving living standards. The new capital fulfilled the same objectives as a modern urban gentrification project. It was a massive construction program. Craftsmen and laborers who came to work on it had their debts forgiven. (It is worth noting that those whose land was acquired for the project were given monetary compensation. The king was not above the law. Some were offered land in other parts of Assyria.)

Around Dur-Sharrukin, olive groves were planted. Olive oil was a scarce resource in Assyria, so this was a practical and potentially profitable move.

Dur-Sharrukin was splendid. It had a citadel with a 165-foot-high ziggurat, a royal palace, and numerous temples. The palace covered twenty-five acres, and its gates were guarded by colossal winged bulls. Its walls were 16,280 Assyrian units in length. That number was important; the Assyrians were great believers in numerology, and 16,280, translated into letters, added up to the name "Sargon." These walls had 157 towers. Temples to Adad, Ningal, Ninurta, Nabu, Shamash, and Sin were erected, and a secondary citadel was built in the southwest corner.

There were also gardens, a central canal, and a huge mound, which was planted with trees and meant to imitate a mountain landscape. However, the city was not completed when Sargon died, and it soon became obsolete.

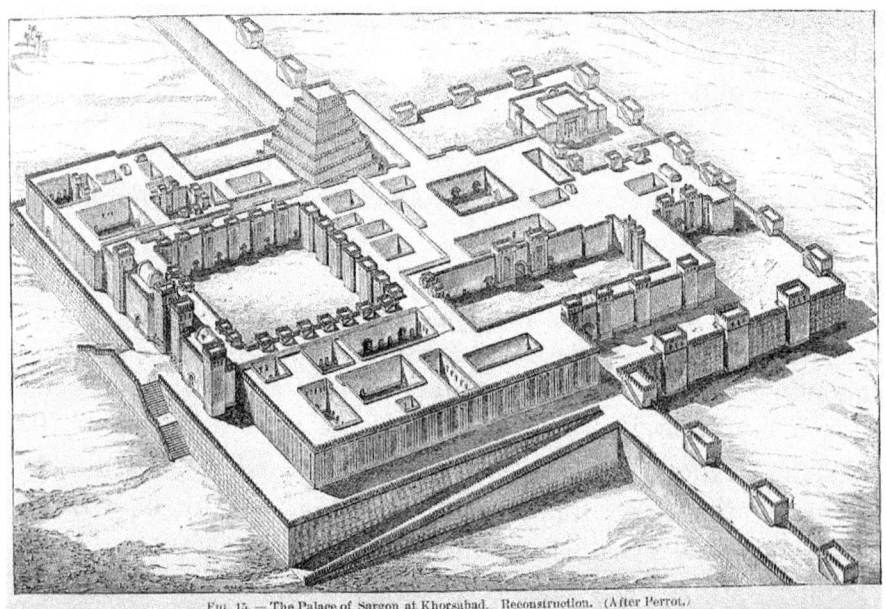

A 1905 artist's impression of the palace at Dur-Sharrukin.[129]

Sargon appeared to have relied a great deal on his close family, such as Crown Prince Sennacherib and his brother and grand vizier, Sin-ahu-usur. Perhaps this, together with the move to Dur-Sharrukin, reflects a feeling of insecurity on Sargon's part. He clearly did not relish the prospect of opposition to his plans in Ashur or Kalhu.

Under Sargon, deportations or resettlements became an even larger feature of Assyrian policy. He deported as many as 600,000 people, seeding new provinces with Assyrians while resettling many of the population of Samaria (conquered in 722) to Assyria. Many of the deportees probably ended up in the region where Dur-Sharrukin was located, working on construction projects or working on new farms. One rebellion in a border area saw five thousand people relocated into the Assyrian heartlands after the insurgency had been put down.

There were three different kinds of provinces in the Assyrian Empire:

- The heartland, where city governors ruled on the king's behalf;
- The border marches to the north and northwest, which were governed by the king's closest officials;
- Annexed foreign lands, which were governed by Assyrian-appointed local rulers.

Assyria had reached the limits of its power. To the west was the Mediterranean, and to the south was the Arabian Desert, both of which presented barriers. The Zagros Mountains blocked the way to Iran. Assyria had become a massive empire, but it faced geographical limits that it was powerless to overcome.

A year after moving to Dur-Sharrukin, Sargon set out on a campaign to Anatolia. He must have been sixty by that point, and he was accustomed to military success. He could have let a general take control of the campaign, but perhaps he had no one he could trust, or perhaps he felt he was invincible. This time, however, he had miscalculated. The enemy broke into his camp, found him, and killed him. Worse, from the Assyrian point of view, his body could not be recovered. He would never join the other kings in the royal tombs of Ashur, and his ghost would wander the world without peace.

Sennacherib succeeded his father, Sargon, in 705. He never moved to Dur-Sharrukin. Maybe he saw it as unlucky, or maybe he thought it was haunted by Sargon's uneasy spirit. He did everything he could to distance himself from his father, whom he must have felt had been cursed. Unlike almost every other legitimate king of Assyria, he never mentioned his father's name in any of his inscriptions. He soon relocated the capital to Nineveh, which he rebuilt extensively.

Sennacherib spent immense amounts on the construction of his new capital, which covered nearly two thousand acres. Nineveh became more than twice the size of both the preceding capitals, Kalhu and Dur-Sharrukin, and was surrounded by a seven-and-a-half-mile-long wall.

Sennacherib's name means "the god Sin has replaced the brothers." This may indicate that he was a long-awaited son since Sargon's other children died in infancy. Later sources state that Sennacherib was afflicted by a demon. The loss of his father might have led to depression. This would make sense; if Sennacherib was a much-longed-for replacement, his father must have been very close to him.

A relief of Sennacherib.[130]

In many ways, Sennacherib can be regarded as the great consolidator who followed Sargon's expansion. He presented himself as a great innovator, an architectural and agricultural inventor, and a metallurgist, who increased the amount of tin used to create bronze. In his palace, he had the sculptors suppress the "extra leg" of the *lamassu*; before this point, they had been shown with four legs on each side, as if they were two reliefs folded together so that when seen at an angle, they appear to have five legs. The new treatment was perhaps less impressive, but it was more naturalistic.

Sennacherib not only rebuilt Nineveh; he also created a huge network of canals around the city. This appears to have developed in four phases, starting relatively small but becoming increasingly ambitious. This construction project included aqueducts, canals, and sluices. Many of the watercourses were subterranean. They were dug into the bedrock and accessed through vertical shafts every forty yards or so. (This kind of channel is still used in parts of the Arabian Peninsula, known as the *qanat* or *falaj*.)

A type of Archimedes screw was used instead of the primitive shaduf (a pivoting pole raising a bucket) to bring water up from one level to another. This was a massive innovation. To make the point about the king's control of the water, relief carvings were often made in the rock next to sluices or wells, showing the king as a patron.

Sennacherib also expressed royal ideology by bringing trees from other parts of the empire to the palace and creating a marsh to imitate the Babylonian marshland. He had brought the extreme ends of the empire to Nineveh. He also planted fruit trees of all kinds, an assertion of fertility that might have referred to the sacred tree shown in Ashurnasirpal's reliefs.

Sennacherib took the title of king of Babylon, going one step further than his father, who only took the title of viceroy; the god Marduk had been recognized as the real king of the city. This could not have gone down well with the Babylonians. Furthermore, Sennacherib didn't turn up for the rite of taking Marduk's hand as his father had done. This was one of Sargon's mistakes that came back to haunt the Assyrian Empire.

A rebellion broke out in Babylon. It probably could have been suppressed quite easily, but Marduk-apla-iddina, sitting comfortably in exile in Elam, saw his chance. He headed straight for Babylon, got rid of the leader of the rebellion, and took control. And this time, thanks to making himself agreeable while in exile, he had backing from Elam.

Sennacherib was forced to invade. The very sensible Marduk-apla-iddina ran to the marshes again. Sennacherib appointed Bel-ibni, a young Babylonian and a hostage who "had grown up like a puppy in my palace" as the new king.[i] Sennacherib plundered Babylon. Perhaps he was determined to do exactly what his father would not have done.

After Bel-ibni proved incapable of suppressing rebellions in the south of his domains (according to some accounts, he actually joined them), Sennacherib replaced him. This time, he kept things in the family, giving his eldest son, Ashur-nadin-shumi, the throne of Babylon.

Then, Sennacherib turned to the Levant. Several Philistine rulers had stopped paying tribute, so a punitive expedition was needed. Sennacherib took Sidon, whose king had fled without defending his city; Ashkelon, where the king was taken captive and sent to Assyria; Ekron; and Lachish, where the siege lasted so long that the archers ran out of metal arrowheads.

Finally, in 701, he blockaded Jerusalem. As usual, diplomacy was tried first. 2 Kings 18 NKJV tells how Sennacherib's *rabshakeh* (chief cup-bearer or vizier) promises the Hebrews that if they join Assyria and leave King Hezekiah, they will receive special treatment. "Make peace with me by a present and come out to me," he says, "and every one of you eat from his own vine and every one from his own fig tree, and every one of you drink the waters of his own cistern; until I come and take you away to a land like your own land, a land of grain and new wine, a land of bread and vineyards, a land of olive groves and honey, that you may live and not die."

This was the way Assyria saw deportation; it was not a punishment but an organized and useful way of settling people on land that could sustain them and support the Assyrian Empire. The ultimate goal was to create a homogeneous "Assyrian" population. Intermarriage was encouraged.

In any case, this promise was not acceptable to the people of Israel, and Sennacherib could not take Jerusalem. However, the blockade worked. Hezekiah eventually decided to pay tribute, and Sennacherib walked away. Or, at least, that's the Assyrian version. There is a rather different ending in the Bible. Instead of Sennacherib making a diplomatic

---

[i] Radner, Karen. *Ancient Assyria: A Very Short Introduction.* Oxford University Press, Oxford, 2015.

decision, God intervened, striking 185,000 Assyrian soldiers dead in the night.

There is something of a puzzle one has to work out when reconciling the two accounts. Perhaps the Hebrews simply didn't believe Sennacherib would give up unless he had to. Sennacherib had probably weighed up the cost of a protracted siege at a time when food resources were becoming stretched, and this enabled a negotiated settlement that both sides could claim as a victory.

In 694, Sennacherib decided to tackle an old enemy, taking a military force to Elam. This would allow him to root out those Babylonian rebels who had escaped to Elam. The Assyrian forces crossed the Persian Gulf on boats crewed by Phoenicians and Greeks. The Assyrians were not a maritime people, but the empire's expansion had brought new skilled workers, and Sennacherib decided to apply them for the first time in warfare. This was a great success, as he conquered a number of Elamite cities.

However, this had unexpected results. The king of Elam, seeing how far Sennacherib was from his capital, decided to go on the offensive and invaded Babylon. The anti-Assyrian faction in Babylon decided to play one enemy off against the other. They handed Ashur-nadin-shumi, their Assyrian-imposed king and the Assyrian crown prince, to the Elamites. He was taken to Elam, and he disappeared from history.

Sennacherib set out for vengeance. He took the new Babylonian king, Nergal-ushezib, captive and brought him to Nineveh. Nergal-ushezib was chained to a wild bear at the gate of the citadel. (This might have been the Assyrians' idea of entertainment.) Sennacherib then invaded Elam for a second time. Though he had success early on, he wasn't prepared for the Persian mountain winter and turned back before being able to end the campaign. The inscriptions in which Sennacherib talks about this journey show very clearly how terrifying the rugged, snowy mountains and passes were for men used to the flat, open steppes of Assyria.

Sennacherib realized he would have to defeat both Elam and Babylon to be secure since the two states would always support each other against him. In 691, an anti-Assyrian coalition of Elamites and Babylonians was put together, and they moved north along the Tigris to threaten Ashur. But Sennacherib was ready for them. At Halule (modern Samarra), he managed to block their advance, and by the following year, he had moved his army south to besiege Babylon. It took fifteen months before the city fell. Sennacherib's troops plundered Babylon, massacred the population, and destroyed the city and its irrigation system. Babylon was no more. This was Sennacherib's fourth campaign against Babylon, and he had finally succeeded in destroying the threat to Assyria.

However, to secure the political achievement, the gods had to be brought into play to affirm the conquest in the divine sphere as well as the earthly sphere. That meant that Babylon's gods had to be absorbed into the Assyrian religion. Sennacherib had Marduk's throne and bed brought to Ashur, and he erected an "Akitu house" modeled on the Babylonian one in Ashur. (The Akitu house is a temple visited by the god Marduk at the New Year festival.) It even included earth taken from the ruins of Babylon in its foundations. Ashur had eaten up Marduk, and Assyria had swallowed Babylon.

Sennacherib never took the title of king of Babylon (again doing the opposite of what his father had done), so the city was left without a ruler.

Sennacherib had probably spent more time out of Assyria than in it by this point, and he might have lost his grasp of domestic politics. Since the crown prince, Ashur-nadin-shumi, had likely been executed in Elam, Sennacherib made Urdu-Mullissi (also written as Arda-Mulissu) crown prince. However, in 684 BCE, he suddenly changed his mind. Sennacherib instead promoted a younger son, Esarhaddon, to the post. Why Esarhaddon? Some historians blame Naqia, his mother, for influencing Sennacherib. Esarhaddon was a mature man when he was chosen, so perhaps he had managed to prove himself to his father.

For a couple of years, things seemed to settle down. Then, for whatever reason, Esarhaddon was sent away from Nineveh to a "secret place." This was most likely intended to ensure his safety. It did not, however, ensure Sennacherib's safety. In October 681 BCE, Urdu-Mullissi and his brother Nabu-shar-usur decided to act. 2 Kings 19 NIV tells the story:

"So Sennacherib king of Assyria broke camp and withdrew. He returned to Nineveh and stayed there. One day, while he was worshiping in the temple of his god Nisrok, his sons Adrammelek and Sharezer killed him with the sword, and they escaped to the land of Ararat. And Esarhaddon his son succeeded him as king."

Esarhaddon, though exiled, was able to march on Nineveh and take the throne. He made sure that everything was done correctly. He was invested as king in Ashur, which remained the religious capital and the home of the god from whom the king of Assyria held his authority. If Sennacherib had been punished for his blasphemy against Marduk and his destruction of the temples in Babylon, Esarhaddon was going to ensure that at least the god Ashur was on his side.

He then got rid of the entire palace security detail. State officials who might have supported his brother were sacked or executed. For the rest of his reign, Esarhaddon was an uneasy man. He regularly asked the oracle of Shamash whether anyone was planning to rebel against him. (His successor, Ashurbanipal, asked the oracle about a number of military operations and political decisions, but Ashurbanipal never seemed to have asked about rebellions. Perhaps he didn't feel he needed to.) Esarhaddon created a state of high vigilance, used agents provocateurs, and encouraged denunciations. His Assyria was, in many ways, a surveillance state.

There were, indeed, rebellions in a number of Assyrian towns, just as Esarhaddon had suspected. His foreign military success contrasted with the unease and plotting at home. Yet, Esarhaddon survived all the plots.

In 677, he seized Sidon and executed its king. He then made a treaty with Tyre. In 674, he made a treaty with Elam, ending the rivalry between the two states and thus securing the eastern border. This allowed him to set his sights on the west and Egypt, which was then ruled by the Nubian (Kushite) dynasty.

Esarhaddon's first attempt on Egypt, in 673 BCE, was a failure, which made him unpopular at home. However, he gathered new allies and attacked Egypt again two years later from Sinai. This time, he was more successful and managed to conquer Egypt as far south as Thebes (about halfway to Egypt's southern border). Egypt became, effectively, a vassal of Assyria since the Kushite King Taharqa fled the field. Esarhaddon installed vassal rulers in Memphis (modern-day Cairo) and Sais (located in the Nile Delta) and took his booty back to Ashur.

Esarhaddon was very unusual to the Egyptians. Every previous foreign ruler of Egypt had adopted the pharaonic titles and dress. The Macedonian Ptolemaic dynasty did so too. But Esarhaddon made no attempt at all to be a pharaoh. Maybe the culture was just too alien to him, or maybe the way Assyria managed vassal states made it unnecessary. Or maybe, having been given his crown by the god Ashur himself, Esarhaddon just didn't see the point of pretending to *be* a god.

Growing increasingly unpopular at home probably did nothing for Esarhaddon's paranoia. The cities of Nineveh and Kalhu became impregnable fortresses, and his obsession with state security continued. Then, in 670, Esarhaddon carried out another purge of his courtiers and officials after an episode of opposition to his rule in northern Syria. The Babylonian Chronicles say, "The king put his officers to the sword in Assyria." It gives no further detail. However, the purge must have been savage. For the first time, there was no high official in place whose name could be used as the eponym for the year's name. It is likely that Ashur-nasir, the chief eunuch who had led the Egyptian campaign, was one of those killed. He was killed just a year after his triumph.

Letters from Esarhaddon's exorcist (who filled roughly the same role as a doctor or psychiatrist would today) suggest that the king was clinically depressed following the death of his wife Esharra-hammat and their baby child. He might have had a form of post-traumatic stress disorder stemming from the assassination of his father.

One sign of Esarhaddon's increasing disturbance was his use of an ancient rite to escape his duties. A substitute king could be used to protect the king from the dangers that came about during a solar eclipse; for a hundred days, a substitute took the king's place. This was intended to blindside the forces of chaos and ensure that, following the eclipse, the king could regain his throne unharmed with no danger to the governance of the Assyrian state.

But Esarhaddon used the rite at least four times, including just a few days after his first victory in Egypt. He didn't use the rite to avoid eclipses; rather, he wanted to be able to hide away from his position as king and retreat into private life. Because he used this ritual, everyone was happy except for the substitute king, who was always killed at the end of the hundred days. Esarhaddon, who was clearly a smart guy, managed to choose political rivals for the position of substitute king.

Under Esarhaddon, Assyria became even more multiethnic and multicultural. Assyrian priests and scholars were joined by Babylonians, and his new conquests saw an Egyptian doctor and Egyptian astronomers and priests join his court.

Sennacherib had a tense relationship with his dead father, and Esarhaddon had a strange relationship with his father. Convinced that Sennacherib had been targeted by the gods for his plunder of Babylon, Esarhaddon set about rebuilding the capital his father had destroyed. The rebuilding of Babylon was Esarhaddon's big building program, rivaling Dur-Sharrukin and Nineveh. For the first time, an Assyrian king funded a huge construction project outside of Assyria, and for the first time, it was funded from outside Assyria too, at least partly. The tribute from Egypt helped pay for the work.

The first stage of construction was clearance. The city had to be cleared of the vegetation that had invaded it, and the river had to be re-channeled into its original course before the area around the city had been flooded.

Assyria was a massive empire with seventy-five provinces. It was perhaps too big for one man to manage, so Esarhaddon decided to separate the two halves of his empire again. In 672, he made his younger son, Ashurbanipal, the crown prince of Ashur, and his older son, Shamash-shumu-ukin, became the crown prince of Babylon. This may seem unusual; surely, the younger son should have been sent to Babylon. An inscription shows why this was the case. Shamash-shumu-ukin was a kind of living sacrifice, a gift to Marduk and the goddess Zarpanitu, the gods of Babylon.

The succession agreement was widely disseminated on steles, in inscriptions, and even in the royal seal, which showed the scene of the king killing a lion in triplicate, representing the triple rule of Esarhaddon and the two princes. However, the demand that officials had to swear in a succession oath was purely to Ashurbanipal, whose mother was Assyrian. Shamash-shumu-ukin's mother was Babylonian.

Esarhaddon died in 669. He was on his way to Egypt again to put down a rebellion under Taharqa. He left an unfinished palace in Kalhu that was built in the Egyptian style. Ashurbanipal inherited a wealthy, successful empire, but there was a hidden death wound. Because of Esarhaddon's two great purges of the civil service, he had destroyed the administration's power to function.

Ashurbanipal (r. 669–631) continued the Assyrian expedition in Egypt. In 667, he invaded, reconquered the country, and installed Necho of Sais as a vassal ruler despite the fact that he had been involved in Taharqa's rebellion. Necho's son Psamtik was also given a high office.

The Kushite dynasty fought back a few years later. Taharqa's successor, Tantamani, surged up the Nile in a fresh offensive, and Necho was killed while defending Memphis. Psamtik fled, but he came back the next year, supported by Ashurbanipal and the Assyrian army.

Ashurbanipal swept through Egypt as far south as Thebes, which he sacked in 663, taking two obelisks back to Assyria, as well as many of the city's inhabitants and a vast amount of gold and silver. Although the archaeological evidence shows that the Assyrians took a good deal of loot, they did not burn the city or destroy buildings. Psamtik was then installed as pharaoh, although he only ruled the top half of Egypt. Ashurbanipal returned to Assyria.

Ashurbanipal probably saw Psamtik as a tame provincial ruler. However, Psamtik reunited Egypt. He founded the Twenty-sixth Dynasty and nearly outlived the Assyrian Empire.

Esarhaddon's succession agreement gave Ashurbanipal the senior role; though his brother was installed as king of Babylon, it was understood that Assyria was the senior kingship. This must have upset his brother, particularly since several major cities in Babylonia (Nippur, Uruk, and Ur) ignored him and dealt directly with Nineveh. After a decade and a half of dutiful administration of what Ashurbanipal saw as simply another Assyrian province, Shamash-shumu-ukin rebelled in 652. He was supported by Elam, though not by all his own subjects.

By 650, things were going wrong for Shamash-shumu-ukin. Ashurbanipal had driven him back, taking Sippar and Borsippa on the way, and was now able to lay siege to Babylon. According to Ashurbanipal's account, Babylon was so sore-pressed that the citizens had resorted to cannibalism, but exaggeration was a regular feature of Assyrian kings' inscriptions. Still, a two-year siege must have reduced living standards in Babylon significantly.

Eventually, the city fell. Ashurbanipal went on a rampage. His inscriptions are full of atrocities, such as carving up bodies to feed them to pigs and dogs. However, they don't say what happened to Shamash-shumu-ukin.

Perhaps the "Tale of the Two Brothers" has the answer. This story is known from a 4th-century Egyptian papyrus (written in both Aramaic and Demotic Egyptian) and tells how Ashurbanipal's and Shamash-shumu-ukin's sister, Sherua-etirat, pleads with her rebellious brother to submit to the king or to burn himself and his family on a pyre together with the Babylonian scholars who tempted him to rebel. He refuses, and when the temple of Marduk is set on fire, he dies in the flames.

Whatever happened to Shamash-shumu-ukin, Ashurbanipal had won. But four years of civil war had left Babylon destabilized and in famine, which destroyed the prestige of Assyria. Babylon, having been destroyed twice in living memory by Assyrian kings, simmered with hatred for its northern rivals.

Elam continued to be a thorn in Assyria's side despite a very successful earlier campaign against Teumman, who had been killed in the Battle of the Ulai River, giving Ashurbanipal a chance to install his own choice of rulers. (Teumman was decapitated; the scene is shown in nauseating detail in the reliefs in Ashurbanipal's palace, and the inscriptions boast of making the rivers run red with blood.) But revolt after revolt occurred in Elam. By 646, Ashurbanipal had decided it was time to put an end to the Elamite problem.

Ashurbanipal probably went further on this campaign than any previous Assyrian king. He might have even taken tribute from some of the Iranian kingdoms. On his way back, he decided to destroy the Elamite capital, Susa. He demolished the temples and the ziggurat, sacked the palace, and "god-napped" no fewer than nineteen Elamite gods. The royal tombs of Elam were destroyed, and the king of Elam was taken to Nineveh, where he had to pull Ashurbanipal's chariot.

The events recounted in these inscriptions appear to justify Frahm's assessment of Ashurbanipal as a "scholar, sadist, hunter, king."[i] Ashurbanipal was proud of his image as a hunter. Reliefs in Ashurbanipal's palace show him killing eighteen lions, which perhaps was a "magic number" since Nineveh has eighteen gates (a lion could protect each of the gates of the city). Ashurbanipal apparently had an arena built specially for lion hunting. The lions might have been sedated.

Ashurbanipal also presented himself as a scholar. This was not unusual in Assyria, as kings were well educated and frequently looked to the past as a precedent for their exploits. The Library of Ashurbanipal at Nineveh was impressive. There were clay tablets and numerous wax tablets. The latter was lost in a fire, but the heat baked and preserved the clay tablets.

Although the library included the only complete text of the *Epic of Gilgamesh*, its key documents concerned rituals, oracles, omens, astrology, and divination. These texts provided materials that could support the king's decision-making. Ashurbanipal not only had scholarly

---

[i] Frahm, Eckart. *Assyria: The Rise and Fall of the World's First Empire*. Basic Books, New York, 2023.

astrological texts, but he also sponsored astrologers to study and record celestial phenomena in what one might call a more scientific way.

The library was also multilingual. It contained Assyrian texts, the Babylonian epic of creation, and texts in Babylonian, Assyrian, and the ancient Sumerian language.

Ashurbanipal was the most erudite of royal collectors, but he inherited much of his library from earlier rulers, maybe as early as Ashur-uballit I. Tukulti-Ninurta I added Babylonian texts to the library, one of the results of his conquest of Babylon.

Still, life was good for the Assyrians during Ashurbanipal's reign. Excavations of the western capital of Dur-Katlimmu show how Shulmusharri, a wealthy man, enjoyed his life in the Red House, with its four courtyards, two floors, two wells, and an effective sewage and drainage system. He had many slaves and three adult sons. In his fifties, he became a "companion" of Ashurbanipal, which was an accredited representative of the king. His house gives a good idea of the luxury in which the truly wealthy of the Neo-Assyrian Empire were able to live.

Ashur's traders voyaged along the Tigris to buy wine in Syria. They brought it back on rafts made of Syrian wood and sold it for timber when they arrived in Assyria. By this time, Assyria held territory all the way from the Mediterranean to the Persian Gulf; it was the unrivaled superpower of its time.

But this was not to last. Perhaps climate change was partly responsible; agricultural yields headed downward again, and elephants became extinct in the region. Perhaps Esarhaddon's purges had led to poor governance and a decline in public infrastructure. The eponym year list ends in 639, and there is a surprising lack of documentation for the last years of Ashurbanipal's reign, suggesting that communications were breaking down.

Perhaps delusions of grandeur were the worst problems that Assyria had to deal with. The economy was starting to teeter, but Ashurbanipal was not paying attention. The market price for grain (calculated from comparing a number of transfer documents) appeared to have been over a thousand times more than the official price. Grain shortages and high inflation forced poor people to sell their children or give them as pledges for loans. However, for the wealthy and for the government, the golden age was still alive and well.

So, when things went wrong, they went wrong very quickly.

In 631 or 630 BCE, Ashurbanipal died or was deposed. Again, there is very limited information; the records were not being kept up to date at this point. He was succeeded by his son, Ashur-etil-ilani, who reigned for three years. Sinsharishkun, another son of Ashurbanipal, then claimed the throne, but this was disputed for some time by the chief eunuch despite the fact that, according to Assyrian tradition, a eunuch was ineligible to rule.

This leadership crisis gave the anti-Assyrian faction in Babylon the opportunity it needed. Nabopolassar, whose origins are unknown, took the throne of Babylon and went on the offensive. There was a battle to the death between Assyria and Babylon.

These battles might have continued indefinitely, but the arrival of a new power, the Medes, to the east changed things. The Iranian tribes had spent 150 years living as fragmented tribes, but they eventually created a confederacy that was able to work together on campaigns. In 614, they captured Ashur, burning the city (this is confirmed by the archaeological record). Ashur's temple, which gave the kings of Assyria their legitimacy, was destroyed, as were the tombs of the kings.

Nabopolassar quickly allied himself with the Medes. Their goal was obvious: to capture the capital of the Assyrian Empire, Nineveh.

In 612, Nineveh fell. King Sinsharishkun disappeared without a trace (it is assumed that he was killed in the battle), and Nineveh appeared to have been abandoned. The soldiers who died defending the Shamash Gate of the city were never buried. Images of the Assyrian kings were disfigured. Their eyes were scratched out, and their noses were broken off. The city was looted and then destroyed. Babylonian engineers redirected Sennacherib's canals to destroy the mudbrick walls of the citadel. Kalhu, too, was completely wrecked and then abandoned. Bodies were thrown into the wells to poison the water and make the city uninhabitable. Irrigation works were destroyed, making it impossible to farm the land. Assyria was in ruins.

With Ashur destroyed, no new king could be rightfully invested. Ashur-uballit II performed his ceremony of investiture at Harran in 612, but it seemed that many considered him only the crown prince. With Egyptian support, he continued an Assyrian state in exile in Harran (far to the north on the modern border between Syria and Turkey). In 610,

Babylon managed to take Harran, and the last inscription to mention Ashur-uballit II dates to 609. He simply disappeared from history after that date, and with him, the Assyrian Empire came to an end. It only took twenty-one years after Ashurbanipal's death for the empire to end.

Nabopolassar and his son Nebuchadnezzar II deported many Assyrians to Babylonia, adopting the Assyrian custom of resettlement. The Neo-Babylonian Empire was on the rise. It even managed to defeat the Egyptians.

Strangely enough, the god Ashur was still worshiped in his temple on the crag overlooking the Tigris under the Persian Achaemenid Empire, which saw an economic, though not political, resurgence in Assyria and later under the Parthians. It was only around 240 CE that the Sasanians captured and sacked Ashur, finally destroying the temple.

Chapter 8: Language Diversity

Ashurbanipal claimed that "Ashur has placed at my disposal all the languages that are spoken from sunrise to sunset."[i] For once, he was not exaggerating, or at least not much. Assyria was a multilinguistic kingdom right from the start.

Assyria inherited a classical language. Sumerian was a language isolate, meaning it was not related to any other languages. It was also the first written language. However, it is important to realize that our knowledge of Sumerian is refracted through Akkadian. Even the name "Sumerian" is Akkadian; the language was *emegir* or "native tongue" to its speakers.

The cuneiform characters in which the language was written started as rough pictographs. Then, the marks became abstract and wedge-shaped, made with a reed stylus pressed into clay. It must have been quite fast to write, particularly compared with Egyptian hieroglyphics. Originally a logographic system, where each sign was a word, it became a mixed system in which the signs could be used for individual syllables. This is similar to modern Japanese, which uses a syllabary together with kanji, Chinese characters that represent a word.

The process of cuneiform development occurred slowly over time, taking at least from 2800 (when the first syllabic signs are dated to but are rare) to 2600 BCE (when they became relatively common). Some signs were also used as unspoken determinatives, that is, signs that denoted

---

[i] Frahm, Eckart. *Assyria: The Rise and Fall of the World's First Empire.* Basic Books, New York, 2023.

what kind of thing the word described. For instance, gods' names were given a star.

The Rassam cylinder, a cuneiform historical document.[181]

List making was an obsession of Sumerian scribal culture, and it remained an important facet of post-Sumerian Mesopotamian culture too. There were lists of trees, lists of animals, lists of professions, and so on. Many of these lists were still being copied hundreds of years after Sumerian had died out as a spoken language.

Hymns often remained in Sumerian even at a late date, though they would have become obscure by then. This is similar to the way Latin was used until the 1950s in Catholic Mass. To help priests who might not have been fluent in Sumerian, some texts had a translation in Assyrian inserted between the lines.

Fluency in written Sumerian was essential for scholars, though. "What kind of scribe is a scribe who does not know Sumerian?" asks a text written four thousand years ago.[i]

The next language to arrive was Akkadian. This was a Semitic language, like Hebrew, Arabic, Aramaic, and some of the Ethiopian languages (Tigrinya and Amharic). It was completely unrelated to Sumerian. Old Assyrian documents are often written in Akkadian.

Both Assyrian and Babylonian developed out of Akkadian, and both languages are sometimes described as Akkadian dialects. They are similar but distinct. Both languages used cuneiform script, though the scripts are not exactly the same. An expert can easily distinguish the two languages just from the writing without reading the words. The Babylonian script was less legible than the more regular Assyrian script. Ashurbanipal had a number of Babylonian texts copied into the Assyrian script.

Reading cuneiform remains a challenge. Different signs can have the same phonetic value, a bit like how "gh," "f," and "ph" can all be read as "f" (such as in the words "enough," "fish," and "phonetic"). However, one sign can have multiple readings. The ability to use signs for concepts, words, and sounds continues. Intriguingly, cuneiform became more complex during the Middle Assyrian period and even more complex during the Neo-Assyrian period, perhaps due to the fact that highly educated scribes felt the need to stress the importance of their profession.

During the Middle Assyrian period, Babylonian—the more prestigious of the languages—was often used for official texts. Under Tukulti-Ninurta II, inscriptions were written in an Assyrian dialect, eschewing Babylonian words and phrases. This constituted a strong assertion of national identity as Assyria fought its way back from chaotic times. Clearly, language was a weapon in the culture wars between Babylonia and Assyria.

During the Old Babylonian period, Sumerian remained the literary and scholarly language. A number of bilingual tablets have been found, such as a list of geographical names in both Sumerian and Akkadian or Assyrian, from which scribes would learn their trade or which they might use for reference.

During the 1ˢᵗ millennium BCE, things changed. Assyrian remained the official language, but Aramaic (another Semitic language) became the language of daily life. Its use began as a commercial language and then

---

[i] Crawford, Harriet. *The Sumerian World*. Routledge, London and New York, 2013. Pg. 95.

spread throughout the empire. However, very few records from Assyrian times survive that are written in Aramaic. There is a reason for this. Assyrian texts were written on clay tablets, but Aramaic was written on leather or papyrus sheets. Most of the Aramaic texts we have come from much later times and were preserved in the Judean Desert, not in Mesopotamia.

It is interesting that several reliefs show pairs of scribes. One of them is shown writing with a pen on a scroll and the other with a stylus on a tablet. The tablet might be made of clay for a permanent record or of wax for temporary notes or calculations that could later be erased. (The wax holders survived in a few cases, with the more luxurious ones being carved out of ivory, but the wax they contained was destroyed by time.)

Aramaic, unlike Assyrian, was written in an alphabetic script that descended from the Phoenician alphabet and was written from right to left (Assyrian went from left to right). Aramaic is still spoken today by Assyrian Christians in the Middle East and in the Assyrian diaspora. Confusingly, it is referred to as "modern Assyrian." It is very distantly related to the Assyrian of Ashurbanipal's day; it would be similar to the relationship between German and modern American English.

One tablet found at Nineveh contains a scribe's speculation on the original forms of later Assyrian cuneiform characters. They are not correct but show that the Assyrians were aware of the long history of their language and were interested in discovering more about it.

Aramaic is not often found on monuments, but Shalmaneser III's palace has Aramaic characters painted on the glazed bricks, probably as a guide to where the bricks needed to go. The bricklayers, or at least the construction manager, might have been able to read or at least identify Aramaic characters but not cuneiform. Aramaic summaries are often appended to the formal Assyrian texts regarding contracts for property sales, and clay tablets in Aramaic were used as IOUs or debt notes.

Literacy appears to have been widespread. Many adult freemen and some women could read. There were more literate people in the Assyrian Empire than in most other societies of the time. Basic literacy could be achieved with the knowledge of just 80 to 120 cuneiform characters in Old Assyrian times; people learning other Middle Eastern scripts had to learn a lot more characters. In Egypt, the use of hieroglyphs limited literacy to a very small percentage of the population. At least 750 hieroglyphs would be needed for even basic communication.

Excavations have found cuneiform tablets in about a third of private houses in Ashur. These are often business documents, but religious and literary texts have been found too. Literacy was widespread in other towns of the empire, both in cuneiform and in the alphabetic Aramaic script.

Kings not only read but also often had editions of scholarly books in their personal libraries. While Ashurbanipal maybe wasn't as great a scholar as he thought, kings were educated well enough to make use of them. Esarhaddon, for instance, often wrote to his scholars for clarification of tricky passages or potential misunderstandings and ambiguities. He obviously paid close attention to the texts he read.

Throughout the Assyrian and Babylonian Empires, there was a great respect for the written word, and it was used to achieve permanence. For instance, the Code of Hammurabi was inscribed on a stele and copied frequently. Copying the code actually became part of the regular curriculum for scribes in training, with the practice still being around a thousand years later. (There was a copy of the Code of Hammurabi in the Library of Ashurbanipal.)

In Ashurnasirpal II's palace, each of the relief panels has the middle portion of the sculpture overwritten with what has become known as the Standard Inscription, which praises the king as the king of the world, priest, and ruler chosen by the gods. The inscription is cut into the relief, so it was clearly done after the relief was carved. The relief would have been considered incomplete without it. (Today, we would be more likely to think that a sculpture has been ruined if something was written over it.)

However, though there was immense respect for the written word in Assyria, there appeared to have been less respect for professional scribes. They never made as much money as traders. One text says, "The house of the chief scribe is miserable, a donkey wouldn't go in there!"[i]

Finally, it is worth stressing that, particularly in the Neo-Assyrian Empire, we often know kings by the Hebrew version of their names, not by their actual kingly names. Tiglath-Pileser, for instance, was named in Assyrian as Tukulti-apil-Esharra, "I trust in the son of Esharra" (the god Ninurta, son of Ashur, whose temple was called Esharra – "world-temple").

Shalmaneser was a name only ever given to kings and might have been taken only after coming to power. Shalmaneser V was referred to as

---

[i] Elayi, Josette. *Esarhaddon, King of Assyria.* Lockwood Press, Columbus, Georgia, 2023.

Ululayu when he was a prince. Again, Shalmaneser is the biblical version; the Assyrian name would have been Shalmanu-ashared, "Shalman is foremost" or "the friendly one is foremost," possibly referring to a manifestation of Ashur. (Intriguingly, the name appears to be related to the Hebrew name Solomon.)

Assyrian is widely considered a dead language. However, Babylonian is not fully dead yet. The first film in Babylonian came out just a few years ago. "The Poor Man of Nippur" was made in 2018 by Cambridge University's Department of Assyriology and tells the comical tale of a poor man getting his revenge on the lazy, sleazy mayor of his city. This story was found on a clay tablet that dates to around 710 BCE. If you would like to see it, it's on YouTube and features a rather lovable (though doomed) goat, as well as some Oscar-level slapstick!

Chapter 9: Religion and Beliefs

The Assyrian religion had much in common with the religions of the rest of Mesopotamia, though some of the details differ. It was a polytheistic religion in which many gods were associated with natural phenomena (sun, moon, storms, etc.) or with particular places.

One of the big themes of religion in Mesopotamia was the conflict between chaos and order. Chaos is what was there before the world. It was often described as a deep abyss or total darkness. The people saw it as a threat that had to be tamed. In the Babylonian creation myth, chaos was represented by Tiamat, goddess of the sea, who gave birth to monsters until she was killed by the god Marduk. After dividing her in two, Marduk separated heaven and earth, creating order out of chaos. He made her ribs into the vault of heaven, and her eyes shed tears that became the Tigris and Euphrates. (In Assyrian versions, it is Ashur who killed Tiamat.)

The figure of the king killing a lion is prevalent in Assyrian art, as it was part of the royal seal. This is a replay of the battle between chaos and order and recreates scenes of the gods killing monstrous creatures.

The myth of the Great Flood, similar to the flood Noah faced in the Bible, is found in Sumerian mythology and was certainly known to the Assyrians. Like Tiamat, the Great Flood symbolized the destructive power of water. Perhaps Sennacherib's destruction of Babylon by opening the sluices was meant to reflect the flood myth.

Demons and monsters were ever-present forces of chaos against which protection needed to be sought from the gods or guardian spirits. The great human-headed winged bulls called *lamassu*, for instance, didn't just form impressive entrances to a king's palace. They also acted as magical protectors. Incantations could also be used to ward off demons.

Lamashtu was an incarnation of chaos. This demon had a lion's head, bird's claws, and a woman's body and sagging breasts. Lamashtu killed young children and sometimes killed mothers in childbirth. To protect against this, expectant mothers made clay figures of Lamashtu and sent them down the Tigris to "send her away."

Pazuzu was the king of the wind demons. He had a lion's face and clawed hands and feet. However, he could be used as a source of good magic, and his figure was often carved on amulets. Other protectors included Ugallu, "great lion," and the urmahlullu, "lion man," who wore bull horns on the front of his helmet as a divine symbol. Lahmu were depicted as bearded men with hair in flowing ringlets. Images of Lahmu are inscribed with the phrase, "Enter, spirit of peace; depart, spirit of evil!" The Apkallu had fish skin cloaks and a fish head as a helmet. They sometimes had bird heads and wings. They were protective spirits despite their monstrous looks.

The importance of demons made exorcism a standard procedure in Assyria since illnesses could be caused by demons or evil magic. The king had his own exorcist, which Assyrians would have seen as no stranger than a CEO nowadays having a therapist.

Magic was practiced by the *mashmashu* or *ashipu*. Magical incantations and spells have been preserved in writings. Amulets could be worn or hung on the wall of a house, and magical figurines were often buried in the foundations. Clay dogs were common foundation figures; they perhaps represented the protective nature of guard dogs. Burning a figurine might be seen as a form of magic. Incantations could be used to rid oneself of witchcraft or evil spirits.

The Assyrians believed in an afterlife of sorts. The underworld was the place where all the dead resided, virtuous or not. The dead ate dust and were blind and powerless. There was no heaven and no hell. All humans were mortal, and their days were numbered. This outlook must have been somewhat depressing.

Although there was no paradise to look forward to, having a decent burial was extremely important, partly to ensure that the dead were happy and did not come back as vengeful ghosts. (A Jewish legend tells how the son of the Babylonian monarch Nebuchadnezzar cut his body into three hundred pieces and fed them to the birds to ensure he could never return.) Houses and palaces had burial chambers in the basement. These were usually vaulted chambers with steps down so that the dead could be visited and given offerings. Grave goods included letters and other documents, jewelry, ivory combs and pins, and carved stone containers.

What was distinctive about Assyria was the god Ashur, the ruler of the city that took his name. Unlike most of the Mesopotamian gods, he did not (originally) have a wife or son. He was not even shown in human form; he was identified with the rock on which his temple was built. He was sometimes known as "lord of the mountain." In contrast, all the Babylonian gods are related to each other. They also all symbolize particular aspects of life, whereas Ashur was, quite simply, the power of the city, nothing else. He has no story; he is just a god of power and omnipotence.

The god Ashur in a winged disk.[132]

Other cities had their own deities. Babylon had the god Marduk, Nippur had the god Enlil, and Arbela had the goddess Ishtar. As Assyria expanded, it indulged in "god-napping," seizing foreign gods' cult statues and relocating them to Ashur in a supernatural equivalent of the resettlement of conquered populations.[i] There was even a divine directory of Ashur telling priests where they could find the relevant god; it

---

[i] Radner, Karen. *Ancient Assyria: A Very Short Introduction*. Oxford University Press, Oxford, 2015.

was a sort of telephone book of the gods.

Ashur's temple was called "Wild Bull: in the time of Erishum I, which suggests that Ashur might have originally been identified with that animal. Ashur was represented on one seal as a four-legged bull-headed rock. He was not given a temple outside the city of Ashur; instead, his weapons were venerated as the "sword of Ashur."

The king had an important part to play in the worship of Ashur, as he was the only go-between for his people. All hymns and prayers to Ashur mention the king prominently. This was not the case, for instance, with Ishtar, who was not a state god of Assyria.

Under Shamsi-Adad I, Ashur came to be conflated with Enlil of Nippur, the chief deity of the Sumerian pantheon. Enlil was known as "wild bull" and "great mountain." Both epithets could also be applied to Ashur. Eamkurkurra, "House, Wild Bull of All Lands," was the name of the new temple that Shamsi-Adad erected. (Hammurabi similarly raised Babylon's city god Marduk in status by stating that Enlil had transferred his powers to Marduk.)

From at least Shamsi-Adad's time, the palace and the temple of Ashur were connected. Other gods, though, were venerated on the other side of the palace toward the city. Even after the royal residence had been relocated to Kalhu and later to Nineveh, the kings of Assyria would come back to Ashur for the spring festival. When they died, they were buried under the old royal palace. The way the kings relied on Ashur is easy to see from the following inscription.

"Sennacherib the great king, mighty king, king of the world, king of Assyria, king of the four quarters, the wise, expert, heroic warrior, foremost among all rulers, the bridle that curbs the disobedient, and the one who smites the enemy with lightning. Ashur, the great god, gave me a kingship without rival; against all those who sit on thrones he made my weapons strong; from the upper sea to the lower sea, he made all the rulers of the world bow down at my feet."[i]

The Great Goddess might have been the main divinity worshiped in all the Assyrian cities at an early date. She was certainly well known in Sumer, where she was called Inanna. She became Ishtar in the Akkadian pantheon. In Babylon, she was known as "Ishtar the Assyrian," and she

---

[i] Cotterell, Arthur. *The First Great Powers: Babylon and Assyria.* Hurst & Company, London, 2019. Pg. 121.

was the goddess of battle fury and sexual desire. She was sometimes called "the splendid lioness."

The goddess Ishtar shown on an Akkadian seal.[133]

Other gods included the following:

- Adad, the weather or storm god, who is sometimes represented by a triple thunderbolt. He was the son of Anum, the sky god. He was much more important in the dry steppes of Assyria than in Babylonia, which did not depend on rain for agricultural production.
- Sin, the moon god.
- Shamash, the sun god. Since he saw everything that happened each day, he was also the god of justice. He was known as Utu in Sumerian.

- Nabu, the god of writing and scribes. He was better known in Babylon than in Assyria.
- Ninurta started as a Sumerian god of grain. In Assyria, he became a warrior god and, as such, was often the patron of the king. Ninurta shot down the chaos eagle Anzu, who had stolen the tablets of destiny on which Enlil relied for his authority.

The gods required service from their worshipers, including sacrifices and libations. Even the earliest temples in Assyria included a blood basin, libation vessels from which beer could be poured, clay incense holders, and sacrificial bowls. Wheat, barley, sesame, fruit, and honey were presented to the gods, as well as meat by ritually pure priests who were clean-shaven (unlike other men, particularly the king).

Menus for the gods have been found on clay tablets, which show how far away some of the foodstuffs were sourced. Since everyone's work should nourish the gods, every Assyrian city and province had to send produce for offerings, which became an act of collective sacrifice. After the gods had taken their sustenance from the aromas, the foodstuffs were divided out among those present. This food was considered to have immense power. "Whoever eats the leftovers will live."[i]

Almost all rituals would have included beer, which had been associated with divinities from early on; intoxication was seen as a divine state.

Votive statues date from Sumerian times but have also been found in Assyrian temples. These figurines of worshipers with folded hands and huge eyes were probably set on mudbrick benches on the long sides of the sanctuary to represent their owners in permanent, unceasing prayer. The cult statue of the god would have been placed in a high, deep niche opposite the entrance, a plan that was found in the earliest temple at Ashur and does not seem to have changed much over the centuries. In the Neo-Assyrian Empire, rulers still set their statues up in such a position that they could adore the god in the temple.

The use of oracles and divination is a characteristic of Mesopotamian religion. Omens were not absolutely determinative; however, they were an indicator of an elevated level of risk, which could be averted by taking action or by ritual or magic. Radner has pointed out that in an absolute

---

[i] Radner, Karen. *Ancient Assyria: A Very Short Introduction.* Oxford University Press, Oxford, 2015.

monarchy, an oracle's answer to a question would have been a useful way to create debate.[i]

Queries might be addressed to Shamash or Adad in a number of ways. Extispicy—divination by examining the internal organs of sacrificed animals—was often used. Archaeologists have found a number of models of animal livers that were marked up so that diviners in training could practice their interpretations.

Other methods included astrology, the study of the weather, the interpretation of dreams, watching smoke from incense, or casting lots. Necromancy (asking questions of the dead) could be used, but this was considered risky. The importance of astrology was one major reason for the development of advanced mathematics; the Sumerians used both the decimal and the sexagesimal system (base sixty), and the Assyrians had tables of reciprocals, square roots, and cube roots.

Precise observation of nature was important. Tables were made of the daily change in the duration of the moon's visibility during the lunar month of the winter solstice, for example.

As one might expect in a culture with great regard for the written word, the questions were usually put in writing. One surviving tablet shows Esarhaddon inquiring of Shamash whether the appointment of Sin-nadin-apli as crown prince was acceptable and pleasing to the god. He also used extispicy to select which crafts workshops should be given commissions for rebuilding Babylonian temples.

Even the coronation ritual was written down. A 12th- or 11th-century BCE tablet described the procession of the monarch to Ashur's temple, where the proclamation "Ashur is king!" was made. After this, the king was addressed. "May Ashur put the crown on your head for a hundred years." At the end of the rite, the court officials gave up their emblems of power, and the king told them to resume their offices, thus ensuring the continued smooth functioning of the civil service. It is a fascinating glimpse of how the religious and bureaucratic aspects of the Assyrian Empire functioned in tandem to ensure the state's continuation.

---

[i] Radner, Karen. *Ancient Assyria: A Very Short Introduction.* Oxford University Press, Oxford, 2015.

Chapter 10: Arts and Architecture

Assyria developed a highly stylized form of art and architecture that was intended to glorify its kings and gods. Art was intended to convey a message about the king's power and wealth and to impress Assyrians and visitors from outside the empire.

Buildings were constructed of mudbrick. There was no other viable choice since Assyria had few trees and very limited rock resources for building. Mudbrick building lends itself to accretion (adding on to or covering over earlier layers). At some sites, numerous different layers have been excavated under a single temple.

The main limitation on the size of buildings was the span of the ceiling beams that could be imported. Only smaller rooms might be vaulted. Beams were sometimes supported on terracotta or bronze-covered wooden fists ("hands of Ishtar"), which, oddly, had five fingers but no thumb. Gates and doors were made of wood and covered with metal bands, which might be highly decorated like the Balawat Gates of Shalmaneser III.

In the glaring sunlight of Mesopotamia, high and relatively narrow rooms were generally lit only by the doorways. This, together with the limits on roof spans, meant that most palaces were made up of various courtyards with large expanses of bare wall. The outside walls were often plastered with gypsum so that they shone gleaming white. The interior walls were decorated with glazed bricks, paint, and stone reliefs. Traces of paint remain on some of the carved stone friezes that survive from the royal palaces.

The palace would have looked like a long, horizontal mass. It was probably considerably higher than other secular buildings in the city. However, ziggurats, which were first developed by the Sumerians, introduced a more vertical focus. Since they were solid (filled with unfired mudbrick), their size was not limited in the same way as palace buildings. Buttresses on walls and ramps and staircases accessing the higher floors created strong accents that further emphasized their bulk.

The royal palaces from the time of Ashurnasirpal II were evidently designed to make an impact on visitors. Reliefs, cut into stone panels that must have been imported at some expense, would originally have been painted, at least partially. Soft Mosul marble—actually a kind of gypsum—is easy to work but hardens after exposure, which enabled Assyrian sculptors to create highly detailed works. On some of the reliefs, fine decorations are incised on the clothes to show the textile patterns of a brocade. There are floral patterns on the edge of the sleeve. A royal robe is decorated with sphinxes, winged bulls, trees of life, and the archetypal scene of the king killing a lion.

The subjects in the sculptures included scenes of subject peoples surrendering, battles, and tribute delivery, complete with a royal audience. Assyrian civility was shown as the assurance of order in a chaotic world. In the battle scenes, chaos is allowed to break out, but order is restored by the king, who is depicted as being in the presence of the god Ashur and his protective spirits.

Ashurbanipal's palace had particularly savage subjects. The scenes of the Battle of the Ulai River against the Elamites show one soldier sawing off the head of Teumman of Elam while another man picks up the royal hat, which has fallen on the ground. A later scene shows an Assyrian soldier waving the head from a chariot. Another scene shows Ashurbanipal lounging on a couch and his wife, Ashur-Sharrat, drinking with him in the garden, which is a highly civilized and very poised scene. However, on the left, a close look will detect the severed head of King Teumman hanging in the branches of a tree.

Ashurbanipal's banquet[134]

A number of conventions were developed. For instance, a fallen enemy (or lion or bull) would be shown beneath the wheels of the king's chariot. An odd form of perspective was used, in which the legs and head would be shown in profile, but the upper half of the body would be shown frontally. Cities were shown as a series of towers or crenelated buttresses. City walls were a sign of civilization and order, as well as a practical form of defense.

Sometimes, the conventions had a political message. No enemy chariots or cavalry are shown in any of Sargon's reliefs, even though his enemies did have these resources. The reliefs maintain the idea of Assyria being technologically and militarily superior.

The king was always shown as a perfect man in the prime of life. The muscles of arms and legs were exaggerated in Assyrian sculpture, and this was the case for animals as well as men. The king's long, curly beard is cut square across the bottom, and his long, curly hair comes down to his shoulders. He is always a figure of power, and in narrative scenes, he always has the grandest beard. Other nobles have shorter beards. Only very young men and eunuchs are shown with clean-shaven faces.

But perhaps the archetypal figures of Assyrian art are the colossal winged bulls and lions that guard the palace gates. They were usually made of a single piece of stone and could weigh up to thirty tons each. A relief from Sennacherib's time shows how they were dragged on sleds by teams of hundreds of men.

Despite the apparent similarity of Assyrian reliefs, connoisseurs have detected some differences between the art of different kings. Artwork made for Ashurnasirpal is impressive and detailed in high relief and very technically assured, while Tiglath-Pileser III commissioned slightly less impressive work in lower relief but with much more varied compositions and more detailed narratives. One room, in particular, showed all the main events of Tiglath-Pileser's reign; effectively, it was a graphic history of his achievements. However, almost all Assyrian work displays a dislike of empty space. Detail is always filled in; for instance, one can find the spiraling waves of a river, the reeds of the marshes, or the texture of cloth in Assyrian art.

Monumental art from the Assyrian Empire is well known since this was the focus of early archaeological investigations. Because a lot of reliefs found their way to places like the British Museum, the Louvre, and the Metropolitan Museum of Art, it's quite accessible; you don't have to go to Iraq to see them. Later digs found more intimate art, such as bronzes, gold jewelry, ivories, and furniture pieces, but a lot of this has stayed in Iraq. Some of these pieces have also been lost, thanks to the plundering of the Iraq Museum in 2003, though some items have been found on the art market and returned to Iraq.

Carved ivories were a luxury that the Assyrians really loved. Max Mallowan found a huge number at Nimrud (called the Nimrud ivories), including some fascinating and lively large-scale carvings. Many were made either outside of Assyria in Phoenicia or in Egypt or by Phoenician and Egyptian craftsmen who had relocated to Assyria. Intriguingly, when the Medes destroyed Kalhu, they had no idea that the ivory was valuable. They stripped off the gold leaf that originally covered many of the ivories and then threw the wrecked pieces into a well.

An ivory masterpiece from the palace at Kalhu.[135]

Another luxury good was glass. In the early period, it was not blown but built up around a core that could then be removed. Later on, it was cast in molds and then finished by grinding and polishing, as if it was stone.

A final typical Mesopotamian art form is the seal. In prehistory, stone amulets were pressed on clay to attest to the ownership and integrity of packages of goods. The cylinder seal, which was rolled across clay to create a rectangular panel, was developed around 3500 BCE. Its use expanded with the introduction of cuneiform script and the use of clay tablets, which could be sealed the way we would sign a letter or document.

However, when Aramaic became widely used, the cylinder seal was not so useful. Stamp seals were created, enabling the sealing of leather or papyrus rolls. Royal stamp seals show the king stabbing a lion. Cylinder seals were more likely to show a number of tiny figures, such as winged bulls, goddesses (surrounded by stars, their *melammu* or divine radiance) and gods, symbols of gods (such as the winged disk or the thunderbolt), and scenes of worship. The work on cylinder seals can be incredibly detailed. A tiny four-centimeter-high seal can show four or five separate figures.

There was another form of art that the Assyrians were experts at: the art of war. No book on the Assyrians would be complete without a mention of Assyrian military equipment and battle tactics, which were redeveloped several times to meet new conditions on the battlefield.

One of the most important weapons was the composite bow, which was a bit more than a yard long. Since it was made of different woods with different compression and release characteristics, it gave greater force to the arrow than a simple bow. Archers were usually mounted, not on a horse but on a chariot. Since a bow requires both hands, the chariot was a two-man team, with a driver to accompany the archer who did the fighting. (The archer would have been the higher one in status, as can be seen from reliefs with the king fighting from a chariot.)

Chariots were maneuverable in the flat lands of Mesopotamia. (Later, when the Assyrians started to fight in the more broken country of the Levant and the Iranian marches, they adopted the cavalry. But even at the start, they used teams, with one man controlling both horses and the other shooting.) The chariots would be used at the beginning of an engagement to smash into the enemy, weakening the line of defense and opening the opposing army's ranks up. The Assyrian infantry would then penetrate through the gaps.

Chariots continued to be upgraded throughout the Neo-Assyrian period. They were made heavier and larger so that they could carry three and, eventually, four men. By Ashurbanipal's time, they were so strong and armored that they were like horse-drawn tanks.

The Assyrians can generally be recognized on reliefs by their panoply of conical helmets. They wore mail shirts of metal plates that were arranged like fish scales on leather and a shield. The shield might be round and made of wood with a metal boss. It could be convex and made of reeds bound with leather or wooden staves, which could cover a man's legs up to the waist. Or shields could be conical; these were used mainly by the king's bodyguard.

The infantry generally used spears and pikes but had a sword or dagger for close-range fighting. Ceremonial mace heads have been found, but these were outdated by the Middle Assyrian Empire since porcelain mace heads could certainly not have been used in war; they would have smashed to bits. They must have been carried purely for ceremonial purposes, just as US Navy officers carry swords today.

Siege warfare was an Assyrian specialty, though they had no artillery and had to operate at close quarters. Reliefs show a plethora of different kinds of battering rams, siege engines, and mobile siege towers, which provided a platform for archers to shoot from, as well as a potential assault base. Palace friezes show Assyrian soldiers climbing ladders to assault the walls. In Sennacherib's palace, the siege of Lachish takes up over six hundred square feet of wall.

Sapping and tunneling were used, and diverting water channels was another frequent technique.

An Assyrian siege engine attacks a city wall.[136]

At Tell el-Duweir, the site of Lachish, there is evidence of a massive fire and an Assyrian siege ramp built of stone. Arrowheads and sling stones were left where they fell.

The cost of such a siege was very high. For the most part, the Assyrians would have tried to secure a negotiated surrender. Promises of amnesty would be made, similar to Sennacherib's offer to the Hebrews. These promises were always honored so enemies knew they could rely on being treated well if they surrendered. Then, the Assyrians would proceed to destroy the orchards, plantations, and irrigation works around the city. Trees take a long time to grow back, so the city's long-term future was at stake. Finally, the Assyrians might execute hostages—usually by impalement—publicly below the walls. Most sieges did not get this far.

Initially, being in the Assyrian army was a seasonal affair. The army could not campaign when there was agricultural work to be done, and the men had to gather at Ashur before setting out. However, the Neo-Assyrian Empire introduced a standing army, which made a huge difference to Assyria's campaigning ability. Now, the army could campaign all year, enabling long-distance operations as far away as Egypt.

Another big change in the late empire was the use of auxiliary troops from subject regions, who can be distinguished by their dress, hairstyles, and weapons in the reliefs. Slingers from Judea formed a useful contingent (remember how David killed Goliath with a slingshot?).

One style that Assyria never really adopted was naval warfare. The first use of ships dates from 694 BCE under Sennacherib, and even then, Assyria used Phoenician and Greek ships and crew. Given the rise of the Greek city-states, many of which became strong maritime powers, this would have been a major handicap had Assyria tried to expand farther west into the Mediterranean.

Taking a territory in war is one thing; holding on to it is quite another. This was where the King's Road came in. This was a postal or messenger service. Each governor was tasked with maintaining the staging posts in their provinces. This served only the state, not private travelers. All nobles had signet rings with the imperial emblem on them; a letter carrying this seal would immediately be identified as a letter requiring urgent transmission. Envoys might also be sent, particularly if the matter was too sensitive to write down, but it was an Assyrian innovation to send a letter without an envoy to get to the receiver quicker. It was slower than USPS, but it was reliable if you had the right signet ring. Without the right stamp on the letter, though, your letter might not get taken anywhere at all.

Conclusion

The Assyrians occupy a crucial place in the history of the world. Without the Assyrians, there might not have been a Neo-Babylonian Empire or a Persian Empire. Alexander the Great might have stayed an unknown Macedonian king, and Rome might never have expanded to take over most of Europe. The very idea of an empire is one of Assyria's legacies.

While Egypt often clung to the past, Assyria managed to adapt to circumstances while always looking back at its roots for inspiration. The development of advanced accounting systems, trade enclaves, and a post office, as well as the mobility of peoples within the empire, were all new developments, and future empires benefited because of it. Assyria became a military empire due to its trading empire, the same way British imperialism grew out of the trading adventures of the East India Company.

Assyria frequently borrowed from Babylonian culture, though it retained its own distinctive language. It was also the first empire to see belonging as more important than ethnic identity. The definition of an Assyrian was quite simply someone who sacrificed to Ashur or provided goods for those sacrifices.

The truly amazing thing about Assyria, though, is that it appears to have been under the control of the same family for almost two thousand years. Compared to Sumerian history, which features incessant, discontinuous change, with cities and dynasties competing for power, Assyria was a stable and orderly empire. It identified itself as a force for order, bringing civilization and the worship of Ashur to other lands.

Temples and palaces were rebuilt time and time again, but they were always on the same site and always included the original foundation inscriptions if they could be found.

When the Persian Empire was created by Cyrus, who conquered Babylon in 539, it used a different language (Elamite, not an Akkadian language). Still, the Persians copied much of their civilization from the Mesopotamian cultures. The *lamassu* flew from Assyria to the Persian capital of Persepolis, and Persian nobles collected Assyrian objets d'art.

More recently, Saddam Hussein co-opted Assyrian monuments into his own style of empire-building. Unfortunately, this made archaeological sites and museums prime targets for the opposition. There was the looting of the Iraq Museum, ISIS's destruction of the ziggurat at Kalhu, and the bulldozing of much of Nineveh. Looking at the 20th-century history of Mesopotamia, one can only conclude that the Assyrian Empire did a pretty good job of running a stable and prosperous state.

If you enjoyed this book, a review on Amazon would be greatly appreciated because it would mean a lot to hear from you.

To leave a review:
1. Open your camera app.
2. Point your mobile device at the QR code.
3. The review page will appear in your web browser.

Thanks for your support!

Here's another book by Enthralling History that you might like

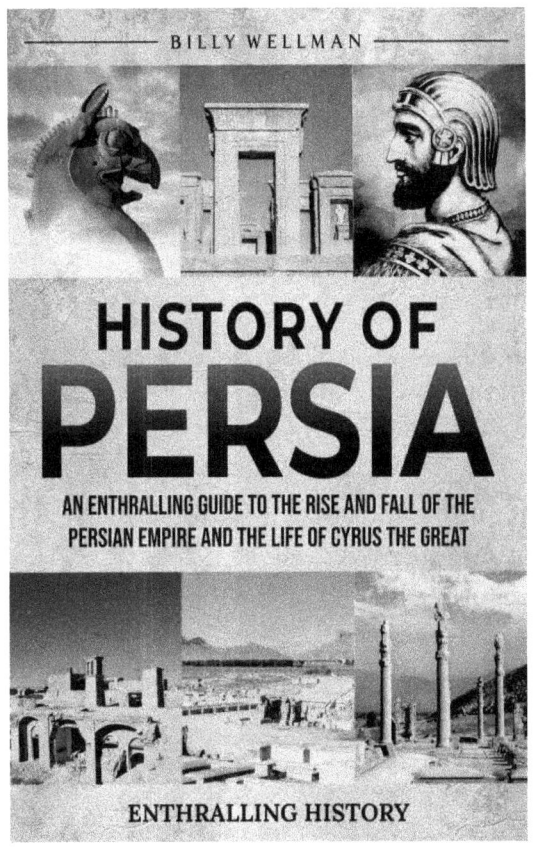

Free limited time bonus

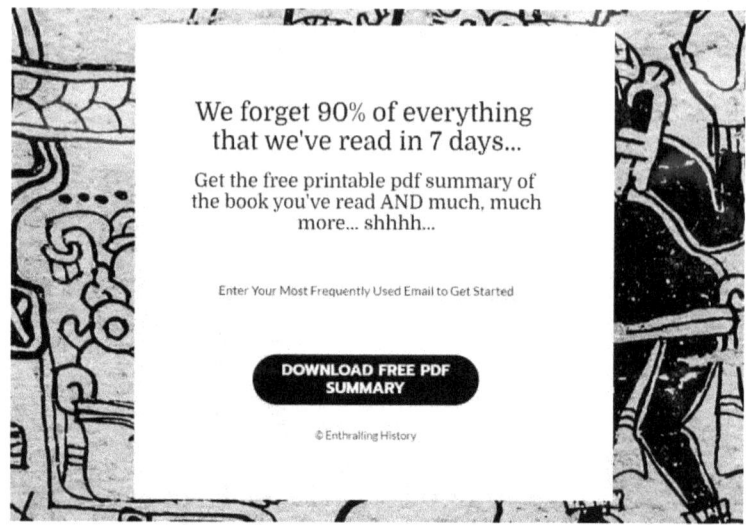

Stop for a moment. We have a free bonus set up for you. The problem is this: we forget 90% of everything that we read after 7 days. Crazy fact, right? Here's the solution: we've created a printable, 1-page pdf summary for this book that you're reading now. All you have to do to get your free pdf summary is to go to the following website: https://livetolearn.lpages.co/enthrallinghistory/

Or, Scan the QR code!

Once you do, it will be intuitive. Enjoy, and thank you!

Bibliography

Part 1
Books

Oxford Encyclopedia of Archaeology in the Near East, Oxford University Press, pp 476 - 483, E.M. Meyers (ed) 1997

Peoples of the Old Testament, Oxford University Press, 1973, DJ Wiseman (ed)

The History and Culture of Ancient Western Asia and Egypt, The Dorsey Press, U.S.A, A Bernard Knapp (ed)

Academic sites used throughout

"(PDF) Re-evaluating the Ubaid: Synchronizing the 6th and 5th millennia." https://www.academia.edu/3751066/Re_evaluating_the_Ubaid_Synchronizing_the_6th_and_5th_millennia_BC_of_Mesopotamia_and_the_Levant_unpublished_MA_thesis_.

"paper: Re-evaluating the Ubaid: Synchronizing the 6th and 5th millennia." 18 Aug. 2020, https://raisinguppharaoh.com/tag/paper-re-evaluating-the-ubaid-synchronizing-the-6th-and-5th-millennia-bc-of-mesopotamia-and-the-levant-77/.

"In search of the genetic footprints of Sumerians: a survey of Y." 04 Oct. 2011, https://www.ncbi.nlm.nih.gov/pmc/articles/PMC3215667/.

"NEW INSIGHTS ON THE ROLE OF ENVIRONMENTAL DYNAMICS SHAPING SOUTHERN." 18 Jul. 2019, https://www.cambridge.org/core/journals/iraq/article/new-insights-on-the-role-of-environmental-dynamics-shaping-southern-mesopotamia-from-the-preubaid-to-the-early-islamic-period/F7084E4BF1171D8B77021B286BFE300C.

"[PDF] NEW INSIGHTS ON THE ROLE OF ENVIRONMENTAL DYNAMICS SHAPING." 18 Jul. 2019, https://www.semanticscholar.org/paper/NEW-INSIGHTS-ON-THE-ROLE-OF-ENVIRONMENTAL-DYNAMICS-Altaweel-Marsh/67e4667f914d7f1b2b6966178f110a8cb629806d.

"AFTER THE UBAID: INTERPRETING CHANGE FROM THE CAUCASUS TO MESOPOTAMIA." https://www.academia.edu/5665737/AFTER_THE_UBAID_INTERPRETING_CHANGE_FROM_THE_CAUCASUS_TO_MESOPOTAMIA_AT_THE_DAWN_OF_URBAN_CIVILIZATION_4500_3500_BC_OFFPRINT.

"Carter 2016_Review of Marro After the Ubaid.pdf - academia.edu." https://www.academia.edu/35253069/Carter_2016_Review_of_Marro_After_the_Ubaid_pdf.

"Marro C. (ed.) 2012. After the Ubaid: Interpreting change." https://www.persee.fr/doc/paleo_0153-9345_2016_num_42_2_5729.

Web References

"Leonard Woolley (Author of The Sumerians) - Goodreads." https://www.goodreads.com/author/show/171163.Leonard_Woolley.

"Sir Leonard Woolley and the Excavations in Ur - SciHi Blog." 17 Apr. 2021, http://scihi.org/leonard-woolley-excavations-ur/.

"Woolley's Excavations - UrOnline." http://www.ur-online.org/about/woolleys-excavations/.

"Thorkild Jacobsen (Author of The Treasures of Darkness)." 02 May. 1993, https://www.goodreads.com/author/show/166860.Thorkild_Jacobsen.

"Selected Writings of Samuel Noah Kramer - Internet Archive." 30 Mar. 2019, https://archive.org/details/KramerStudies19461990.

"THE SUMERIANS - Oriental Institute." https://oi.uchicago.edu/sites/oi.uchicago.edu/files/uploads/shared/docs/sumerians.pdf.

"Sumerian Mythology Index - Sacred-Texts.com." https://www.sacred-texts.com/ane/sum/.

"Samuel Noah Kramer | Open Library." 30 Sept. 2020, https://openlibrary.org/authors/OL398202A/Samuel_Noah_Kramer.

"The Sumerians: Their History, Culture, and Character." https://oi.uchicago.edu/research/publications/misc/sumerians-their-history-culture-and-character.

"AS 20. Sumerological Studies in Honor of Thorkild Jacobsen on His Seventieth Birthday." https://oi.uchicago.edu/research/publications/as/20-sumerological-studies-honor-thorkild-jacobsen-his-seventieth-birthday.

"THE SUMERIANS - The Oriental Institute of the University of Chicago."
https://oi.uchicago.edu/sites/oi.uchicago.edu/files/uploads/shared/docs/sumerians.pdf.

"Nippur - The Oriental Institute of the University of Chicago."
https://oi.uchicago.edu/research/projects/nippur-sacred-city-enlil-0.

"Cuneiform Studies | Near Eastern Languages and Civilizations."
https://nelc.uchicago.edu/cuneiform-studies.

"The Sumerians - University of Chicago Press."
https://press.uchicago.edu/ucp/books/book/chicago/S/bo27481022.html.

"Expedition Magazine - Penn Museum."
https://www.penn.museum/sites/expedition/ur-and-its-treasures/.

Chapter 1

"The Ubaid Period (5500–4000 B.C.) | Essay | The Metropolitan Museum of Art."
https://www.metmuseum.org/toah/hd/ubai/hd_ubai.htm.

"Ubaid Period | Mesopotamian history | Britannica."
https://www.britannica.com/topic/Ubaid-Period.

"Ubaidian Culture and the Roots of Mesopotamia - ThoughtCo." 07 Sept. 2018,
https://www.thoughtco.com/ubaidian-culture-ubaid-roots-mesopotamia-173089.

"Ubaid period - Wikipedia." https://en.wikipedia.org/wiki/Ubaid_period.

"Cultures | Ubaid Period - Ancient Mesopotamia."
https://ancientmesopotamia.org/cultures/ubaid-period.php.

"Ancient Reptilians: The Unanswered Mystery of the 7,000-Year-Old Ubaid Lizardmen." 26 Feb. 2022, https://www.ancient-origins.net/unexplained-phenomena/ubaid-lizardmen-001116.

"Ubaid Period: Culture & Explanation | Study.com." 06 Feb. 2022,
https://study.com/academy/lesson/ubaid-period-culture-lesson-quiz.html.

"Tell al-Ubaid - Academic Dictionaries and Encyclopedias."
https://mesopotamia_enc.en-academic.com/360/Tell_al-Ubaid.

"Tall al-'Ubayd | archaeological site, Iraq | Britannica."
https://www.britannica.com/place/Tall-al-Ubayd.

"TELL AL-'UBAID."
https://rootshunt.com/angirasgautam/archaeologicalsitesiniraq/tellalubaid/tellalubaid.htm.

"Hereafter - Tell al-Ubaid - Our Ancient World."
http://ourancientworld.com/Settlement.aspx?id=81.

"Tel al 'Ubaid Ceramics: Photographs from Neutron Activation Analysis."

https://core.tdar.org/image/373029/tel-al-ubaid-ceramics-photographs.

"Tell al-'Ubaid Copper Lintel - Joy of Museums Virtual Tours." https://joyofmuseums.com/museums/united-kingdom-museums/london-museums/british-museum/tell-al-ubaid-copper-lintel/.

"Tell al-`Ubaid Wiki." https://everipedia.org/Tell_al-%2560Ubaid.

"Tell al-'Ubaid | Detailed Pedia." 24 May. 2022, https://www.detailedpedia.com/wiki-Tell_al-%27Ubaid.

Chapter 2

"Fertile Crescent - HISTORY." 20 Dec. 2017, https://www.history.com/topics/pre-history/fertile-crescent.

"Fertile Crescent | National Geographic Society." 20 May. 2022, https://www.nationalgeographic.org/encyclopedia/fertile-crescent/.

"Fertile Crescent | Definition, Location, Map, Significance, & Facts." https://www.britannica.com/place/Fertile-Crescent.

"The Sumerians of the Fertile Crescent." https://www.gardencity.k12.ny.us/cms/lib/NY01913305/Centricity/Domain/671/8%20Mesopotamia.pdf

"A Functional and Fertile Crescent: Technological Advancements." 03 Aug. 2018, https://www.ancient-origins.net/history-important-events/fertile-crescent-0010488.

"Fertile Crescent - Cradle of Civilization (Collection) - World History." 23 Nov. 2018, https://www.worldhistory.org/collection/26/fertile-crescent---cradle-of-civilization/.

"The White Temple and the Great Ziggurat in the Mesopotamian City of Uruk." 17 Oct. 2016, https://www.ancient-origins.net/ancient-places-asia/white-temple-and-great-ziggurat-mesopotamian-city-uruk-006835.

"Art: Ruins of the White Temple and Ziggurat - Annenberg Learner." https://www.learner.org/series/art-through-time-a-global-view/the-urban-experience/ruins-of-the-white-temple-and-ziggurat/.

"White Temple of God Anu in Sacred Precinct of Kullaba at Uruk." 10 Oct. 2016, https://www.ancientpages.com/2016/10/10/white-temple-of-god-anu-in-sacred-precinct-of-kullaba-at-uruk/.

"Uruk - Wikipedia." https://en.wikipedia.org/wiki/Uruk.

"The White Temple - Artefacts." https://www.artefacts-berlin.de/portfolio-item/uruk-visualisation-project-the-white-temple/.

"Reconstruction of the White Temple – Ancient Art." 24 Apr. 2015, https://ancientart.as.ua.edu/reconstruction-of-the-white-temple/.

"Hamoukar (Syria) | Jason Ur - Harvard University." https://scholar.harvard.edu/jasonur/pages/hamoukar.

"Hamoukar, Great City of Old – StMU Research Scholars." 15 Sept. 2016, https://stmuscholars.org/hamoukar-great-city-of-old/.

"Evidence of battle at Hamoukar points to early urban development." http://chronicle.uchicago.edu/070118/hamoukar.shtml.

"Is it true the first known battle was in Hamoukar? If it is, why did it occur, and who were the combatants?" https://www.quora.com/Is-it-true-the-first-known-battle-was-in-Hamoukar-If-it-is-why-did-it-occur-and-who-were-the-combatants.

"Hamoukar - Wikipedia." https://en.wikipedia.org/wiki/Hamoukar.

"The Lost City of Hamoukar | Edward Willett." https://edwardwillett.com/2000/05/the-lost-city-of-hamoukar/.

"Site of Earliest Known Urban Warfare Threatened by Syrian War." 24 Jun. 2013, https://www.livescience.com/37672-ancient-urban-warfare-site-threatened.html.

"Hamoukar - Oriental Institute." https://oi.uchicago.edu/sites/oi.uchicago.edu/files/uploads/shared/docs/08-09_Hamoukar.pdf.

"Uruk - World History Encyclopedia." 28 Apr. 2011, https://www.worldhistory.org/uruk/.

"Uruk Period Mesopotamia: The Rise of Sumer - ThoughtCo." 21 Apr. 2019, https://www.thoughtco.com/uruk-period-mesopotamia-rise-of-sumer-171676.

"Cultures | Uruk Period - Ancient Mesopotamia." https://ancientmesopotamia.org/cultures/uruk-period.php.

"Uruk period - Wikipedia." https://en.wikipedia.org/wiki/Uruk_period.

"Tell Brak Home." https://www.tellbrak.mcdonald.cam.ac.uk/.

"Tell Brak (Syria) | Jason Ur - Harvard University." https://scholar.harvard.edu/jasonur/pages/tell-brak.

"Tell Brak - Wikipedia." https://en.wikipedia.org/wiki/Tell_Brak.

"Tell Brak - Mesopotamian Capital in Syria - ThoughtCo." 08 Mar. 2017, https://www.thoughtco.com/tell-brak-mesopotamian-capital-syria-170274.

"Syria: Tell Brak - World Archaeology." 28 Apr. 2012, https://www.world-archaeology.com/features/syria-tell-brak-3/.

Chapter 3

"Early Dynastic Period of Sumer - Ancient Mesopotamia." https://ancientmesopotamia.org/cultures/early-dynastic-period-of-sumer.php.

"Sumer - HISTORY." 07 Dec. 2017, https://www.history.com/topics/ancient-middle-east/sumer.

"Sumer Timeline - World History Encyclopedia." https://www.worldhistory.org/timeline/sumer/.

"Ancient Sumer & The Sumerian Civilization: Here's What We Know." 02 Dec. 2020, https://www.thecollector.com/ancient-sumer-civilization/.

"EARLY DYNASTIC/AKKADIAN/UR III SUMER: 2." https://www.unm.edu/~gbawden/328-rel/328-rel.htm.

"Early Dynastic Sumer Research Papers - Academia.edu." https://www.academia.edu/Documents/in/Early_Dynastic_Sumer?page=5.

"Sumer (Early Dynastic Period) with Assyrian Border Style 11." 27 Sept. 2021, https://archive.org/details/SumerEarlyDynasticPeriodArabicWithAssyrianBorderStyle11.

"Early Dynastic Sumer Research Papers - Academia.edu." https://www.academia.edu/Documents/in/Early_Dynastic_Sumer?page=3.

"Cultures | Early Dynastic Period of Sumer." https://ancientmesopotamia.org/cultures/early-dynastic-period-of-sumer.

"Early Dynastic Period (Mesopotamia) - Wikipedia." https://en.wikipedia.org/wiki/Early_Dynastic_Period_(Mesopotamia).

"Old Sumerian Period (c. 3000 BC - Ancient Civilizations." https://anciv.info/mesopotamia/old-sumerian-period.html.

"Sumer (Early Dynastic Period) with Assyrian Border Style 11." 27 Sept. 2021, https://archive.org/details/SumerEarlyDynasticPeriodArabicWithAssyrianBorderStyle11.

"Sumerian Religion - The Spiritual Life." https://slife.org/sumerian-religion/.

"Jemdet Nasr - Oxford Reference." https://www.oxfordreference.com/view/10.1093/oi/authority.20110803100019282.

"List of Place Names from Jemdet Nasr (Illustration) - World History." 07 Apr. 2016, https://www.worldhistory.org/image/4852/list-of-place-names-from-jemdet-nasr/.

"Historic Overview of Early Mesopotamian Civilization." https://www.unm.edu/~gbawden/328-sumhist/328-sumhist.htm.

"Defining the style of the period: Jemedt Nasr, 1926-28."

https://ehrafarchaeology.yale.edu/ehrafa/citation.do?method=citation&forward=browseAuthorsFullContext&id=mh62-001.

"Jemdet Nasr: a Pleiades place resource."
https://pleiades.stoa.org/places/733910291.

"The Jemdet-Nasr Period - Penn Museum."
https://www.penn.museum/documents/publications/bulletin/10-3_4/jemdet-nasr_period.pdf.

"Jemdet Nasr: The Site and the Period | The Biblical Archaeologist
https://www.journals.uchicago.edu/doi/10.2307/3210314.

"Jemdet Nasr Period - 3300-2900 BC - GlobalSecurity.org." 07 Sept. 2011, https://www.globalsecurity.org/military/world/iraq/history-jemdet-nasr.htm.

"Jemdet Nasr - Wikipedia." https://en.wikipedia.org/wiki/Jemdet_Nasr.

"Mesannepada | ruler of Ur | Britannica."
https://www.britannica.com/biography/Mesannepada.

"Ancient Mesopotamian Gods and Goddesses - Mesopotamian history: the basics." http://oracc.museum.upenn.edu/amgg/mesopotamianhistory/index.html.

"Sumerian King of the First Dynasty of Ur - Ancient Pages." 14 Apr. 2016, https://www.ancientpages.com/2016/04/14/helmet-of-meskalamdug-sumerian-king-of-the-first-dynasty-of-ur/.

"List of Rulers of Mesopotamia | Lists of Rulers | Heilbrunn Timeline."
https://www.metmuseum.org/toah/hd/meru/hd_meru.htm.

"Ancient Mesopotamian Gods and Goddesses - An/Anu (god)."
http://oracc.museum.upenn.edu/amgg/listofdeities/an/index.html.

"History of Mesopotamia - First historical personalities | Britannica."
https://www.britannica.com/place/Mesopotamia-historical-region-Asia/First-historical-personalities.

"Mesannepada - Wikipedia." https://en.wikipedia.org/wiki/Mesannepada.

"Ur-Nanshe | king of Lagash | Britannica."
https://www.britannica.com/biography/Ur-Nanshe.

"Sumerian People | Ur-Nanshe - Ancient Mesopotamia."
https://ancientmesopotamia.org/people/ur-nanshe.php.

"Ur-Nanshe - Wikipedia." https://en.wikipedia.org/wiki/Ur-Nanshe.

"Ur-Nanshe [CDLI Wiki]." https://cdli.ox.ac.uk/wiki/doku.php?id=ur-nanshe.

"Sumerian Plaque Dedicated To King Ur-Nanshe, The Founder Of The 1st Dynasty of Lagash." 05 Dec. 2018,
https://www.ancientpages.com/2018/12/05/sumerian-plaque-dedicated-to-king-ur-nanshe-the-founder-of-the-1st-dynasty-of-lagash/.

"Ur-Nanshe Biography - King of Lagash | Pantheon."
https://pantheon.world/profile/person/Ur-Nanshe/.

"Lagash | ancient city, Iraq | Britannica."
https://www.britannica.com/place/Lagash.

"Records of the Past, 2nd series, Vol. I: The Inscriptions of Telloh."
https://sacred-texts.com/ane/rp/rp201/rp20112.htm.

"Enmebaragesi | king of Kish | Britannica."
https://www.britannica.com/biography/Enmebaragesi.

"Enmebaragesi - Wikipedia." https://en.wikipedia.org/wiki/Enmebaragesi.

"Enmebaragesi Biography - Ancient Mesopotamian king | Pantheon."
https://pantheon.world/profile/person/Enmebaragesi/.

"Enmebaragesi, King of Kish - geni family tree." 06 Sept. 2016,
https://www.geni.com/people/Enmebaragesi-King-of-Kish/6000000006277541149.

"8 kings descended from heaven and ruled for 241,200 years." 08 May. 2022,
https://mysteriesrunsolved.com/2020/11/the-sumerian-king-list-8-kings-ruled-241200-years.html.

"History of Mesopotamia - First historical personalities | Britannica."
https://www.britannica.com/place/Mesopotamia-historical-region-Asia/First-historical-personalities.

"Holy City of God Enlil and One of the Oldest Cities of Sumer, Ancient Pages." 08 Jun. 2020,
https://www.ancientpages.com/2020/06/08/nippur-holy-city-of-god-enlil-and-one-of-the-oldest-cities-of-sumer/.

"Kish | ancient city, Iraq | Britannica." https://www.britannica.com/place/Kish.

Chapter 4

"The Akkadian Period (ca. 2350–2150 B.C.) | Essay | The Metropolitan Museum of Art."
https://www.metmuseum.org/toah/hd/akka/hd_akka.htm.

"Mesopotamian art and architecture - Akkadian period | Britannica."
https://www.britannica.com/art/Mesopotamian-art/Akkadian-period.

"Akkadian Period - Oxford Reference."
https://www.oxfordreference.com/view/10.1093/oi/authority.20110803095359204.

"Cultures | Akkadian Empire - Ancient Mesopotamia."
https://ancientmesopotamia.org/cultures/akkadian-empire.php.

"Akkadian Empire - Wikipedia."

https://en.wikipedia.org/wiki/Akkadian_Empire.
"Explaining the Fall of the Great Akkadian Empire - Ancient Origins." 10 Jan. 2021, https://www.ancient-origins.net/ancient-places-asia/akkadian-empire-0011871.
"Chapter Six - Sealing Practices in the Akkadian Period." https://www.cambridge.org/core/books/seals-and-sealing-in-the-ancient-world/sealing-practices-in-the-akkadian-period/81775349C1B2C3BD7E6567C21D9F9B74.
"The Akkadian Period: Empire, Environment, and Imagination." https://www.lettere.uniroma1.it/sites/default/files/3109/6_MCMAHON%202012.pdf.
"(PDF) The Use of Sumerian and Akkadian during the Akkadian Period." 10 May. 2022, https://www.academia.edu/78905915/The_Use_of_Sumerian_and_Akkadian_during_the_Akkadian_Period_The_Case_of_the_Elites_.
"Akkad Timeline - World History Encyclopedia." https://www.worldhistory.org/timeline/akkad/.
"Akkadian Empire: The first Semitic-speaking empire of Mesopotamia." 21 Mar. 2020, https://www.ancient-civilizations.com/akkadian-empire/.
"Cuneiform - Wikipedia." https://en.wikipedia.org/wiki/Cuneiform.
"Akkad | People, Culture, History, & Facts | Britannica." https://www.britannica.com/place/Akkad.
"Akkad - World History Encyclopedia." 28 Apr. 2011, https://www.worldhistory.org/akkad/.
"Akkad (city) - Wikipedia." https://en.wikipedia.org/wiki/Akkad_(city).
"Akkadian Empire: The first Semitic-speaking empire of Mesopotamia." 21 Mar. 2020, https://www.ancient-civilizations.com/akkadian-empire/.
"The Akkadian Period (ca. 2350–2150 B.C.) | Essay | The Metropolitan Museum of Art." https://www.metmuseum.org/toah/hd/akka/hd_akka.htm.
"The history of AKKAD." http://akkad.org/.
"The Akkadian Empire - History." https://www.historyonthenet.com/the-akkadian-empire.
"Agade | ancient city, Iraq | Britannica." https://www.britannica.com/place/Agade.
"Kingdoms of Mesopotamia - Agade / Akkad - The History Files." https://www.historyfiles.co.uk/KingListsMiddEast/MesopotamiaAkkad.htm.
"About: Ur-Zababa." https://live.dbpedia.org/resource/Ur-Zababa.

"Sargon and Ur-Zababa | Mesopotamian Gods & Kings." http://www.mesopotamiangods.com/sargon-and-ur-zababa/.

"Ur-Zababa Biography | Pantheon." https://pantheon.world/profile/person/Ur-Zababa/.

"Ur-Zababa - Wikipedia." https://en.wikipedia.org/wiki/Ur-Zababa.

"Lugalzagesi | ruler of Uruk | Britannica." https://www.britannica.com/biography/Lugalzagesi.

"Lugal-zage-si - Wikipedia." https://en.wikipedia.org/wiki/Lugal-zage-si.

"Ambitious King Who United Sumer - Ancient Pages." 30 Apr. 2020, https://www.ancientpages.com/2020/04/30/infamous-end-of-lugalzagesi-ambitious-king-who-united-sumer/.

"King Sargon of Akkad—facts and information - Culture." 18 Jun. 2019, https://www.nationalgeographic.com/culture/article/king-sargon-akkad.

"Sargon of Akkad - Wikipedia." https://en.wikipedia.org/wiki/Sargon_of_Akkad.

"Sargon | History, Accomplishments, Facts, & Definition | Britannica." https://www.britannica.com/biography/Sargon.

"Sargon of Akkad: The Orphan Who Founded an Empire." 04 Mar. 2022, https://www.thecollector.com/sargon-of-akkad-akkadian-empire/.

"The Legend of Sargon of Akkad - World History Encyclopedia." 30 Aug. 2014, https://www.worldhistory.org/article/746/the-legend-of-sargon-of-akkad/.

"Sargon - Encyclopedia of The Bible - Bible Gateway." https://www.biblegateway.com/resources/encyclopedia-of-the-bible/Sargon.

"Sargon the Great and the World's First Professional Army." 18 Apr. 2016, https://warfarehistorynetwork.com/2016/04/18/professional-soldiers-king-sargon-of-akkads-expanding-empire/.

"Sargon of Agade - penn.museum." https://www.penn.museum/documents/publications/bulletin/10-3_4/sargon_agade.pdf.

"Enheduanna - New World Encyclopedia." https://www.newworldencyclopedia.org/entry/Enheduanna.

"Enheduanna - Poet, Priestess, Empire Builder - World History Encyclopedia." 12 Oct. 2010, https://www.worldhistory.org/article/190/enheduanna---poet-priestess-empire-builder/.

"Enheduanna – the world's first known author - World History Edu." 20 Mar. 2022, https://www.worldhistoryedu.com/enheduanna-the-worlds-first-known-author/.

"Enheduanna - Virginia Tech." https://cddc.vt.edu/feminism/Enheduanna.html.

"Enheduanna -The Akkadian Princess who became the world's first female author." 14 Feb. 2022, https://www.historyofroyalwomen.com/the-royal-women/enheduanna-the-akkadian-princess-who-became-the-worlds-first-female-author/.

"Elamite | Rimush." https://ancientmesopotamia.org/people/rimush.

"Rimush - Wikipedia." https://en.wikipedia.org/wiki/Rimush.

"Elamite | Rimush - Ancient Mesopotamia." https://ancientmesopotamia.org/people/rimush.php.

"Rimush, 2nd King of Akkadian Empire - Geni.com." 05 Apr. 2021, https://www.geni.com/people/Rimush-King-of-the-Akkadian-Empire/6000000047190539827.

"Rimush Biography | Pantheon." https://pantheon.world/profile/person/Rimush/.

"People | Manishtusu - Ancient Mesopotamia." https://ancientmesopotamia.org/people/manishtusu.php.

"Manishtushu - Wikipedia." https://en.wikipedia.org/wiki/Manishtushu.

"People | Manishtusu." https://ancientmesopotamia.org/people/manishtusu.

"Manishtusu | king of Akkad | Britannica." https://www.britannica.com/biography/Manishtusu.

"First Sumerian Revolt - Ancient Pages." 09 Nov. 2020, https://www.ancientpages.com/2020/11/09/story-behind-the-first-sumerian-revolt/.

"Manishtushu Biography | Pantheon." https://pantheon.world/profile/person/Manishtushu/.

"Naram-Sin - World History Encyclopedia." 07 Aug. 2014, https://www.worldhistory.org/Naram-Sin/.

"Naram-Sin of Akkad - Wikipedia." https://en.wikipedia.org/wiki/Naram-Sin_of_Akkad.

"Akkadian Empire - History - Origins - Naram-Sin | Technology Trends." https://www.primidi.com/akkadian_empire/history/origins/naram-sin.

"Naram Sin: Victory Stele & Concept | Study.com." 07 Feb. 2022, https://study.com/academy/lesson/naram-sin-victory-stele-lesson-quiz.html.

"Sumerian People | Naram-Sin - Ancient Mesopotamia." https://ancientmesopotamia.org/people/naram-sin.php.

"Shar-kali-sharri | king of Akkad | Britannica." https://www.britannica.com/biography/Shar-kali-sharri.

"Sumerian People | Shar-Kali-Sharri." https://ancientmesopotamia.org/people/shar-kali-sharri.

"Shar-Kali-Sharri - Wikipedia." https://en.wikipedia.org/wiki/Shar-Kali-Sharri.

"(DOC) Sargon and Shar-Kali-Sharri | Damien Mackey - Academia.edu." 08 Jun. 2019, https://www.academia.edu/39473281/Sargon_and_Shar_Kali_Sharri.

"MS 4556 - The Schoyen Collection." https://www.schoyencollection.com/history-collection-introduction/sumerian-history-collection/king-shar-kali-sharri-ms-4556.

"Shar-Kali-Sharri in Italian - English-Italian Dictionary | Glosbe." https://glosbe.com/en/it/Shar-Kali-Sharri.

Chapter 5

"Gutians - World History Encyclopedia." 27 Oct. 2021, https://www.worldhistory.org/Gutians/.

"Gutians." http://www.realhistoryww.com/world_history/ancient/Misc/Sumer/Gutians.htm.

"GUTIANS - Encyclopedia Iranica." 15 Dec. 2002, https://www.iranicaonline.org/articles/gutians.

"Cultures | Gutium - Ancient Mesopotamia." https://ancientmesopotamia.org/cultures/gutium.php.

"Gutian rule in Mesopotamia - Wikipedia." https://en.wikipedia.org/wiki/Gutian_rule_in_Mesopotamia.

"Kingdoms of Mesopotamia - Gutians / Gutium - The History Files." https://www.historyfiles.co.uk/KingListsMiddEast/MesopotamiaGutium.htm.

"Gutian people in Zagros mountains; pale in complexion and blonde." https://cof.quantumfuturegroup.org/events/5390.

"Gudea - The Gutians." http://realhistoryww.com/world_history/ancient/Sumer_Iraq_3.htm.

"Guti | people | Britannica." https://www.britannica.com/topic/Guti.

Chapter 6

"Ur-Nammu - World History Encyclopedia." 16 Jun. 2014, https://www.worldhistory.org/Ur-Nammu/.

"Ur-Nammu - Wikipedia." https://en.wikipedia.org/wiki/Ur-Nammu.

"The Code of Ur-Nammu: The Oldest Law in the World?." 04 May. 2022, https://www.historicmysteries.com/code-of-ur-nammu/.

"Ur-Nammu | king of Ur | Britannica." https://www.britannica.com/biography/Ur-Nammu.

"Code of Ur-Nammu - World History Encyclopedia." 26 Oct. 2021, https://www.worldhistory.org/Code_of_Ur-Nammu/.

"The Legacy of Ur-Nammu - History of Kurdistan." 09 Oct. 2016, http://historyofkurd.com/english/2016/10/09/the-legacy-of-ur-nammu/.

"Sumerian People | Ur-Nammu - Ancient Mesopotamia."

https://ancientmesopotamia.org/people/ur-nammu.php.

"The Code of Ur-Nammu: When Ancient Sumerians Laid Down the Law." 15 Sept. 2021, https://www.ancient-origins.net/artifacts-ancient-writings/code-ur-nammu-sumerians-009333.

"Utu-khegal | king of Uruk | Britannica." https://www.britannica.com/biography/Utu-khegal.

"Utu-hengal - Wikipedia." https://en.wikipedia.org/wiki/Utu-hengal.

"The Victory of Utu-hegal (Poem of Utu-ḫeĝal)." https://www.mesopotamiangods.com/poem-of-utu-%E1%B8%ABegal/.

"Vase of Utu-Hegal of Uruk - World History Encyclopedia." 28 Feb. 2018, https://www.worldhistory.org/image/8195/vase-of-utu-hegal-of-uruk/.

"Shulgi of Ur - World History Encyclopedia." 17 Jun. 2014, https://www.worldhistory.org/Shulgi_of_Ur/.

"Shulgi | king of Ur | Britannica." https://www.britannica.com/biography/Shulgi.

"Shulgi of Ur Timeline - World History Encyclopedia." https://www.worldhistory.org/timeline/Shulgi_of_Ur/.

"People | Shulgi." https://ancientmesopotamia.org/people/shulgi.

"The Mighty Deeds of King Shulgi of Ur, Master of Mesopotamian Monarchs." 11 Mar. 2019, https://www.ancient-origins.net/history-famous-people/king-shulgi-0011602.

"Shulgi - Forgotten Realms Wiki." https://forgottenrealms.fandom.com/wiki/Shulgi.

"Shulgi: First Great Athlete? | Ancient Greek Sport." 27 Feb. 2017, https://sites.psu.edu/camskines442/2017/02/27/shulgi-first-great-athlete/.

"Shulgi Biography - Sumerian King | Pantheon." https://pantheon.world/profile/person/Shulgi/.

"Shulgi - Wikipedia." https://en.wikipedia.org/wiki/Shulgi.

"Amar-Sin - Wikipedia." https://en.wikipedia.org/wiki/Amar-Sin.

"Shu-Sin | king of Ur | Britannica." https://www.britannica.com/biography/Shu-Sin.

"The oldest love poem of the world | Arts & History." 30 Aug. 2015, https://artsnhistory.com/2015/08/30/sumerian/.

"Shu-Sin - Wikipedia." https://en.wikipedia.org/wiki/Shu-Sin.

"A Door Socket with King Shu-Sin Inscription (Illustration) - World History." 25 Sept. 2014, https://www.worldhistory.org/image/3083/a-door-socket-with-king-shu-sin-inscription/.

"DUMUZI - the Sumerian God of Farming (Mesopotamian mythology)."
https://www.godchecker.com/mesopotamian-mythology/DUMUZI/.
"Dumuzi-Abzu | Sumerian deity | Britannica."
https://www.britannica.com/topic/Dumuzi-Abzu.
"Dumuzi." http://www.mesopotamia.co.uk/gods/explore/dumuzi.html.
"Dumuzi / Tammuz the Shepherd, Son to Enlil & Ninsun, Slide-Show."
https://www.mesopotamiangods.com/dumuzi-the-shepherd-son-to-enki-ninsun/.

Chapter 7

"Amorite | people | Britannica." https://www.britannica.com/topic/Amorite.
"Cultures | Amorites - Ancient Mesopotamia."
https://ancientmesopotamia.org/cultures/amorites.php.
"What do we know about the Amorites? - CompellingTruth.org."
https://www.compellingtruth.org/Amorites.html.
"Amorites - Wikipedia." https://en.wikipedia.org/wiki/Amorites.
"Amorite - World History Encyclopedia." 28 Apr. 2011,
https://www.worldhistory.org/amorite/.
"Amorites, an introduction − Smarthistory." 06 Apr. 2022,
https://smarthistory.org/amorites-an-introduction/.
"Ebla | ancient city, Syria | Britannica." https://www.britannica.com/place/Ebla.
"Ebla - Wikipedia." https://en.wikipedia.org/wiki/Ebla.
"Ebla - New World Encyclopedia."
https://www.newworldencyclopedia.org/entry/Ebla.
"Ebla in the Third Millennium B.C. | Essay | The Metropolitan Museum of Art." https://www.metmuseum.org/toah/hd/ebla/hd_ebla.htm.
"First Kingdoms: The Forgotten Mesopotamian Kingdom of Ebla." 21 May. 2019,
https://www.ancient-origins.net/ancient-places-asia/ebla-0011940.
"Ebla: Its Impact on Bible Records - Institute for Creation Research."
https://www.icr.org/article/ebla-its-impact-bible-records/.
"Cultures | Ebla." https://ancientmesopotamia.org/cultures/ebla.php.
"Shulgi | king of Ur | Britannica." https://www.britannica.com/biography/Shulgi.
"Shulgi of Ur Timeline - World History Encyclopedia."
https://www.worldhistory.org/timeline/Shulgi_of_Ur/.
"The Mighty Deeds of King Shulgi of Ur, Master of Mesopotamian Monarchs." 11 Mar. 2019,
https://www.ancient-origins.net/history-famous-people/king-shulgi-0011602.

"SHULGI - mesopotamia.en-academic.com." https://mesopotamia.en-academic.com/314/SHULGI.

"Shulgi - Wikipedia." https://en.wikipedia.org/wiki/Shulgi.

"Ibbi-Sin | king of Ur | Britannica." https://www.britannica.com/biography/Ibbi-Sin.

"Ibbi-Sin - Wikipedia." https://en.wikipedia.org/wiki/Ibbi-Sin.

"Ibbi-Sin Biography | Pantheon." https://pantheon.world/profile/person/Ibbi-Sin/.

"IBBI-SIN." https://mesopotamia.en-academic.com/182/IBBI-SIN.

"Martu - Wikipedia." https://en.wikipedia.org/wiki/Martu.

"Amurru (god) - Wikipedia." https://en.wikipedia.org/wiki/Amurru_(god).

"Amurru | ancient district, Egypt | Britannica." https://www.britannica.com/place/Amurru.

"Amarru: the home of the Northern Semites." 31 Dec. 2014, https://archive.org/details/amarruhomeofnort00clay.

"Ur - Wikipedia." https://en.wikipedia.org/wiki/Ur.

"Ur - World History Encyclopedia." 28 Apr. 2011, https://www.worldhistory.org/ur/.

"Ur | City, History, Ziggurat, Sumer, Mesopotamia, & Facts." https://www.britannica.com/place/Ur.

"The Ancient City of Ur - HeritageDaily - Archaeology News." 05 Oct. 2020, https://www.heritagedaily.com/2020/10/the-ancient-city-of-ur/135753.

"Ur | Ur Region Archaeology Project." https://www.urarchaeology.org/ur/.

"Ancient World History: City of Ur." https://earlyworldhistory.blogspot.com/2012/01/city-of-ur.html.

"Ur, Sumeria. - Ancient-Wisdom." http://www.ancient-wisdom.com/iraqur.htm.

"Qatna, Syria - World Archaeology." 07 Jan. 2006, https://www.world-archaeology.com/features/qatna-syria/.

"The Kingdom of Qatna - HeritageDaily - Archaeology News." 29 May. 2020, https://www.heritagedaily.com/2020/05/the-kingdom-of-qatna/129581.

"Elam - World History Encyclopedia." 27 Aug. 2020, https://www.worldhistory.org/elam/.

"Elam | History, Definition, & Meaning | Britannica." https://www.britannica.com/place/Elam.

"Elam - Wikipedia." https://en.wikipedia.org/wiki/Elam.

"The Elamites - The Early History of Elam and Its People (Part 1)." 26 Aug. 2020, https://www.worldhistory.org/video/2088/the-elamites----the-early-history-of-elam-and-its/.

"Ancient World History: Medes, Persians, and Elamites." https://earlyworldhistory.blogspot.com/2012/03/medes-persians-and-elamites.html.

"Elamite Empire: Art & Culture | Study.com." https://study.com/academy/lesson/elamite-empire-art-culture.html.

"Publications - Matt Konfirst - Google Search." https://sites.google.com/site/mattkonfirst/publications.

"Did Climate Change Bring Sumerian Civilization to an End?." 05 Dec. 2012, https://www.biblicalarchaeology.org/daily/biblical-sites-places/biblical-archaeology-places/did-climate-change-bring-sumerian-civilization-to-an-end/.

"Acid rock drainage and climate change - ScienceDirect." 01 Feb. 2009, https://www.sciencedirect.com/science/article/pii/S0375674208000861.

"Climate Shift May Have Silenced Ancient Civilization - HuffPost." 04 Dec. 2012, https://www.huffpost.com/entry/sumerian-language-drought-climate-change_n_2238058.

"Kindattu - Wikipedia." https://en.wikipedia.org/wiki/Kindattu.

"History of Mesopotamia - Ur III in decline Britannica."https://www.britannica.com/place/Mesopotamia-historical-region-Asia/Ur-III-in-decline.

"People | Ibbi-Sin - Ancient Mesopotamia." https://ancientmesopotamia.org/people/ibbi-sin.php.

Chapter 8

"Sumerian Language - Mesopotamia." https://guides.lib.uw.edu/c.php?g=341420&p=2298733.

"The Sumerian King List and the Early History of Mesopotamia." https://www.academia.edu/10052536/The_Sumerian_King_List_and_the_Early_History_of_Mesopotamia.

"Sumerian - Oxford Reference. The Sumerian King List - Livius." https://www.livius.org/sources/content/anet/266-the-sumerian-king-list/.

"The Sumerian King List." https://rebirthoftheword.com/the-sumerian-king-list/.

"The Sumerian King list - Earth-history." 14 May. 2022, https://earth-history.com/sumer/the-sumerian-king-list.

https://www.oxfordreference.com/view/10.1093/oi/authority.20110803100541919.

"Sumerian King List - Wikipedia." https://en.wikipedia.org/wiki/Sumerian_King_List.

"The Antediluvian Patriarchs and the Sumerian King List." 01 Dec. 1998, https://answersingenesis.org/bible-history/the-antediluvian-patriarchs-and-the-sumerian-king-list/.

"15 facts about the Sumerian King List: When gods ruled Earth." 22 May. 2022, https://www.ancient-code.com/15-facts-about-the-sumerian-king-list-when-gods-ruled-earth/.

"Was Alulim, First King of Sumer and Eridu Biblical Adam?." 14 Mar. 2019, https://www.ancientpages.com/2019/03/14/was-alulim-first-king-of-sumer-and-eridu-biblical-adam/.

"Alulim - Wikipedia." https://ro.wikipedia.org/wiki/Alulim.

"Hebrew Codec." https://yhvh.org/.

"Who Was the First King in the World? - WorldAtlas." 11 Mar. 2020, https://www.worldatlas.com/who-was-the-first-king-in-the-world.html.

"Before the Great Deluge, Eighth Antediluvian Kings Ruled for 241,200 Years - Ancient Code." 20 Apr. 2022, https://www.ancient-code.com/before-the-great-deluge-eighth-antediluvian-kings-ruled-for-241200-years/.

"Mesopotamia - THE WORLD ALOHA." https://www.theworldaloha.com/world/mesopotamia.

"The Early Dynastic Period in Ancient Mesopotamia." 14 Oct. 2019, https://brewminate.com/the-early-dynastic-period-in-ancient-mesopotamia/.

"Mesh-ki-ang-gasher Biography - Sumerian ruler priest of Inanna." https://pantheon.world/profile/person/Mesh-ki-ang-gasher.

"Meshkiangasher - Wikipedia." https://en.wikipedia.org/wiki/Meshkiangasher.

"Enmerkar | Mesopotamian hero | Britannica." https://www.britannica.com/biography/Enmerkar.

"Enmerkar - Wikipedia." https://en.wikipedia.org/wiki/Enmerkar.

"Enmerkar: Legendary Sumerian Founder and Ruler of Uruk and Grandson of God Utu." 23 Mar. 2020, https://www.ancientpages.com/2020/03/23/enmerkar-legendary-sumerian-founder-and-ruler-of-uruk-and-grandson-of-god-utu/.

"Enmerkar and the Lord of Aratta | Mesopotamian Gods & Kings." http://www.mesopotamiangods.com/enmerkar-and-the-lord-of-aratta/.

"Enmerkar and the Lord of Aratta - TheAlmightyGuru." 28 Apr. 2020, http://www.thealmightyguru.com/Wiki/index.php?title=Enmerkar_and_the_Lord_of_Aratta.

"Enmerkar - Bible History." https://bible-history.com/links/enmerkar-2556.

"Gilgamesh | Epic, Summary, & Facts | Britannica." https://www.britannica.com/topic/Gilgamesh.

"Gilgamesh - World History Encyclopedia." 29 Mar. 2018, https://www.worldhistory.org/gilgamesh/.

"Gilgamesh - Wikipedia." https://en.wikipedia.org/wiki/Gilgamesh.

"The Myth of Gilgamesh, Hero King of Mesopotamia - ThoughtCo." 20 Aug. 2019, https://www.thoughtco.com/gilgamesh-4766597.

"Epic of Gilgamesh - Ancient Texts." http://www.ancienttexts.org/library/mesopotamian/gilgamesh/.

"The Epic of Gilgamesh | World Epics - Columbia University." https://edblogs.columbia.edu/worldepics/project/gilgamesh/.

"What the Bible says about Gilgamesh." https://www.bibletools.org/index.cfm/fuseaction/Topical.show/RTD/CGG/ID/775/Gilgamesh.htm.

"BBC NEWS | Science/Nature | Gilgamesh tomb believed found." 29 Apr. 2003, http://news.bbc.co.uk/2/hi/science/nature/2982891.stm.

"Gilgamesh | Essay | The Metropolitan Museum of Art | Heilbrunn Timeline." https://www.metmuseum.org/toah/hd/gilg/hd_gilg.htm.

"Queen Kubaba: The Tavern Keeper Who Became the First Female Ruler in History." 23 Feb. 2021, https://www.discovermagazine.com/planet-earth/queen-kubaba-the-tavern-keeper-who-became-the-first-female-ruler-in-history.

"Brooklyn Museum: Kubaba." https://www.brooklynmuseum.org/eascfa/dinner_party/heritage_floor/kubaba.

"All Hail the Divine Ruler, Queen of Kish - ThoughtCo." 30 May. 2019, https://www.thoughtco.com/kubaba-a-queen-among-kings-121164.

"Kubaba | Anatolian deity | Britannica." https://www.britannica.com/topic/Kubaba.

"Queen Kubaba: The Tavern Keeper Who Became the First Female Ruler in History." 08 Mar. 2022, https://headtopics.com/us/queen-kubaba-the-tavern-keeper-who-became-the-first-female-ruler-in-history-24609982.

"Ku-Bau: The First Woman Ruler – Semiramis-Speaks.com." 10 Dec. 2011, http://semiramis-speaks.com/ku-bau-the-first-woman-ruler/.

"Kubaba — Google Arts & Culture." https://artsandculture.google.com/entity/m04dk_d.
"Kubaba (goddess) - Wikipedia." https://en.wikipedia.org/wiki/Kubaba_(goddess).
"Kubaba - Wikipedia." https://en.wikipedia.org/wiki/Kubaba.
"Eannatum | king of Lagash | Britannica." https://www.britannica.com/biography/Eannatum.
"People | Eannatum." https://ancientmesopotamia.org/people/eannatum.
"Eannatum - Wikipedia." https://en.wikipedia.org/wiki/Eannatum.
"King Destroys Those on his Hit List, One by One – Eannatum: The First Conqueror." 06 Mar. 2017, https://www.ancient-origins.net/history/king-destroys-those-his-hit-list-one-one-eannatum-first-conqueror-part-i-007666.
"Eannatum The Conqueror | Classical Wisdom Weekly." 28 May. 2013, https://classicalwisdom.com/politics/enemies/eannatum-the-conqueror/.
"Sumer (Eannatum) - Civilization V Customisation Wiki." 03 Jun. 2016, https://civilization-v-customisation.fandom.com/wiki/Sumer_(Eannatum).
"Eannatum the Great." https://sumerianshakespeare.com/37601.html.
"Eannatum - Wikiquote." https://en.wikiquote.org/wiki/Eannatum.
"Eannatum - Bible History." https://bible-history.com/links/eannatum-2516.
"Stele of the Vultures - Ancient World Magazine." 14 Aug. 2017, https://www.ancientworldmagazine.com/articles/stele-vultures/.
"Stele of the Vultures - Wikipedia." https://en.wikipedia.org/wiki/Stele_of_the_Vultures.
"Stele of the Vultures | Ancient monument, Sumer | Britannica." https://www.britannica.com/place/Stele-of-the-Vultures.
"Sumerian Stele of the Vultures: Oldest Known Historical Records Carved on Limestone." 01 Sept. 2016, https://www.ancientpages.com/2016/09/01/sumerian-stele-of-the-vultures-oldest-known-historical-records-carved-on-limestone/.
"Sumerian war chariots deconstructed." 12 Jan. 2012, http://sumerianshakespeare.com/84201.html.
"The Wheels of War: Evolution of the Chariot - History." https://www.historyonthenet.com/the-wheels-of-war-evolution-of-the-chariot.
"Chariot - War Mesopotamian Civilization." https://sites.google.com/site/mesopotamianwarfare/weapon-innovations-in-mesopotamia/sumer/chariot.
"A model of a Sumerian War Chariot." 14 Mar. 2021, http://sumerianshakespeare.com/1273801.html.

"The Wheels of War: Evolution of the Chariot - History."
https://www.historyonthenet.com/the-wheels-of-war-evolution-of-the-chariot.

"SUMERIAN TROOPS | Weapons and Warfare." 22 May. 2020,
https://weaponsandwarfare.com/2020/05/22/sumerian-troops/.

"Warfare in Sumer - Wikipedia."
https://en.wikipedia.org/wiki/Warfare_in_Sumer.

"The Sumerian Military: Professionals of Weaponry and Warfare." 17 Jun. 2016,
https://www.ancient-origins.net/history/sumerian-military-professionals-weaponry-and-warfare-006115.

"SUMERIAN TROOPS | Weapons and Warfare." 22 May. 2020,
https://weaponsandwarfare.com/2020/05/22/sumerian-troops/.

"Ancient Mesopotamian Warfare | Akkad and Sumer."
https://sites.psu.edu/ancientmesopotamianwarfare/.

Chapter 9

"9 Ancient Sumerian Inventions That Changed the World - HISTORY." 01 Aug. 2019,
https://www.history.com/news/sumerians-inventions-mesopotamia.

"Top 10 Sumerian Inventions and Discoveries - Ancient History Lists." 20 Nov. 2019,
https://www.ancienthistorylists.com/mesopotamia-history/top-10-sumerian-inventions-followed-many-civilizations/.

"Razor - Wikipedia." https://en.wikipedia.org/wiki/Razor.

"Who Were the Ancient Sumerians? | Discover Magazine." 10 Nov. 2020,
https://www.discovermagazine.com/planet-earth/who-were-the-ancient-sumerians-and-what-are-they-known-for.

"History of the Sumerians: The 'First' of the Mesopotamians." 06 Dec. 2019,
https://www.realmofhistory.com/2019/12/06/sumerians-first-mesopotamian/.

"What are some of the other things the Sumerians invented?"
https://ask.mrdonn.org/meso/43.html.

"The History of Wet Shaving - OriginalShaveCompany.com." 22 Mar. 2016,
https://originalshavecompany.com/the-history-of-wet-shaving/.

Chapter 10

"Sumerian Myths - Grand Valley State University."
https://faculty.gvsu.edu/websterm/SumerianMyth.htm.

"Sumerian creation myth - Wikipedia." https://en.wikipedia.org/wiki/Sumerian_creation_myth.

"Sumerian Mythology Index - sacred-texts.com." https://www.sacred-texts.com/ane/sum/.

"Death and Afterlife in Sumerian Beliefs - Ancient Pages." 12 May. 2017, https://www.ancientpages.com/2017/05/12/death-and-afterlife-in-sumerian-beliefs/.

"What Is Sumerian Mythology? | Only Slightly Biased." https://onlyslightlybiased.com/what-is-sumerian-mythology.

"Sumerian creation myth | Religion Wiki | Fandom." https://religion.fandom.com/wiki/Sumerian_creation_myth.

"Mesopotamian Creation Myths | Essay | The Metropolitan Museum of Art." https://www.metmuseum.org/toah/hd/epic/hd_epic.htm.

"Eridu Genesis - World History Encyclopedia." 07 May. 2020, https://www.worldhistory.org/Eridu_Genesis/.

"CREATION MYTHS – AKKADIAN – BABYLONIAN – SUMERIAN - lc5827wdp." 05 Apr. 2013, https://lc5827wdp.wordpress.com/2013/04/05/creation-myths-akkadian-babylonian-sumerian-april-2013/.

"Inanna: A Sneak Peek into the Rebel Ancient Sumerian Goddess." https://www.timelessmyths.com/mythology/inanna/.

"Sumerian Gods & Goddesses - Transcendence Works!" https://www.transcendenceworks.com/blog/sumerian-gods-goddesses/.

""Sumerian Mythology and the Controversy That Surrounds the Anunnaki." 11 Oct. 2020 https://rebirthoftheword.com/sumerian-mythology-and-the-controversy-that-surrounds-the-anunnaki/.

"The origins of human beings according to ancient Sumerian texts." 26 Feb. 2019 https://www.ancient-origins.net/news-human-origins-folklore/origins-human-beings-according-ancient-sumerian-texts-0065

"Ancient Mesopotamian Gods and Goddesses - An/Anu (god)." http://oracc.museum.upenn.edu/amgg/listofdeities/an/.

"Anu | Mesopotamian god | Britannica." https://www.britannica.com/topic/Anu.

"Ninhursag - Wikipedia." https://en.wikipedia.org/wiki/Ninhursag.

"Ninhursag - World History Encyclopedia." 26 Jan. 2017, https://www.worldhistory.org/Ninhursag/.

"Ninhursag | Mesopotamian deity | Britannica."
https://www.britannica.com/topic/Ninhursag.

"Enlil - World History Encyclopedia." 24 Jan. 2017,
https://www.worldhistory.org/Enlil/.

"Enlil - Wikipedia." https://en.wikipedia.org/wiki/Enlil.

"Enlil - Mesopotamian God of Wind and Breath | Mythology.net." 31 Oct. 2016,
https://mythology.net/others/gods/enlil/.

"Ancient Mesopotamian Gods and Goddesses - Enlil/Ellil (god)."
http://oracc.museum.upenn.edu/amgg/listofdeities/enlil/index.html.

"Enki - Wikipedia." https://en.wikipedia.org/wiki/Enki.

"Enki - World History Encyclopedia." 09 Jan. 2017,
https://www.worldhistory.org/Enki/.

"Who was the Sumerian God Enki? | Gaia." 29 Nov. 2019,
https://www.gaia.com/article/who-was-sumerian-god-enki.

"Enki & Enlil - Annunaki." https://www.annunaki.org/enki-enlil/.

"Enki and the world order: translation - University of Oxford."
https://etcsl.orinst.ox.ac.uk/section1/tr113.htm.

"Enki and the World Order (Version 1) - Mesopotamian Gods."
http://www.mesopotamiangods.com/enki-the-world-order-version-1/.

"Enki and the World Order - Earth-history." https://earth-history.com/Sumer/enki-worldorder.htm.

"Myth, Ritual, and Order in Enki and the World Order."
https://www.academia.edu/14523257/Myth_Ritual_and_Order_in_Enki_and_the_World_Order

Part 2

"Akkadian Military." *Weapons and Warfare: History and Hardware of Warfare.* 2019. https://weaponsandwarfare.com/2019/09/21/akkadian-military

Bertman, Stephen. *Handbook to Life in Ancient Mesopotamia.* Oxford: Oxford University Press, 2005.

Botsforth, George W., ed. "The Reign of Sargon." *A Source-Book of Ancient History.* New
York: Macmillan, 1912, 27-28.
http://www.thelatinlibrary.com/imperialism/readings/sargontablet.html

Carter, R., and Graham Philip, eds. *Beyond the Ubaid: Transformation and Integration in the Late Prehistoric Societies of the Middle East.* Chicago: The Oriental Institute, University of Chicago, 2010.

Chavalas, M. W., ed. *The Ancient Near East: Historical Sources in Translation.* Malden, MA: Blackwell Publishing, 2006.

Clarke, Joanne, Nick Brooks, Edward B. Banning, Miryam Bar-Matthews, Stuart Campbell, Lee Clare, Mauro Cremaschig, et al. "Climatic Changes and Social Transformations in the Near East and North Africa during the 'Long' Fourth Millennium BC: A Comparative Study of Environmental and Archaeological Evidence." *Quaternary Science Reviews* 136, (2016), 96-121, https://doi.org/10.1016/j.quascirev.2015.10.003

Cooper, Jerrold S. "Sumerian and Akkadian in Sumer and Akkad." *Orientalia* 42 (1973):

239-46. http://www.jstor.org/stable/43079390

Cooper, Jerrold S., and Wolfgang Heimpel. "The Sumerian Sargon Legend." *Journal of the American Oriental Society* 103, no. 1 (1983): 67-82. https://doi.org/10.2307/601860

Cserkits, Michael. "The Concept of War in Ancient Mesopotamia: Reshaping Carl von Clausewitz's Trinity." *Expeditions with MCUP,* United States Marine Corps University Press, 2022. https://doi.org/10.36304/ExpwMCUP.2022.01

Dalley, Stephanie. *Myths from Mesopotamia Creation, the Flood, Gilgamesh, and Others.*

Oxford: Oxford University Press, 2008.

Delougaz, P. "A Short Investigation of the Temple at Al-'Ubaid." *Iraq* 5 (1938): 1-11.

https://doi.org/10.2307/4241617

Edens, Christopher. "Dynamics of Trade in the Ancient Mesopotamian 'World System.'" *American Anthropologist* 94, no. 1 (1992): 118-39. http://www.jstor.org/stable/680040.

Editors. "The World's Oldest Writing." *Archaeology,* May/June 2016.

https://www.archaeology.org/issues/213-features/4326-cuneiform-the-world-s-oldest-writing

Enthralling History. *Ancient Mesopotamia: An Enthralling Overview of Mesopotamian History,*

Starting from Eridu through the Sumerians, Akkadian Empire, Assyrians, Hittites, and

Persians to Alexander the Great. Columbia: Joelan AB, 2022.

Eppihimer, Melissa. "Assembling King and State: The Statues of Manishtushu and the Consolidation of Akkadian Kingship." *American Journal of Archaeology* 114, no. 3 (2010): 365-80. http://www.jstor.org/stable/25684286

Eppihimer, Melissa. *Exemplars of Kingship: Art, Tradition, and the Legacy of the Akkadians.* New York: Oxford University Press, 2019.

Foster, Benjamin R. *The Age of Agade: Inventing Empire in Ancient Mesopotamia.* New
York: Routledge, 2016.

Foster, Benjamin R. *Before the Muses: An Anthology of Akkadian Literature.* Bethesda:
CDL Press, 2018.

"Gilgamesh and Aga: Translation." *The Electronic Text Corpus of Sumerian Literature*, Oxford: Faculty of Oriental Studies, University of Oxford, 2000. https://etcsl.orinst.ox.ac.uk/section1/tr1811.htm

Grayson, A. K. "The Empire of Sargon of Akkad." *Archiv Für Orientforschung* 25 (1974): 56-64. http://www.jstor.org/stable/41636304

Gurney, O. R. "The Sultantepe Tablets: VII. The Myth of Nergal and Ereshkigal." *Anatolian Studies* 10 (1960): 105-31. https://doi.org/10.2307/3642431

Hritz, Carrie, Jennifer Pournelle, Jennifer Smith, and سميث جنيفر. "Revisiting the Sealands: Report of Preliminary Ground Reconnaissance in the Hammar District, Dhi Qar and Basra Governorates, Iraq." *Iraq* 74 (2012): 37-49. http://www.jstor.org/stable/23349778

Jacobsen, Thorkild. "The Assumed Conflict between Sumerians and Semites in Early Mesopotamian History." *Journal of the American Oriental Society* 59, no. 4 (1939): 485-95. https://doi.org/10.2307/594482

Kantor, Helene J. "Landscape in Akkadian Art." *Journal of Near Eastern Studies* 25, no. 3 (1966): 145-52. http://www.jstor.org/stable/543262

King, Leonard W. *A History of Sumer and Akkad: An Account of the Early Races of Babylonia from Prehistoric Times to the Foundation of the Babylonian Monarchy.* New York: Amulet Press, 2015 (first published 1910)

Lawrence, D., A. Palmisano, and M. W. de Gruchy. "Collapse and Continuity: A Multi-proxy Reconstruction of Settlement Organization and Population Trajectories in the Northern Fertile Crescent during the 4.2kya Rapid Climate Change Event. *PLoS One.* 16 (1) (2021). https://pubmed.ncbi.nlm.nih.gov/33428648

Lenzi, Alan. *An Introduction to Akkadian Literature.* University Park: The Pennsylvania State University Press, 2019.

Lenzi, Alan, ed. *Reading Akkadian Prayers and Hymns: An Introduction.* Atlanta: Society of Biblical Literature, 2011.

Levin, Yigal. "Nimrod the Mighty, King of Kish, King of Sumer and Akkad." *Vetus Testamentum* 52, no. 3 (2002): 350-66. http://www.jstor.org/stable/1585058

Lewis, Brian. *The Sargon Legend: A Study of the Akkadian Text and the Tale of the Hero Who was Exposed at Birth.* Philadelphia: American Schools of Oriental Research, 1980.

Lloyd, Seton, Fuad Safar, and Robert J. Braidwood. "Tell Hassuna Excavations by the Iraq Government Directorate General of Antiquities in 1943 and 1944." *Journal of Near Eastern Studies* 4, no. 4 (1945): 255-89. http://www.jstor.org/stable/542914

Luckenbill, D. D. "Akkadian Origins." *The American Journal of Semitic Languages and Literatures* 40, no. 1 (1923): 1-13. http://www.jstor.org/stable/528139

Mark, Joshua J. "The Legend of Cutha." *World History Encyclopedia.* 2021. https://www.worldhistory.org/article/1869/the-legend-of-cutha/.

Moore, A. M. T. "Pottery Kiln Sites at al' Ubaid and Eridu." *Iraq* 64 (2002): 69-77. https://doi.org/10.2307/4200519

Moorey, P. R. S. "The 'Plano-Convex Building' at Kish and Early Mesopotamian Palaces." *Iraq* 26, no. 2 (1964): 83-98. https://doi.org/10.2307/4199767

Nadali, Davide. *Representations of Battering Rams and Siege Towers in Early Bronze Age Glyptic Art.* Universitat Autonoma de Barcelona:39-52. https://ddd.uab.cat/pub/historiae/historiae_a2009n6/historiae_a2009n6p39.pdf

Nemet-Nejat, Karen Rhea. *Daily Life in Ancient Mesopotamia.* Westport, Connecticut: Greenwood Press, 1998.

Nigro, Lorenzo. "The Two Steles of Sargon: Iconology and Visual Propaganda at the Beginning of Royal Akkadian Relief." *Iraq* 60 (1998): 85-102. https://doi.org/10.2307/4200454

Nowicki, Stefan. "Sargon of Akkade and His God: Comments on the Worship of the God of the Father among the Ancient Semites." *Acta Orientalia Academiae Scientiarum Hungaricae* 69, no. 1 (2016): 63-82. http://www.jstor.org/stable/43957458

Petrovich, Douglas. "Identifying Nimrod of Genesis 10 with Sargon of Akkad by Exegetical and Archaeological Means." *Journal of the Evangelical Theological Society* 56, no. 2 (2013): 73-305. https://www.etsjets.org/files/JETS-PDFs/56/56-2/JETS_56-2_273-305_Petrovich.pdf

Powell, Marvin A. "The Sin of Lugalzagesi." *Wiener Zeitschrift Für Die Kunde Des Morgenlandes* 86 (1996): 307-14. http://www.jstor.org/stable/23864744

Rubio, Gonzalo. "On the Alleged 'Pre-Sumerian Substratum.'" *Journal of Cuneiform Studies* 51 (1999): 1-16. https://doi.org/10.2307/1359726

Sackrider, Scott. "The History of Astronomy in Ancient Mesopotamia." *The NEKAAL Observer* 234. https://nekaal.org/observer/ar/ObserverArticle234.pdf

Speiser, E. A. "Some Factors in the Collapse of Akkad." *Journal of the American Oriental Society* 72, no. 3 (1952): 97-101. https://doi.org/10.2307/594938

Stol, Marten. "Women in Mesopotamia." *Journal of the Economic and Social History of the Orient* 38, no. 2 (1995): 123-44. http://www.jstor.org/stable/3632512

Sumerian King List. Translated by Jean-Vincent Scheil, Stephen Langdon, and Thorkild Jacobsen. Livius. https://www.livius.org/sources/content/anet/266-the-sumerian-king-list/#Translation

Teall, Emily K. "Medicine and Doctoring in Ancient Mesopotamia." *Grand Valley Journal of History* 3:1 (2014), Article 2. https://scholarworks.gvsu.edu/gvjh/vol3/iss1/2

"The Akkadians." *Weapons and Warfare: History and Hardware of Warfare.* 2019. https://weaponsandwarfare.com/2019/07/29/the-akkadians

The Code of Hammurabi. Translated by L.W. King. The Avalon Project: Documents in Law, History, and Diplomacy. Yale Law School: Lillian Goldman Law Library. https://avalon.law.yale.edu/ancient/hamframe.asp

The Curse of Agade. Translated by Jerrold S. Cooper. Baltimore: Johns Hopkins University Press, 1983.

The Epic of Atrahasis. Translated by B. R. Foster. Livius. https://www.livius.org/sources/content/anet/104-106-the-epic-of-atrahasis

The Epic of Gilgamesh. Academy of Ancient Texts. https://www.ancienttexts.org/library/mesopotamian/gilgamesh

"The Legend of Sargon of Akkadê." *Ancient History Sourcebook*. New York: Fordham University, 1999. https://sourcebooks.fordham.edu/ancient/2300sargon1.asp

"The Sargon Geography." Translated by Wayne Horowitz. *Mesopotamian Cosmic Geography*. Winona Lake: Eisenbrauns 1998 http://www.aakkl.helsinki.fi/melammu/database/gen_html/a0000526.php

The Tummal Chronicle. Livius. https://www.livius.org/sources/content/mesopotamian-chronicles-content/cm-7-tummal-chronicle

Van Buren, E. Douglas. "Discoveries at Eridu." *Orientalia* 18, no. 1 (1949): 123-24. http://www.jstor.org/stable/43072618

Van De Mieroop, Marc. *A History of the Ancient Near East ca. 3000 - 323 BC*. Hoboken: Blackwell Publishing, 2006.

Wall-Romana, Christophe. "An Areal Location of Agade." *Journal of Near Eastern Studies* 49, no. 3 (1990): 205-45. http://www.jstor.org/stable/546244

Weidner Chronicle (ABC 19). Livius, 2020. https://www.livius.org/sources/content/mesopotamian-chronicles-content/abc-19-weidner-chronicle

Weiss, Harvey. *Megadrought and Collapse*. New York: Oxford University Press, 2017.

Weiss, H., M. A. Courty, W. Wetterstrom, F. Guichard, L. Senior, R. Meadow, and A. Curnow. "The Genesis and Collapse of Third Millennium North Mesopotamian Civilization." *Science* 261, no. 5124 (1993): 995-1004. http://www.jstor.org/stable/2881847

West, M. L. "Akkadian Poetry: Metre and Performance." *Iraq* 59 (1997): 175-87. https://doi.org/10.2307/4200442

Westenholz, Joan Goodnick. "Heroes of Akkad." *Journal of the American Oriental Society* 103, no. 1 (1983): 327-36. https://doi.org/10.2307/601890

Westenholz, Joan Goodnick. *Legends of the Kings of Akkade: The Texts*. Winona Lake: Eisenbrauns, 1997.

Wilford, John Noble. "Ancient Clay Horse is Found in Syria." *The New York Times*, January 3, 1993. https://www.nytimes.com/1993/01/03/world/ancient-clay-horse-is-found-in-syria.html

Wilkinson, T. J., B. H. Monahan, and D. J. Tucker. "Khanijdal East: A Small Ubaid Site in Northern Iraq." *Iraq* 58 (1996): 17-50. https://doi.org/10.2307/4200417

Woolley, C. Leonard. "Excavations at Ur." *Journal of the Royal Society of Arts* 82, no. 4227 (1933): 46-59. http://www.jstor.org/stable/41360003

Ziskind, Jonathan R. "The Sumerian Problem." *The History Teacher* 5, no. 2 (1972): 34-41. https://doi.org/10.2307/491500

Part 3

Assyrian King List. Livius. https://www.livius.org/sources/content/anet/564-566-the-assyrian-king-list/

Alstola, Tero. "Judean Merchants in Babylonia and Their Participation in Long-Distance Trade." *Die Welt Des Orients* 47, no. 1 (2017): 25–51. http://www.jstor.org/stable/26384887.

Beaulieu, Paul-Alain. *A History of Babylon, 2200 BC-AD 75*. Pondicherry: Wiley, 2018.

Beaulieu, Paul-Alain. *Reign of Nabonidus, King of Babylon (556-539 BC)*. New Haven: Yale University Press, 1989.

Bertman, Stephen. *Handbook to Life in Ancient Mesopotamia*. Oxford: Oxford University Press, 2005.

Boivin, Odette. *The First Dynasty of the Sealand in Mesopotamia*. Volume 20: Studies in Ancient Near Eastern Records. Boston: De Gruyter, 2018.

Broad, William J. "It Swallowed a Civilization." *New York Times*, October 21, 2003. https://www.nytimes.com/2003/10/21/science/it-swallowed-a-civilization.html

Carter, R., and Graham Philip, eds. *Beyond the Ubaid: Transformation and Integration in the Late Prehistoric Societies of the Middle East*. Chicago: The Oriental Institute, University of Chicago, 2010.

Chavalas, M. W., ed. *The Ancient Near East: Historical Sources in Translation*. Malden, MA: Blackwell Publishing, 2006.

Chronicle of Early Kings (ABC 20). Livius.
https://www.livius.org/sources/content/mesopotamian-chronicles-content/abc-20-chronicle-of-early-kings

Cserkits, Michael. "The Concept of War in Ancient Mesopotamia: Reshaping Carl von Clausewitz's Trinity." *Expeditions with MCUP,* United States Marine Corps University Press, 2022. https://doi.org/10.36304/ExpwMCUP.2022.01

Cuneiform Texts from Babylonian Tablets in the British Museum: Part XIII. Piccadilly: Longmans and Co., 1901.

Dalley, Stephanie. *Myths from Mesopotamia Creation, the Flood, Gilgamesh, and Others*. Oxford: Oxford University Press, 2008.

Da Riva, Rocío. "The Figure of Nabopolassar in Late Achaemenid and Hellenistic Historiographic Tradition: BM 34793 and CUA 90." *Journal of Near Eastern Studies* 76, no.1.
https://www.journals.uchicago.edu/doi/full/10.1086/690464

Deams, A. and K. Croucher. "Artificial Cranial Modification in Prehistoric Iran: Evidence from Crania and Figurines." *Iranica Antiqua* 42 (2007):1-21.

De Boer, Rients. "Beginnings of Old Babylonian Babylon: Sumu-Abum and Sumu-La-El." *Free University of Amsterdam*. American Schools of Oriental Research.
https://www.jstor.org/journal/jcunestud

De Graef, Katrien. "Dual Power in Susa: Chronicle of a Transitional Period from Ur III via Šimaški to the Sukkalmaḫs." *Bulletin of the School of Oriental and African Studies*, University of London 75, no. 3 (2012): 525-46. http://www.jstor.org/stable/41811207.

"Descent of the Goddess Ishtar into the Lower World." In *The Civilization of Babylonia and Assyria*, Morris Jastrow, Jr., 1915. https://www.sacred-texts.com/ane/ishtar.htm

Enthralling History. *Ancient Mesopotamia: An Enthralling Overview of Mesopotamian History,*

Starting from Eridu through the Sumerians, Akkadian Empire, Assyrians, Hittites, and Persians to Alexander the Great. Coppell, Texas: Joelan AB, 2022.

Enthralling History. *The Akkadian Empire: An Enthralling Overview of the Rise and Fall of the Akkadians.* Coppell, Texas: Joelan AB, 2022.

Finkel, Irving. "The Lament of Nabû-šuma-ukîn." In *Focus Mesopotamischer Geschichte, Wiege früher Gelehrtsamkeit, Mythos in der Moderne.* Saaerbrücken, 1999.

George, Andrew. "Ancient Descriptions: The Babylonian Topographical Texts." In *Babylon*, edited by I. L. Finkel and M. J. Seymour. New York: Oxford University Press, 2008, 161-165.

George, Andrew. "The Poem of Erra and Ishum: A Babylonian Poet's View of War." In *Warfare and Poetry in the Middle East,* edited by Hugh Kennedy, 39-71. London: I. B. Tauris, 2013.

George, Andrew. "The Tower of Babel: Archaeology, History and Cuneiform Texts." *Archiv für Orientforschung,* 51 (2005/2006): 75-95.
https://eprints.soas.ac.uk/3858/2/TowerOfBabel.AfO.pdf

Grayson, A. K. *Babylonian Historical-Literary Texts: Toronto Semitic Texts and Studies, 3.* Toronto: University of Toronto Press, 1975.

Herodotus. *Capture of Babylon.* Livius.
https://www.livius.org/articles/person/darius-the-great/sources/capture-of-babylon-herodotus

Hritz, Carrie, Jennifer Pournelle, Jennifer Smith, and سميث جنيفر. "Revisiting the Sealands: Report of Preliminary Ground Reconnaissance in the Hammar District, Dhi Qar and Basra Governorates, Iraq." *Iraq* 74 (2012): 37-49. http://www.jstor.org/stable/23349778.

Huber, Peter J. *Astronomical Dating of Babylon I and Ur III.* Cambridge: Harvard University, 1982.

Jacobsen, Thorkild. "The Assumed Conflict between Sumerians and Semites in Early Mesopotamian History." *Journal of the American Oriental Society* 59, no. 4 (1939): 485-95. https://doi.org/10.2307/594482.

Jastrow, Jr., Morris. "Did the Babylonian Temples Have Libraries?" *Journal of the American Oriental Society* 27 (1906): 147-182. https://www.jstor.org/stable/pdf/592857.pdf

Jones, Tom B. "By the Rivers of Babylon Sat We Down." *Agricultural History* 25, no. 1 (1951): 1-9. http://www.jstor.org/stable/3740293.

Kerrigan, Michael. *The Ancients in Their Own Words*. London: Amber Books, 2019.

King, Leonard W. *A History of Sumer and Akkad: An Account of the Early Races of Babylonia from Prehistoric Times to the Foundation of the Babylonian Monarchy*. New York: Amulet Press, 2015 (first published 1910).

Koppen, Frans van. "The Old to Middle Babylonian Transition: History and Chronology of the Mesopotamian Dark Age." *Ägypten Und Levante / Egypt and the Levant* 20 (2010): 453-63. http://www.jstor.org/stable/23789952

Lawrence, D., A. Palmisano, and M. W. de Gruchy. "Collapse and Continuity: A Multi-proxy Reconstruction of Settlement Organization and Population Trajectories in the Northern Fertile Crescent during the 4.2kya Rapid Climate Change Event." *PLoS One*. 16 (1) (2021). https://pubmed.ncbi.nlm.nih.gov/33428648

Leemans, W. F. "The Trade Relations of Babylonia and the Question of Relations with Egypt in the Old Babylonian Period." *Journal of the Economic and Social History of the Orient 3*, no. 1 (1960): 21-37. https://doi.org/10.2307/3596027

Levin, Yigal. "Nimrod the Mighty, King of Kish, King of Sumer and Akkad." *Vetus Testamentum* 52, no. 3 (2002): 350-66. http://www.jstor.org/stable/1585058.

Lambert, W. G. "Studies in Marduk." *Bulletin of the School of Oriental and African Studies, University of London* 47, no. 1 (1984): 1-9. http://www.jstor.org/stable/618314.

Mansfield, D.F. "Plimpton 322: A Study of Rectangles." *Foundations of Science* 26 (2021): 977-1005. https://doi.org/10.1007/s10699-021-09806-0

Mark, Joshua J. "Ashurnasirpal II." *World History Encyclopedia*. https://www.worldhistory.org/Ashurnasirpal_II

Mark, Joshua J. "The Marduk Prophecy." *World History Encyclopedia*. 2016. https://www.worldhistory.org/article/990/the-marduk-prophecy

Marriage of Martu. The Electronic Text Corpus of Sumerian Literature. Oxford: University of Oxford. https://etcsl.orinst.ox.ac.uk/section1/tr171.htm

Moore, A. M. T. "Pottery Kiln Sites at al' Ubaid and Eridu." *Iraq* 64 (2002): 69-77. https://doi.org/10.2307/4200519

Nemet-Nejat, Karen Rhea. *Daily Life in Ancient Mesopotamia.* Westport, Connecticut: Greenwood Press, 1998.

Prayer of Nabonidus (4Q242). Livius.
https://www.livius.org/sources/content/dss/4q242-prayer-of-nabonidus

Sackrider, Scott. "The History of Astronomy in Ancient Mesopotamia." *The NEKAAL Observer* 234. https://nekaal.org/observer/ar/ObserverArticle234.pdf

Stol, Marten. "Women in Mesopotamia." *Journal of the Economic and Social History of the Orient* 38, no. 2 (1995): 123-44.
http://www.jstor.org/stable/3632512

Sumerian King List. Translated by Jean-Vincent Scheil, Stephen Langdon, and Thorkild Jacobsen. Livius. https://www.livius.org/sources/content/anet/266-the-sumerian-king-list/#Translation

Teall, Emily K. "Medicine and Doctoring in Ancient Mesopotamia." *Grand Valley Journal of History* 3:1 (2014), Article 2.
https://scholarworks.gvsu.edu/gvjh/vol3/iss1/2

The Chronicle Concerning the Reign of Nabonidus (ABC 7). Livius, 2020.
https://www.livius.org/sources/content/mesopotamian-chronicles-content/abc-7-nabonidus-chronicle

The Chronicle Concerning Year Three of Neriglissar (ABC 6). Livius, 2006.
https://www.livius.org/sources/content/mesopotamian-chronicles-content/abc-6-neriglissar-chronicle

The Code of Hammurabi. Translated by L.W. King. The Avalon Project: Documents in Law, History, and Diplomacy. Yale Law School: Lillian Goldman Law Library. https://avalon.law.yale.edu/ancient/hamframe.asp

The Epic of Atrahasis. Translated by B. R. Foster. Livius.
https://www.livius.org/sources/content/anet/104-106-the-epic-of-atrahasis

The Tanakh: Full Text. Jewish Virtual Library: A Project of AICE. 1997.
https://www.jewishvirtuallibrary.org/the-tanakh-full-text

The Tummal Chronicle. Livius.
https://www.livius.org/sources/content/mesopotamian-chronicles-content/cm-7-tummal-chronicle

Van De Mieroop, Marc. *A History of the Ancient Near East ca. 3000 - 323 BC.* Hoboken: Blackwell Publishing, 2006.

Van De Mieroop, Marc. *King Hammurabi of Babylon: A Biography.* Hoboken: Blackwell Publishing, 2005.

Verse Account of Nabonidus. Translated by A. Leo Oppenheim. Livius.
https://www.livius.org/sources/content/anet/verse-account-of-nabonidus

Vlaardingerbroek, Menko. "The Founding of Nineveh and Babylon in Greek Historiography." *Iraq* 66 (2004): 233-41. https://doi.org/10.2307/4200577.

Weiershäuser, Frauke, and Jamie Novotny. *The Royal Inscriptions of Amēl-Marduk (561-560 BC), Neriglissar (559-556 BC), and Nabonidus (555-539 BC), Kings of Babylon* (PDF). Winona Lake: Eisenbrauns, 2020.

Weidner Chronicle (ABC 19). Livius, 2020.

https://www.livius.org/sources/content/mesopotamian-chronicles-content/abc-19-weidner-chronicle

Weiss, Harvey. *Megadrought and Collapse.* New York: Oxford University Press, 2017.

Weiss, H., M. A. Courty, W. Wetterstrom, F. Guichard, L. Senior, R. Meadow, and A. Curnow. "The Genesis and Collapse of Third Millennium North Mesopotamian Civilization." *Science* 261, no. 5124 (1993): 995-1004. http://www.jstor.org/stable/2881847.

Woolley, C. Leonard. "Excavations at Ur." *Journal of the Royal Society of Arts* 82, no. 4227 (1933): 46-59. http://www.jstor.org/stable/41360003.

Year Names of Ibbi-Suen. CDLI Wiki. University of Oxford. https://cdli.ox.ac.uk/wiki/doku.php?id=year_names_ibbi-suen

Xenophon. *Cyropaedia: The Education of Cyrus.* Translated by Henry Graham Dakyns. Project Gutenberg EBook. https://www.gutenberg.org/files/2085/2085-h/2085-h.htm

Part 4

Cotterell, Arthur. *The First Great Powers: Babylon and Assyria.* Hurst & Company, London, 2019.

Crawford, Harriet. *The Sumerian World.* Routledge, London and New York, 2013.

Crawford, Vaughn E; Harper, Prudence O; Pittmann, Holly. *Assyrian Reliefs and Ivories in the Metropolitan Museum of Art: Palace Reliefs of Ashurnasirpal II and Ivory Carvings from Nimrud.* Metropolitan Museum of Art, New York, 1980.

Curtis, JE and Reade, JE. *Art and Empire: Treasures from Assyria in the British Museum.* British Museum Press, London, 1995.

Düring, Bleda S. *The Imperialisation of Assyria: An Archaeological Approach.* Cambridge University Press, Cambridge, 2020.

Elayi, Josette. *Sargon II, King of Assyria.* SBL Press, Atlanta, 2017.

Elayi, Josette. *Esarhaddon, King of Assyria.* Lockwood Press, Columbus, Georgia, 2023.

Elayi, Josette. *Sennacherib, King of Assyria.* SBL Press, Atlanta, 2018.

Frahm, Eckart. *A Companion to Assyria.* Wiley Blackwell, Malden MA, 2017.

Frahm, Eckart. *Assyria: The Rise and Fall of the World's First Empire.* Basic Books, New York, 2023.

Kramer, Samuel Noah. *The Sumerians: Their History, Culture and Character.* University of Chicago Press, Chicago, 1963.

Melville, Sarah C. *The Campaigns of Sargon II, King of Assyria, 721-705 BC.* University of Oklahoma Press, Norman, Oklahoma, 2016.

Radner, Karen. *Ancient Assyria: A Very Short Introduction.* Oxford University Press, Oxford, 2015.

Image Sources

[1] *Map Ubaid culture-en.svg: NordNordWestderivative work: Rowanwindwhistler, CC BY-SA 4.0* https://creativecommons.org/licenses/by-sa/4.0 *via Wikimedia Commons;* https://commons.wikimedia.org/wiki/File:Map_Ubaid_culture-es.svg

[2] *Zunkir, CC BY-SA 4.0* https://creativecommons.org/licenses/by-sa/4.0 *via Wikimedia Commons;* https://commons.wikimedia.org/wiki/File:Shallow_dish_-_Ubaid.jpg

[3] *tobeytravels, CC BY-SA 2.0* https://creativecommons.org/licenses/by-sa/2.0 *via Wikimedia Commons;* https://commons.wikimedia.org/wiki/File:White_Temple_ziggurat_in_Uruk.jpg

[4] https://commons.wikimedia.org/wiki/File:Augenidole_Syrien_Slg_Ebn%C3%B6ther.jpg

[5] *Ciudades_de_Sumeria.svg: Cratesderivative work: Phirosiberia, CC BY 3.0* https://creativecommons.org/licenses/by/3.0 *via Wikimedia Commons;* https://commons.wikimedia.org/wiki/File:Cities_of_Sumer_(en).svg

[6] *Metropolitan Museum of Art, CC0, via Wikimedia Commons;* https://commons.wikimedia.org/wiki/File:Met_(2)_-_Administrative_tablet,_Jamdat_Nasr,_Uruk_III_style_-_3100%E2%80%932900_B.C_(d%C3%A9tail).jpg

[7] *Osama Shukir Muhammed Amin FRCP(Glasg), CC BY 4.0* https://creativecommons.org/licenses/by/4.0 *via Wikimedia Commons;* https://commons.wikimedia.org/wiki/File:Wall_plaque_showing_libation_scene_from_Ur,_Iraq,_2500_BCE._British_Museum_(adjusted_for_perspective).jpg

[8] https://commons.wikimedia.org/wiki/File:Relief_Im-dugud_Louvre_AO2783.jpg

[9] https://commons.wikimedia.org/wiki/File:Blau_Monument_British_Museum_86260.jpg

[10] *Hans Ollermann, CC BY-SA 2.0* https://creativecommons.org/licenses/by-sa/2.0 *via Wikimedia Commons;* https://commons.wikimedia.org/wiki/File:Mask_of_Sargon_of_Akkad.jpg

[11] *Middle_East_topographic_map-blank_3000bc_crop.svg: Fulvio314. The original uploader was Fulvio314 at Italian Wikipedia. Italian labels: YiyiEnglish labels: Kanguole, CC BY 3.0 https://creativecommons.org/licenses/by/3.0 via Wikimedia Commons; https://commons.wikimedia.org/wiki/File:Near_East_topographic_map_with_toponyms_3000bc-en.svg*

[12] *Louvre Museum, CC BY-SA 4.0 https://creativecommons.org/licenses/by-sa/4.0 via Wikimedia Commons; https://commons.wikimedia.org/wiki/File:Tablet_of_Lugalannatum.jpg*

[13] *Steve Harris, source, CC BY-SA 2.0 https://creativecommons.org/licenses/by-sa/2.0 via Wikimedia Commons; https://commons.wikimedia.org/wiki/File:King_Ur-Nammu.jpg*

[14] *Attar-Aram syria, CC BY-SA 4.0 https://creativecommons.org/licenses/by-sa/4.0 via Wikimedia Commons; https://commons.wikimedia.org/wiki/File:Third_Mari.png*

[15] *Gary Todd, CC0, via Wikimedia Commons; https://commons.wikimedia.org/wiki/File:Cuneiform_Clay_Tablets_from_Amorite_Kingdom_of_Mari,_1st_Half_of_2nd_Mill._BC.jpg*

[16] *Ashmolean Museum, CC BY-SA 4.0 https://creativecommons.org/licenses/by-sa/4.0 , via Wikimedia Commons; https://commons.wikimedia.org/wiki/File:Sumerian_King_List,_1800_BC,_Larsa,_Iraq.jpg*

[17] *Osama Shukir Muhammed Amin FRCP(Glasg), CC BY-SA 4.0 https://creativecommons.org/licenses/by-sa/4.0 , via Wikimedia Commons; https://commons.wikimedia.org/wiki/File:Gilgamesh_in_a_Sculptured_Vase,_Shara_Temple,_Tell_Agrab,_Iraq.jpg*

[18] *Background: Kikuyu3Elements: Eric Gaba (User: Sting) Composite: पाटलिपुत्र (talk) 10:52, 30 April 2020 (UTC), CC BY-SA 4.0 https://creativecommons.org/licenses/by-sa/4.0 ,via Wikimedia Commons; https://commons.wikimedia.org/wiki/File:Stele_of_the_Vultures_in_the_Louvre_Museum_(enhanced_composite).jpg*

[19] *Istanbul Archaeology Museums, CC0, via Wikimedia Commons; https://commons.wikimedia.org/wiki/File:Ur_Nammu_code_Istanbul.jpg*

[20] *Nic McPhee from Morris, Minnesota, USA, CC BY-SA 2.0 https://creativecommons.org/licenses/by-sa/2.0 , via Wikimedia Commons; https://commons.wikimedia.org/wiki/File:Flickr_-_Nic%27s_events_-_British_Museum_with_Cory_and_Mary,_6_Sep_2007_-_185.jpg*

[21] *Osama Shukir Muhammed Amin FRCP(Glasg), CC BY-SA 4.0 https://creativecommons.org/licenses/by-sa/4.0 via Wikimedia Commons; https://commons.wikimedia.org/wiki/File:Bull%27s_head_of_the_Queen%27s_lyre_from_Puabi%27s_grave_PG_800,_the_Royal_Cemetery_at_Ur,_Southern_Mesopotamia,_Iraq._The_British_Museum,_London..JPG*

[22] *British Museum, CC BY-SA 3.0 https://creativecommons.org/licenses/by-sa/3.0 via Wikimedia Commons; https://commons.wikimedia.org/wiki/File:Reconstructed_sumerian_headgear_necklaces_british_museum.JPG*

[23] *Zzztriple2000 at English Wikipedia, CC BY 3.0 <https://creativecommons.org/licenses/by/3.0>, via Wikimedia Commons https://commons.wikimedia.org/wiki/File:Royal_game_of_Ur,at_the_British_Museum.jpg*

[24] *Vassil, CC0, via Wikimedia Commons;*
https://commons.wikimedia.org/wiki/File:British_Museum_Middle_east_14022019_Panel_Imdug ud_2500_BC_3640.jpg

[25] *Nic McPhee from Morris, Minnesota, USA, CC BY-SA 2.0*
https://creativecommons.org/licenses/by-sa/2.0 *via Wikimedia Commons;*
https://commons.wikimedia.org/wiki/File:Adda_Seal_Akkadian_Empire_2300_BC.jpg

[26] https://commons.wikimedia.org/wiki/File:Copia_de_Enki.jpg

[27] https://commons.wikimedia.org/wiki/File:Entemena_vase_motif.jpg

[28] *Map modified: zoomed in, and labels of cultures added. By Jolle - This file was derived from Jarmo to Ubaid 7000-4500.jpg, CC BY 3.0,*
https://commons.wikimedia.org/w/index.php?curid=78287238

[29] https://commons.wikimedia.org/wiki/File:Hassuna_redware_bowl.jpg

[30] *Osama Shukir Muhammed Amin FRCP(Glasg), CC BY-SA 4.0*
<https://creativecommons.org/licenses/by-sa/4.0>, *via Wikimedia Commons*
https://commons.wikimedia.org/wiki/File:Neck_of_a_painted_jar_from_Tell_Hassuna,_Iraq,_belonging_to_Samarra_culture._5000_BCE._Iraq_Museum.jpg

[31] *Osama Shukir Muhammed Amin FRCP(Glasg), CC BY-SA 4.0*
<https://creativecommons.org/licenses/by-sa/4.0>, *via Wikimedia Commons*
https://commons.wikimedia.org/w/index.php?curid=90674882

[32] *ALFGRN, CC BY-SA 2.0* <https://creativecommons.org/licenses/by-sa/2.0>, *via Wikimedia Commons* https://en.wikipedia.org/wiki/Ubaid_period#/media/File:Ubaid_III_pottery_jar_5300-4700_BC_Louvre_Museum.jpg

[33] *Osama Shukir Muhammed Amin FRCP(Glasg), CC BY-SA 4.0*
<https://creativecommons.org/licenses/by-sa/4.0>, *via Wikimedia Commons*
https://commons.wikimedia.org/wiki/File:Pottery_bowl_from_Telul_eth-Thalathat,_Iraq._Ubaid_period,_c._5000_BCE._Iraq_Museum.jpg

[34] *Zunkir, CC BY-SA 4.0* <https://creativecommons.org/licenses/by-sa/4.0>, *via Wikimedia Commons* https://commons.wikimedia.org/wiki/File:Golden_dagger_and_sheath_-_Ur_RT.jpg

[35] https://commons.wikimedia.org/wiki/File:Cylinder_seal_lions_Louvre_MNB1167.jpg

[36] https://commons.wikimedia.org/wiki/File:Standard_of_Ur_chariots.jpg

[37] https://commons.wikimedia.org/wiki/File:Enki(Ea).jpg

[38] https://en.wikipedia.org/wiki/File:O.1054_color.jpg

[39] *CC BY-SA 3.0,* https://commons.wikimedia.org/w/index.php?curid=1084105

[40] *Michel wal (travail personnel (own work)), CC BY-SA 3.0*
<https://creativecommons.org/licenses/by-sa/3.0>, *via Wikimedia Commons*
https://commons.wikimedia.org/w/index.php?curid=7801508O

[41] *Attribution-ShareAlike 2.5 Generic, CC BY-SA 2.5* < https://creativecommons.org/licenses/by-sa/2.5/deed.en> https://commons.wikimedia.org/w/index.php?curid=18438114 *Map modified: location of Euphrates and Tigris rivers and the possible location of Agade noted.*

⁴² Hans Ollermann, CC BY-SA 2.0 <https://creativecommons.org/licenses/by-sa/2.0>, via Wikimedia Commons https://commons.wikimedia.org/wiki/File:Mask_of_Sargon_of_Akkad.jpg

⁴³ ALFGRN, CC BY-SA 2.0 <https://creativecommons.org/licenses/by-sa/2.0>, via Wikimedia Commons https://commons.wikimedia.org/w/index.php?curid=77514888

⁴⁴ Map modified: zoomed-in, labels of seas and regions added. Middle_East_topographic_map-blank.svg: Sémhur (talk)derivative work: Zunkir, CC BY-SA 3.0 <https://creativecommons.org/licenses/by-sa/3.0>, via Wikimedia Commons https://commons.wikimedia.org/wiki/File:Moyen_Orient_3mil_aC.svg

⁴⁵ Metropolitan Museum of Art, CC0, via Wikimedia Commons https://commons.wikimedia.org/wiki/File:Head_of_a_ruler_ca_2300_2000_BC_Iran_or_Mesopotamia_Metropolitan_Museum_of_Art_(dark_background).jpg

⁴⁶ Map modified: zoomed-in, names of regions added, outline of expanded territory inserted. Enyavar, CC BY-SA 4.0 <https://creativecommons.org/licenses/by-sa/4.0>, via Wikimedia Commons https://commons.wikimedia.org/wiki/File:Ancient_Near_East_2300BC.svg

⁴⁷ Map modified: zoomed-in, regions and seas added, an outline of expanded territory inserted. Enyavar, CC BY-SA 4.0 <https://creativecommons.org/licenses/by-sa/4.0>, via Wikimedia Commons https://commons.wikimedia.org/wiki/File:Ancient_Near_East_2300BC.svg

⁴⁸ Rama, CC BY-SA 2.0 FR <https://creativecommons.org/licenses/by-sa/2.0/fr/deed.en>, via Wikimedia Commons https://commons.wikimedia.org/wiki/File:Naram-Sin.jpg

⁴⁹ https://commons.wikimedia.org/wiki/File:John_Henry_Haynes_The_Nippur_temple_excavation._1893.jpg

⁵⁰ Bertramz, CC BY 3.0 <https://creativecommons.org/licenses/by/3.0>, via Wikimedia Commons https://commons.wikimedia.org/wiki/File:TellBrakTW-W.jpg

⁵¹ ALFGRN, CC BY-SA 2.0 <https://creativecommons.org/licenses/by-sa/2.0>, via Wikimedia Commons https://commons.wikimedia.org/wiki/File:Prisoner_of_the_Akkadian_Empire_period_possibly_Warka_ancient_Uruk_LOUVRE_AO_5683.jpg

⁵² Vania Teofilo, CC BY-SA 3.0 <https://creativecommons.org/licenses/by-sa/3.0>, via Wikimedia Commons https://commons.wikimedia.org/wiki/File:Female_statuette_Empire_d%27Akkad_Louvre_-1.jpg

⁵³ Gary Todd, CC0, via Wikimedia Commons https://commons.wikimedia.org/wiki/File:Diorite_Male_Statue%2C_found_in_Assur_%28next_to_the_Anu-Adad_Temple%29%2C_c._2300-2200_BC_%28Akkadian_Period%29.jpg

⁵⁴ Map modified: names of seas and regions added. Arrows added to show trade routes. Middle_East_topographic_map-blank.svg: Sémhur (talk)derivative work: Zunkir, CC BY-SA 3.0 <https://creativecommons.org/licenses/by-sa/3.0>, via Wikimedia Commons https://commons.wikimedia.org/w/index.php?curid=17330302

⁵⁵ Rama, CC BY-SA 3.0 FR <https://creativecommons.org/licenses/by-sa/3.0/fr/deed.en>, via Wikimedia Commons https://commons.wikimedia.org/wiki/File:Victory_stele_of_Naram_Sin_9066.jpg

⁵⁶ *Osama Shukir Muhammed Amin FRCP(Glasg), CC BY-SA 4.0* <https://creativecommons.org/licenses/by-sa/4.0>, *via Wikimedia Commons* https://commons.wikimedia.org/wiki/File:The_rock-relief_of_Naram-Sin_at_Darband-i_Gawr,_Qaradagh_Mountain,_Sulaymaniyah,_Kurdistan,_Iraq.jpg

⁵⁷ *Louvre Museum, CC BY 3.0* <https://creativecommons.org/licenses/by/3.0>, *via Wikimedia Commons* https://commons.wikimedia.org/w/index.php?curid=25852586

⁵⁸ *Jans, G. / Bretschneider, J. 1998: "Wagon and Chariot Representations in the Early Dynastic Glyptic. "They came to Tell Beydar with wagon and equid"". In M. Lebeau (ed.), About Subartu. Studies Devoted to Upper Mesopotamia. Turnhout, 155-194., CC BY-SA 4.0* <https://creativecommons.org/licenses/by-sa/4.0>, *via Wikimedia Commons* https://commons.wikimedia.org/wiki/File:Beydar-1.png

⁵⁹ *Sting, CC BY-SA 3.0* <http://creativecommons.org/licenses/by-sa/3.0/>, *via Wikimedia Commons* https://commons.wikimedia.org/wiki/File:Stele_of_Vultures_detail_01a.jpg

⁶⁰ https://commons.wikimedia.org/wiki/File:Cylinder_seal_of_the_scribe_Kalki.jpg

⁶¹ *Mbzt 2011, CC BY 3.0* <https://creativecommons.org/licenses/by/3.0>, *via Wikimedia Commons* https://commons.wikimedia.org/wiki/File:Impression_of_an_Akkadian_cylinder_seal_with_inscription_The_Divine_Sharkalisharri_Prince_of_Akkad_Ibni-Sharrum_the_Scribe_his_servant.jpg

⁶² *Eric de Redelijkheid from Utrecht, Netherlands, CC BY-SA 2.0* <https://creativecommons.org/licenses/by-sa/2.0>, *via Wikimedia Commons* https://commons.wikimedia.org/wiki/File:Bronze_head_of_an_Akkadian_ruler,_discovered_in_Nineveh_in_1931,_presumably_depicting_either_Sargon_or_Sargon%27s_grandson_Naram-Sin_(Rijksmuseum_van_Oudheden).jpg

⁶³ https://commons.wikimedia.org/wiki/File:Bassetki_statue.jpg

⁶⁴ *ALFGRN, CC BY-SA 2.0* <https://creativecommons.org/licenses/by-sa/2.0>, *via Wikimedia Commons* https://commons.wikimedia.org/wiki/File:Sargon_of_Akkad_and_dignitaries.jpg

⁶⁵ *MapMaster, CC BY-SA 4.0* <https://creativecommons.org/licenses/by-sa/4.0>, *via Wikimedia Commons* https://en.wikipedia.org/wiki/Sippar#/media/File:Hammurabi's_Babylonia_1.svg

⁶⁶ https://en.wikipedia.org/wiki/Rimush#/media/File:Fragments_of_the_Victory_Stele_of_Rimush_(Heuzey).jpg

⁶⁷ *Shonagon - Own work, CC0,* https://commons.wikimedia.org/w/index.php?curid=61159609

⁶⁸ *Daderot, CC0, via Wikimedia Commons* https://commons.wikimedia.org/wiki/File:El,_the_Canaanite_creator_deity,_Megiddo,_Stratum_V_II,_Late_Bronze_II,_1400-1200_BC,_bronze_with_gold_leaf_-_Oriental_Institute_Museum,_University_of_Chicago_-_DSC07734.JPG

⁶⁹ *Prioryman, CC BY-SA 4.0* <https://creativecommons.org/licenses/by-sa/4.0>, *via Wikimedia Commons* https://commons.wikimedia.org/wiki/File:Tablet_of_Shamash_relief.jpg

⁷⁰ *User1712, CC BY-SA 4.0* <https://creativecommons.org/licenses/by-sa/4.0>, *via Wikimedia Commons* https://commons.wikimedia.org/wiki/File:Nergal-b.jpg

⁷¹ https://en.wikipedia.org/wiki/Tiamat#/media/File:Chaos_Monster_and_Sun_God.png

[72] *British Museum, CC0, via Wikimedia Commons*
https://commons.wikimedia.org/wiki/File:British_Museum_Queen_of_the_Night.jpg

[73] *Map modified: added labels of cultures, rivers, and the Persian Gulf. Credit: Jolle, CC BY 3.0*
https://creativecommons.org/licenses/by/3.0 *via Wikimedia Commons;*
https://commons.wikimedia.org/wiki/File:Mesopotamian_Prehistorical_cultures.jpg

[74] *Osama Shukir Muhammed Amin FRCP(Glasg), CC BY-SA 4.0*
https://creativecommons.org/licenses/by-sa/4.0 *via Wikimedia Commons;*
https://commons.wikimedia.org/wiki/File:Lizard-headed_nude_woman_nursing_a_child,_from_Ur,_Iraq,_c._4000_BCE._Iraq_Museum_(retouched).jpg

[75] *Photo modified: zoomed-in, place names added. Credit: Erinthecute, CC BY-SA 4.0*
https://creativecommons.org/licenses/by-sa/4.0 *via Wikimedia Commons;*
https://commons.wikimedia.org/wiki/File:Umma2350.svg

[76] *Daderot, CC0, via Wikimedia Commons;*
https://commons.wikimedia.org/wiki/File:Cylinder_seal_-_Oriental_Institute_Museum,_University_of_Chicago_-_DSC07233.JPG

[77] *Hans Ollermann, CC BY-SA 2.0* https://creativecommons.org/licenses/by-sa/2.0 *via Wikimedia Commons;* https://commons.wikimedia.org/wiki/File:Mask_of_Sargon_of_Akkad.jpg

[78] *Rama, CC BY-SA 2.0 FR* https://creativecommons.org/licenses/by-sa/2.0/fr/deed.en *via Wikimedia Commons;* https://commons.wikimedia.org/wiki/File:Naram-Sin.jpg

[79] *Dosseman, CC BY-SA 4.0* https://creativecommons.org/licenses/by-sa/4.0 *via Wikimedia Commons;* https://commons.wikimedia.org/wiki/File:Damascus_National_Museum_worshipper_from_Amorite_city_of_Mari_5327.jpg

[80] *Metropolitan Museum of Art, CC0, via Wikimedia Commons;*
https://commons.wikimedia.org/wiki/File:Ibbi-Sin_enthroned.jpg

[81] *Rowanwindwhistler, GFDL <*http://www.gnu.org/copyleft/fdl.html*>, via Wikimedia Commons*
https://commons.wikimedia.org/wiki/File:Mesopotamia_en_el_segundo_milenio-es.svg

[82] *Serge Ottaviani, CC BY-SA 3.0* https://creativecommons.org/licenses/by-sa/3.0 *via Wikimedia Commons;* https://commons.wikimedia.org/wiki/File:Royal_portrait_-_Hamurabi_-_King_of_Babylon_-1900_before_JC_-.JPG

[83] https://commons.wikimedia.org/wiki/File:Worshipper_Larsa_Louvre_AO15704.jpg

[84] *MapMaster, CC BY-SA 4.0* https://creativecommons.org/licenses/by-sa/4.0 *via Wikimedia Commons;* https://commons.wikimedia.org/wiki/File:Hammurabi%27s_Babylonia_1.svg

[85] https://commons.wikimedia.org/wiki/File:Marduk_and_pet.jpg

[86] *Goran tek-en, CC BY-SA 4.0 <*https://creativecommons.org/licenses/by-sa/4.0*>, via Wikimedia Commons* https://commons.wikimedia.org/wiki/File:N-Mesopotamia_and_Syria_english.svg

[87] *MapMaster, CC BY-SA 4.0* https://creativecommons.org/licenses/by-sa/4.0 *via Wikimedia Commons;* https://commons.wikimedia.org/wiki/File:Kassite_Babylonia_EN.svg

[88] *Metropolitan Museum of Art, CC0, via Wikimedia Commons;*
https://commons.wikimedia.org/wiki/File:Cylinder_seal_and_modern_impression-male_worshiper,_dog_surmounted_by_a_standard_MET_ss1985_357_44.jpg

⁸⁹ https://commons.wikimedia.org/wiki/File:%E2%80%98Aqar_Q%C5%ABf.jpg

⁹⁰ https://commons.wikimedia.org/wiki/File:Kudurru_Melishipak_Louvre_Sb23_n02.jpg

⁹¹ *Near_East_topographic_map-blank.svg: Sémhurderivative work: Zunkir, CC BY-SA 3.0* https://creativecommons.org/licenses/by-sa/3.0 *via Wikimedia Commons;* https://commons.wikimedia.org/wiki/File:M%C3%A9dio-assyrien.png

⁹² *Gary Todd, CC0, via Wikimedia Commons;* https://commons.wikimedia.org/wiki/File:Babylonian_Limestone_Boundary_Stele_(Kudurru),_Reign_of_Nebuchadnezzar_I.jpg

⁹³ *Carole Raddato from FRANKFURT, Germany, CC BY-SA 2.0* https://creativecommons.org/licenses/by-sa/2.0 *via Wikimedia Commons;* https://commons.wikimedia.org/wiki/File:Exhibition_I_am_Ashurbanipal_king_of_the_world,_king_of_Assyria,_British_Museum_(31033563287).jpg

⁹⁴ https://commons.wikimedia.org/wiki/File:Iraq;_Nimrud_-_Assyria,_Lamassu%27s_Guarding_Palace_Entrance.jpg

⁹⁵ *Osama Shukir Muhammed Amin FRCP(Glasg), CC BY-SA 4.0* https://creativecommons.org/licenses/by-sa/4.0 *via Wikimedia Commons;* https://commons.wikimedia.org/wiki/File:Tiglath-pileser_III,_an_alabaster_bas-relief_from_the_king%27s_central_palace_at_Nimrud,_Mesopotamia.,JPG

⁹⁶ https://commons.wikimedia.org/wiki/File:Skythian_archer_plate_BM_E135_by_Epiktetos.jpg

⁹⁷ *Patrick Gray, CC BY 2.0* https://creativecommons.org/licenses/by/2.0 *via Wikimedia Commons;* https://commons.wikimedia.org/wiki/File:Battle_of_Carchemish.png

⁹⁸ *User: Hahaha, CC SA 1.0* http://creativecommons.org/licenses/sa/1.0/ *via Wikimedia Commons;* https://commons.wikimedia.org/wiki/File:Pergamonmuseum_Ishtartor_05.jpg

⁹⁹ *Mary Harrsch from Springfield, Oregon, USA, CC BY 2.0* https://creativecommons.org/licenses/by/2.0 *via Wikimedia Commons;* https://commons.wikimedia.org/wiki/File:A_mu%C5%A1%E1%B8%ABu%C5%A1%C5%A1u,_the_sacred_animal_of_the_Mesopotamian_god_Marduk_on_the_Ishtar_Gate_of_Babylon_reconstructed_with_original_bricks_at_the_Pergamon_Museum_in_Berlin_575_BCE_(32465090312).jpg

¹⁰⁰ *British Museum, CC BY 3.0* https://creativecommons.org/licenses/by/3.0 *via Wikimedia Commons;* https://commons.wikimedia.org/wiki/File:Nabonidus.jpg

¹⁰¹ https://commons.wikimedia.org/wiki/File:Defeat_of_Croesus_546_BCE.jpg

¹⁰² *Carlo Raso, CC BY-SA 2.0* <https://creativecommons.org/licenses/by-sa/2.0>, *via Wikimedia Commons,* https://commons.wikimedia.org/w/index.php?curid=74758953

¹⁰³ *Osama Shukir Muhammed Amin FRCP(Glasg), CC BY-SA 4.0* https://creativecommons.org/licenses/by-sa/4.0 *via Wikimedia Commons;* https://commons.wikimedia.org/wiki/File:Man_and_woman,_Old-Babylonian_fired_clay_plaque_from_Southern_Mesopotamia,_Iraq.jpg

¹⁰⁴ https://commons.wikimedia.org/wiki/File:Marduk-apla-iddina_II.jpg

[105] Photo modified: zoomed-in: Osama Shukir Muhammed Amin FRCP(Glasg), CC BY-SA 4.0 https://creativecommons.org/licenses/by-sa/4.0 via Wikimedia Commons; https://commons.wikimedia.org/wiki/File:Old-Babylonian_plaque_of_a_standing_woman_holding_her_child,_from_Southern_Mesopotamia,_Iraq.jpg

[106] Mbmrock, CC BY-SA 4.0 https://creativecommons.org/licenses/by-sa/4.0 via Wikimedia Commons; https://commons.wikimedia.org/wiki/File:(Mesopotamia)_Hammurabi.jpg

[107] https://commons.wikimedia.org/wiki/File:William_Blake_-_Nebuchadnezzar_(Tate_Britain).jpg

[108] https://en.wikipedia.org/wiki/Bull_of_Heaven#/media/File:O.1054_color.jpg

[109] Александр Михальчук, CC BY-SA 4.0 https://creativecommons.org/licenses/by-sa/4.0 via Wikimedia Commons; https://commons.wikimedia.org/wiki/File:The_Tower_of_Babel_Alexander_Mikhalchyk.jpg

[110] https://commons.wikimedia.org/wiki/File:Hanging_Gardens_of_Babylon_by_Ferdinand_Knab_(1886).png

[111] Hammurabi, CC BY 3.0 https://creativecommons.org/licenses/by/3.0 via Wikimedia Commons; https://commons.wikimedia.org/wiki/File:P1050763_Louvre_code_Hammurabi_face_rwk.JPG

[112] Hammurabi, CC BY 3.0 https://creativecommons.org/licenses/by/3.0 via Wikimedia Commons; https://commons.wikimedia.org/wiki/File:F0182_Louvre_Code_Hammourabi_Bas-relief_Sb8_rwk.jpg

[113] Drawn by Henri Faucher-Gudin after Austen Henry Layard, Public domain; https://commons.wikimedia.org/wiki/File:Ramman.png

[114] https://commons.wikimedia.org/wiki/File:Passing_lion_Babylon_AO21118.jpg

[115] Osama Shukir Muhammed Amin FRCP(Glasg), CC BY-SA 4.0 https://creativecommons.org/licenses/by-sa/4.0 via Wikimedia Commons; https://commons.wikimedia.org/wiki/File:God_Ea_holding_a_cup._From_Nasiriyah,_Iraq._2004-1595_BCE._Iraq_Museum.jpg

[116] TYalaA, CC BY-SA 4.0 https://creativecommons.org/licenses/by-sa/4.0 via Wikimedia Commons; https://commons.wikimedia.org/wiki/File:Marduk_Tiamat_Battle_from_Enuma_Elish_-_repaired_version.png

[117] https://commons.wikimedia.org/wiki/File:Illustrerad_Verldshistoria_band_I_Ill_034.jpg

[118] https://commons.wikimedia.org/wiki/File:Artist%E2%80%99s_impression_of_Assyrian_palaces_from_The_Monuments_of_Nineveh_by_Sir_Austen_Henry_Layard,_1853.jpg

[119] Goran tek-en, CC BY-SA 4.0 <https://creativecommons.org/licenses/by-sa/4.0>, via Wikimedia Commons; https://commons.wikimedia.org/wiki/File:N-Mesopotamia_and_Syria_english.svg

[120] Hardnfast, CC BY 3.0 <https://creativecommons.org/licenses/by/3.0>, via Wikimedia Commons; https://commons.wikimedia.org/wiki/File:Ancient_ziggurat_at_Ali_Air_Base_Iraq_2005.jpg

[121] https://commons.wikimedia.org/wiki/File:Sargon_of_Akkad_(1936).jpg

[122] https://commons.wikimedia.org/wiki/File:Gudea_of_Lagash_Girsu.jpg

[123] Jononmac46, CC BY-SA 3.0 <https://creativecommons.org/licenses/by-sa/3.0>, via Wikimedia Commons; https://commons.wikimedia.org/wiki/File:Assyrian_lions.png

[124] Hammurabi, CC BY 3.0 <https://creativecommons.org/licenses/by/3.0>, via Wikimedia Commons; https://commons.wikimedia.org/wiki/File:P1050763_Louvre_code_Hammurabi_face_rwk.JPG

[125] https://commons.wikimedia.org/wiki/File:Iraq;_Nimrud_-_Assyria,_Lamassu%27s_Guarding_Palace_Entrance.jpg

[126] Osama Shukir Muhammed Amin FRCP(Glasg), CC BY-SA 4.0 <https://creativecommons.org/licenses/by-sa/4.0>, via Wikimedia Commons; https://commons.wikimedia.org/wiki/File:Ashurnasirpal_II_performs_religious_rituals_before_the_sacred_tree._From_Nimrud,_Iraq._865-860_BCE._British_Museum.jpg

[127] https://commons.wikimedia.org/wiki/File:Tell_Ahmar,_mural_palacio_rey_Tiglatpileser_audiencia_sicglo_VIII.jpg

[128] Osama Shukir Muhammed Amin FRCP(Glasg), CC BY-SA 4.0 <https://creativecommons.org/licenses/by-sa/4.0>, via Wikimedia Commons; https://commons.wikimedia.org/wiki/File:Tiglath-pileser_III,_an_alabaster_bas-relief_from_the_king%27s_central_palace_at_Nimrud,_Mesopotamia..JPG

[129] https://commons.wikimedia.org/wiki/File:Reconstructed_Model_of_Palace_of_Sargon_at_Khosrabad_1905.jpg

[130] Timo Roller, CC BY 3.0 <https://creativecommons.org/licenses/by/3.0>, via Wikimedia Commons; https://commons.wikimedia.org/wiki/File:Sanherib-tr-4271.jpg

[131] Photograph: Anthony HuanText: George Smith in 1871 (Public domain), CC BY-SA 2.0 <https://creativecommons.org/licenses/by-sa/2.0>, via Wikimedia Commons; https://commons.wikimedia.org/wiki/File:Rassam_cylinder_with_translation_of_the_First_Assyrian_Conquest_of_Egypt,_643_BCE.jpg

[132] https://commons.wikimedia.org/wiki/File:Ashur_god.jpg

[133] Sailko, CC BY 3.0 <https://creativecommons.org/licenses/by/3.0>, via Wikimedia Commons; https://commons.wikimedia.org/wiki/File:Ishtar_on_an_Akkadian_seal.jpg

[134] Allan Gluck, CC BY 4.0 <https://creativecommons.org/licenses/by/4.0>, via Wikimedia Commons; https://commons.wikimedia.org/wiki/File:Assyrian_Relief_of_the_Banquet_of_Ashurbanipal_From_Nineveh_Gypsum_N_Palace_British_Museum_01.jpg

[135] British Museum, CC BY-SA 3.0 <https://creativecommons.org/licenses/by-sa/3.0>, via Wikimedia Commons; https://commons.wikimedia.org/wiki/File:Inlaid_and_gilded_panel_-_WA_127412_-_British_Museum.JPG

[136] Osama Shukir Muhammed Amin FRCP(Glasg), CC BY-SA 4.0 <https://creativecommons.org/licenses/by-sa/4.0>, via Wikimedia Commons; https://commons.wikimedia.org/wiki/File:Assyrian_siege-engine_attacking_the_city_wall_of_Lachish,_part_of_the_ascending_assaulting_wave._Detail_of_a_wall_relief_dating_back_to_the_reign_of_Sennacherib,_700-692_BCE._From_Nineveh,_Iraq,_currently_housed_in_the_British_Museum.jpg

www.ingramcontent.com/pod-product-compliance
Lightning Source LLC
Chambersburg PA
CBHW071107160426
43196CB00013B/2495